W9-AXF-950

MORAL EVIL

Humber College Library
3199 Lakeshore Blvd. West
Toronto, ON   M8V 1K8

1

Selected Titles from the MORAL TRADITIONS SERIES

James F. Keenan, SJ, *Editor*

The Acting Person and Christian Moral Life
Darlene Fozard Weaver

*Aquinas, Feminism, and the
Common Good*
Susanne M. DeCrane

*Aquinas on the Emotions:
A Religious Ethical Inquiry*
Diana Fritz Cates

*Catholic Moral Theology in the
United States: A History*
Charles E. Curran

*The Church and Secularity:
Two Stories of Liberal Society*
Robert Gascoigne

*Creative Conformity: The Feminist Politics
of U.S. Catholic and Iranian Shi'i Women*
Elizabeth M. Bucar

*The Critical Calling: Reflections on Moral
Dilemmas since Vatican II*
Richard A. McCormick

*Defending Probabilism: The Moral
Theology of Juan Caramuel*
Julia Fleming

Family Ethics: Practices for Christians
Julie Hanlon Rubio

Heroes, Saints, and Ordinary Morality
Andrew Flescher

*John Cuthbert Ford, SJ: Moral Theologian
at the End of the Manualist Era*
Eric Marcelo O. Genilo, SJ

*Kinship across Borders:
A Christian Ethic of Immigration*
Kristin E. Heyer

*Law's Virtues: Fostering Autonomy and
Solidarity in American Society*
Cathleen Kaveny

Living the Truth: A Theory of Action
Klaus Demmer

*Loyal Dissent: Memoir of a
Catholic Theologian*
Charles E. Curran

The Origins of War: A Catholic Perspective
Matthew A. Shadle

*Overcoming Our Evil: Human Nature and
Spiritual Exercises in Xunzi and Augustine*
Aaron Stalnaker

*Prophetic and Public: The Social
Witness of U.S. Catholicism*
Kristin E. Heyer

*The Sexual Person: Toward a
Renewed Catholic Anthropology*
Todd A. Salzman and
Michael G. Lawler

*The Social Mission of the U.S. Catholic
Church: A Theological Perspective*
Charles E. Curran

*Theological Bioethics: Participation,
Justice, and Change*
Lisa Sowle Cahill

*United States Welfare Policy:
A Catholic Response*
Thomas J. Massaro, SJ

MORAL EVIL

Andrew Michael Flescher

Georgetown University Press
Washington, DC

HUMBER LIBRARIES LAKESHORE CAMPUS
3199 Lakeshore Blvd West
TORONTO, ON. M8V 1K8

DISCARD

Cover image: M. C. Escher's "Circle Limit IV," © 2013 The M. C. Escher Company—The Netherlands. Used by permission. All rights reserved.

© 2013 Georgetown University Press. All rights reserved. No part of this book may be reproduced or utilized in any form or by any means, electronic or mechanical, including photocopying and recording, or by any information storage and retrieval system, without permission in writing from the publisher.

Library of Congress Cataloging-in-Publication Data

Flescher, Andrew Michael, 1969-
Moral evil / Andrew Michael Flescher.
pages cm.—(Moral traditions)
Includes bibliographical references and index.
ISBN 978–1-62616–010–1 (pbk. : alk. paper)
1. Good and evil. 2. Good and evil—Religious aspects—Christianity. 3. Theodicy. I. Title.
BJ1401.F57 2013
170—dc23

2013002331

This book is printed on acid-free paper meeting the requirements of the American National Standard for Permanence in Paper for Printed Library Materials.

15   14   13   9   8   7   6   5   4   3   2   First printing

Printed in the United States of America

CONTENTS

Acknowledgments   vii

INTRODUCTION
"Evil" and Evil   1
    Defining Evil   4
    Four Models of Moral Evil   8

CHAPTER ONE
Evil versus Goodness: Satan and other "Evildoers"   23
    The Standard View of Evil   23
    Manicheanism and the Idea of Satan   27
    The Manichean Theological Tradition   33
    Evil Naturalized   38
    Evil and the Apocalypse   43
    "Evil Genes"   48
    The Manichean Model under Scrutiny   53

CHAPTER TWO
**Evil as the Good in Disguise: Theodicy and the Crisis
of Meaning**   67
    "With or Against, but Not Without"   68
    The Great Conundrum   72
    Theodicy *Simpliciter*: The Innovation of Gottfried Leibniz   77
    The Educative Theodicy: From Job to Irenaeus and Lactantius   83
    The Free Will Theodicy   95
    Theodicy under Scrutiny: Some Broader Issues   101

CHAPTER THREE

Evil as "Evil": Perspectivalism and the Construction of Evil   117
  Beyond Convention   117
  Subjectivism   120
  Nietzsche   124
  The Intellectual Legacy of Nietzsche   129
  Taoism, Zen Buddhism, and Perspectivalism   138
  Positive Psychology   145
  Is Evil Illusory? Model Three under Scrutiny   147

CHAPTER FOUR

**Evil as the Absence of Goodness: Privation and the Ubiquity
of Wickedness**   164
  Evil and Character   164
  Evil in the Mind of Augustine: The Will and Difficult Freedom   170
  Broadening Augustine's Account of Evil   180
  Neo-Augustinians   192
  The Privation Account under Critical Scrutiny   197

CHAPTER FIVE

**Evil as Inaction: Augustine, Aristotle, and Connecting the
Thesis of Privation to Virtue Ethics**   207
  Overcoming Evil Situations   207
  Aristotle, Self-Deception, and the Will   217
  The Privation Thesis, Virtue Ethics, and the Case of Fukushima   226
  The Connection between Augustine and Aristotle under Scrutiny   232
  Undoing Wickedness   237
  Evil: Our Problem   245

Bibliography   255

Index   271

ACKNOWLEDGMENTS

THIS BOOK is the fruit of thinking hard over the last ten years with students and colleagues about the nature of evil and the moral recommendations to which specific understandings of evil lead. Today scholars have come to realize that the central problem of evil is not theology or philosophy's classical preoccupation with theodicy, which asks how there can be an all-powerful, redeeming deity in light of human suffering, but rather how one might best and most compassionately live one's life in light of the irremovability of injustice, suffering, and brutality from normal life. Of course, to arrive at this insight is still to leave open many avenues for inquiring how one is to take real responsibility and live a meaningful life in a world in which cruelty reigns more often than it should. The specific approach I explore in pursuit of this inquiry ties Augustine's conception of evil as privation, as absence of goodness, to a certain sort of virtue ethic that encourages altruistic habit-forming. To this end, I relate the thought of Augustine and Aristotle in a manner that I believe is, to date, unexplored. The four models of moral evil I attempt to describe in this book en route to establishing this connection are themselves, while part of a typology also of my own making, refinements of refinements. Each is the result of valuable conversations with smart individuals in both academic and nonacademic contexts during periods in which I worked in the Department of Religious Studies at California State University, Chico, and subsequently in the Center for Medical Humanities, Compassionate Care, and Bioethics at Stony Brook University.

I could not have conceived, researched, and written this book without some small grants and a sabbatical awarded by Chico State in 2007 and 2008, or without an additional grant awarded by the Templeton Foundation in 2009. I am deeply grateful to comments from anonymous reviewers who provided constructive commentary on a paper I delivered to the Society of Christian Ethics in 2004. Their feedback helped me to frame the four models approach I ultimately adopted. I thank Aaron Stalnaker, Bruce Grelle, Barney Twiss, John

Kelsay, Loren Lybarger, Jung Lee, Charles Mathewes, Jim Swan-Tuite, and Doug Tarnopol for providing me with indispensable advice for how to make an age-old topic maximally relevant to current inquiries under way in the field of comparative religious ethics. I owe Ronald Green a particular debt of gratitude for carefully reading a draft of my first three chapters (one on the model of theodicy, a topic on which he is probably the world's expert) and thank Jock Reeder for reading the whole manuscript at the last minute and giving me so many thoughtful suggestions for clarification. I thank Alycia La Guardia, Leslie La Guardia, and especially Nicole Fuschetti for their editorial assistance.

Aside from Bruce Grelle, I want to thank some other colleagues at Chico State who participated in a reading group devoted to topics related to the problem of evil, many that surface in one form or another in this book, or who otherwise spent significant time discussing my project with me one on one. Robert Burton, Jason Clower, Marcel DaGuerre, Laird Easton, Eric Gampel, Richard Houchin, Troy Jollimore, Edward Pluth, Olav Smith, Wai-hung Wong, Daniel Veidlinger, and Becky White contributed to my thinking about what sources to emphasize, what key problems to raise, and where to beware of looming thorny issues in my treatment of the models I would consider. At Stony Brook, I have been fortunate to have brilliant colleagues who have helped me reframe questions about moral psychology in light of some of the most recent evidence emerging in neuroscience and neuropsychology. I particularly thank Stephanie Brown, Stephen Post, and Michael Roess for helping me become aware of some of the most salient examples of this contemporary research.

My experience with Georgetown University Press continues to be wonderful. I am so appreciative of Richard Brown, James Keenan, and the anonymous reviewers of the Moral Traditions series from whose invaluable feedback I consistently benefit. They take seriously the process of nurturing their authors through the process of book writing from conception to completion. Finally, I want to acknowledge my loving family, who always push me to do my best work with their warmth and support. This book is dedicated to Robert and Joyce Flescher, and Ethan, Ellen, Benjamin, Samuel, and Rachel Foxman.

Introduction

"Evil" and Evil

"But I think once you quit hearing sir or ma'am,
the rest is soon to foller."
—SHERIFF ED TOM BELL, *No Country for Old Men* (film)

DEFEATED AND EXHAUSTED from the fruitless pursuit of the ruthless Anton Chigurh, who got away and who is sure to continue to elude capture, Sheriff Ed Tom Bell utters these words to a fellow befuddled colleague. Chigurh is the consummate psychopath, clever and self-reliant but lacking the capacity to feel empathy or indeed an interest in forming any sort of connection with other people. Chalking a good many of his deeds up to fate, Chigurh confesses to his future victims that it is nothing personal: the ability to choose otherwise is beyond even him. Cormac McCarthy's efficient, relentless murderer, a sure survivor against the unlikeliest of odds, is equal to the creepiest of characters thought up in all of literature, and made all the more eerie by Javier Bardem's depiction of him in the Coen Brothers' award-winning film of the same title. Sheriff Ed Tom Bell's observation connects psychopathy to mundane selfishness. The unstoppable, anonymous assassin is the predictable upshot of the waning of courtesy, kindness, and love of one's neighbor. Evil, like entropy, has the edge over hard-won virtues such as compassion and mercy.

Two memorable moments of *No Country for Old Men* underscore the seasoned sheriff's reflection. The first occurs in the middle of the film, when the protagonist Llewelyn Moss is badly injured and needs the assistance of three men to help him sneak over the border into Mexico for cover, for which he needs a temporary disguise. The second takes place at the end of the film, when Chigurh is hit by a car as he is leaving the scene of his latest crime and needs one of the boys who has witnessed the accident to give him the shirt off his back to

1

serve as a sling that will hold his badly broken arm in place. In both cases, the Good Samaritanship of would-be assisters lapses into an occasion for opportunism. One of the men Moss encounters on his way into Mexico wants to see how much more money he can get for the half-empty beer bottle needed to sell the disguise, beyond what Moss has already paid for the jacket he needs to cloak his wounds. In the second instance, the boy's friend matter-of-factly informs him that he had better plan on sharing the hundred dollars Chigurh has just paid for the shirt. The audience cannot help but notice that in neither of these instances do the ones requesting more money pay much attention to the fact that someone has been critically injured. They are interested in the opportunity that has arisen as a result of their introduction to someone desperate for their help. These two episodes occupy only a few minutes of a film that is more than two hours long and introduce characters who are not to appear again, yet their presence is as deliberate as the most climactic scene. The three men and two boys are the viewers, people who also look for easy ways to make money and who often act on base, selfish instincts. In turn we, at least potentially, are Anton Chigurh, an individual past the point of no return, incorrigible in and resigned to his evil. If we are not careful, evil will overtake us too. As *No Country for Old Men* suggests, evil is inescapably with us and at least in one sense not the mirror opposite of goodness. Unlike goodness, evil does not require planning or perseverance. Although we have the propensity to be good and evil, we are more easily evil. Our biological hardwiring does not ensure our participation in wrongdoing, but we are at some point likely to be drawn into the vortex of evil by default. Evil, in other words, has its way of finding us.

The point extends to occurrences that are explained as nature's whim. In the summer of 2008, I was in New Orleans and took the Hurricane Katrina Tour, on which I was able to visit the areas most affected by the storm, such as the Lower 9th Ward, St. Bernard, and Lakeview. There I was surprised to learn that most residents who lived through the aftermath insist that what they experienced was not a natural disaster but a "man-made catastrophe," caused as much by human inaction as by nature's action. A June 2007 report released by the American Society of Civil Engineers reveals that the failures of the federally built levies in New Orleans were found to be the result of system design flaws, the lion's share of which were known and repeatedly identified in advance as areas in need of attention.[1] The failure of local and federal agencies to fortify the levies known to be compromised, the poor planning surrounding the evacuations during the crisis, the long time it took for relief to arrive to the survivors, the inefficiency with which resources were distributed when they did arrive, and the inability in general on the part of FEMA (the Federal Emergency Management Agency) and other governmental agencies to organize a more effective response to the crisis in the aftermath of the hurricane are by now all well documented. Conservative estimates indicate that about 165 square miles (80 percent of the city)—an area equivalent to more than seven Manhattans—flooded. In most of the affected areas, surging water full of sewage submerged homes. The disaster took lives, ruined neighborhoods, displaced families, and raised serious questions about whether residents of a major American city could ever return home. Although of course none of this was intended, most of it was the result of a collective and pervasive passivity that transpired before, during, and after the catastrophe. Such is the case with many instances of evil: It arrives suddenly, leaving carnage in its wake that is entirely out of proportion to the culpable neglect that invited it.

What are the ways of explaining, if not justifying, the harm wrought by Katrina? Some interpreted the hurricane's destruction in the same light as other disasters forecast in apocalyptic literature: a cataclysmic event not only predictable but also indicative of a new era of crisis for which to be on the lookout. Some went so far as to say that Katrina was divine retribution for human misdeeds. A wrathful God invoked Satan's services to teach human beings a lesson.[2] Others similarly saw Katrina as pedagogical on God's part, but interpreted it as an event in service of a larger, loving objective, one perceivable only from a vantage point grander than that within current human grasp. New Orleans, which in the final analysis was not destroyed, is now a safer city because we have learned—finally—what can occur as a result of human neglect. Catastrophes in this analysis become a way of averting even greater disasters by redirecting the course of history in a way that leads to human betterment. Terrible ills lead to a larger good. A third way of understanding the evil of Katrina is that the devastation it caused was considered bad from the perspective of some, but not of everyone. In this view the idea that suffering is a state to be universally avoided is a myth. No such thing as an objectively recognizable oppressed victim around whom to rally exists, no kind of sympathy translates into "the only" sensible human response to some experienced pain. Suffering, evil, devastation are idiosyncratically experienced phenomena that, despite what they seem, can never be defined in advance as the same thing from person to person. A fourth way of understanding Katrina grants that the calamity may indeed have been the cause of real, universally recognizable suffering, but this suffering was exacerbated because of an absence rather than a presence. In this case Katrina reveals immoral inaction, a failure to seize the opportunity to promote and protect the good in advance of a predictable crisis. Evil becomes a reflection of preparations for flourishing not undertaken, lapses of action and conscience. These, then, are at least four possible ways of looking at the meaning of the evil of Katrina: It was Satan's bad work; it was God's good work; it is an event, despite appearances, that lends itself to no universal interpretation; it is an event of sufficiently stressful magnitude that it exposes other aspects of attention to human flourishing that have somehow gone missing. A similar analysis can be applied to one we identify as the "evildoer." We may see the one who performs evil as the torturer who is ineluctably given to maleficent wrongdoing, causing others to suffer for the sake of it; the agent of tough love whose seeming maliciousness serves a higher good purpose; the one judged as destructive from one perspective but not all (e.g., one man's freedom fighter is another man's terrorist); the bystander identified by inaction and missed opportunity whose failure indicates our own. The first way of characterizing evil restricts the idea of evildoers to moral monsters of a pure black heart; the fourth way, by contrast, broadens our understanding of evil to include the most ordinary sorts of neglects of responsibility. In the second and third ways no such thing as an "evildoer" really exists to begin with: evil really is the good, or it is entirely illusory.

Defining Evil

Identifying which experiences justify when the word *evil* is to be used as a descriptor is no easy matter. Consider several examples of those participating in harmful acts and determine for yourself whether their deeds rise to the level of evil or whether they deserve the label of evildoer: a psychologically disturbed woman who eviscerates her neighbor's abdomen so she can steal the near-term fetus and raise the baby as her own; a soldier who bombs a village of innocents out of obedience to a superior officer; an incompetent government official whose inability to act efficiently in a crisis leads to the death of additional thousands; a miser who refuses to offer aid and shelter to his suffering neighbors in the aftermath of a crisis; an insane man who murders his beloved daughter in the name of the God to whom he offers her as a sacrifice; a mid-level account manager in a prominent advertising firm who cheats and lies to win a coveted promotion; a suicide bomber motivated by the utilitarian reasoning that his actions are a last resort to procuring social justice; a serial killer who tortures for pleasure before doing away with his victims. Only the last of these is unambiguous, but they are all stories from real life. Raw malice motivates the torturer. The rest of the examples call our attention to a medley of activities that can be characterized in a wide range of ways. We have garden-variety selfishness, mental illness, obedience to authority, culpable negligence, unchecked ambition, religious zealotry, and, in the case of the suicide bomber, spurious moral reasoning. In some of the examples, a mix of motivations arguably fermented in the context of a larger narrative. Were the actors pressed to explain their actions, I suspect we would encounter substantial diversity in the justifications they offered for why they acted as they did. In how many of these examples have we described evil or identified evildoers? How would we know?

The notion that we could with consistency locate the line that separates the justifiably bad from the inexcusably evil, either with respect to actions or persons, is ridiculous. This is because most often, evil is not fixed, located in a single act. Nor is it something easily recognized in advance of our encounter with it. Like kindness, evil begins with the repetition of small acts that eventually come to define the actor. This is not to say that there is no such thing as a bad apple. There are in this world psychopaths and moral monsters beyond the pale. The much more representative metaphor, however, is that of a good apple gone bad. Philip Zimbardo proposes this thesis in *The Lucifer Effect*, arguing that evil is not only banal, as Hannah Arendt famously noted in her study of Adolf Eichmann, but also situational, the result of long-term effects of a "bad barrel" on unwitting fruit.[3] Zimbardo defines evil as a "going wrong" and invokes M. C. Escher's *Circle Limit IV* to highlight the illustration. Escher depicts devils and angels—equally plausible outcomes of human moral development. Their outlines, Zimbardo explains, are "permeable and nebulous" and mutually form the contours of one another. The drawing thus provocatively implies that human beings are both good and evil entities at the same time. We travel in the direction of goodness or wickedness depending on the circumstances, sometimes aware that we could have traveled otherwise. Zimbardo elaborates that evil caused by "behaving in ways that harm, abuse, demean, dehumanize, or destroy innocent others" includes not acting to alter the currently existing "systemic powers" that permit such outcomes.[4]

Because in Zimbardo's definition evil is propelled by inertia, it thrives under conditions of passivity. Painfully reflecting on the prison experiments he conducted at Stanford University in the early 1970s, Zimbardo considers the curious ease with which his prisoners and his guards accepted the premises of their situations: "They no longer object to or rebel against anything they are told or commanded to do. They are like Method actors who continue to play their roles when offstage and off camera, and their role has come to consume their identity. It must be distressing to those who argue for innate human dignity to note the servility of the former prison rebels, the heroes of the uprisings, who have been reduced to beggars. No heroes are stepping out of this aggregation."[5]

Zimbardo's reflections demonstrate how easily the benign can become malignant for unsuspecting participants whose intentions and self-understandings are initially good. What emerged from the Stanford experiments was a "powerful illustration of the potentially toxic impact of bad systems and bad situations in making good people behave in pathological ways that are alien to their nature."[6]

Zimbardo's observations are useful for rebutting excuses put forward by those in leadership positions who refuse to take responsibility for their charge, for example, the insistence by some in the Pentagon that the Abu Ghraib scandal was the result of a few bad apples in an otherwise good barrel. Zimbardo's bad barrel counterhypothesis, unlike the military's explanation, provides an answer to the question of how ordinary people come to act in extraordinarily bad ways.[7] Under conditions of systematic dehumanization, inhumanity becomes a reflection of "humanity under pressure."[8] If Zimbardo is right, then the obsession with evil that so characteristically occupies our attention as spectators is misplaced. The extent to which we participate in evil is variable, determined by our response to our situational handicaps. Although evil might accurately be described as alien to who we essentially are, it is not embodied in something wholly other in the context of human existence. Instead, evil, like kindness, begins with small, often unnoticed acts. What starts off as bad becomes, invisibly, evil.

In keeping with Zimbardo's reflections, the distinction between "evil" and evil is significant. "Evil" is used for political or rhetorical purposes by governments, the media, and ordinary people as a conversation stopper to vilify alien others being defined in contrast to familiar selves. Evil, on the other hand, is a reality constitutive of the human condition, and maybe even human nature. Evil has a global rather than a local flavor. It is ubiquitous, an underlying feature of our lives, which is why it is not a helpful descriptor of specific religious practitioners, ethnic tribes, ideological groups, or nation states. Furthermore, evil does not appear instantaneously, out of nowhere. Even the most extreme of the examples of evil noted earlier is the result of a series of occurrences. Evil, in other words, is a state rather than a single act or character trait. It has a narrative and is produced by a specific chain of events.

That we ought to be aware of the uses and misuses of the word *evil*, therefore, is not to suggest that evil itself is mere perspective, a contextually relative designation according to which what is bad for some is good for others. Evil is real. The staggering diversity of normative commitments among human beings in the world, which compel different cultures to value the same things differently, is no argument against the existence of some (man-caused and natural) occurrences that are terrible for everyone everywhere. A television commercial I recently watched hyping a show about hunting animals that strikes me as cruel anticipates a seasonal tradition for others. Some happenings, however, such as the carnage wrought in the targeting of innocents in a war, or the mendacious betrayal of a friend, we would be hard-pressed ever to describe as good, or even morally ambiguous. Such occurrences we ought not to mischaracterize as excusable in view of some greater picture. Dostoevsky's Ivan Karamazov insists that no justification can be made for the brutal treatment of even one vulnerable child, rightly recognizing that mature, thoughtful believers will at some point have to face what theologians refer to as "crises of disconfirmation." This recognition extends to the natural world too as, for example, when a tsunami lures its victims by first teasing them with a dramatically receding shoreline and then substituting the curious phenomenon with a disastrous tidal wave, or when loved ones are taken from us for no reason at all far before their time. The structure of the world is such that it inevitably tests the mental resolve of anyone who is not completely naïve. Evil defies what we can creatively imagine and forces us to question the possibility of meaning within a human situation. What strikes us as bad sometimes becomes less bad in time, and occasionally can come to be seen as a blessing in disguise. Evil stays evil.

I have enumerated the important difference between the rhetorical use of "evil" and the reality of evil, as well as the difference between the concept of bad, which is revisable, and evil, which is permanent. I have not, however, yet elaborated on the extremely significant distinction mentioned so far only in passing between natural and moral evil. The distinction is important because it bears on the relationship between human agency and evil. "Natural evil" pertains to the calamitous events beyond human control that devastate societies, lead to suffering and death, and shake our faith to its core. "Moral evil" pertains to the evil we *cause*, whether the harm that ensues is a result of deliberate maleficent actions or the absence of beneficent motives. Just like natural evil, moral evil leads to suffering and death and forces us to reexamine our faith in the divine or, more broadly (i.e., secularly), in the very idea of a world that contains meaning.

Although the difference between "natural" and "moral" is clear enough, that there is a difference poses problems for the way we think about evil. Is what is distinctive about evil its consequences or that it is intended?[9] Accounts of evil that emphasize the harm evil causes tend not to make as much of the difference between natural and moral evil as those which strongly identify evil with the knowing commission of wrongdoing.[10] How much solace is it to sufferers to know that their suffering is not deliberate or personally earmarked? In some theologies, the difference between natural and moral evil is not that important, because even if evil is primarily associated with maleficent intent, humanly willed, God created humans to have free will, therefore allowing evil to be part of the human condition. For many committed to the project of theodicy, then, both natural and moral evil obtain in crises of faith that challenge the dominant metaphor of an all-loving, all-powerful divinity. Likewise, for a nontheist such as Camus, according to whom the underlying absurdity of our encounter with a universe that is indifferent to our concerns governs all of human life, the distinction between natural and moral evil is not so great.[11] For, whatever its ramifications for theories about moral agency, the characterization of an evil act as natural or moral little affects the impact of the magnitude of human suffering, or makes much of a difference with regard to our attempts to understand why we are alive and how our lives can contain meaning. According to Heidegger, Camus's existentialist contemporary, the crueler our experiences, at the hand of either nature or man, and the blunter their force, the more the notion of "thrown-ness"—our being thrust into a world under circumstances not of our own choosing—substitutes for any proffered explanation about the purposefulness of evil.[12] The analysis I undertake here, then, despite the title of the book, does not necessarily hinge on a qualification that I am talking about only moral, and not natural, evil. Indeed, when we are talking about evil's victims, moral evil becomes but just another instance of a natural evil. We are in either case helpless to prevent the evil encounter from taking place.[13]

This said, I am ultimately concerned with human beings as acting subjects, not merely as passive victims. I am therefore also concerned with the extent to which an evil in which we have the propensity to become actively involved influences our participation in the good. This is an occurrence over which we do have some say. Acknowledging that moral evil can be understood as an instance of natural evil, I focus primarily on the portion of evil that is beyond the guaranteed inheritance of human suffering meted out in the cosmic lottery. My discussion thus turns on the related question of how much free will we have, and whether we are in a position to live better lives once we become sufficiently self-aware of our potential to be evil. My hunch at the outset is that the answer lies somewhere between a deterministic view, that we have no freedom, and a radically self-determinate one, in which evil's influence over us is something from which we can free ourselves.

Four Models of Moral Evil

The work that has been done on the problem of evil is staggering, and carried out from multiple perspectives by a variety of scholars.

In the last four decades sociologists and anthropologists have undertaken scores of investigations into the question of how ordinary people with good traits can come to do terrible things.[14] Other social scientists, in tandem with contemporary deconstructionists and postmodernists, have pioneered a field of what is sometimes called "evil studies." They study the way in which the word *evil* is rhetorically deployed within certain evangelical groups preoccupied with Messianic themes in anticipation of a forthcoming apocalypse, often exploring the ironic thesis that evil ensues precisely when one sets out to vanquish evil.[15]

Some historians hone in on the connection between evil and modernity, often concluding that the Enlightenment ideal of progress is unrealistic in light of the record of the twentieth century, the bloodiest in human history.[16] Religious studies and biblical scholars have recently revived the commitment begun by the early church fathers to reconcile the problem of evil with the traditional notion of a providential divinity that has our best interests at heart.[17] This trend occurs in response to a counter effort among "recovering" believers who have formed an alliance with the "new atheists," attempting to demonstrate that not only does the Bible not rescue God from the critique that he is not all-loving, but that if God did exist, then on the basis of the scriptural evidence, he would have to be found guilty of promoting human misery as well as acting in a morally repugnant fashion.[18]

The most recent group of thinkers to become interested in the concept of evil are scientists conducting brain research. In the last ten years fMRI studies of psychopaths have established that callous behavior is a result of a dysfunction of the amygdala, an area in the middle of the brain that is largely responsible for emotional processing.[19] In the same way some scientists wonder whether identifying the regions of the brain responsible for empathetic identification will lead to amplified altruistic activity, they hypothesize that medical technology will soon be available to treat this part of the brain, and, as a result, decrease the propensity for humans with borderline or Machiavellian personality disorders to engage in harmful conduct.[20] The scientific awakening to the problem of evil offers a fresh justification for the wisdom in the ethicist's age-old appeal to the Delphic Oracle's admonition, know oneself. Human fulfillment begins with anthropological excavation in all its forms.

Scholars in all these camps remind us of the importance of keeping in the forefront of our minds our susceptibility to self-deception, whether in connection with utopian ideas of progress, naïve religiosity, or even pretensions to biological self-sufficiency. Reading this literature over the last four to five years has been humbling, to say the least.

I account for the surge in the focus on the problem of evil, however, by thinking about another humbling realization, namely, that in spite of all the ways in which technology has advanced, in which we have with all due global sensibility gained an exposure to those unlike us, and in which the media immediately and graphically identifies for us the threats for which we have to be on the lookout—in spite of all of these contemporary developments that would seem to mitigate the blunt force of evil's blow—things are not all well in this life, and they are perhaps less well than they were in a time before. Evil remains a problem no closer to being solved than it has ever been. Millions among us still suffer terribly due to the proactive cruelty and callous inaction of others. The reach of the havoc wrought by malicious human beings extends further than ever before. The proportion of sufferers to the world's population is, as a whole, growing.[21] The increased disparity between the wealthy few and the impoverished many, combined with the unprecedented threat of mass destruction and heightened resentment of the West on the part of inhabitants of developing nations, threatens the security even of the most sheltered inhabitants of the most civilized nations. For the more impoverished and war-torn citizens of the world, the matter is considerably worse.

Thus, against the backdrop of the optimism shared by some recent contributors to the study of evil, in the proposition that the evil we experience will lessen in proportion with our discovery of its root causes, I undertake this study with the rather traditional conviction that evil is here with us to stay, in a measure at least no less than that of previous generations. Evil is one of the constants of the human condition. Rather than asking about its quantitative reduction or qualitative reinterpretation, I am interested in what we do with the fact of evil. What is a morally constructive model for dealing with the problem of evil? What are the best resources within our religious and moral traditions for thinking about evil in a manner conducive to human flourishing? Whence the motivation for another book about evil.

In the following chapters I explore the available options for thinking about evil to subsequently weigh the advantages and disadvantages of each approach. Specifically, I focus on four dominant models for understanding the concept of moral evil within the field of comparative religious ethics, locating the genesis for these models in particular religious and moral traditions, and tracing historically their conceptual trajectory to the contemporary era. The first four chapters of this book are devoted, respectively, to the four models and include a discussion of the proponents and critics of each. The principal descriptive virtue of this volume is its ambition to bring these models into focus alongside one another in a synthesized typology. Although the different ways of understanding evil are nothing new, my way of characterizing and contrasting them with one another is.

I now lay out the four models in some detail. The first is evil as the presence of badness (i.e., evil as substantively and radically separate from the good—Manicheanism). The second is evil as the presence of goodness (i.e., evil as tantamount to the good—theodicy). The third is evil as the absence of badness (i.e., evil as an invention, a designated contrast to the good—thorough-going perspectivalism). The fourth is evil as the absence of goodness (i.e., evil as what occurs in lieu of the good—privation or Augustinianism). The four models are my own synthesis, and I have thought hard about how best to characterize them for the better part of the last ten years. Together they form a comprehensive typology: At least one of the four, if not some combination of them, seems to capture the way in which the many scholars working on the problem of evil have understood their subject. The first four chapters in this book discuss these models in turn and are followed by a fifth chapter that, in concluding, links the fourth model—evil as privation—to a certain sort of virtue ethic to achieve moral betterment throughout the course of our lives. I thus move from the descriptive to the normative, drawing some hitherto unconsidered connections between Augustine and Aristotle.[22] Specifically, I tie Augustine's conception of evil as privation—an absence of compassion and goodness—to a neo-Aristotelian emphasis on altruistic habit-forming.

Chapter 1 explores the dichotomy between evil and good in the Manichean model and looks at Satan as a type. It examines the role of the devil in biblical and contemporary theological narratives, attempting to explain genealogically the advent of the popular contemporary referent *evildoer*. The chapter begins with the oldest and most basic theological worldview, which is both dualistic and deterministic, and traces this tradition to the twenty-first century by examining some of the literature emerging today in the fields of psychology and neurology. Martin Luther King Jr. once exhorted his followers to "love the person who commits the evil deed while hating the deed itself." In this view, there is malevolence in the world but there are not truly malevolent people. Chapter 1 engages those who take the greatest exception to this judgment from their conviction that in fact persons ineluctably committed, one might say programmed, to harm others are indeed in our world. As such, the chapter explores what today is still a standard popular understanding of evil, namely, that evil exists independently of—and correspondingly seeks always to undo—the good. In the Manichean model forces of light are opposed by forces of darkness, evil regarded as something to eliminate if we can, but as something whose essence we are unable to modify. Notwithstanding Judaism's and Christianity's by and large official rejection of Manicheanism on theological grounds because it implicitly denies the omnipotence of God, many Jews and Christians still find themselves attracted to the binary logic of the "two poles" to which human beings naturally drift. This portrait is especially endorsed in certain Christian denominations that rely heavily on prophesies outlined in the book of Revelation. Drawn to an idea of a dangerous and seductive Satan who instrumentally serves as a foil to the figure of Jesus in narratives about the Second Coming, many evangelicals, anticipating the end of days, read into newspaper headlines a drama being played out on earth that reflects one already being played out on a grander scale. Chapter 1 discusses the popularity of apocalypticism and looks at the rapture culture that has swept over some portions of the United States, engaging the work of, among others, Amy Frykholm and Paul Boyer.

Chapter 1 thus strives to account for the seductive appeal as well as the historical endurance of the Manichean model. Beginning with some writings of the Gnostics and early Manicheans, the chapter offers an account of why the Manichean understanding of evil has endured over the last seventeen hundred years, examining along the way some contemporary defenders of the Manichean view in the Jewish and Christian traditions. The chapter also takes up the Manicheanism of some classic and contemporary secular thinkers, such as Thomas Hobbes, the Marquis de Sade, Joseph Conrad, and Samuel Huntington, and concludes with an examination of some unexpected and compelling scientific evidence currently emerging that supports the two poles thesis. To what theological and ethical ends does an understanding of evil as a substantive presence commit its defender? After drawing some conclusions about the appeal of the Manichean view of evil, chapter 1 looks at some of the criticisms leveled against it: essentialism, pessimism, self-righteousness, self-deception, and warmongerism.

Chapter 2 deals with the classic religious treatment of evil in the West, focusing on theodicies, that is, vindications of the divine in light of the terrible suffering human beings experience. Specifically, the chapter examines the brand of thinking in religious and philosophical literature that sees evil, especially moral evil, as necessary for realizing the good. In the second model the evil that leads to goodness and suffering is seen as redemptive. Although it had plenty of biblical precedent, Gottfried Leibniz officially introduced the term *theodicy* into the discourse of theological ethics in his seminal essay, "Theodicy: An Essay on the Benevolence of God, the Free Will of Man, and the Origin of Evil," published in 1710. After considering Leibniz's innovation, chapter 2 delves into the story of Job and then focuses on the two church fathers who integrated the problem of evil into Christian theology: Irenaeus, a second-century bishop and apologist in what is now Lyon, and Lactantius, an early fourth-century Christian apologist. Lactantius's classic formulation of the conundrum has become a template for theodicists. Invoking Epicurus, Lactantius lays out the basic problem: "God either wishes to take away evils and cannot, or he can and does not wish to, or he neither wishes nor is able, or he both wishes to and is able."[23] In any of these scenarios, God cannot be thought to be all-loving and all-powerful if at the same time evil is acknowledged to be genuinely evil, that is, not the good in disguise. Thus began the long attempt in church history to explain away evil as something other than evil. Chapter 2 presents in their most convincing forms some of the most prominent contemporary solutions to Lactantius's conundrum. Historically, the vindications appear in both simple (e.g., God's ways are hidden; God rights all wrongs in the eschaton) and more subtle arguments (e.g., pain and loss are inextricably bound up with joy; anger toward God is legitimate expression of faith; free will requires the possibility of evil, which is our problem not God's). The chapter analyzes each of the major versions of theodicy critically, with an eye to the present day, asking whether theodicy is still plausible in the wake of the brutalities of the twentieth century—the worst in human history—and in light of the threats that loom in the twenty-first century. What are the descriptive and normative selling points of understanding evil through the lens of theodicy? What are the problems with doing so? How prevalent is theodicy today? Chapter 2 concludes by examining some of theodicy's detractors, who expound on the problematic positions to which theodicy leads, such as idealism and quietism.

In contrast to the view that evil is the manifestation of the devil in concrete guise, and equally challenging the view that evil is part and parcel of a greater good, the currently fashionable conviction holds that evil as a concrete concept is illusory, lacking either substantive, metaphysical status or real psychological purchase. Chapter 3 explores the claim that evil is mere orientation, a perspective from which we can wrest ourselves with the right sort of self-reinvention. In *Beyond Good and Evil*, Nietzsche writes,

> Not to remain stuck to a person—not even the most loved—every person is a prison, also a nook. Not to remain stuck to a fatherland—not even if it suffers most and needs help most—it is less difficult to sever one's heart from a victorious fatherland. Not to remain stuck to some pity—not even for higher men into whose rare torture and helplessness some accident allowed us to look. Not to remain stuck to a science—even if it should lure us with the most precious finds that seem to have been saved up precisely for us. Not to remain stuck to one's own detachment, to that voluptuous remoteness and strangeness of the bird who flees even higher to see ever more below him—the danger of the flier. Not to remain stuck to our own virtues and become as a whole victim of some detail in us, such as our hospitality . . . One must know how to *conserve oneself*: the hardest test of independence.[24]

According to Nietzsche, we may be required to sacrifice any loyalty to an ethic, habit, belief, joy, or identity to rise above those conventional norms and institutions that impede the progress of the mediocre majority. The strong person never remains stuck, even in the malaise that afflicts him or her from within. By implication, evil can be, in Nietzsche's phrase, "actively forgotten," a past that is erased if we can manage only to examine our current predicament in a new, different light. Evil, in lieu of any legitimate authority that can objectively distinguish good from evil, can be demythologized as the illusion it in fact is. Evil thereby becomes something we can will away.[25] It does not as such exist.

Chapter 3 thus challenges the traditional association of evil with what is objectively bad, and delves into the tradition Nietzsche spawned in the West when he recommended that we move "beyond good and evil." The chapter also looks at classical texts from Eastern traditions (e.g., Chuang-Tzu's *Inner Chapters* and Dōgen's "Shobogenzo Gejokoan") that, supporting the Nietzschean line of thought, assert that distinctions themselves, including the one between good and evil, can never be accessed in any meaningful way because of the limitations of language. In turn, chapter 3 examines the writings of Michel Foucault ("value is bound up with power"), Hermann Hesse ("there is beauty in everything if you look at it the right way"), as well as Eastern traditions, which suggest either that we are the creators of what we value (e.g., Nietzsche, Hesse, Foucault) or that we are illusorily locked into standard perceptions about good and evil because of the limitations of language (e.g., Dōgen, Chaung-Tzu). Chapter 3 scrutinizes an approach to understanding evil that emphasizes language and power, as well as one that prizes the triumph of the aesthetic over the normative. The chapter closes by examining opponents of perspectivalism who argue in defense of an enduring reality to the sting of death and the loneliness of despair, experiences to which we can respond as beings with free will, but over whose advent we often have no control. Denying suffering, this objection runs, does not amount to eliminating it.

Chapter 4 considers the model that defines evil as an absence, a vacuum of goodness, rather than a presence. The chapter asks whether it is possible to resist seeing evil as tantamount to the good (against theodicists) and to simultaneously steer between the extremes of Manicheanism, in which evil is thought to exist substantively apart from the good, and perspectivalism, which sees evil as not existing substantively. It then considers the Augustinian understanding of evil as privation, or absence of goodness, as the view that might well be this *via media*. According to the privation thesis, evil is what occurs in lieu of God, or more generally, the good. Evil, to paraphrase Hannah Arendt, is the fungus that grows in dark corners where light has been missing for too long, a fungus by which we are all susceptible of being seized. Evil is in this sense more accurately characterized as thoughtlessness than as undiluted monstrousness, though it can be monstrous. It is mundane, banal, an affliction with which ordinarily and extraordinarily wicked people are familiar.

Chapter 4 offers a careful presentation and analysis of the privation thesis classically proposed by St. Augustine in book 3, chapter 7 of *The Confessions* and then again in books 6 and 12 of *City of God*. After spending time with Augustine himself, through texts that show the maturation of his thinking on the problem of evil, chapter 4 examines religious and secular heirs of the Augustinian tradition, including Reinhold Niebuhr, Albert Camus, and Hannah Arendt. Despite their varying degrees of religiosity, these thinkers share certain presuppositions about the nature of moral evil. First, as human beings, we have a natural tendency to inconstancy and corruption. Augustine and his theological descendants explain this defect as an inherited liability which, due to the Fall, we are unable to overcome apart from God. Secular thinkers like Camus and Arendt call our attention to the dangers that accrue in proportion to our distance from the good. In both constructions, however, at the start of our existence, something crucial is already missing, something worth trying to recover. Second, these thinkers emphasize that knowing oneself as defective, as existing in the first place in a state of inconstancy, is the impetus that might motivate us to do away with our complacent dispositions. Third, it is in attending to our human nature (or in the case of Camus and Arendt, our human condition) that we acquire human dignity. Repairing our fallen selves, closing the distance between ourselves and God (or ourselves and the good) is the quintessential human task. Evil, according to the privation thesis, is correspondingly the deprivation of human dignity, the condition that overtakes the human being who has yet to live up to his or her humanity.

The Augustinian picture is controversial. It arouses our attention because of the general problem of recognition it invites. Because evil refers to what is not present, it is hard in this conception to imagine how we might defend ourselves against the causes of our ruination at evil's behest. In the Augustinian approach we do not have the luxury of identifying human monsters as a first stage in preparation for later vanquishing them. We cannot even reliably separate evil and good actors into distinct categories to better clarify to ourselves the sorts of people with whom we should try to empathize. The privation thesis accommodates the chillingly descriptive observation that normal people are capable of dastardly as well as wonderful things. Human beings pine in the direction of good and evil. That is, we are in our essence problematic and, as a result, must work on this problem. Augustine's diagnosis of evil confronts us as human agents qua agents and is for this reason more demanding than its alternative models, in which one is construed either as passive (Manicheanism, theodicy) or unrestrained (perspectivalism) in one's freedom. In Augustinian theological anthropology, we are free, but our freedom is, as the Judaic philosopher Emmanuel Levinas puts it, "difficult."[26] Chapter 4, like the three that precede it, is primarily descriptive and does not aspire to make an argument for the Augustinian view.

Chapter 5, which concludes the book, takes the normative turn, connecting the descriptive account of evil as privation endorsed by Augustine to an Aristotelian theory of virtue that sees altruistic habit-forming as the crux of the well-lived moral life. The purpose of chapter 5 is twofold. First is to make the argument that the Augustinian account is to be preferred over its alternatives. Second is to draw a hitherto underexplored connection between Augustine and Aristotle, that is, between the privation thesis and character development. The descriptive account of evil as privation, which commits us to a "difficult freedom," leads to a demanding normative claim: Avoiding our participation in evil, to the albeit limited extent it is possible in this life for us to do so, amounts to hard moral work, but work we nonetheless ought to do. According to the privation thesis, evil is more ubiquitous and less eradicable than we might expect. It follows that if we are not careful, we might fall under its sway. Thus we ought always to be on moral guard. If evil is the effect of a lack, then it is something that we overcome through investment, not divestment. Through sustained effort—not through mere avoidance of wrongdoing—we can protect ourselves from evil's subsuming influence. The absence of goodness—evil—to which, due to our nature, we are always in danger of succumbing, can in this sense be seen as a descriptive prognosis that has a normative implication. We ought, as much as possible, to build the good into our lives.

Chapter 5 makes this connection between the Augustinian understanding of evil as privation and Aristotelian ethics. Both, and not just the latter, emphasize virtue. Left to mere inertia, we will drift away from righteousness and eventually become participants in the dehumanizing trends that have time and time again characterized the darkest of human sagas. By reminding us of the ugly selves we each potentially are, the privation thesis can be interpreted as an inducement to seek virtue in a society that obligates us to adhere only to the moral minimal. An Augustinian understanding of evil implicates everyone. If this is true, we should seek the good beyond the level that common sense morality, a morality built on the avoidance of wrongdoing, requires of us.

A word needs to be said about my intended audience as well as about my way of using the figures I choose to focus on in this book. I hope to reach not only specialists, but also an educated public capable of understanding conceptual differences among ways of construing moral evil. To borrow a distinction from Richard Rorty, I am trying to engage not in *historical reconstruction*, the replication of historical figures' ideas strictly in their terms, betraying an explicit awareness each time I invoke them of the latest debates occurring in the secondary scholarship (although I do try to do this as much as possible), but in *rational reconstruction*, the application of such figures' ideas to broader normative issues in terms contemporaneous with how those issues are currently being discussed.[27] Thus I bring seminal classical figures such as Augustine or Nietzsche into the company of recent thinkers working in the tradition of their predecessors but not necessarily sharing all of their views in important respects. To take one example, current scholarship seems decisively to have veered away from characterizing Nietzsche as a subjectivist, or even an intellectual radical, for whom the "revaluation of values" implies an irretrievable rejection of any stable notion of "truth." Although I have taken efforts not to construe Nietzsche this way, for some of the thinkers with whom I put him in conversation, such as Hermann Hesse, the matter is not as settled. In dealing with Nietzsche and Hesse together in my chapter on the perspectivalist model, I risk giving the impression I hope not to give, and thereby running afoul of the theorist who acknowledges only the legitimacy of historical reconstruction. I am aware of this methodological hazard, which I nevertheless take to establish, through family resemblance constructions, distinct conceptual models that stand in helpful contrast to one another. In my defense in this regard, I do have some precedent, because many scholars with more than a historical preoccupation with their subjects take a constructive interest in the past to encourage fresh avenues for normative inquiry.

One more qualification bears mentioning. Although the four models in my typology are distinguishable from one another, in some instances they overlap. Manicheanism could be construed as but another theodicy in which God is insulated from having to answer for human suffering because evil is not within his purview to begin with. The theodicist's conviction that we are of a radically different order than God, unable to speculate about divine intentions, is consistent with an Augustinian claim about the constancy of God, who exists in a category apart from all other relative goods. The four models are surely more complicated than I have so far presented them, and none should be dismissed too readily. Each has its share of intelligent defenders and it is important not to make straw men out of any of the models' main supporters. This acknowledged, I lead in this chapter toward several conclusions for how we ought to think of evil. Among them are the following:

> Like altruism, evil can neither be explained through reference exclusively to genetic traits nor without some understanding of its biological underpinnings. Evil is an irremovable part but not exclusively determinative of human nature. Save but a few exceptions, human beings are not accurately characterized as good seeds or bad seeds but rather as creatures with the capacity for good and evil, these traits often surfacing in response to situations that facilitate their emergence. As the work of Milgram, Zimbardo, and others has demonstrated, ordinary people who display virtuous traits can act in extraordinarily malicious ways under certain environmental pressures.

> That we have the capacity for evil, however, does not mean that our participation in evil is necessarily the result of the dehumanizing situations into which we are thrown. Rather, as with our participation in the

good, it is also the upshot of nurture working on nature, and vice versa. Although correct that even the best of us are corruptible in the face of systemic pressures that blunt our capacity to resist wrongdoing, Zimbardo's bad barrel theory does not fully explain why ordinary persons do extraordinarily terrible things. In a crisis situation, under virtually the same circumstances, some bystanders become villains, others become heroes, and still others remain bystanders. Our decision to pursue moral betterment within the context of our religious and moral traditions has something to do with how or whom our character shapes up to be. A rejection of a binary view of good and evil should not be understood to imply a situational determinism of a different sort.

> We are therefore, in spite of all that is beyond our control, endowed with the capacity to prepare ourselves for the terrible things that are to come and in which we are in danger of participating, including natural disasters that arrive out of nowhere, the systems in which we get caught up without our knowing it, and our own biological proclivities for selfish and even overtly harmful behavior. Free will, despite the extent to which it has arguably been exaggerated in theology, philosophy, and legal theory, is not a myth, although it may turn out that free will does not apply to the extent we thought it did with regard to the worst among us, for instance, psychopaths.

> Free will, in the context of discussions about evil, pertains to the human potential to form certain moral habits. It implies that we have an opportunity, in consultation with mentors, spiritual leaders, and others in whom we have located a virtuous character, proactively to become compassionate people. Evil is constant, but how we respond to evil is variable, and depends on our developing character. It is in this sense that a theory of evil as privation, as the absence of goodness, is tied to empathy, fellow-feeling, and altruism. What this means is that discussions about evil have ramifications in ethics beyond theology and human anthropology. They also lay the ground for an endorsement of an ethic of virtue that sees the crux of the well-lived moral life as the acquisition of other-regarding habits.

Within these four claims I fuse the insights of two figures often opposed to one another in ethics and theology: Augustine and Aristotle. Augustine's pessimistic account of human anthropology, which plays down free will and our capacity to participate in the creation of the good, stands in some tension with Aristotelian notions of self-love that deemphasize humility, contrition, and sin. Nevertheless, I think it is possible to combine insights from both thinkers to form the complex view of the relationship between evil and free will that I have outlined. With Augustine, I subscribe to the notion that evil is ontologically inevitable as well as more phenomenally common than we are wont to recognize. Not even the most saintly among us go through life unscathed. As human creatures, we are in this respect not completely free. With Aristotle, I maintain that our "difficult freedom" nonetheless puts the burden more rather than less heavily on our shoulders to take responsibility for what is within our control, and in this respect, as Aristotle reminds us in *The Nicomachean Ethics*, to strive, in spite of our mortality, to be immortal.[28] Evil is a stain on the human being that can never be fully wiped away, but it is for this reason no less a spur to wisdom, the communal, and, finally, the good.

At the end of *No Country for Old Men*, Anton Chigurh is alone, but Sheriff Ed Tom Bell, who has survived Chigurh's killing spree, is not. Nor are we. Evil might be a reason for inescapable concern, even despair, but this does not make it a justification to resign to an ethic of futility despite the casualties that evil claims from human communities. No account of evil that is honestly descriptive will permit us to whitewash the destructive threat under which we remain in everyday human experience. At the same time, under this oppressive umbrella of constraint endure dignity, hope, and the opportunity for connection between human beings who need one another, perhaps without yet realizing it.

Notes

1. On April 5, 2006, months after independent investigators had demonstrated that levee failures were not caused by natural forces beyond intended design strength, Lieutenant General Carl Strock testified before the US Senate Subcommittee on Energy and Water that "We have now concluded we had problems with the design of the structure." See www.cbsnews.com/stories/2006/06/01/storm/main1675244.shtml. He also testified that the US Army Corps of Engineers did not know of this mechanical design failure before August 29, 2005. The claim of ignorance is refuted, however, by the National Science Foundation investigators hired by the Army Corps of Engineers, who point to a 1986 study also conducted by the Corps of Engineers that found such flaws possibly existed in the I-wall design. As late as two full years after the tragedy, only $40 million of the $854 million allocated for disaster victims had been used (as reported by the *Los Angeles Times*, August 29, 2007), more evidence of the inefficiency of the governmental agencies overseeing the recovery effort.

2. On *The 700 Club*, Pat Robertson blamed Hurricane Katrina on the permissibility of abortions in the United States. Robertson and Jerry Falwell made similar claims about the connection between promiscuity and homosexuality in the United States and the attacks on September 11, 2001. Robertson, ever consistent, attributed the devastating earthquake in Haiti in January 2010 to a pact Haitians made with the devil. On Robertson and Katrina, see www.time.com/time/specials/packages/article/0,28804,1953778_195 3776_195377 1,00.html.

3. Arendt, *Eichmann in Jerusalem: A Report*, Zimbardo, *Lucifer Effect*, x.

4. Zimbardo, *Lucifer Effect*, 5, 1.

5. Ibid., 143.

6. Ibid., 195.

7. Ibid., x, 226.

8. Walzer, *Just and Unjust Wars*, 4.

9. Claudia Card offers a wonderful analysis of these two classical ways of understanding evil and classifies them under the rubrics of the utilitarian and stoic (or Kantian) approaches, respectively. Her definition fuses the two aspects: evil is a foreseeable harm that is both "culpably inflicted (or tolerated, aggravated, or maintained)" and "deprives, or seriously risks depriving, others of the basics that are necessary to make a life possible and tolerable or decent (or to make a death decent)." *Atrocity Paradigm*, 16.

10. Socrates thought that it was impossible knowingly to commit wrongdoing because, he believed, we could not know the good and then fail to act on it. This is sometimes referred to as the Socratic Paradox. Socrates establishes this strong link between knowledge and virtue in Plato's dialogue, *Protagoras*. See Plato, *Protagoras*, 355A–58D.

11. Camus, *Myth of Sisyphus*. See especially chapter 3.

12. Heidegger, *Being and Time*, 175.

13. Even by acknowledging a category of natural evil at all, I open myself to the charge of ontologizing evil, i.e., giving it a substantive existential status apart from the choices we make as moral agents. This is problematic for, for example, Kantians and even some teleological thinkers for whom a category of natural evil by default risks underemphasizing the critical role of responsibility in human conduct. Although sympathetic to this concern, I nevertheless defend the use of the term *natural evil* on the basis of the capacity of some natural disasters and calamities to be so severe that they threaten the very notion of meaning within the human context. This said, I agree that moral evil as a category takes primacy over natural evil, hence the book title. I thank Ron Green for helping me think more critically about the usefulness of employing a category of natural evil.

14. A mere sampling of some of the most important examples include Baumeister, *Evil*; Browning, *Ordinary Men*; Conroy, *Unspeakable Acts, Ordinary People*; Cooper, *Dimensions of Evil*; Goldhagen, *Hitler's Willing Executioners*; Kelman and Hamilton, *Crimes of Obedience*; Milgram, *Obedience to Authority*; Straub, *Roots of Evil*; Waller, *Becoming Evil*; Zimbardo "Pathology of Imprisonment"; Zimbardo, *Lucifer Effect*.

15. On the anticipation of an apocalypse, see Boyer, *When Time Shall Be*; Frykholm, *Rapture Culture*; Phillips, *Terrors and Experts*; Sandler, *Righteous*. On the irony thesis, see, for example, Bernstein, *Abuse of Evil*, 11; Frankfurter, *Evil Incarnate*, 5–12.

16. See Glover, *Humanity*.

17. For a wonderful resource for examining the ways theodicy emerges in liturgy, see Laato and de Moor, *Theodicy in the World of the Bible*.

18. Four references stand out here: Dawkins, *God Delusion*; Harris, *End of Faith*; Hitchens, *God Is Not Great*; Ehrman, *God's Problem*. Ehrman was a once committed Christian and still writes as an insider, albeit a recovering one, whereas Dawkins, Harris, and Hitchens, critics from the outside, are sometimes collectively referred to among Christian intellectuals as the unholy Trinity.

19. Kiehl et al., "Limbic Abnormalities"; see Oakley, *Evil Genes*, 89–93.

20. Oakley, *Evil Genes*, 39–48; Trout, *Empathy Gap*. Mounting evidence suggests that psychopathic behavior manifests itself in children, leading researchers to speculate optimistically about new prospects for treating psychopathy, because the younger the brain, the more malleable it is thought to be. See Viding et al., "Substantial Genetic Risk."

21. I am aware of the strong nature of these claims and do not want nostalgically to romanticize a safer, less vicious human past. Nevertheless, there are reasons to believe the twentieth century poet Philip Larkin, who, in "MCMXIV," commenting on the legacy of two world wars, wrote "Never such innocence again." Larkin's warning, quoted by Jonathan Glover on page 3 of *Humanity*, is used as an overarching theme in the context of the advent of a technology that makes possible unprecedented population growth, the killing of very large numbers of people at a distance, access by the masses to guns, and the forced proximity of disparate tribes within the confines of a small space in an ever-closing global context. Genocide alone is arguably a modern phenomenon so massive in scope and carefully planned that it simply could not have been organized in prior epochs. These facts, Glover is right to point out, at the very least call into question the neo-Enlightenment ideal of human progress. Neither I nor Glover would argue that human beings have changed essentially. If anything, the conditions of the contemporary age have pressed the urgency of engaging in an accurate human anthropology. Notwithstanding my suspicion of the Enlightenment ideal of steady betterment on the aggregate level, I share Glover's cautious optimism that the development of the moral imagination, spurred into action now as never before, might provide us with the resources to combat "the festival of cruelty" (Nietzsche's phrase) to which we have always been given. See Glover, *Humanity*, 31–44.

22. One thinker who does relate Aristotle to Augustine is Oliver O'Donovan; however, O'Donovan primarily criticizes an Aristotelian virtue ethics. See *Problem of Self-Love*, 18.

23. Lactantius, *Minor Works*, 92–93.

24. Nietzsche, *Beyond Good and Evil*, 52.

25. Independent of his insistence on our moving beyond the linguistic baggage typically associated with human flourishing, it is important to appreciate Nietzsche's indispensable spur provided by the "revaluation of values" to question conventional labels. Nietzsche is surely right about the temptation to become beholden to a pattern that reifies existing judgments about good and bad, right and wrong, and so on. Thus, the careful reader of Nietzsche acknowledges that he is methodologically committed to undermine himself constantly in the pursuit of a radical intellectual freedom. The wise Buddhist practitioner knows that the raft is not the shore. Likewise, the nimble self-examiner realizes that the overman is a pedagogical prod rather than an end in itself and is intended to help the self to become truer by periodically overcoming itself. I thank Doug Tarnopol and Jim Swan-Tuite for helping elucidate this distinction.

26. Levinas, *Difficult Freedom*.

27. Rorty, "Historiography of Philosophy." Van Harvey's work on Feuerbach invokes Rorty's distinction to suggest that sometimes the best rational reconstruction occurs through close historically sensitive analysis, as it did in his retrieval of Feuerbach. This is not to say that rational reconstruction needs historical reconstruction in every

case. See Harvey, *Feuerbach and the Interpretation of Religion*, 15–20, 231. Whether one can get at the issues historical figures address without fully spelling out the context of their advent is, of course, in question. I thank Jock Reeder and Jim Swan Tuite for helping me think about how to frame my use of examples in this book.

28. Aristotle, *Nicomachean Ethics*, 1177b35.

CHAPTER ONE

Evil versus Goodness

Satan and Other "Evildoers"

"If I've learned anything through these many years of research, it's that Carolyn's choices were a bit like the choices a tree on a windy shoreline has in deciding how tall and how bent to grow. Sure, others, as for example, George Washington and Mahatma Gandhi, were probably able to produce real changes in their neurobiological makeup through their conscious choices— strengthening their top-down control even if they were unable to adjust their bottom-up passions. . . . But what of those, like Carolyn, who don't seem to have the requisite neural apparatus to understand that there is a problem, not with drinking, or with others, but rather, with themselves? What motivation could such a person have to even attempt a change?"

—Barbara Oakley, *Evil Genes*
(commenting on her sister's apparent lack of free will)

The Standard View of Evil

The idea of moral evil has always held a special place in philosophical and theological systems of thought because the existence of evil has implications for the dignity with which and the limits within which we act. Moral culpability is made possible by our ability to choose to do terrible things or to refrain from doing good things. Philosophically, the categories of moral praiseworthiness and blameworthiness depend on the prospect of our being able to act or not act one way when we have the capacity to act otherwise. Theologically, the whole point to being humans made in God's image is that we are neither beasts enslaved to act on appetite alone nor automatons whose actions are exhaustively predetermined by mechanisms of which we are not aware. This means that among the things implied in the standard view of free will is the notion that when we act we also create. Through our own volitional force we change the world in important, if small, ways. Were it not for our decision making, the course of human history would have proceeded differently, according to an endless chain of events begun long ago and beyond anyone's capacity to alter. All human dignity is bound up with the human ability and human desire to make that little difference. Clearly, regardless of whether we in fact have free will, we are motivated to acknowledge free will. With free will come independence, responsibility, and dignity. Because these are features of creaturely existence that elevate us, they have become important aspects of how evil is recognized and understood. In the standard view, the concepts of moral evil and moral agency therefore go hand in hand. When we talk about moral evil in the standard view, we are also talking about personal responsibility, which depends on our being able to make meaningful choices about how to act and live.

The standard view recognizes that at times we are helpless. At such moments we lack the moral resources to overcome the default course of events. On these occasions we encounter evil from the outside as the advent of horrific circumstances for which we are not morally responsible, and of such an overwhelming magnitude that we are simply unable to interpret our encounter as something any milder. When this occurs, our freedom is limited and we are at our most like the other animals. According to the standard view, however, our encounter with evil is not exhaustively characterized by such encounters. Evil so great that every time we encountered it we also succumbed would impinge on human freedom and dignity too extensively for us to afford a recognizably human picture of ourselves. The upshot of the standard view, which embraces a robust notion of free will, is a "thesis of containment" according to which evil exists but can also be fought. Evil is not so debilitating that we become impotent to respond to it, or so overbearing that we cannot survive it. Rather, in the standard view, evil is understood as a character-defining test that pushes human virtue and resilience to their limits. A world in which evil is mere nuisance is as pointless as a world in which evil inevitably destroys everything in its path.

It follows that theodicy is compatible with the standard view. Within the framework of theodicy, evil is the means by which meaning is affirmed within human existence: Our dignity accrues in proportion to our wherewithal to endure a trial whose advent is beyond our control, but whose duration we have the capacity to outlast. William James captures the optimistic flavor of the thesis of containment at work within most religious worldviews in a passage from *The Varieties of Religious Experience*: "In the Louvre there is a picture, by Guido Reni, of St. Michael with his foot on Satan's neck. The richness of the picture is in large part due to the fiend's figure being there. The richness of its allegorical meaning also is due to his being there—that is, the world is all the richer for having a devil in it, *so long as we keep our foot upon his neck*."[1] Religion's secret, James asserts, is its ability outwardly to accept evil as a perennial condition of human existence but inwardly to provide practitioners with the faith that this evil is to "be permanently overcome."[2] Secularized theodicies come more in the form of accessible aphorisms such as "everything happens for a reason," or "without pain we would not know pleasure," but retain the prophetic character of traditional theodicies. In both cases, faith in a future "both here and not yet" trumps a present characterized by suffering and rampant injustice. Indeed, suffering is redemptive. According to James, we are in the big picture better off with a world that has evil, as long as the forces of evil do not gain too much control. The extent to which what I have called the thesis of containment does empirical justice to the range and depth of suffering human beings experience in this world is a matter of considerable debate and will become a primary issue in chapter 2. However, the thesis already needs to be underscored, to emphasize the counterintuitive observation that under the right parameters evil not only is not necessarily conducive to despair, it also actually reinforces the idea that this world ultimately has meaning. What this, in turn, means is that in spite of the multiple times we will as a matter of course stumble upon evil, we also have a motivation to model and remodel evil—to introduce it—as problematic within our religious traditions and as a recognizable obstacle within the larger cultural milieu.

This process of modeling evil is not without its dangers. David Frankfurter, a historian of religion examining the phenomenon of satanic cults (which he suggests the media and others helped create), argues that our drive to participate in the extermination of evil is so powerful that we actually create conflict where there previously was none.

> Evil is a *discourse*, a way of representing things and shaping our experience of things, not some force in itself. The most horrible atrocities . . . can and must be rendered sensible as human actions with proper contexts. . . . If there is an irony, then it lies not in my having to describe the experience of evil in its extreme but rather in the fact that, in every one of the historical cases I address, it was a myth of evil conspiracy that mobilized people in large numbers to astounding acts of brutality against accused conspirators. That is, the real atrocities of history seem to take place *not* in the perverse ceremonies of some evil cult but rather in the course of *purging* such cults from the world. Real evil happens when people speak of evil.[3]

Frankfurter seeks to expose "demonic conspiracies" whose participants are obsessively preoccupied with cults and heretics. Their understanding of evil, he argues, deflects attention from the cumbersome, ongoing burden of self-reflection and regards our existing norms as beyond reproach.

Frankfurter's criticism of the way in which the word *evil* is so often rhetorically deployed leads to a second key feature of the standard view central to the project of modeling evil. This is the assumption that evil pertains to something that exists substantively, apart from the self, prowling with impunity and without permission as an uninvited intruder on the human scene. Some thinkers' term of choice for this referent is the "Gothic," wherein evil is understood to be a grotesque, suprahuman force whose candidate for membership among human beings qua human beings is out of the question.[4] To us, the evil other is as a cancer whose reasons we neither fully manage nor care to understand. Like cancer, it attacks without explanation. It paradigmatically manifests itself in the faceless terrorist or the serial rapist. We cannot get through to the evil other, but we do not need to do so, for what is essential is to protect ourselves from its impingement on our world.

No doubt it behooves us to recognize that some individuals and groups are so given to cruelty that they relinquish their potential to be gripped by any appeal to empathize with their victims. Still, it is instructive that once the Gothic model as a template for our understanding of evil takes hold, it easily gives way to a set of binaries. These binaries are reflected in the familiar slogans of our headlines. Columbine is recast as a battle between believers of Christ and an underground that has forsaken him; the war on terror is characterized as a matter of the defenders of freedom versus freedom's deniers. Often this dichotomizing results in a simplified ideology of essentialism, which, in the political sphere, translates into what freelance writer Danny Postel has termed an "ontology of alterity."[5] Postel uses this phrase in a review of John Gray's book *Al Qaeda and What It Means to Be Modern*, in which he criticizes Gray for treating certain ethnic and religious entities as monolithic, and for dismissing out of hand ecumenical hopes of peaceful coexistence among diverse cultures and civilizations. Gray's diatribe against universalism reminds Postel of Samuel Huntington's controversial but popular thesis about the belief in the incommensurability of Arab culture and the West.[6] Postel takes both authors to task for suggesting that we are long past the era of trying to grasp one another in our particularity, and for insisting that today the stakes are too high not to accept that groups of human beings are ineluctably given to divergent, clashing values. An upshot of such othering is the shunning of nuance and self-examination.[7] Evil remains a linguistic weapon used to demonize whatever the current "them" is with which "we" happen to be concerned. Evil, runs this criticism, is rhetorically deployed to help avoid the burden of turning inward and engaging in genuine self-judgment. The concern, then, is that the Gothic view of evil is both descriptively false and normatively evasive.

On the other hand, something about evil is strange and life-stultifying, in that encounters with evil interrupt the rhythm and comfortable dependability of normal existence. Also, hypothetically, reflections about evil that result from our fear of it do not have to devolve into a dichotomization between an *us* and a *them*. Indeed, evil could be conceived as a dark, unwelcome, substantive intrusion within the self. As the psychologist Terry Cooper notes, it is plausible that we have a shadow self, our own Mr. Hyde who corresponds to a more recognizable Dr. Jekyll, who, the more we suppress and try to quarantine him or her, hates us back the more and manifests in rebellious and self-sabotaging ways.[8] In Cooper's account, evil is essentially a "hatred of others that may very well begin with a hatred of ourselves."[9] According to Cooper, we are all susceptible to this shadow self, which becomes increasingly diabolical and inhuman the more we ignore it.[10] Cooper's observation suggests, without identifying explicit perpetrators and victims, the possibility of a depoliticized understanding of evil along Gothic lines in which evil is understood to attack human beings ubiquitously, from without. In this case evil might lose its tribal dimension but nevertheless retain an impenetrable and unalterable character. Evil would still not be collapsible into the good, but neither would it be easily dismissible by critics as mythologization.

Is this more charitable view of a Gothic understanding of evil intellectually sustainable? What are the advantages of construing evil as the opposite of good, as the presence of badness, as I characterized the Manichean view in the introduction? With what system of thought did such a model gain traction and why does it continue to hold such an appeal today?

Manicheanism and the Idea of Satan

Attempting to guide the healing of Asclepius, god of medicine, the ranking deity Hermes Trismegistus prophetically warns,

> You must not then, my pupils, speak as many do, who say that God ought by all means to have freed the world from evil. To those who speak thus, not a word ought to be said in answer; but for your sake I will pursue my argument, and therewith explain this. It was beyond God's power to put a stop to evil, and expel it from the universe; for evil is present in the world in such sort that it is manifestly an inseparable part thereof. . . . I will say that there are daemons who dwell with us here on earth, and others who dwell above us in the lower air, and others again, whose abode is in the purest part of the air, where no mist or cloud can be, and where no disturbance is caused by the motion of any of the heavenly bodies. And the souls which have transgressed the rules

of piety, when they depart from the body, are handed over to these daemons, and are swept and hurled to and fro in those strata of the air which teem with fire and hail. The one safeguard is piety. Over the pious man neither the evil daemon nor destiny has dominion; for God saves the pious from every ill. Piety is the one and only good among men.[11]

In this passage Hermes Trismegistus forecasts the conditions under which evil was meant to be countered according to second-century BCE Gnostic cosmology: as something from which to flee or as something to eradicate, but in either case something we are fundamentally unable to alter.[12] Existing independently of and correspondingly seeking always to undo the good, evil, in the Gnostic view, justified a culture of fear that inspired the narrow remedy of obedient cultic observance. Once firmly in the grip of the King of Darkness, there was nothing for a mortal to do, the Gnostics believed, but languish. Salvation for most mortals remained available via consultation with specialized esoteric teachings that emphasized the spiritual over the material—*gnosis*—and featured fasting, meditation, sexual abstinence, and ascetic withdrawal.[13] In lieu of pursuing this elevated form of existence, one would by default succumb to one of Satan's seductive minions, to which all human beings were thought to be susceptible by virtue of the embodied, lustful nature of fleshly existence.

Manicheans, like the Gnostics, embraced a dualistic worldview. They believed, however, even more strongly than the Gnostics did in the idea of two independent and opposing forces of good and evil that had little control over one another, and toward which, as if by gravitational force, all living entities under them would be lured, in one direction or the other. Founded by the prophet Mani (210–276 CE), the tradition of Manicheanism began in Persia and spread rapidly both east and west, incorporating aspects of its predecessor, Zoroastrianism, as well as a Christian emphasis on spiritual redemption and the Buddhist idea of transmigration of souls, but famously becoming most known for its controversial innovation, namely, the idea that because an independent evil entity exists against which God battles, God is not omnipotent.[14] Whence one of the earliest and most influential theological motifs in Western thought: that of the cosmic, ongoing conflict between the spiritual realm of light and the material realm of darkness, the former constantly under attack by the latter. The following, taken from the Manichean psalm, "Light Your Lamps," appears in a psalter believed to be originally written by Mani himself:

Many are the ships that have gone down after they were near to mooring to the bank; a number of houses have fallen after the parapet had been reached. So it is also, my brethren, that there

is a soul that shall fight at first and the storm arises upon it and
the waves seize it.
There is none that can fight if he is committed to both sides.
The insidious and the meddlers never find God;
but they that have shut their eyes to the good,
for them how greatly I care that they should repent.[15]

The author notes the futility of even the best-intended soul wresting itself
free once in the grip of dark forces and calls our attention to the helplessness
of fence-straddling. Notably absent is any appeal made to an omnipotent God
to save at the last minute. The battle between the devil and God is real, and
only the lesser observer of the narrative concludes that we know in advance
who will prevail. Because the notion that God will prevail is not taken for
granted, the divinity is understood, by logical extension, to be imperfect. He is
genuinely threatened by his divine counterpart. Moreover, as the quoted passage indicates, we as humans are the principal domain of the battle zone. The
devil can score points against God by appealing to humanity's base, material
nature and by corrupting human souls. As one fourth-century Manichean theologian argued, the "body does not belong to God, but to matter . . . it is dark
and must be kept in the dark."[16] Because we can do nothing about the fact that
we are embodied, evil is a perennial threat. The devil, strange as he is with all
of those Gothic descriptors, is assured an even more enduring familiarity by
virtue of his staying power. Although embodied as concrete darkness, Satan
remains an ongoing presence in human existence. Powerful, infectious with
influence, durable, and irredeemable, he is the epitome of evil. Those not yet
turned by him should fear what he will do.

What are the ethical, sociological, political, and scientific ramifications of
such a model? What advantages of dualism account for the contemporary appeal
of narratives that center around the persona of Satan? In its favor, the Manichean model sticks close to the apparent facts about life: It makes the most
sense of an ordinary human experience routinely marred by terrible occurrences.[17] Counting honest description as an intellectual virtue of the model,
the seventeenth-century French philosopher Pierre Bayle skeptically noted that
"Travel gives continual lessons of this. Monuments to human misery and weakness are found everywhere—prisons, hospitals, gallows, and beggars. Here you
see the ruins of a flourishing city; in other places you cannot even find the
ruins."[18]

As if to anticipate the massive Lisbon earthquake that would soon devastate
Europe's faith in the Enlightenment ideal of progress, as well as the comfortable sense that things happen for a reason, Bayle—the son of a Calvinist minister who converted to Catholicism and then reconverted to Calvinism—gave

Manicheanism its theological due.[19] That evil existed in itself, not just as a mere disguise for the good, could not be denied. The idea that evil was attributable to Satan rather than God, though it defied God's rationality and omnipotence, at least preserved the notion of a noncruel God in evil's wake. Furthermore, because Satan's existence lay outside the purview of the divine, in the Manichean view, believers could avoid the mental paralysis that afflicted others who tried to comprehend God's pedagogical purpose in creating or at least allowing plague, war, famine, pain, and all trouble in the world.[20] The more one appreciates what Satan is capable of, the less one is forced to turn to God to explain the mystery of a divine purpose. Satan makes evil, in this crude sense, understandable.

The power attributed to Satan is linked to his status as a rogue agent with independent motives. It is he who tested Job and tried to lure Jesus away in the wilderness. In the Manichean psalms he is identified as Jesus's main adversary, the leader of a variety of anthropomorphized beasts all of whom draw on their inherent creativity to terrorize. In literature, Satan is accorded an exalted, if ignoble presence. For Milton and Dante, he is the proud monarch of Hell expelled from heaven whose raison d'être is to tempt the prized creature of God to act further on his already healthy penchant for disobedience. Commenting on Milton's protagonist, the philosopher and acclaimed writer Mary Midgley has this to say: "Barring the difference of scale, Satan's role is comparable to that of human instigator. He is in fact that arch-instigator of all time, having just carried off to ruin a third of the heavenly host, and—merely from spite—he is about to lure the human race to wreck its happiness as well."[21] Satan's promise to himself and to the world that he will play out the hand he has been dealt has become immortalized in the realm of literature in the commitment Milton poignantly voices on his behalf:

> All good to me is lost;
> Evil be thou my good: *by thee at least*
> *Divided empire with Heaven's King I hold,*
> By thee, and more than half perhaps will reign,
> As Man ere long, and this new world shall know.[22]

"Evil be thou my good" establishes all of Satan's future motives, which will be governed by norms that operate *expressio unius est exclusio alterius* (the expression of one thing is the exclusion of another). Henceforth, Satan is to be known by what he is not. Entirely Manichean in character, the point of the passage, Midgley elucidates, is "not that evil has been suddenly perceived to have greater value than good, nor that an existential decision can confer that value on it, but simply—as [Milton's] italicized words show—that it looks as if it might provide an empire independent of and corresponding to that of God."[23] This motif of virtue for the sake of vice, an arguably sadistic delight in mischief, is consistent with the etymology of the word *Satan*. According to the medievalist Jeffrey Burton Russell: The Hebrew word *satan* derives from a root meaning "oppose," "obstruct," or "accuse." It was translated by the Greek *diablos*, meaning 'adversary," whence it passed into Latin *diabolus*, German *Teufel*, and English *devil*. The basic meaning of the term, then, is "opponent."[24]

Not only does the postulation of an entity that seeks to undo God's works make sense in the realm of moral evil—if there is an active, positive effort made to destroy what God creates on the part of a powerful and self-determining entity, then one is not left puzzled as to what God must be up to in allowing evil—but even natural evil is also no longer chalked up to destructive, gratuitous entropy. To the contrary, along with moral evil, it too becomes purposeful and creation-denying.

This idea of Satan as deliberately tempting human beings and destroying creation feeds into a thesis that he is mainly here not for our pedagogical benefit, as the theodicists imagine, but rather for his own sake. The only appropriate response is to fear him. We have here neither Job's Satan, ultimately a puppet to God's puppeteer, nor the image William James invokes of Reni's devil contained by a stronger force. Despite the popularity among some literary theorists of romanticizing him as a creative self-actualizer, Satan is in the final analysis singly determined to undo the good, constrained not to give any other objective greater priority. No divinity can keep him in check and he could not change if he wanted to: something for which to be on the lookout indeed. This connection between the depiction of Satan as an independent and powerful agent and the "culture of fear" it begets actually helps explain some of the theological, literary, and even political appeal of the Manichean account.[25]

Satan is a menace because he comes to delight in his own private good, a good apart from that afforded by God's creative prowess.[26] The narrative roughly supplied by dualism—from Zoroastrianism to Gnosticism to Manicheanism, and later picked up by Milton and others—construes Satan as a fallen angel cast out of heaven and plays out in a drama that unfolds as if things could not have been otherwise. That God is causally linked to Satan's demise, his ensuing resentment, and our consequent undoing, however, does not necessarily imply that God continues to be either the explanation or authority responsible for Satan's works.[27] In other words, if God is a creator, Satan has become a formidable "subcreator," enough to pose a genuine challenge to rival God's designs.[28] Satan is to be feared precisely because he has left the fold; he is a rogue with whom it is in principle impossible to reason. Symbolic of our loss of control, Satan has a certain irredeemable quality, winning his battles by removing individuals from the domain of those to whom we can appeal for compassion.

It is this aspect of Satan—his capacity to affect the demonic turn—that renders the Manichean account so accessible, because Satan's rebellion provides a straightforward explanation for the existence of evildoers in the world. Gordon Graham notes an Ockham's razor–like attractiveness to this idea of incorrigible, Satanic evil. It has a powerfully explanatory answer for calamitous events like Columbine, for example, as well as for noteworthy serial murders caused by killers such as Jeffrey Dahmer. Graham notes,

> In short there is a (relatively) simple explanation of what went on at Columbine. This was yet another instance of something most peoples at most times have believed in—the battle between elemental forces between good and evil—a battle in which the Prince of Darkness was on this occasion assisted by the wealth of technology readily available to those who were, as a result of their engagement with it, more readily seduced into becoming his agents. By this account, the regular watching of violent videos did not *cause* their subsequent action, a contention, let it be repeated, for which there is no satisfactory evidence. Rather, it made them ready targets for someone else's 'crafts and assaults.'[29]

According to Graham, neither Klebold nor Harris ought to be dismissed too easily, either as God's unwitting agents, or as countercurrent teen nomads exiled to the underground, who, had we listened to them more closely, might have acted otherwise.[30] To see them in the first way is to call evil good, whereas to see them in the second is to imply that no such thing as evil exists. The first explanation does not square with the reality that the destruction of evil outweighs the merit of any ensuing goods, and the second ignores the intent of Klebold and Harris. Graham suggests that something larger is at work: a cosmic drama between opposing supernatural forces, the outcome of which—by extension—governs the interplay among humans on earth. Although this is perhaps not a fashionable explanation in today's world for what motivates murderous teens, Graham argues, it is to be commended for its honesty in not confusing what is evil for an outcome that could have been prevented in more favorable environmental circumstances.[31] Evil, to repeat, is evil in part because it is wholly out of our control. Graham alludes to Augustine's reference to the corrupted will to point out that, like Satan, people can "come to be their own good."[32] Like satellites of a dying star that has overwhelming gravitational pull, people under a demonic influence can learn to refine newly acquired malfeasance, and, in turn, come into their own idiosyncratic, destructive "subcreative" mode. Satan is to be feared not only because he is the most formidable other, but also because of his spectacular ability to recruit. The Manichean account of evil insists on a rejection of the idea of unity as well as the eventual reconciliation between what is good and bad. In this it offers the sufferer an answer for why there is no answer for the betrayer, torturer, malicious tyrant, and the one to whom reason, compassion, and empathy are lost. At the same time, it is in just this sense, surprisingly, that theologians attracted to the Manichean model of evil see the possibility for redemption in the prospect of choosing sides, decisively, in a cosmic battle under way. Correctly identified as unalterable, we can free ourselves to devote our energy to vanquish evil and defend the good as best we can, seeking redemption in the critical assumption that we are on the side of the good.

To the extent that a model is to be favored on the grounds of eschewing unrealistic idealism, it would be hard to recommend a characterization of evil more highly than the Manichean one. Among the possible accounts of evil, nothing is more simple or straightforward. With regard to the clarity with which the battle lines are drawn, the Manichean model is also a structurally efficient account of evil. (The first step in dealing with one's enemies is to recognize them for who they are). Identifying for all to see where the external source of evil resides, the Manichean account affirms wherein lie the zones of safety and danger, resisting any facile or politically correct attempts to conflate the two.

The Manichean Theological Tradition

If Ockham's razor were not enough to endorse it on the grounds that it offers the clearest and most succinct description of the facts of life as we know them, one could draw on a more sophisticated theological benefit to the Manichean tradition to explain its historical endurance. This might seem odd given the dominant theological view that dualism impugns the majesty of God by positing a divinity not in complete control of the world he has created. Defenders of the Manichean model resist this traditional wisdom. They protest that a dualistic theology gives God credit in a way that competing *creatio ex nihilo* narratives never could, for, they aver, only a contest whose outcome is uncertain is one in which the victor yields his full share of credit. Because Satan, or something like him, was a formidable presence in creation out of the primal cosmos, God is to be prized even more for prevailing on our behalf.

The Jewish biblical scholar Jon Levenson proposes that God's creation of the world is a consequence rather than a condition of his brutal struggle with and eventual victory over evil. Evil, in his view, is not something that came after the fact but rather part of the primordial cosmic soup on which ordered goodness would subsequently be built. What is more, as Levenson states, evil, as understood in the context of the Hebrew Bible, was not mere nothingness or chaos:

> It seems more likely that [the biblical sources] identified "nothing" with things like disorder, injustice, subjugation, disease and death. To them, in other words, "nothing" was something—something negative. It was not privation of being (as evil is the privation of good in some theodicies), but a real, active force, except that its charge was entirely negative. When order emerges where disorder had reigned unchallenged, when justice replaces oppression, when disease and death yield to vitality and longevity, this is indeed the creation of something out of nothing. It is the replacement of the negative by the positive every bit as much as is the erection of a majestic royal palace where there had once been only sewers, dung, and garbage. This crucial point will be lost on us if we follow the long-standing philosophical tradition of identifying God with perfect being, so that his opposite is non-being, or "nothing" in the sense of a void.[33]

A God who creates and recreates over again at all moments, ex nihilo, displays no real theological prowess. Indeed, Levenson points out, if God's rival powers never acquire any real control, then whence the undiluted jubilee at the thought of God's vanquishing them, or the need to vanquish them to begin with?[34] The effect of the perfectionist view of the divinity favored in the nondualist view, Levenson argues, is that creation is trivialized and the creator is crowned without allowing any time to consider why he should be glorified. The Platonic idea of God as an unmoved, perfect divinity deprives God and his creatures of real agency, as on this account everyone becomes the passive beneficiary of unmotivated action, rather than viable junior partners in a soteriological drama that has real battles to be won.[35]

According to Levenson, this is not merely sound theology; it is good biblical interpretation too. Despite the implication of Genesis 1, God did not create the behemoths that emerged out of the chaos. Rather, God became the most powerful force in the universe by taming them, or rather by setting a border between him (goodness and light) and them (darkness and evil). Psalm 74:12–17, for example, alludes to a colossal confrontation between God and aquatic monsters in which God triumphed and set "all the boundaries of the earth" (74:17).[36] Levenson is interested in those parts of the Bible in which God is highly anthropomorphized, a valiant warrior relying on recognizable if superhuman resources to prevail over all that threatens to undo the world, as, for example, in Genesis

9, in which we are told how his intervention protects us from the ongoing threat of another flood (never fully eradicated), as well as in Isaiah 24–27, where death, kept at bay for the moment, still looms. The divine endeavor is not undertaken without effort. Isaiah's wail, indicative of the reality that all is not well, beckons a supreme and paternal God who will as a rule rescue us, but who sometimes appears to be absent. We can be hopeful but never certain that God will rush in on our behalf. Thus God's victory is there just as much to assure as it is to remind us that a cosmic evil lurks in the distance, waiting to pounce, leading to a kind of apocalyptic logic that pertains to the everyday evil we experience. As Levenson explains, the "evil that occurs in history is symptomatic of a larger suprahistorical disequilibrium that requires, indeed invites, a suprahistorical correction. As evil did not originate with history, neither will it disappear alto-gether *in* history, but rather *beyond* it, at the inauguration of the coming world."[37] Creation is fragile and unstable. Evil is a condition of existence. This is as metaphysically beyond God's control as it is beyond our own.

The Christian theologian Catherine Keller finds the ex nihilo metaphor equally problematic. She argues for a new tehomic Christian theology—*tehom* refers to the dark, oceanic primordial chaos out or on top of which everything else was created—that, like Levenson's, sees creation not as a fait accompli but as indicative of a sustained divine determination. Omnipotence, the effective denial of independent evil, wipes out the existence of or even the need for the creator's creative pallet, and by extension, on a micro level, genuine free will. Keller writes, "To render the biblically 'all-powerful' deity formally omnipotent was to close out the primal space, the khora or chaos, of creaturely spontaneity. Without that space, human freedom and natural chance are themselves directed by a Lord—who is thereby responsible for the havoc they wreak. A tehomic theology seeks . . . a theological alternative to the dangerously unavowed amor-ality of omnipotence."[38]

In their rush to glorify God, Keller argues, prominent Christian thinkers—from church fathers like Irenaeus to modern theologians like Karl Barth—have had trouble dealing with the underemphasized description in Genesis 1:2 of an earth marred by "darkness upon the face of the deep," a darkness that existed before God approached it. In the service of maintaining God's omnipotence and unconditional sovereignty, unrivaled by any competitor, the doctrine of *creatio ex nihilo* was forced on foundational biblical passages, such as Genesis 1:2, that did not readily suggest it.[39]

Keller, a feminist and process theologian, is primarily interested in the sup-pressed tehomic elements of the creation myth in Christian theology to empha-size a chauvinism she believes has governed the theopolitics of her tradition for centuries. But the Manichean account of good and evil to which her tehomic account leads also has independent theological advantages to recommend it. By acknowledging an original evil that subsists alongside an original good, we do not dismiss the challenge of making do in a world constantly under threat from the forces that seek to destroy it. Such an acknowledgment, in turn, far from leading to a deterministic worldview, opens avenues for human responsibility and freedom. Assertions of ex nihilo, by contrast, are unproductive conversation-stoppers. Because God is the ultimate author of everything, and God has his reasons, what of meaning is there really left to discuss? Keller goes so far as to argue that the ex nihilo model is coercive, a political and unilateral imposition of God's will that deprives human beings of the drama, dignity, and space within which to develop their character amid genuine struggle. We are a far way indeed from the classical view of dualism as pessimistic and resistant to a robust acknowledgment of human agency.

As mentioned earlier, Gordon Graham concurs with the notion that the possibility of hope first requires an acknowledgment of substantive evil that is woven into the fabric of the natural world, for such acknowledgment is tantamount to bracing ourselves for an all-important contest in which we must engage, whether we know it or not. Graham further suggests that notwithstanding the good many moral issues on which disagreement is widespread and irresoluble, the consensus that an (admittedly small) class of occurrences, such as rape or slavery, that constitute absolute wrongs does exist testifies to the inappropriateness of automatically attributing all that is wrong in the world to a divine plan.[40] Only by seeing evil as wholly irreducible, truly other, can we begin to marshal a defense against what threatens us. Thus even if he has problems with their conclusions, Graham would welcome the findings of Milgram, Zimbardo, Browning, and Hannah Arendt, each preoccupied with accounting for the sadistic behavior of seemingly ordinary, often compassionate adults, who, away from their evil deeds, made good mothers and fathers and otherwise blended well into society.[41] According to Graham, such perpetrators of evil neither suffered from split personalities nor were "banal." Rather, they became possessed by a darker force greater than them. Here characterized is a threat worthy of a response no less than a crusade of epic proportions. The sinner—certainly the one for whom sin has become habitual—loves the sin, enough so that he or she cannot reform through normal means. The only alternative becomes forcibly to remove the sinner from civil society. Graham bemoans the underuse of the revelation of St. John in Christian theology, a book from scripture whose purpose is to exhort Christians to prepare for an ensuing battle.[42] Harkening back to centuries when the text was more emphasized than it is among theologians today, Graham calls for return to the interpretation of the resurrection as the inspirational instance of good triumphing over evil, Jesus prevailing and in so doing liberating us from the enemy.[43]

In selecting theological allies from history, there is no shortage of church fathers from whom to choose who were attracted to the formidable construction of evil in the dualist narrative. In one well-known instance, commenting on the recurring appearance of the damned, the twelfth-century pope Innocent III alludes to a psalm: " 'They are laid in hell like sheep; death will feed on them' (Psalms 48:15). This text is based upon the similarity of damned souls to beasts of burden, who do not tear up the grass by the roots but only chew the top, so that the grass grows again for pasture. Thus the wicked, as if eaten by death, spring to life again to die once more, and so are eternally dying."[44]

In their love of and commitment to wrongdoing, the wicked lose the trait of existing in God's image, and so, by default, form an army opposing him. Pope Innocent III's judgment is consistent with Calvin's subsequent and more dire observation that, after the fall, our originally good nature becomes forever lost whereby "the whole of man is overwhelmed—as by a deluge—from head to foot, so that no part is immune from sin and all that proceeds from him is to be imputed to sin."[45] Although this judgment is not, strictly speaking, Manichean— Calvin was vocal in condemning the Manichean failure to locate evil as naturally residing within man and thus as something not attributable to God—it does, in contrast even to Luther, emphasize our legitimate denunciation before God owing to a depravity of which we were never in a position to shed ourselves. Like Pope Innocent III's, Calvin's view of evil was Manichean at least in flavor, dividing souls into the saved and the damned, the former constituting a conspicuously graced minority. Thus, although the Calvinist account does not incorporate a strict substantive binary between the forces of light and the forces of darkness, a significant and recognizably intuitive normative dichotomy between the favored insider and the forsaken other nevertheless remains. Moreover, in keeping with the discussion about Satan's infectious influence, Calvin recognizes a "perversity [that] never ceases in us, but continually bears new fruits— the works of flesh that we have already described—just as a burning furnace gives forth flame and sparks, or water ceaselessly bubbles up from a spring."[46] Calvin describes a real evil, in the form of sin, that explicitly stands in opposition to the good and is beyond our capacity to alter. Because we cannot undo having veered from our originally good condition, the separation between those saved, via grace, and the far greater population of those damned becomes all important. What Gordon Graham, Pope Innocent III, and John Calvin have in common, consistent with their endorsement of the first model of evil described in this chapter, is what looks like a pessimistic outlook of human nature in light of the prominent place evil holds in any human drama. Their opting for this model of evil may seem indicative of a depressing quietism, but for them marks the condition of redemption. Knowing the devil is the precondition for vanquishing him.

Evil Naturalized

A theologized Manicheanism foretells of a battle between two supernatural forces, one light and one dark, the former prevailing but not without significant effort. In such an account the world—and by extension the human condition—is on an ongoing basis susceptible to evil, which is thought to be built into the natural structure of things. It is also possible to conceive of an "originary" evil, innate to human experience, without the theological trappings. In such a case evil is still ontologically substantive despite its extraction from a theological narrative. In such a characterization, evil remains the profoundly other, a serious threat built into the nature of things, that continues to predict an impending colossal battle between two formidable forces.

Two political philosophers, Niccolò Machiavelli and Thomas Hobbes, writing at the dawn of the Enlightenment, were concerned with how it could be possible to maintain power in human societies that had a penchant for lapsing into chaos and conflict. Machiavelli and Hobbes were, to say the least, cynical about the character of persons in the state of nature. Machiavelli believed that because human beings were at base fundamentally lacking a just disposition, they had to be contained by a ruler who would know how to use vice instrumentally to quell the tendency for them to group into unruly masses when left unchecked. Hobbes, in kind, imagined a Leviathan in the form of a ruling government that through the right tactical deployment of reason, cunning, and power could tame a population otherwise headed for a "war of all against all." Much of the attention devoted to these two figures has focused on their innovative political philosophy, their advice for how to use prudential reason in governing, and their sometimes pessimistic justifications for the use of power in reining in a species often in need of being tamed. What is significant with regard to Machiavelli and Hobbes, however, is the assumption they share about human nature that lays the foundation for their political philosophies. They maintain that we are, at base, fallen creatures, naturally given to selfish desires and lacking any impartial sense of right and wrong. One of the implications of this dour prognosis is that because vice plays such a central role in forming the motivations for our actions, we ought to acknowledge it for what it is and put it to good use, if possible. Machiavelli makes an interesting case in *The Prince*—and a persuasive one if his assumptions about human nature are correct—in favor of avoiding the reputation of being vice-ridden while conceding that vice is, nevertheless, a necessary resource that any savvy ruler will have to avail himself of over the long haul:

> You have to be astute enough to avoid being thought to have those evil quali-
> ties that would make it impossible for you to retain power; as for those that
> are compatible with holding on to power, you should avoid them if you can;
> but if you cannot, then you should not worry too much if people say you have
> them. Above all, do not be upset if you are supposed to have those vices a
> ruler needs if he is going to stay securely in power, for, if you think about it,
> you will realize there are some ways of behaving that are supposed to be
> virtuous [*che parrà virtù*], but would lead to your downfall, and others that are
> supposed to be wicked, but will lead to your welfare and peace of mind.[47]

Machiavelli's argument is reminiscent of that forwarded by some defenders of the Second Amendment, who point out that given the widespread presence of guns on so many urban corners, which can never all be retrieved, more guns become necessary to defend ourselves. There is no putting the genie back in the bottle. What is not disputed in this sort of defense of the right to bear arms is the evil nature of guns themselves. The realistic pragmatism in this judgment is in effect a concession to the way things are, albeit we would wish them other-wise. Machiavelli's prince may not be responsible for humanity's deficiency of compassion, but as long as that deficiency exists, he had better tactically avail himself of merciless and self-serving deeds when they become necessary.

Hobbes echoes Machiavelli's cynical belief in the unavoidability of partici-pating in necessary evils, attributing the concession to the external world we inhabit. Just to live, Hobbes points out, is to labor under several handicaps at once. Human beings require scarce resources to get by and for the most part exist in a state of perennial insecurity. Surviving in this harsh world requires us to seek even the slightest advantage over one another. When we do seek this advantage, we will harness, if unwittingly, those vices that lead us not to think of the one in need. In the Hobbesian picture, competition is the reigning activ-ity among human beings. The hope we naturally possess in "attaining our Ends" sets individuals equal in ability against one another, vying for the same goods, and resorting to foul play and deceit to satisfy their organic impulse. When more than one person desires the same thing that both cannot enjoy, "they become enemies; and in the way to their End, which is principally their owne conservation, and sometimes the delectation only, endeavor to destroy, or subdue one another."[48] In Hobbes's view, our competitive disposition, which ceteris paribus occurs between opposing equal parties, mirrors that depicted in the Manichean account of combating deities both of whom want to subjugate the other. The ensuing power struggle is an ancient trope.

Machiavelli and Hobbes therefore endorse the Manichean picture of good and evil in an attempt to know ourselves as human subjects better. In the same way a psychotherapist of Freudian persuasion analyzes a dream to bring a dangerous compulsion under control, the stately prince or Leviathan benefits society by adopting a ruling strategy based on a native understanding of what human beings are truly capable of and why. No one is better off by acting as if evil is not a central part of the larger picture. Not just in theological speculations about the eschaton, but also in the real world the Manichean model prepares us best for the facts of life.

The idea that evil is an organic part of human experience is emphasized more explicitly by two other modern figures who set out to examine the topic aesthetically. Bearing in mind the Miltonic aphorism "evil be thou my good," the Marquis de Sade and Charles Baudelaire explore the Manichean notion that pleasure comes from pain and sweetness from what is bitter. The Marquis de Sade presses the Manichean position to its logical maximum, writing in *Justine* that not only does nature itself encourage homicide, hatred, revenge, violent conflict, betrayal, and all other crimes, but also that because destruction is "one of the chief laws of Nature" it cannot, in the final analysis, be "criminal."[49] Because they are justified by nature, crimes cannot be deemed iniquitous. Rather, the murderer "does but alter forms, [and] gives back to Nature the elements whereof the hand of this skilled artisan instantly re-creates other beings: now, as creations cannot but afford delight to him by whom they are wrought, the murderer thus prepares for Nature a pleasure most agreeable, he furnishes her material, she employs them without delay, and the act fools have had the madness to blame is nothing but meritorious in the universal agent's eye."[50]

A murder is but a natural transfer among goods in nature.[51] It is one of nature's frequent inevitabilities to which only fools do not resign themselves. Murder, thus described, becomes a deed purified of guilt, a deed to be celebrated in its honesty, as tribute to the life force bigger than the creature who participates in it.[52] Without destruction, nature would lose its creative capacity. The same goes for inner turmoil. Conflict is not only necessary but it is good and should be counted alongside nature's other pleasures. With regard to this last judgment, Charles Baudelaire ups the ante. Romanticizing evil, Baudelaire waxes poetic in "The Flowers of Evil" about evil's seductive floral siren:

> Gangs of demons are boozing in our brain—
> ranked, swarming, like a million warrior-ants,

they drown and choke the cistern of our wants;
each time we breathe, we tear our lungs with pain.[53]

To resist evil is neither savvy nor consonant with our inner temperament.
Better to give in to it than commit to a false, priggish austerity. Here the morbid
horror of nature's vivid destructiveness is also beautiful, not arbitrarily beautiful—not beautiful because beauty is to be enjoyed in any experience so long as
we choose to look at it in a certain light—but because the subject in question
is evil and not something else. We have little choice about what we are drawn
to, and evil is objectively attractive. Although it was the intention of neither,
the Marquis de Sade's and Charles Baudelaire's lyrical tributes to objects of
destructive taboo brings vividness to the theological warnings about the attractiveness of the devil. Evil is here, as it is in Manichean theology, very much a
presence and not an absence.

The dualistic naturalism to which the Marquis de Sade and Charles Baudelaire implore us to surrender anticipates the Gothic emphasis on night typical
of the Victorian age in the late nineteenth and early twentieth century. Joseph
Conrad's *Heart of Darkness* is a good literary example of an expression of the
Manichean form of a seductive, though no less horrific, evil. The heart of darkness is the Belgian Congo, both a jungle and, metaphorically, the subconscious
nucleus of the human psyche. We learn of the jungle and the evil that lurks
within it through the reports of Marlow, Conrad's protagonist who happens into
Africa and suddenly finds himself drawn in the direction of the powerful white
trader Kurtz. Over the course of the novel, Marlow becomes obsessed with
Kurtz, who, despite Kurtz's impenetrable nature, he comes to know intimately.
Kurtz is portrayed by Conrad as a shadow self. He is a fellow Englishman who
is also an honorary native to the tribal population in the Congo, as well as Marlow's own shadow: timeless, mysterious, authoritative, and persuasive. At the
same time, the shadow is depicted as a product of our own design: "All Europe
contributed to the making of Kurtz, and by and by I learned that most appropriately the International Society for the Suppression of Savage Customs had
entrusted him with the making of a report for its future guidance."[54] The
shadow is both the uninvited guest and the host, the hidden ruler of the forest
about whom, at the same time, everybody has heard. Finally, the shadow is
itself a manifestation of something larger, older, and more enduring than it. As
our narrator notes near the conclusion, "I tried to break the spell—the heavy,
mute spell of the wilderness—that seemed to draw him to its pitiless breast by
the awakening of forgotten and brutal instincts, by the memory of gratified and
monstrous passions. This alone, I was convinced, had driven him out to the
edge of the forest, to the bush, towards the gleam of fires, the throb of drums,

the drone of weird incantations; this alone had beguiled his unlawful soul beyond the bounds of permitted aspirations."[55]

Evil is with us and draws us into its breast.[56] Thus, darkness is ultimately not unseen. It is a tangible reality, a jungle that contrasts with the light of civilization. It is the other, and therefore strange to us, but also the other with which it is our destiny to collide as it encroaches on our territory and we encroach on its.

Although Joseph Conrad was no colonialist—indeed, writing at the turn of the twentieth century, some Conrad scholars have asserted that *Heart of Darkness* is in fact a critique of imperialism—certainly an observation is to be made about the "clash of civilizations" depicted in the text, one civil and the other savage.[57] Kurtz used to be part of Marlow's world, but now is not, and, as Marlow's journey up the Congo makes manifest, the two worlds cannot exist together. One might read into the premise a strategic maxim: If we want our (safe) world to survive, we had better do something about the other one. While constraints of space prohibit me from moving too far onto the terrain of politics and foreign policy, connections are to be drawn between the depiction of two clashing worlds implied in the literary portrayal of the Manichean worldview at the turn of the twentieth century and a well-known thesis that continues to have a strong influence in America and indeed in the West more than a hundred years later. This is Samuel Huntington's clash of civilizations thesis. Huntington argues that the globe human beings inhabit is divided into people of cultural and religious identities that are fundamentally at odds with one another, and that, given the growing population density combined with the expansionist mindset of some of these cultures in the post–Cold War era, the world's civilizations are, by default, set on a crash course with one another, a meeting that implies the ascension of one set of civilizations and the decline if not elimination of another.[58]

Huntington is worried, in particular, about a radical Islamicism that has seized the Muslim world. Like the other imagined in the Manichean account, the Islamic Muslim cannot be altered or gotten through to. We are, in Huntington's view, helpless to modify the theocratic designs of the suicide bomber who wants to destroy societies in the West and threaten the assumption that citizens of such societies can live in freedom and safety. Hence, Huntington puts the West on notice: We fail to heed that "Islam has bloody borders" at the expense of our own security and well-being.[59] The foreign policy implications of Huntington's thesis are clear. The West can either fight back or allow itself to be wiped out. Harmony within a mosaic landscape is not an option.

Nine days after the terrorist attacks of September 11, 2001, Huntington's thesis was given an authoritative stamp in the voice of the president of the

United States in what has now come to be known as the Bush doctrine: "Every nation, in every region, now has a decision to make. Either you are with us, or you are with the terrorists." Taking to heart the old Manichean supposition that the forces of darkness wield powerful influence, Bush committed the United States to its most decisively proactive stance to date against perceived threats abroad. In the process, distinctions rendered too subtle, such as those between terrorists and the ones who harbored them, became passé. The doctrine of deterrence that the Bush doctrine replaced became a dated defense against an enemy recharacterized as to never recognize rational discourse. A foreign policy that waged war only in self-defense was deemed naive in the neo-Manichean mindset. It underestimated Satan's impenetrability as well as the massive gravitational force by which he recruited others to his cause. In declaring a new world order, with new, fierce enemies, George W. Bush tapped into a long-standing anxiety that had begun to assume unusual relevance in contemporary society. This anxiety signals a failure of ecumenicalism. In a world growing smaller and smaller, pushing disparate cultures, with incommensurable values, ever closer to one another, inevitably victors and victims will emerge. The division feeds into a cultural narrative that imagines a class of those saved and those left behind.

Evil and the Apocalypse

The Manichean worldview envisions the earth's inhabitants locked in a battle to the death on which not just the lives of individual creatures, but the fate of the societies of which they are a part, hang in the balance. In the last ten years, scholars have noticed and written voluminously about the emergence of enclaves of communities awaiting the rapture whose members are striving to be counted among those whom God will save before a final, colossal contest between good and evil unfolds. The rapture technically refers to an event described in 1 Thessalonians 4:15–17 and John 14:2–3, but also elsewhere where Saint Paul anticipates the Lord's assurance of the secret second arrival of Jesus to collect those who have been loyal to him.[60] Jesus's return will be glorious, followed by mayhem on earth.[61]

Professor of literature and cultural studies and author of *Rapture Culture: Left Behind in Evangelical America*, Amy Johnson Frykholm, summarizes this mayhem as it is depicted in the series.[62] As the saved are escorted up to heaven, the world they leave behind "is plunged into chaos. Cars and airplanes crash; buildings crumble; people search in vain for loved ones. [O]ver the seven years . . . [of] tribulation, the world suffers plague and famine. A dictator, the Antichrist, emerges as a world leader and tortures and kills those who oppose him. At last Christ comes again. This time he comes in glory, defeats the Antichrist, and reigns over the earth."[63] Herein described is the very archetype of a contest between good and evil. To the extent that one takes such an apocalyptic world-view seriously, one commits oneself to an ethos of erecting boundaries and choosing sides. The apocalypse, the saving revelation to a graced few at the end of days, implies by definition the redemption of a minority and the damnation of a far greater majority.

In biblical literature the four most conspicuous apocalyptic passages occur in Ezekiel and Daniel (Old Testament) as well as in the "little apocalypse" of Mark 13 and the book of Revelation of St. John (New Testament). Each of these passages consist of revelatory literature that spells out in detail Messianic eschatology, and in particular an account of how the Messiah's arrival on earth affects the salvation of the religious practitioner.[64] The four passages are quint-essentially Manichean, confidently declaring, not just speculating on, "what is and what is to take place" (Revelation 1:19). They dwell on a cosmic dualism between superhuman angels and demons and offer a deterministic historical perspective in which neither rulers of the secular state nor individuals them-selves have much say about what is to transpire when the Antichrist arrives. The Revelation of St. John, the most important and descriptive of these texts, characterizes the Antichrist as an irreverent and grotesque beast with seven heads and ten horns, rising from the sea, having the characteristics of a lion, a bear, and a leopard, and identified by the number 666 (Revelation 1:13–14). The arrival of the Antichrist is foreshadowed by settings and events that evoke connotations of the Gothic through and through: riders on colored horses, prophesies of doom, prayers of martyrs, various catastrophes, the sounding of trumpets, heavenly bodies darkened, and so forth.[65] Through the evocation of fear and exertion of force, the beast wins several followers, and those who resist are brutally murdered. He gains authority and dominance especially among those who are attached to worldly goods. That he will not prevail, however, is signaled by the demise of Babylon (Revelation 1:18), a city known for its opu-lence, promiscuity, aesthetic allure, healthy culture of trade, and also symbolic of everything evil in humanity.[66] After songs praising Babylon's destruction, the book of Revelation moves to the climactic confrontation between good and evil, Jesus emerging from heaven "in full battle array, mounted on a white steed," indeed a "warrior king," a far cry from the modest carpenter preaching on a mount.[67] Jesus defeats Satan, ushering in the era of the "new Jerusalem" (Reve-lation 1:21), just as earthly ruin gives way to heavenly reward for those individu-als that have been judged to be men and women of genuine faith.

In terms of the extensiveness and the intensity of its readership, the book of Revelation is, bar none, the most addictive piece of literature ever penned. Its rich, classically ominous, sometimes quirky details are known and parsed down to the last adjective. What is its stark appeal, and why does the beast play such a prominent part in the narrative? In *When Time Shall Be No More*, Paul Boyer chronicles the rising number of Christians fervently anticipating the end of days in recent years. He attributes the rise in "doomsday chic" not only to an obsession with the unveiling of what is hidden in a world bereft of new frontiers, but also to a renewed interest believers have betrayed in garnering an advantage in the very competitive process of salvation.[68] The expected final battle of Armageddon between good and evil is epic, a narrative in which Jesus prevails, but the saved are few compared with the many who are doomed. Although the upshot of the battle between good and evil is known in advance, what individuals are ultimately chosen by which side is not yet clear.

The book of Revelation offers its readers a key to history and to the eschaton as well as proof of divine providence trumping calamity and ushering in an era of a new utopia.[69] Boyer notes that just as the author of Revelation and the other apocalyptic texts wrote during times of crisis, so has such prophetic literature gained the most traction among its readership during trying eras.[70] Boyer suggests that this is because it is comforting, during such moments, to know with clarity what is good and what is evil and where, by the end of the crisis, the chips will fall. Hence the inspiration of Revelation 21:4: "And God shall wipe away all tears from their eyes; and there shall be no more death, neither sorrow, nor crying, neither shall there be any more pain; for the former things are passed away."[71] Albeit deterministic, the final battle between good and evil, thus construed, represents its own theodicy, for though we are helpless to prevent evil, the threat of evil makes the good all the more worth coveting. In addition, prophetic literature leaves the impression that to the extent one accepts the general structure and timeline for how the contest between good and evil unravels, one will find oneself on the side of good. Statistics be damned—a seniority, as it were, applies to the tradition of apocalyptic and prophetic literature, according to which, to the extent one is familiar with the forecasted narrative, one will find oneself among the saved despite the odds. In millenialist communities, insiders reinforce the beliefs of one another, not the least of which is that the chaos of evil is precursor to the harmony of a new heavenly age. Contemporary social unrest, the threat of terrorism and economic collapse, the ever-increasing scarcity of resources as well as the disparity in the distribution of what little resources there are—all of these conditions are necessary for ushering in the new utopia. Anything less would not signal the coming of the Antichrist, whose presence is tantamount to the final battle.[72] A theodicy indeed.

The Manicheanism inherent in apocalyptic literature suggests a totality, a comprehensive narrative to which people cling to feel better about very real and distressing social conditions that would otherwise thrust those insecure about their future prospects into deep despair. In this sense, the detailed prophesy of the rapture induces the experience of our bracing for terror, an experience that is preferable to the experience of terror itself. The book of Revelation features a narrative in which the actions and motives of all of the main characters are public and transparent, the forces of good and bad clearly demarcated. Such disclosure affords a therapeutic certainty, because it gives anxious and otherwise helpless individuals the feeling of some measure of control over their predicament. In this sense, the prophecy becomes a blueprint and the prophet becomes the authority who shelters narrative-insiders from the terror they would experience without the luxury of consulting an expert. As the psychologist Adam Phillips argues, in this way fear is transformed into meaning and becomes a form of anticipation. Our expectations managed, evil consoles rather than terrorizes us by, once decoded, playing a central part in the explanation of how everything will turn out to be.[73] We—not the evildoers—are to be on the lookout, but we are also in the know. If Phillips is right, then adopting the Manichean account of evil affords a Freudian benefit: In such a model the evil we experience ironically becomes the means by which the unknown is revealed and the arbitrariness of life is controlled. Calamities suffered at nature's whim and harm experienced at the hand of another have a sudden purpose. Everything that happens in the real world metaphorically corresponds to events that have taken place or are predicted in the narrative. The collapse of Wall Street, the increasing instances of erratic weather, and the explosion of violent global unrest are but signs for which it behooves the careful reader of the coveted prophesy to be on the lookout.

Here, then, is a further clarification for the appeal of apocalyptic narratives: They furnish one with a sense of active participation over one's destiny, a destiny over which one does not have any real control. In her study of the evangelical youth movement, the journalist Lauren Sandler captures the sense of belonging provided by membership in evangelical groups who deliberately self-identify with the cause of good in a cosmic battle already under way:

> This is a religious movement where for everyone the spiritual is personal and the personal political. It is a crusade that wraps action in emotion, activism in salvation. People at Cornerstone tell me they are soldiers in a holy war, a culture war, a civil war for souls on American soil. They enlist for belonging.

They enlist for love. Some convert to the pro-life movement before they accept Christ as their Savior, drawn into the movement . . . by the arbitrariness of their birth. . . . Many, though, are just kids who need a community organized around an ethic that provides their lives with a purpose.[74]

Notwithstanding the determinism of a worldview that predicts a war and its outcome, channeling Jesus represents a concrete way for one, especially a young adult in search of a life-purpose, to participate actively in the drama that determines how she or he, and everyone, will end up. The noticeable culture clash between left and right in contemporary society strikes the spiritual warrior as a plausible microcosm of a conflict being carried out on a much larger scale. The tangibility of evil is crucial, for it is what concretely inaugurates the spiritual warrior's activism and provides the possibility for order against the backdrop of a rapidly changing world where one is constantly in danger of losing one's footing. Amy Johnson Frykholm, who focuses specifically on the appeal of the *Left Behind* series in contemporary American society, concurs with Sandler:

In the midst of turmoil over the rapid changes in cultural life that were the result of capitalist expansion, new technologies, scientific discoveries, and large-scale immigration, the narrative of the rapture came to hold an important place. In an atmosphere where conservative Protestants sensed a loss of cultural control, the doctrine of rapture promised an escape. In a complex and confusing social arena, the rapture divided the saved from the unsaved. As a vivid story of justification, the rapture became a way for these Christians to reject a disorienting new terrain. The Antichrist, the suffering of the tribulation, and the battle at Armageddon were all the just desserts of a corrupt modern world and the logical end of modernity's godless ways.[75]

The *Left Behind* series, which takes place in the future, offers a theory about ultimate meaning in a confusing world. If present-day chaos really is representative of a larger macrocosm, then we do not need to despair, for we should expect airplanes flying into buildings, an abundance of emerging questions about the ethics of stem-cell research or human cloning, blurred lines with regard to matters of sex and gender, a deep secular resistance to a Christian way of life, and so on. What used to make sense still does make sense if the end-time during which souls divide into one camp or another is upon us. It is important that the characters of the novel who are "left behind" bear a recognizable mark, making it obvious who is damned, on the one hand, and who is saved but must suffer through the tribulation, on the other.[76] Within the framework of the story, what is good and what is evil are not judgments that are up for discussion. Description and explanation are one. No hermeneutic is required.

One way of evaluating the adequacy of the Manichean model is by determining whether evil is something correctly characterized as immediately identifiable when we encounter it. Consider, on this score, its stance in contrast to the other three models yet to be considered, none of which identify evil as easily. The view of theodicy is that evil is instrumentally in the service of good, and in some cases already the good in disguise. Perspectivalism claims, even more strongly, that evil is really just "evil," a construction that could be defined as good from a different perspective. The fourth, the Augustinian view of privation, according to which evil is defined as the absence of good, acknowledges that evil is real, but places the locus of evil in what is not present, that is, in lapses of piety, conscience, and virtue. Only in the Manichean account is evil clearly defined and easily recognized. Evil is with us because Satan is with us. Humans do evil because Satan causes them to do evil. It is a mistake, on the Manichean view, to mischaracterize evil as something less than evil (as traditional theodicies and Nietzschean deconstructions do), or to imply that we can reduce the amount of evil in the world by building the good into our lives (as the privation model assumes). It would seem, then, that serious consideration of the Manichean account presses its defender to show that evil is irreducibly and substantively in the world, present at the beginning of things, independent of the attitudes, perspectives, or habits we adopt. Are we hardwired for evil?

"Evil Genes"

Is the tendency toward evil something we can avoid if we try? In the modern era from Kant on, the traditional view has been grounded in the assumption that human beings, through recourse to free will, have a significant say over their actions, however difficult it might be to do the right thing or avoid the wrong thing on a particular occasion. A recent study of twins is the first serious challenge from the scientific community to this standard Enlightenment assumption.[77] It demonstrated that antisocial behavior is strongly inherited in children with psychopathic tendencies such as callousness and reduced empathetic capacity. The study, along with a subsequent one, established not only that those who bore psychopathic tendencies as adults and those who did not differed psychologically, but also that such adults could be predicted with remarkable accuracy to turn out to become psychopaths when they were still children, in some cases as early as three years old.[78] Weighing in on the nature versus nurture debate, the authors of the twin study conclude that

> exhibiting high levels of callous-unemotional traits (CU) at 7 years, as assessed by teachers at the end of the first year of school, is under strong genetic

influence. Minimal shared environmental influences on callous-unemotional traits were detected, suggesting that at the age of 7, environmental factors common to both members of the twin pair (such as socio-economic status, school and neighborhood) do not account for extreme CU. Moreover, antisocial behavior (AB) for children who are high on CU (i.e. children with psychopathic tendencies) is highly heritable. In contrast, the extreme AB of those without psychopathic traits was under strong environmental influence— shared as well as non-shared.[79]

Children who exhibit antisocial behavior but lack the critical tendency for callous-unemotional traits, like normal children, have a healthy capacity to morally develop in a nurturing learning setting as well as to be influenced by their surrounding environments. Children in whom psychopathic traits are identified at an early age, by contrast, are strongly disposed to become adult psychopaths regardless of their environment. The implication of this research is that we have the capacity to become more loving, giving, and in general empathetic toward others than we currently are at a particular point in our lives, as long as we have not inherited antisocial behaviors associated with the most serious forms of callous-unemotional tendencies. Human beings have the capacity for goodness, in other words, to the extent that evil does not stand in the way, in which case we cannot do much about our moral destiny, either by availing ourselves of free will or placing ourselves (or being placed) in the right sorts of environments.

This conclusion is consistent with the thesis of J. D. Trout's recent work, *The Empathy Gap*. Trout argues that though many of us may be endowed with "Dalai Lama neurons" that send a helping impulse when we see other people suffer, human beings, in varying degrees, are also disposed to have flaws in the brain that incline them to tie their capacity for empathy to egocentric motives, to attribute other peoples' shortcomings to character flaws and their own to bad luck, and to be subject to irrational, emotional biases that hamper reason's clear direction to not neglect suffering individuals right in front of us.[80] Science provides evidence, in other words, that an original goodness inherent in our creation would endow us with the ability to become more altruistic as we discovered people in this life who needed our help, were it not for the several, consistently predictable mechanical failures in the brain that mar this process and cause many of us to not act on this innate ability.[81] We are not necessarily aware that we are subject to the moral constraints of our brains' mechanical failures, in which case there is not much we can do about our moral destiny.[82] If we happen to be one of the bad seeds then we will turn out, despite free will, to be neglectful, overconfident, callous, and in many cases display tendencies toward criminal behavior. To the theological Manichean, Trout's observations confirm the suppositions of a deterministic universe indicative of a larger evil at work, despite the intentions we may wish to attribute to others.

In her recent book *Evil Genes: Why Rome Fell, Hitler Rose, Enron Failed, and My Sister Stole My Mother's Boyfriend,* Barbara Oakley engages in a sustained study of some of history's worst offenders in an attempt to make the case that they each suffered from some debilitating personality disorder, which the evidence indicates was to a significant extent inherited, a personality disorder that probably caused their dreadful behavior. Synthesizing the most up-to-date research, Oakley suggests that although in such figures an evil future was not a fait accompli at birth, a group of genetic deficiencies or in some cases excesses that we can now identify due to the genome project, and not merely free will, were responsible for their antisocial, psychopathic, and sadistic behavior. Machiavelli, Hitler, Stalin, Mao Tse Tung, Pol Pot, Idi Amin, and Slobodan Milosevic—all of whom Oakley considers—were because of their genes much more susceptible than the rest of us to becoming the notorious villains they ultimately became. Spelling out her thesis, Oakley writes,

> We know that there is no single gene known to create a psychopath, or to cause someone to suffer from antisocial personality disorder, or to generate more sinisterly successful variants of either one of these disorders. But there *are* a number of genes and gene complexes that have been found to affect brain function—most importantly, for our purposes, regarding traits such as impulsivity, mood, and anxiety. Through the use of sophisticated new techniques and concepts as imaging genetics and intermediate phenotypes, researchers are discovering how alleles of particular genes can help underpin the dysfunctional behavior that can lead to a problematic personality or full-blown clinical pathology. In a sense, you might call these *evil genes.*[83]

Evil people are not created solely, or even primarily, by their environment.[84] *Evil Genes* is full of descriptions of the various chemical deficiencies, hormonal imbalances, and genetic abnormalities that, triggered by the right circumstances (e.g., stress, compromised immune system), lead to disparate though often overlapping personality disorders that present as psychopathological behavior.[85] Hence Oakley determines of her own sister, who motivated her to write the book in the first place, "Carolyn's strange, uncaring attitude was not a conscious choice but was almost certainly due to shaky neural underpinnings, in all probability caused by a perfect storm of neural damage due to the poliovirus infection, extraordinary stress from the consequent social isolation and ostracization, and underneath it all, a genetic predisposition."[86]

Constraints of space prevent me from discussing the many personality disorders into which Oakley delves in great detail. Her emphasis on the genetic

heritability of some of these disorders, however, reveals something very interesting: Sometimes gene strands are peculiarly clustered to produce noteworthily
good and bad traits in the same individual, which explains why the Hitlers,
Stalins, and Chairman Maos of the world can rise to power. Hitler's ruthless-
ness, for instance, could not have had much effect were it not for the charisma
that led him to be taken seriously by so many people. Oakley contends that
each of these historical villains betray a Machiavellianism to a certain degree.
Like her conniving but charming sister, it is no accident that each of these
figures, as the firsthand accounts of them affirm, had an uncanny ability to win
over their respective audiences, slowly, over a period of years, garnering the
support they would need to rise to power. It is as if evil and good are waging
their own private war within the brains of these unusual individuals. What is
more, just as a good trait can double as a bad one, a vice can turn out to be a
virtue. As Oakley notes of Churchill, "In the dark days of 1940 and '41, when
the Nazis seized the bulk of Europe and the lonely little islands of Britain were
the next target, it was Churchill's convincing, egotistically certain manner that
rallied the troops and the populace around the idea of standing fast rather than
continuing with fruitless appeasement."[87]

The point is neither that genetics provides a new account for how the most
ordinary among us come to do the most terrible things, nor that nothing is black
or white only, but rather that Hitler and Churchill became world leaders who
played the roles they did for a reason. Their genetic makeup made them excellent candidates to enter the world stage precisely as they did. The more we
know about what the brain looks like on an fMRI readout, the more accurately
we can predict what the upshot will be in the contest between the good and
bad genetic influences on our personalities. This means, among other things,
that one of the most effective ways to "treat" evil is directly to attend to the
physical abnormality, once we can detect what it is. To many of the scientists
working on psychopathology and the problem of "empathy gaps" in human
beings, such a conclusion is a warrant to adopt a hopeful, optimistic attitude.
Evil is a real and formidable encumbrance to the emergence of good within the
human psyche, but to the extent that it is correctly identified it can also be
dealt with.

In an important sense, this conclusion supports one of the key maxims of
Manicheanism: Evil is a substantive entity that can be vanquished or quelled
but not fundamentally altered. To the Manichean theologian, the battle
between good and evil in the brain, again, suggests yet another microcosm of a
cosmic contest to the finish. If Oakley has interpreted the recent science correctly, then the standard belief in the importance of free will in the process of
moral decision-making may have to be revisited. Granting that our personalities

are not solely the result of environmental decisions combined with the force and effect of our volition, the question remains: Just how determinative are genes and the bodies we have been given at birth in predicting how good or bad a person we will turn out to be? Oakley ends *Evil Genes* with a reflection along these lines in the case of her sister: "If I've learned anything through these many years of research, it's that Carolyn's choices were a bit like the choices a tree on a windy shoreline has in deciding how tall and how bent to grow." Although in some extraordinary individuals, "neural shifts can take place through long-term conscious efforts," in those who are especially susceptible to morally debilitating personality disorders, the crucial neural apparatus that makes one aware of one's shortcomings is itself not there to motivate one to work on one's character in the first place. Oakley asks, "What if the ability to exert focused mental effort is itself dysfunctional as a result of some varying combination of genetic predisposition and environmental factors, as was probably the case with Carolyn?"[88]

Oakley's question is similar to one once asked by Aristotle, one of the great classic defenders of the idea that forming the right habit can, and indeed does, have the most decisive effect on our developing characters. Anticipating the critic's challenge to his view, Aristotle pessimistically ponders, "Someone might raise this puzzle: 'What do you mean by saying that to become just we must first do just actions and to become temperate we must first do temperate actions? For if we do what is just or temperate, we must be already just or temperate?' "[89] What resources are at the disposal of the one already morally handicapped to work on his or her character, if the motivation for that ambition depends on one's being able to recognize one's deficiency in the first place?[90] Aristotle's answer to his question strongly emphasizes the importance of being surrounded by the right mentors and being reared in the right sorts of ways. He therefore stresses the connection between the one morally developing and the trusting relationship that individual chooses to have with a proven, virtuous authority. But if genes play a larger role in determining personality than Aristotle could have been aware, the adequacy of this answer is called into question.

This is not to deny the possibility of free will altogether. It is, however, to suggest, as Adrian Raine notes, that free will exists "on a continuum, with some people having almost complete freedom in their actions, while others have little freedom of will."[91] Those susceptible to harmful behavior at an early age in life due to genetic and biological mechanisms beyond their control additionally grow up unable to overcome their brain dysfunction. We can with confidence predict that they will engage in evil sorts of actions. This conclusion is consistent with Bernard Harcourt's 2007 finding that America's higher than average prison population compared with that of other countries is inversely related to the number of involuntary patients we commit to our mental institutions.[92] Evil, it appears, runs deeper than our awareness of our commission of evil acts. Free will, correspondingly, seems more available to the individual who has the supporting mental equipment to act on it.

If this Manichean understanding of the genetic disposition toward evil within the human brain is correct, then one can easily imagine the far-reaching ethical and legal implications for how we ought to define personal responsibility, as well as for how to punish those who fail to exercise it. Later in this book, particularly when I consider the model of privation, I revisit the question of the contingency of good and bad behavior. Elsewhere I have committed myself to the notion that regardless of what moral traits we are naturally endowed with, we always have the capacity to become better people than we initially are, a view that is decisively not deterministic.[93] I am therefore naturally skeptical of attempts to jettison the important role that the will plays in moral development. This said, having now read articles written by scientists who have used magnetic imaging to demonstrate that deficiencies of empathy are a result of physical abnormalities in some human brains, I am more persuaded than I used to be that the only way to "fix" the evil in some individuals is to develop technology that will repair their damaged brains.[94] The extent to which one might fix this kind of deficiency on one's own, it is beginning to seem clear, is beyond one's moral control, certainly if self-awareness is required to effectuate moral motivation. If the consensus of the research presented by Oakley can be relied on—if the fMRIs to which neurologists and psychologists have recently resorted truly reveal structural deficiencies in the brains of their criminal subjects, already measurable when these subjects are young children—then evil is not going to go away by itself or through our individual efforts.[95] It must be located, battled, and eliminated. Insofar as their understanding of evil is concerned, it would seem, Christians evangelical about the end of days and scientists who remain naturalists to the core have become unlikely bedfellows. Evil is not only real metaphysically, evidence of its physical existence can be located and identified on an x-ray.

The Manichean Model under Scrutiny

Criticisms of the Manichean view abound, not only because Manicheanism is a heresy in Western religious traditions, because it implies God is not omnipotent, but also because a Manichean understanding of evil affirms a questionably binary view of the world that is too simple to do justice to a phenomenon that comes in so many forms and emerges out of so many sources. A number of issues arise along descriptive lines. Is evil really never a product of our own

making or God's, but rather something that exists in the world independently
of us? Is this independent source really so recognizable after all? Is all evil cut
from the same cloth, all part of the same destructive force that seeks to undo
created goodness? The Manichean view of evil promotes a form of self-identity
according to which we define ourselves not by who we are or what values we
espouse, but by what we are not. Correspondingly, it pays little attention to our
participation in evil. Furthermore, it ignores the possibility that sometimes evil
is gratuitous, altogether without meaning.

An ethical dimension to the criticism of the Manichean account of evil pertains to the sanitary manner in which an acceptable self is set in contrast to an
unacceptable other. Evil, in the Manichean view, is incorrigible, governed by
its own logic, and inimical to anything recognizably human. The one who commits evil is a foreigner entity, an outcast Beowulf, whose inclusion in the human
community is out of the question. Such a characterization is fine for myths,
but in the real world the assumption precipitates cognitive dissonance, self-
righteousness, self-deception, and finally the combative spirit that underlies
war. Those who subscribe to the Manichean view do not merely resign themselves to a forthcoming contest of epic proportions, they anticipate it. The battle
against evil becomes a noble crusade, justified by the formidable opponent that
threatens to contaminate the ones who legitimately line up on the side of the
good. On normative grounds, critics harbor misgivings about the chain of events
to which the us-versus-them assumption in the Manichean view leads. To the
extent that conflict resolution requires humility, self-reflection, and an ability
to see a narrative from the other's point of view, the Manichean account seems
to offer few resources for processes of reconciliation between vying parties.
Social justice is often the consequence of compromise and forgiveness. The
Manichean style of conceiving of the enemy offers a thin blueprint for restoring
a global commitment to fostering tolerance, dialogue, and understanding.

Finally, critics tend to point out, Manicheanism is essentially pessimistic in
its denial that evil can become good, serve a larger good, or even be mitigated
with the adoption of a positive attitude. According to the Manichean account,
evil inflexibly remains external and unalterable. As such, in a sense we never
acquire the luxury of relinquishing an attitude of dread in the face of evil. Evil
eternally encroaches on us. To understand the true nature of evil is to always
be on call, cautious, straining to protect what we value against the ongoing
threat of evil's destructiveness. In light of the threat evil poses, it becomes
permissible, indeed appropriate, to live in fear. One might say that to not live
fearfully—to fail to show a proper reverence for terror—is to betray a self-
destructive naïveté and possibly to reveal that one's loyalties are not where they
should be in the battle of good versus evil. In concrete terms this means, for

example, that the "war on terror" can never be won, because a state of war is metaphysically built into the conditions of the proposed Manichean binary. Community, global dialogue, interdependence, peace are all occurrences, in essence, that are ruled out for any sustained basis. Such a conclusion, critics suggest, leads to a profoundly unhopeful state of affairs. One might say that Manicheanism is in a sense spiritually frustrating, lacking the resources to provide for prophetic redemption. In the Manichean view, we are consigned to play out our roles in the cosmic and microcosmic dramas that pit groups of individuals against one another. This commitment renders the ideal of overcoming widespread and violent conflict incoherent.

The three sorts of criticisms just enumerated—that the Manichean account of evil is descriptively not exhaustive in its characterization of evil, normatively not conducive to the virtues required to bring us out of conflict and toward a lasting reconciliation, and spiritually not hopeful in its resignation to a future laden with conflict and strife—are given voice by a number of important thinkers, religious and secular. In this final section of the chapter, for economy of space, I discuss primarily theological criticisms of the Manicheanism position, especially that of Saint Augustine, keeping in mind that I return to Augustine at much greater length in chapter 4. My aim is therefore not to provide a comprehensive critique and rebuttal of the Manichean view, but simply to introduce avenues for reflection for the student and scholar interested in the broader enterprise of weighing the advantages and disadvantages of the models of evil considered in this book.

One of the reasons Saint Augustine is hailed as a seminal thinker in Western thought, particularly with regard to his contributions on the subject of evil, is that he appreciates and thinks through the merits of one of the principal motivations of the Manichean account of evil, namely, the desire to provide a logically straightforward answer to the question of how a world of inherent goodness could simultaneously contain such irreducibly horrific occurrences. Manicheanism, Augustine saw, did not redescribe evil as something else. It did not, for example, dismiss, as some church fathers did, the suffering of the afflicted as collateral damage in service of God's larger plan. In the Manichean view, evil is decisively not good, and to this extent the model is descriptively in tune with what sufferers claim they experience when they encounter the worst there is to experience in life.

But Augustine also points out that in positing a source for human suffering—a source quite apart from God or the good creatures created in his image—the Manichean model paints a rigid and consequently inaccurate picture of the human being, for a human being is a far more complicated creature than one whose placement in one category or the other allows. What Augustine notices, in other words, is that in its way of preserving the crucially descriptive feature of evil's reality by positing an independent source of evil, the Manichean model forgoes a human anthropology that captures us in our complexity, as beings who are fallible and therefore corruptible. In adamantly insisting on the irreducibility of evil, the Manichean account succumbs to an inflexible picture of the human being, presumed to be born one way or another. By contrast, Augustine's alternative to this solution preserves the distinction between evil and goodness but allows the human capacity to have plenty to do with both. Resisting the Manichean binary by reminding us that no human being is perfect, Augustine writes,

> Beings that suffer corruption are nevertheless good. If they were supremely good, they could not be corrupted, but unless they were good they could not be corrupted. If they were supremely good, they would be incorruptible, and if they were not good at all, there would be nothing in them to be corrupted. Corruption damages a thing, and it would not suffer damage unless its good were diminished. Therefore, either corruption damages nothing, and this cannot be, or whatever suffers corruption is deprived of some good.[96]

In Augustine's alternative solution, there are no purely good or purely bad human beings, only corruptibly good human beings, whose corruption indicates a higher goodness before that corruption. This is another way of saying that, at least in terms of moral evil, human beings are in their inception good but also disposed to become involved with evil. One might infer that in this solution how nature and nurture combine to form the moral sensibilities of a particular individual matter a great deal in determining just how corruptible one is relative to another. Although every being created by God has goodness, some beings are more good than others.[97] We are in any case complex beings, and our collective disposition to be corrupted to some extent ought also to furnish us with a sense of humility about who is to be labeled, simply, as good or bad, without additional qualification.

This picture of human nature is not obviously compatible with some of the scientific evidence emerging today on behalf of the Manichean thesis. What of the seven-year-olds for whom psychopathological behavior can be accurately predicted once they become adults? Surely Gordon Graham's Ockham's razor–like explanation of the villains in Columbine and elsewhere who massacred their victims has some power? Perhaps it is that though nature and nurture combine to determine how altruistic most of us will be, the same is not true with regard to the worst of us.[98] The objection to the Augustinian response maintains an asymmetry between good and evil, for while it is plausible that no one is born purely good, and that nature and nurture always combine in some fashion to produce the best sorts of people, there are, nevertheless, some evil seeds regardless of environment.

The objection is well taken. When it comes to moral goodness, the saints are not born one way that distinguishes them from the rest of us, but are rather extremely virtuous individuals who are more morally developed than we yet are, journeying further along the same road we are meant to travel. When it comes to moral evil, however, it may turn out that there are truly evil seeds who are born differently than the rest of us.

In response it becomes important, I think, to appreciate the Augustinian distinction between something that is necessarily and immutably bad and something that has become, even at the outset of its existence, corrupted. A damaged brain might be an instance of the latter and not the former. Such a rejoinder would be consistent with what the scientific researchers sometimes say is motivating them, namely, a desire to treat these damaged brains with the current technology in hopes of being able to "fix" evil. But the rejoinder works on a metaphysical level as well. Correctly working brains, no one disputes, reflect organs designed to pursue the good. That the template is one geared for goodness emphasizes Augustine's point about the human capacity to veer, inevitably, from that good, albeit in different degrees. That people are born with damaged brains, therefore, ultimately does not excuse them from the process of reform and rehabilitation, though it may make that process more difficult.

Another facet of the Augustinian objection to the Manichean description of evil pertains to the external manner in which good and evil are designated, a process that obfuscates the connection between the notions of evil and responsibility. "Corruptibility," which for Augustine is the upshot of the inevitability of sin, implies, among other things, an inward turn on the part of the self, that is, a realization that one is capable of harboring—and therefore responsible for harboring—a variety of attitudes and actions, not all of them good. Without such an intentional focus on who one is, the concepts of accountability and free will become unintelligible, for in such a case one is deprived of any mechanism of self-determination. If we are inclined to grant that accountability and free will in fact exist, that we are not beings whose every action is predetermined, then some corresponding notion of introspection and interiority needs to be at work when one understands oneself as good or evil, otherwise these terms become no more than labels. Good and evil, in other words, should be predicated on something besides an identity established based on group membership. Because it seems phenomenologically true that the vast majority of human beings are in fact capable of and do question themselves, form moral intentions, wonder how well they are living their lives, and, in lieu of doing these things adequately, acquire feelings of inadequacy and guilt, it would also seem to be that these occurrences matter in terms of how we go about characterizing moral goodness and badness. Moral meaning transcends mere labeling. It is not clear that the Manichean account of evil allows for the sort of self-reflection and self-determination on which moral culpability and praiseworthiness depend.

This descriptive observation segues into a normative criticism of the Manichean account of evil, the second sort of criticism mentioned earlier. To the extent that we adopt a deterministic attitude, and deny free will, we distance ourselves from our shortcomings. In turn, our resistance to internal reflection is tantamount to self-deception and moral evasion. This makes sense if we see moral evil not as a thing but as a process, specifically a turning away from the good—for Augustine, a turning away from God.[99] Manicheanism involves a flight from the self insofar as its labeling in advance of what is good and what is not heads off at the pass the very possibility that one can fall from grace, that one has the capacity to turn away. The concern is that Manicheanism's purely external orientation has no mechanism for inducing in the morally developing agent the self-critical virtues such as contrition, remorse, and repentance, all of which are necessary to repair a weakened will. Indeed, without some notion of interiority at work, the very notion of a will becomes untenable. Rowan Williams has this to say about the normative inadequacy of an exclusively external orientation to evil: "A discord on a musical instrument is not the result of the instrument being interfered with by an external agency *called* discord, it is a function of the workings of what is there, of what constitutes the instrument itself. . . . far from undermining the idea of moral personality, this scheme in fact seeks to defend the integrity of personal agency from a mythological conception of something outside that agency displacing the person's own responsibility."[100]

Moral evil, according to Williams, is not a feature of human nature revealed by examining the relationship between two disparate entities but rather one that becomes manifest in comparing an ailing to a healthy self. This insight is crucial to such things we value in society as conflict-reconciliation, distributive justice, social and economic equity, and the tolerance and respect of others, all of which depend on some earnest attempt on the part of the self to identify with others. On the Manichean account, evil is not a state of the self, but an objective description of some selves in toto, in contrast to other selves—most likely ourselves—who are understood to be completely bereft of evil. As such, the fight against evil is divorced from the project of contrition, empathy cultivation, and ultimately moral development.

The Manichean tendency to reject the link between the project of identifying and ridding the world of evil and character development has a deeper and more disturbing consequence. This is the tacit concession such an account yields to a deterministic view of things, according to which the processes of enlightenment, reform, and redemption—all remedies for despair—are essentially rendered moot. This leads to the third critique of Manicheanism, that it is lacking a certain sort of spiritual inspiration that has the wherewithal to console anguished and afflicted sufferers. In the Manichean worldview, it is assumed that a cosmic drama is under way, needs to be played out, and to the extent that we participate in this drama we participate as actor-witnesses whose charge it is to fulfill the roles assigned to us. It is unclear whether we are actors empowered to have any real effect on the drama's outcome. Evil, as truly other, lies outside the purview of our agency.

One here might invoke Karl Barth's identification of *Das Nichtige* (roughly translated as nothingness) with evil to draw out this criticism. According to Barth, moral evil is a function of our sinfulness, that is, of our capacity to harbor the menacing and self-alienating impulse to deny God's creative grace. This is a rejection that neither God nor any other force chooses for us but rather one we choose for ourselves.[101] This means that nothingness, in Barth's theology, is not exactly nothing; it is a part of human self-making that draws us away from the creator and leaves us all alone.[102] To attribute evil to a creative force outside ourselves is in this sense not only to commit an evasive ethical breach by unduly relinquishing moral agency.[103] It is also to eclipse the spiritual possibility of our being delivered from a situation in which we are left by ourselves. By contrast, evil as nothingness is self-condemnation, which makes it not as hopeless as other forms of condemnation. It can be, if not undone, mitigated by turning toward what is not nothing.

The responsibility for our participation with nothingness, to be sure, rests on our shoulders alone, for "the concrete form in which nothingness becomes active" and becomes apparent "is the sin of man as his personal act and guilt, his aberration from the grace of God and its command, his refusal of the gratitude he owes to God and the concomitant freedom and obligation, his arrogant attempt to be his own master, provider, and comforter, his unhallowed lust for what is not his own, the falsehood, hatred and pride in which he is enmeshed in relation to his neighbour, the stupidity to which he is self-condemned, and a life which follows the course thereby determined on the basis of the necessity thus imposed."[104]

A strong indictment indeed, yet we are all the more spiritually fortunate for the condemnation being of this sort rather than one in essence beyond our control. Being a personal act, evil is ours to undo. That evil is *Das Nichtige* is for Barth beneficial insofar as it serves as a reminder of the possibility of our being redeemed by getting outside ourselves. Within the framework of Barth's Christocentric theology, such a spiritual return is uniquely doable through surrendering to Jesus Christ, whose conquering of sin made the possibility of salvation a reality. The larger point, however, is that seeing evil as an absence with which we can actively replace a presence removes the despair of a vicarious existence in which we, in the face of evil, are basically helpless to participate in our, and for that matter the world's, reformation.

All three of the criticisms—the descriptive, the normative, and the spiritual—allege that the Manichean model adopts an understanding of human agency that is restricted and, insofar as it plays down our volitional capacities, undignified. The Manichean may respond that wishing for a more optimistic depiction does not make it so. Although we may sympathize with what is motivating these objections, it may well be that we are less free than we think. For all the mythology in which the dualistic narrative is couched, it may be that the Manichean is the realist at the end of the day. Certainly the Manichean is to be credited for not painting too rosy a picture of human existence and for not watering down our painful encounter with evil. Counter to good, evil poses a threat to the very idea of meaning with which human beings have to reckon. This assumption, that evil is inimical to meaning, is precisely one with which the principal figures to be examined in chapter 2, the theodicists, are poised to take issue.

Notes

1. James, *Varieties of Religious Experience*, 33.
2. Ibid.
3. Frankfurter, *Evil Incarnate*, 11–12.
4. See, for example, Mathewes, *Evil and the Augustinian Tradition*, 34–35.
5. Postel, "Gray's Anatomy."
6. Huntington, *Clash of Civilizations*.
7. Mathewes, *Evil and the Augustinian Tradition*, 35.
8. Cooper, *Dimensions of Evil*, 157.
9. Ibid., 157–58.
10. On the shadow self, see also Sanford, *Evil*, and *The Strange Trial*; Kopp, *Mirror, Mask, and Shadow*, 16. Cooper considers at length the work of both Sanford and Kopp in his analysis.
11. Letter III to Asclepius (ascribed to) Hermes Trismegistus, in Rorty, *Many Faces of Evil*, 24–25.
12. The Gnostics were made up of disparate, related sects in the early Christian era. They emphasized that gnosis, or esoteric knowledge, is the linchpin to salvation and deliverance from suffering. Gnostics were primarily located in Syria and Egypt and

adopted a more moderate dualism than that of their Manichean counterparts, who predominantly inhabited Persia. Dualistic theologies always posit opposing forces of good and evil, and additionally, in varying degrees, employ other dualisms such as that between spirit and flesh.

13. In light of the discussion of the Gothic, consider the detailed and altogether strange manner in which the King of Darkness is described in the Gnostic tradition in the first-century Mandean Ginza texts: he "assumed all the forms of earthly creatures: the head of the lion, the body of the dragon, the wings of the eagle, the back of the tortoise, the hands and feet of a monster. He walks, crawls, creeps, flies, screams, is insolent, threatening, roars, groans, gives (impudent) winks, whistles, and knows all the languages of the world. . . . [H]e is mightier than his words, stronger and more numerous than all of them and more powerful than all his creatures and stronger than they. . . . The thickness of his lips measures 144,000 parasangs. The breath of his jaws melts iron, and the rocks are scorched by his breath. He lifts up his eyes and the mountains quake, the whisper of his lips makes the plains shudder. He mused with himself, deliberated in his foolish heart, and plotted in his crafty mind" (Rorty, *Many Faces of Evil*, 27). Unrecognizable yet uniquely threatening, the King of Darkness overmatches everything short of the source of all goodness in the world.

14. The seven or eight known books originally written by Mani, of which only fragments remain, were discovered relatively late, in the 1900s. Most were written in Syriac and presented in a comprehensive volume called *Manichaeische Dogmatik aus chinesischen und iranischen Texten* (Manichean Dogma from Chinese and Iranian texts), published in Berlin in 1933. The most accessible translation of the Manichean writings in English can be found online at *The Gnostic Archive*: www.gnosis.org/library/manis.htm. For most of modernity and the entirety of the Middle Ages what we knew of Manicheanism we knew from its critics. For the most thorough treatment of these, including Mani's repudiation of the historical Jesus and his endorsement of radical dualism, see the Catholic Encyclopedia, www.newadvent.org/cathen/09591a.htm. Manichean cosmogony begins with an account of two separate powers that could have lived in peace had the King of Darkness, incarnated as Satan, not chosen to encroach on God's realm of light.

15. "Light Your Lamps," *The Gnostic Archive*, www.gnosis.org/library/manis.htm.

16. Gardner and Lieu, *Manichaean Texts*, 184.

17. Neiman, *Evil in Modern Thought*, 118.

18. Bayle, *Historical and Critical Dictionary*, 146, quoted by Neiman, *Evil in Modern Thought*, 119.

19. Neiman, *Evil in Modern Thought*, 120.

20. Ibid., 124.

21. Midgley, *Wickedness*, 133.

22. As quoted by Midgley, *Wickedness*, 134.

23. Ibid.

24. Russell, *The Devil*, 189. Russell traces the development from *satan* as a nonproper noun that referred to a threatening human opponent to the currently accepted sense of him as an accusing, obstructing divinity conveyed in the apocalyptic texts. In the Hebrew Bible, Satan refers to the obstruction of one's path (Numbers 22:22) but does not yet appear as a demonic entity responsible for all evil until the apocryphal texts.

25. The phrase Barry Glassner helped popularize makes sense within the context of the reception of Manichean theology as well. See Glassner, *Culture of Fear*.

26. See also St. Augustine's similar characterization in Augustine, *City of God*, book 12, 471–73.

27. Graham, *Evil and Christian Ethics*, 201.

28. My thanks to Audrey Allas in suggesting this term.

29. Graham, *Evil and Christian Ethics*, 159, 123, 203.

30. If Graham is right that there is something demonic about Klebold and Harris, it doesn't necessarily mean that nothing is to be learned from tapping into the counterculture undercurrent of which these two are representative. For an excellent treatment of the two sorts of narratives that converged in the wake of the Columbine tragedy, one theological and the other sociological, see Pike, "Dark Teens and Born-Again Martyrs." Pike, a sociologist of religion, argues against seeing Columbine only through the lens of Protestant evangelical captivity narratives (of the sort Graham, for example, favors), for the event also invites a discourse of troubled youth and calls attention to a need to integrate the disparate parties who coexist at the margins of "normality" in society.

31. Ibid., 170.

32. Ibid., 203.

33. Levenson, *Creation and the Persistence of Evil*, xxi.

34. Ibid., xxi–xxii.

35. Ibid., xxvi.

36. As quoted by Levenson, *Creation and the Persistence of Evil*, 7.

37. Ibid., 39.

38. Keller, *Face of the Deep*, 49.

39. Ibid., 28.

40. Graham, *Evil and Christian Ethics*, 96. Graham makes a sustained argument against theodicy on 165, ff.

41. Milgram, *Obedience to Authority*; Zimbardo, "Pathology of Imprisonment"; Browning, *Ordinary Men*; Arendt, *Eichmann in Jerusalem*.

42. Graham, *Evil and Christian Ethics*, 180.

43. Ibid., 181.

44. Quoted in Rorty, *Many Faces of Evil*, 81.

45. Calvin, *Institutes of the Christian Religion*, 2.1.9.

46. Ibid., 2.1.8.

47. Machiavelli, *The Prince*, 48–49.

48. Hobbes, *Leviathan*, 98–99.

49. Quoted in Rorty, *Many Faces of Evil*, 194.

50. Ibid., 194.

51. Some might interpret this inversion of good and bad as an indication that the Marquis de Sade, rather than betraying a view that is conducive to the Manichean model, subscribes to the third model to be explored in chapter 3, according to which evil is really only "evil," a perspective that depends entirely on the point of view of the one denoting. Yet, the Marquis de Sade assigns murder a positive valuation. By substituting bad for good, he clearly acknowledges the conceptual distinction between the two. Thus, there is here no agnosticism about merit, but an out and out reversal, and hence still a dualism posited between good and evil.

52. The Marquis de Sade seems to articulate a similar life philosophy as that of Jack London's brutal sea captain, Wolf Larsen, for whom all of life is but the brief "crawling and squirming" of selfish beings quite understandably vying to fulfill their biological urges. The competition, according to Wolf Larsen, is not only permissible but commendable, precisely because it is natural. See London, *Sea Wolf*, 35.

53. Quoted in Rorty, *Many Faces of Evil*, 217.

54. Conrad, *Heart of Darkness*, 50.

55. Ibid., 65.

56. Consider Mary Midgley's observation that the shadow self bears a Manichean flavor both foreign and native: Evil traits "are not just something alien. In one sense they are simply qualities of the person who owns them, though in another they are indeed something extraneous which has attacked him. This duality is a most puzzling feature of the mental life, and a continual practical as well as a theoretical problem. We try to avoid 'owning' our bad motives . . . because we feel that to own or acknowledge is to accept. We dread exposure to the hidden force whose power we sense." Midgley, *Wickedness*, 113–14.

57. See, for example, Hawkins, "Conrad's Critique of Imperialism."

58. See Huntington, *Clash of Civilizations*. The historian Bernard Lewis, who has greatly influenced Huntington's thesis, introduced the phrase "clash of civilizations" in a 1990 article in *The Atlantic*.

59. Huntington, "Clash of Civilizations?"

60. See Philippians 3:20–21; 2 Thessalonians 2:1–7; Matthew 24:36–41.

61. The precise manner in which the Antichrist returns to earth and believers are saved while nonbelievers are condemned is heavily debated in Christian theology. There are camps and divisions within these camps. Peterists maintain that the Revelation pertains to events that have already taken place in the first century, the Apocalypse pertaining only to unsaved Jews, whereas Futurists maintain that the Revelation has yet to unfold in history and will do so only just prior to the Second Coming. Futurists, who make up the majority of Christians, believe in a period of tribulation: a seven year span of time during which Christians will be persecuted by nonbelievers and prove their worthiness as loyalists to Jesus Christ. Within the futurist camp there is some dispute about when the rapture will occur. Pre-tribulationists hold that believers will be taken up to meet Christ before the Tribulation begins; mid-tribulationists hold that the rapture will take place at the mid-point of the Tribulation; and post-tribulationists believe that believers will enter the Kingdom of Christ only after the rapture, at the end of the period of Tribulation. There is also a debate about precisely when Jesus Christ returns to earth, and whether he literally reigns for a full thousand years before the final battle.

62. The *Left Behind* series has sold more than 50 million copies and, by virtue of its popularity, can be taken to be a fair amalgamation of many evangelicals' beliefs about the details of the rapture

63. Frykholm, *Rapture Culture*, 3–4. The series adheres to a pre-tribulation account of the rapture according to which believers are already, by the story's start, distinguished from nonbelievers who bear the mark of the beast and who can, in turn, do nothing about their forthcoming condemnation. The series in this sense deemphasizes the importance of the performance of good works in the process of salvation. It is also less

concerned with the injunction to love the neighbor, provide care for the one least well off, or with any communal orientation in general. Instead it focuses narrowly on the epic battle between good and evil and the salvation of those individuals who are good. One could argue that in this sense the view of Revelation adopted by the series is particularly Manichean, even more than accounts already focused on the Rapture and the Apocalypse.

64. For more on the Messianic eschatology featured in the book of Revelation, see Boyer, *When Time Shall Be*, 23. For a wonderful discussion of the use of Revelation as "war-time literature," see Pagels, *Revelations*.

65. For more, see Boyer, *When Time Shall Be*, 36.

66. In historical context, Babylon, a worldly power symbolic of spiritual oppression, is in the era of antiquity thought to be Rome, and today America. See Boyer, *When Time Shall Be*, 43, 246–47.

67. Ibid., 41.

68. Ibid., 11.

69. Ibid., 297–98, 318.

70. Ibid., 312. See Pagels, *Revelations*, 1–36.

71. Boyer, *When Time Shall Be*, 318.

72. Ibid., 322.

73. Phillips, *Terrors and Experts*, 50.

74. Sandler, *Righteous*, 33–34.

75. Frykholm, *Rapture Culture*, 19.

76. Ibid., 46.

77. Viding et al., "Evidence for Substantial Genetic Risk."

78. Glenn et al., "Temperamental and Psychophysiological Precursors."

79. Viding et al., "Evidence for Substantial Genetic Risk," 596.

80. Trout, *Empathy Gap*, 29.

81. The neuroscientists Dharol Tankersley, C. Jill Stowe, and Scott Huettel have shown that especially compassionate people have more than the usual amount of activity in the posterior superior temporal cortex of the brain, a region specifically responsible for perceiving the designs and actions of others. In other words, empathy, which depends on our ability to see and thus grasp others' motivations the way we understand our own, depends on correct neural functioning. See Tankersley, Stowe, and Huettel, "Altruism Is Associated." One way to define psychopathology is by the short-circuitry of the neurons in the posterior superior temporal cortex, which deprives affected individuals of being able to feel empathy. Adrian Raine and Yaling Yang discuss the various ways this occurs in "Neuroanatomical Bases of Psychopathy," 278–95.

82. Recent experiments seem to have isolated an area of the brain that is responsible for producing feelings of consciously intending to do something as well as the feeling of having done it—all without actually doing it. A different part of the brain is responsible for actually doing actions, and when these two parts of the brain aren't allowed to communicate, the subject performs actions without being aware of it, and thinks they've done things they haven't. I thank Richard Houchin for alerting me to this point. See http://scienceblogs.com/notrocketscience/2009/05/electrical_stimulation_produces_feelings_of_free_will.php?utm_source = networkba nner&utm_me dium = link.

83. Oakley, *Evil Genes*, 68–69.

84. Ibid., 175. Oakley sees herself in a school with Steven Pinker, Judith Rich Harris, and others who have staked their reputations on debunking the vogue thesis that nurture (rather than some combination of nurture acting upon nature) is what is decisively important in determining human behavior. See also Pinker, *Blank Slate*, 260; Harris, *Nurture Assumption*, 14–32.

85. Oakley considers too many examples to mention them all here, but see especially *Evil Genes*, 78–88; 90–105; 131–49; 179–205.

86. Ibid., 327.

87. Ibid., 59, 207, 277, 303–4n, 42, 310–22, 292–93.

88. Ibid., 327–28.

89. Aristotle, *Nicomachean Ethics*, 1105a18–22.

90. I discuss this conundrum in Flescher, *Heroes, Saints*, 265–66.

91. Raine, "Psychopathy, Violence, and Brain Imaging," 50–51, quoted in Oakley, *Evil Genes*, 329.

92. Harcourt, "Institutionalization vs. Imprisonment." I was made aware of Harcourt's research through Oakley, *Evil Genes*, 330.

93. See Flescher, *Heroes, Saints*; Flescher and Worthen, *Altruistic Species*.

94. See especially Kiehl, "A Cognitive Neuroscience Perspective." Kiehl has studied the brains of psychopathic criminals, whom he ranks on a forty-point scale, from Western New Mexico Correction Facility and, using fMRI technology, has demonstrated a difference between the amygdalas of their brains, the regions thought to be responsible for "emotional intelligence," and those of normal people. What is interesting is that although fMRIs showed less activity in the amygdalas of psychopaths, in some cases they revealed more activity in the frontal lobes, indicating that such subjects knew the difference between right and wrong—they were not insane according to the technical definition—but just did not care about this difference.

95. The question, of course, remains about whether the studies referenced manage to establish the causation and not merely correlation between damaged brains and psychopathological behavior. At least two sorts of objections linger for the one who wants to conclude that damaged brains cause psychopathology. First is a directional one that worries about whether the causal process works in reverse, in this case asking whether it is possible that criminal behavior is itself what causes the brain damage detected on fMRIs. Second is a third-variable objection that questions the conclusion that damaged brains directly lead to psychopathological behavior, suggesting that perhaps a third variable may be at work in the whole process. It may be, for example, that damaged brains cause certain sorts of behaviors and that it is other people's reaction to these behaviors that then causes psychopathological behavior. That many of the studies supporting the stronger thesis of causation are longitudinal, measuring the behavioral shifts in subjects as they mature from callous and unemotional children to criminal psychopaths, addresses the directional objection but not necessarily the third-variable objection.

96. *Confessions of Saint Augustine*, 7.12.18, 172.

97. Mann, "Augustine on Evil and Original Sin," 43.

98. As Daniel Worthen and I argue in *Altruistic Species*, 245.

99. Williams, "Insubstantial Evil," 105.

100. Ibid., 112–13.

101. Barth, *Church Dogmatics*, 310, 351.

102. Ibid., 349.

103. In contrast, for example, to Jon Levenson and Catherine Keller, as discussed earlier, for whom such an attribution elevates rather than lowers our conception of the divinity. Here Barth establishes quite clearly that he is not Manichean. "Nothingness" is precisely what God has not elected to create (Barth, *Church Dogmatics*, 351).

104. Ibid., 305.

CHAPTER TWO

Evil as the Good in Disguise

Theodicy and the Crisis of Meaning

"Have you ever been to Florence, Reyes?"

Felipe sat back, open-mouthed with disgusted incomprehension.

"No," he said acidly. "I haven't felt much like touring, Sir."

"You should go. There's a series of sculptures there by Michelangelo that you should see. They are called *The Captives*. Out of a great formless mass of stone, the figures of slaves emerge: heads, shoulders, torsos, straining toward freedom but still held fast in the stone. There are souls like that, Reyes. There are souls that try to carve themselves from their own formlessness. Broken and damaged as he is, Emilio Sandoz is still trying to find meaning in what happened to him. He is still trying to find God in it all."

It took Felipe Reyes, blinking, several moments to hear what he'd been told, and if he was too stiff-necked to look at Giuliani for the time being, he was able at least to admit that he understood. "And by listening, we help him."

"Yes. We help him. He will have to tell it again and again, and we will have to hear more and more, until he finds the meaning." In that instant, a lifetime of reason and moderation and common sense and balance left Vincenzo Giuliani feeling as weightless and insubstantial as ash. "He's the genuine article, Reyes. He has been all along. He is still held fast in the formless stone, but he's closer to God right now than I have ever been in my life. And I don't even have the courage to envy him."

—MARY DORIA RUSSELL, *The Sparrow*

"With or Against, but Not Without"

A VICTIM OF UNSPEAKABLE TORTURE and humiliation, having borne witness to a mass slaughter in which he took unwitting part, the once devout and still compassionate Emilo Sandoz is a broken man by the time Vincenzo Giuliani, the father general of the Society of Jesus, interviews him. Sent to the planet Rakhat along with seven others to investigate the possibility of intelligent life, Sandoz is the sole survivor in a hopeful mission that unravels into catastrophe for everyone involved. Mary Doria Russell's novel about a believer forsaken by a God in whom his faith had never before wavered is tragic and humane. By the time Felipe Reyes and Vincenzo Giuliani hear Sandoz's story, the reader is already well aware of the details, details that provide at least strong circumstantial evidence—if not a smoking gun—that God is not only cruel but deliberate in his cruelty. Russell's title, *The Sparrow*, is an unveiled reference to Matthew 10:29, which speaks to God's omniscience and, we may presume as well, his omnibenevolence and omnipotence. Not a single sparrow falls from the sky without God knowing it and therefore willing it. Asked whether it is God who is rightfully to be blamed, Sandoz's conclusion draws out the unanticipated implications of the biblical logic:

> "You see, that is my dilemma. Because if I was led to love God, step by step, as it seemed, if I accept that the beauty and the rapture were real and true, then the rest of it was God's will too, and that, gentlemen, is cause for bitterness. But if I am simply a deluded ape who took a lot of old folktales far too seriously, then I brought all this on myself and my companions and the whole business becomes farcical, doesn't it. The problem with atheism, I find, under these circumstances," he continued with academic exactitude, each word etched on the air with acid, "is that I have no one to despise but myself. If, however, I choose to believe that God is *vicious*, then at least I have the solace of hating God."[1]

For Sandoz, damaged as he is, meaning and purpose are tied to the persistence with which he maintains his relationship with God, a God he does not have the luxury of jettisoning in the wake of even the most brutal experiences life has to offer. "I can be with God or against God, but not without God," Elie Weisel once said in response to a questioner who asked him why he didn't lose faith after the Holocaust.[2] When one commits in faith, one has no choice but to fall where one's leap lands him. However damning, one must embrace the consequence of one's full spiritual investment. As Sandoz points out, the alternative would betray a "farcical" absence of authenticity.

What Emilo Sandoz does not explicitly say but we are inevitably left to con-clude in the quoted passage, however, is how hollow the prospect is of believing in a God one has legitimate grounds to despise, for believing in this sort of God arguably offers the struggling believer little solace. Sandoz probably knows what Russell's readers know: In spite of his rhetoric to the contrary, the choice to hate God is not sufficient compensation for the pain he causes that makes him worth hating. If we believe in God and something dreadful transpires, and it seems as though it is God who has led us there, we are left with a nagging, unanswerable mystery that threatens to engender feelings of despair and aban-donment. The dreadful occurrence is both painful in itself as well as a reminder of what fools we can sometimes be for thinking everything will turn out to be okay, as if some insight we have yet to experience could justify a dehumanizing reality standing right in front of us. Evil, real evil, does not easily lend itself to forgiveness or redemption. It is not necessarily or even often prologue to a deeper understanding, or any resolution, really, that repairs the damage incurred by a traumatized victim. Forgiveness and understanding sometimes occur in the wake of atrocity, but never to an extent that the victim's world looks anything like it did before the atrocity took place.

How meaning can be possible—how an affirmation of God, and, more broadly, the good, can take place following the affliction of overwhelming suf-fering—is the subject of chapter 2. Whence the challenge of theodicy: The effort to see evil in the broader service of the good when evil's description as a blessing in disguise strikes its victim as offensively off base. Can a life-stultifying experience, one that calls meaning itself into question, legitimately be considered to be part of a larger good? Can humans manage evil?

According to the thesis of containment, which we will recall is a key explana-tory rubric in the standard view, evil is something that implies an arduous trial but is at the end of the day under human control. This is so for both the evil we experience and the evil we cause. First, with regard to the evil we experi-ence (as victims), the thesis of containment asserts that human beings have in general the ability to endure those trials that cause us to suffer, no matter their duration and their intensity. Outlasting the trial may come to require the sort of stoic patience that is unusual among ordinary men and women, but, according to the standard view, trials are time-bound, and when worse comes to worst and the disguised blessing remains opaque or inaccessible, our existence after this life is always there to consider. Ultimately, we emerge stronger or happier for having been tested. This first sense of control over evil is Jamesian in character and implies a faith in the idea of a meaningful human existence that we have the capacity to ascertain in retrospect.[3] Such a meaning is all the more affirmed when it is hard-won. As Guido Reni's painting of St. Michael's foot on the dcvil's ncck implies, we are better off for having evil in the world, as long as evil is not afforded the last word.

Second, with regard to the evil we cause (as moral subjects), evil is also under our control because of the robust notion of personal responsibility built into the understanding of human agency at work in the standard view. This second sense of control, which refers to the evil we decide to perpetrate, is Kantian. Evil is the upshot of the habitual corruption of the will, our succumbing to a degenerative process whereby, over time, we substitute the essential obligation to do what is right (by virtue of which we are morally compelled to act but do not always do) with a desire to act on inclination instead.[4] In Kantian terms, evil is a perversion of our maxims.[5] It is a problem of our making, and, as such, one that we have in principle the resources to address by ourselves. Thus, unlike original sin, which according to Kant is inevitable, moral righteousness lay within human jurisdiction and could be achieved by keeping the temptation of inclination at bay. Indeed, for Kant it is the possibility of evil that makes the will real. Kant did not believe that evil could ultimately be explained or understood as the good; strictly speaking, Kant was not a theodicist. For Kant, evil remained, and had to remain, a mystery, otherwise humans would have no space within which to act according to genuine moral choice: for if every time suffering occurred as a response to immoral human action, God entered into history and rescued the world from its consequences, people could have no real notion of human accountability. But for this very reason, Kant did believe, like James, that evil was a necessary, even sensible, part of human existence and was, moreover, crucial to making the human experience meaningful. In this broader sense Kant's orientation toward moral evil is consistent with the project of theodicy, understood not as a vindication of the divine but at least as a justification, or even argument in favor of, the existence of evil. The lure of inclination, and in turn a will that can become radically corrupted, makes possible the will's dignity, for the will has a capacity for self-legislation in direct proportion to its susceptibility to maxim-inversion.

The combined impression of the Jamesian-Kantian view is that evil is ultimately necessary for the good. The evil we experience grants us the opportunity to display fortitude and benefit from hidden blessings (James). Correspondingly, our penchant for causing evil, a handicap under which we inevitably labor because we are innately sinful, affords us, in contrast to the other animals, the chance to become creatures who have genuine accountability (Kant). The thesis of containment, which draws on William James and Immanuel Kant in the manner I have explained, thus has the potential to be not only appealing but also descriptively convincing as an account of how evil fits into the larger human picture. For such an account to be plausible, however, evil must at some point actually give way to good. Evil is conducive to the good only if at some juncture we can see what would irretrievably be lost without it, or at least that on balance with evil we are better off in the long run even if we are worse off for the time being. The best defenses of the descriptive claim about the complementarity between evil and good do not ignore the empirical realities that seem to count against this complementarity. They acknowledge a victim's trauma or a community's dissemination and then go on, despite these potentially disconfirming crises, to argue that evil is nevertheless structurally necessary for meaning and flourishing. Whether such arguments are persuasive remains to be seen. The basic descriptive question with regard to theodicies, therefore, is whether evil leads or is already the good in the hardest sorts of cases.

A normative question about theodicies warrants careful consideration. The thesis of containment assumes that the notion of the will, through which human beings acquire moral agency, and in turn dignity, depends on the genuine human susceptibility to the commission of wrongdoing. It is not clear, however, that this assumption can be sustained. Granting that a notion of free will logically necessitates a world that contains the possibility of evil does not, at the same time, imply that that evil also has to allow for the possibility of a type of suffering so severe that it denies to its victim the very conditions of agency the existence of evil is purportedly needed to protect. The point can be put theologically. Was it really necessary for God, who created evil out of a deeper love for his creature (in order to provide free will), to organize the world so harshly that innocents would be tortured and communities destroyed? Could not free will be preserved without the consequence of suffering on such a widespread and intense scale? The Kantian response is no. For free will to be genuine, God must stay out of human affairs. By definition this implies that anything, including the worst of things, can possibly transpire. In this case, though, we must begin to question, as does Ivan Karamazov in the challenge he issues to his younger brother Alyosha,[6] whether free will is worth the price. The thesis of containment may overreach. It may turn out that the autonomy-enabling and pedagogical benefits of evil do not justify their toll in suffering, especially in view of the examples of evil that have emerged in recent history.[7] Thus, for the project of theodicy to be successful, it must both make the descriptive case that evil and good have a positive relationship with one another and the normative case that the human condition is better off by virtue of that relationship. This chapter looks at and evaluates some of the best attempts to have undertaken this project, both as an intellectual effort and as apologetics.[8]

The Great Conundrum

Discussions about theodicy tend to begin with a familiar conundrum of three premises held by the committed believer in traditional Western religious contexts. Two are articles of faith and the third an empirical fact:

> God is all-loving (omnibenevolence).
> God is all-powerful (omnipotence, which implies omniscience).
> Evil exists.

For nonbelievers in the traditional sense who nonetheless fundamentally trust that there is a larger "sense to it all," the first two premises collapse into a single affirmation and the last is unchanged:

> There is ultimately meaning in this world.[9]
> Evil exists.

All of those engaged in the project of theodicy try to reconcile the apparent contradiction in these groupings. How could a God who infinitely loves us and has the unlimited power to keep us safe, if not always happy, act directly to cause or allow us indirectly to be afflicted by experiences that are an assault on our well-being? How can faith in an ultimately meaningful existence be reconciled with encounters the most honest descriptions of which characterize them as meaning-denying? As suggested, the challenge is not merely intellectual, requiring a conceptually plausible way out of a seemingly irresolvable tension. It also beckons the holder of the premises to defend the worldview to which he or she has so far committed in the form of a kind of apology issued either on behalf of the author who made the world the way it is, or of the world itself (presumed within a secular context to have inherent meaning from its inception). In both cases, theodicists are resoundingly committed to not relinquishing their faith in a goodness that not only exists but also prevails in the world. This requires them to demonstrate that the good stands in some sort of symbiotic, if subtle, relationship to evil. Thus evil can still exist but it is trumped, subsumed, or represented by the good. For those who deny the existence of evil, or harbor the atheist (or nihilist) view that God (or meaning) is a reflection of wish fulfillment, the conundrum evaporates but along with it so does the problem of theodicy. Unlike uncritical theists on the one hand and atheists on the other, most theodicists are sophisticated and confront the existential dilemma of evil directly. They resist the temptation to making it easier to resolve either by abandoning a realistic attitude toward suffering or by softening their faith in a higher purpose and meaning. Sophisticated theodicists, in other words, set out to be neither empirically aloof nor despairingly resigned. Satisfying both of these ambitions requires a bit of mental gymnastics, inviting a constructive theology that involves redescribing, reinterpreting, and remanaging expectations.

Vexing though the conundrum is, there is no shortage of proposed solutions. As we have just seen, perhaps the most typical tack is, rather than to modify the traditional picture of God, to qualify the nature of evil as, if not insignificant, reinterpretable.[10] Evil is either tantamount to the good or already the good camouflaged. We simply lack the full panoramic perspective within which to view God's divine plan—or, secularly, to ascertain in full the unfolding of meaning within the universe. Indeed, to think that we do not lack such a perspective is a sign of our arrogance. Because evil is understood as necessary to either know or lead to the good, the best sort of universe would naturally include it. God, for example, permits us to suffer so we will know joy better, or permits us to suffer as a form of grace so we will understand more vividly our need of him. In other versions of the solution that seeks a qualification of the empirical premise, evil, no matter how severe, is justified either as a consequence of some past violation (e.g., as applied through some principle of retributive justice or karma), or as a pedagogical prod intended to teach or toughen or improve us in ways we could not otherwise without our involvement with it. Still some other solutions to the conundrum do not qualify the evil we experience as much as they qualify the time during which we experience it. The idea here is that everything in the present is hors d'oeuvre for the future. That which is wrong becomes righted in the afterlife. Last is the free will defense, according to which evil, no matter how bad, is justified on the grounds that the best kind of life is one in which no force would obstruct our autonomy even in the most dire circumstances. The free-willist claims that our decisions are capable of possessing moral content, not in spite of but because we are beings capable of deciding in favor of despicable sorts of actions. The free will defense is particularly important for our purposes here because it is intimately tied to the question of moral evil.

Another category of solutions to the Great Conundrum focuses not on the qualifications to or the justifications for evil but on the nature of God, or at least on the nature of the fundamental goodness presumed to be present in the human situation. Theologically, this category of solutions questions whether God is really all-loving or all-powerful. In *After Auschwitz*, Richard Rubenstein, in the wake of genocide, refuses to give an inch when it comes to relaxing our description of evil as evil. Taking issue with Emil Fackenheim as well as other traditional Jewish theologians, he argues that the Holocaust is too great a cost for human beings to have to have endured at the behest of God, divine plan or not. He jettisons the idea of an all-loving deity, hypothesizing instead that God is the unknowable other, the *Ein Sof*, to use the Hebrew term, who, like the tide of the ocean, moves of his own accord, without regard to what is in the best interests of humans.[11] In *Models of God*, Sallie McFague, in response to a similar concern, forgoes all-powerful rather than all-loving. In view of contemporary technology, which includes the existence of nuclear weapons powerful enough to destroy all life, she claims it is high time we replace the paternalistic model of an omnipotent deity in favor of a loving one whose body, the earth, can be injured by our irresponsibility.[12] Rubenstein's commitment to the nonrevisability of evil beckons him to consider whether God might be an elusive, ineffable force sufficiently beyond the categories of goodness or badness to act in favor of petty human interests. McFague's revision to the traditional model, on the other hand, imagines a maternal deity as a creator of the world, without, at the same time, being its preserver, in which case humans alone are responsible for what ensues after creation. For both thinkers, God is "remodeled" to no longer be both all-loving and all-powerful, thereby resolving the apparent contradiction introduced by the existence of evil.

In some non-Western, nontheistic traditions, such as the various subtraditions of Buddhism, no God exists in the first place to be all-loving or all-powerful; instead, the self alone has the essential purpose, over a course of successive lifetimes, to undergo transformation, and eventually transcendence, at which point the very categories of evil and good themselves become defunct. Some subtraditions within Hinduism as well as shamanistic religions that feature divinities of myth assert that God, in his quirky comprehensiveness, cannot be restricted only to good in himself. The God Eshu from Yoruba mythology, who intentionally established the world to include violent conflict, is a good example of this.[13] In this case God is all-loving, but he is not only all-loving. He is also equally, or at least comparatively, wicked. There are thus several possibilities for modifying the nonempirical premises in the theological version of the Great Conundrum, any one of which explains how there can be an evil in the world.

In the nontheological formulation, solutions that do not address the nature of evil modify what ultimate meaning is so that it accords with the harsh empirical facts of the universe. In this case the conundrum is sometimes resolved by supplanting a reverence for, or deeper meaning to, life with mere consciousness or there-ness. Or, in the face of evil, one might remain skeptical about whether any dignity is within humanity or whether one even has the ability to live one's life genuinely—as opposed to experiencing it inauthentically, as is the case, for example, in the "life" that humans experience in the vats in which their minds are contained in the movie *The Matrix*. Or perhaps there is goodness in the world, but it is never less superficial than hedonistic satisfaction or Kierkegaard-ian immediacy. In each of these instances, when the nonempirical premise of the nontheological version of the Great Conundrum is modified, "goodness" exists, but remains in quotation marks because it is shallow, or fleeting, or arbitrary, or in some way lacking in depth. It is not a goodness strong enough to justify evil or a goodness that manages to compensate for the suffering and despair we inevitably experience. It is possible that ultimate meaning pertains to no more than human solidarity, the capacity for humans to rise from the ashes and rebuild what has been destroyed, forming individual and communal bonds in the process.[14] This, again, is an interpretation of ultimate meaning that does not contradict the existence of evil but raises questions about whether something significantly less than profound has been substituted for what the phrase might have been meant to connote.

In regard to this second category of solutions, which both in their theological and nontheological versions attempt to modify the faith-premises of the conun-drum, a few issues arise that enable us to dismiss them, not as illegitimate in themselves, but as not viable within the context of theodicy. The first has to do with the manner in which the theological (God) or secular (ultimate meaning) referent is altered. If God does not exist (as in nontheistic traditions) or is thought not to be both all-powerful and all-loving (as in reconstructed Western theologies), then the very condition of ultimate goodness that the tension inher-ent in the conundrum presumes dissolves. An evil, in other words, is only a problem to begin with if one posits a specific sort of good that that evil threatens to undo. The source of goodness must not only ensure human existence but also ensure human flourishing, which (again, from a theological perspective) only an all-loving, all-powerful God could do. A God that does not have the capacity or desire to redeem, or a God that is in some other respect significantly limited in his abilities, is not a God capable of preserving the good in a way we would expect a divinity to do. The point being made here is descriptive: in most traditions, at a certain point remodeling the divine strips God of his divinity. In a similar respect, it is not clear that a notion of ultimate meaning that is signifi-cantly watered down still pertains to a good that is good enough to explain away evil. A good that narrowly refers to human solidarity, for example, pertains to a redemptive experience in a limited sense, but solidarity is arguably not redemp-tive enough to compensate for life's crushing, meaning-denying episodes. Soli-darity, in other words, is not quite a theodicy. It would thus appear that in both the theological and nontheological versions of the Great Conundrum, when one attempts to solve the problem by altering the nonempirical (faith)-premises, one calls into question the strength of the goodness that is in the first place threatened by the introduction of evil.

A second problem arises, however, when one sets out to alter the faith-premises of the Great Conundrum, and goes beyond the descriptive objection just mentioned. This issue surfaces when one proposes a solution that fails to appreciate the thing believers in God tend to care most about preserving in their theologies. I learned of this objection firsthand in discussing the problem of evil with a diverse group of freshmen in an introduction to religion course I teach from time to time. On reviewing some of the proposals that have arisen in attempts to solve the Great Conundrum, such as Rubenstein's and McFague's, many of my more religious students explained that they would rather become atheists than forgo either the all-loving or all-powerful divine attributes, for it is the presence of these attributes that furnishes them with a real sense of hope during the toughest of times. In the words of one student, "if God is not all-loving and all-powerful, I might as well give up on the idea of God altogether. It seems simpler and more honest than it would be to conveniently rearrange my idea of God just so I can address evil." Despite the best intentions and open-mindedness many of my believing students displayed when thinking about evil, they could not on an emotional-affective level accept that an only all-loving or an only all-powerful God could answer their prayers, procure their salvation, or convince them that the world was a world of goodness. The belief they were interested in maintaining entailed an unconditional trust in a God that would both be able to and want to shepherd them through the worst life might bring. When I pressed them on behalf of Rubenstein and McFague to be more theologically creative, suggesting with Rubenstein and McFague that the empirical reality of evil rendered the idea of an all-loving and all-powerful divinity implausible, one student replied, "well then I might as well pull a Camus." He felt on an intuitive level that Camus's atheistic humanism offered more redemptive power than what he regarded to be the "half-asked" theodicies of Rubenstein or McFague. (In their defense, Rubentein and McFague do not necessarily see themselves as offering a theodicy.)

My point in relating this teaching encounter is not to consider whether Camus's atheism is better or worse than the models of divinity proposed by theological revisionists, but rather to convey a problem with solutions to the Great Conundrum that make room for the existence of evil by revising the nature of God. Their solutions not only cease to remain descriptively credible to religious insiders, they also fail to meet the pastoral burden of providing comfort to the prospective sufferers for whom they are intended. If theodicy is not only about solving an intellectual puzzle, but also about assuring a believer in crisis that his or her God is real and responsive, then what the believer has identified as redemptive about this God must survive whatever modifications one introduces to the traditional notions of the divine.

A similar point can be made about secular solutions to the problem of evil that irreversibly alter the source of goodness thought to ground meaningful human experience. The idea that such a goodness is possible begins to seem unlikely when one removes metaphysical assurances of certain features of our experience that underlie a meaningful life, such as insulation from violent outburst, or material security, or opportunity for social interaction, or ability to form loving relations with others.[15] Only so many concessions to ultimate meaning can be made before the term becomes a description of a different sort of referent. If the existence of evil is shown to thwart the presence of the features tantamount to human fulfillment and flourishing, so much so that in response we modify the good to mean something diffuse, such as mere existence, or something else very narrow, such as food and shelter, then the good has not really been preserved and the proposed solution to the theodicy has failed.

In light of such issues, it would seem that the only course is to deal directly with the problem of evil. Along the way, I consider at greatest length the most defensible and important kind of theodicy—that of free will. The free will defense is significant not only because it is the best available explanation for why evil must also exist in a good world but also because it makes specific reference to the idea of moral evil, the evil that occurs as a result of deliberate action and inaction. Free will theodicists point out that evil is a matter of the commission or omission of deeds the decisions for which are under our control. Conversely, an enabling condition of human agency that entails genuine free will must entertain the possibility of our committing evil. In this sense evil—the evil we cause to happen—is a morally justified condition of human existence because without it we would not be human beings who are genuinely free. Thus evil is part of a far greater good.

Theodicy *Simpliciter*: The Innovation of Gottfried Leibniz

Although the problem of evil is thought to go back as far as the Greek philosopher Epicurus, the term *theodicy* formally entered our nomenclature at the turn of the eighteenth century, when a German idealist picked up the gauntlet dropped by a French critic.[16] This philosopher-critic, Pierre Bayle, was perhaps iconoclastic as a proto-Enlightenment figure who nevertheless sought to engender a healthy skepticism in the linear view of history and progress for which the Enlightenment was known. At issue for Bayle was the popular belief that the hardships in this life but lead to the doorstep of a happier one in the next. I alluded in chapter 1 both to Bayle's reluctance to accept the optimism in this sentiment uncritically and to his having praised Manicheanism for its earnest acknowledgment of the empirical reality of human misery. In postulating two independent sources of good and evil, neither of which had dominion over the other, the Manichean solution to where evil came from had the virtue, in Bayle's view, of not engaging in any sort of philosophical wish fulfillment. In his comprehensive and highly influential *Historical and Critical Dictionary*, first published in 1697, Bayle attacked Christianity for promoting a distorted view of history. Disabusing the reader of the fantasy he thought it provided, Bayle insisted the problem of unwarranted suffering that could furnish an astute student of history with any feeling of contentment had no neat solution: "If an historian were to relate truthfully all the crimes, weaknesses and disorders of mankind, his readers would take his work for satire rather than for history."[17]

Impressed by his wit and sophistication, but dissatisfied with what he took to be a penchant for exaggeration, G. W. Leibniz honed in on Bayle's empirical assumptions about the frequency and severity of misery, particularly Bayle's metaphor that more "prisons than houses" were in the streets of this world. Leibniz recognized in Bayle's resignation an allusion to Romans 3, when St. Paul worried about the extent to which unrighteousness, especially humanly caused unrighteousness, might be indicative of a God in kind. His reply invokes the greatness of divine foresight, the smallness of human perspective, and the futility of evaluating the former in light of the limitations presented by the latter:

> The apostle, [the prelates] say (Rom iii.8), is right to disapprove of the doing of evil that good may come, but one cannot disapprove that God, through his exceeding power, derive from the permitting of sins greater goods than such as occurred before the sins. It is not that we ought to take pleasure in sin, God forbid! but that we believe the same apostle when he says (Rom. v. 20) that where sin abounded, grace did much more abound; and we remember that we have gained Jesus Christ himself by reason of sin. Thus we see that the opinion of these prelates tends to maintain that a sequence of things where sin enters in may have been and has been, in effect, better than another sequence without sin.[18]

Leibniz raises the example of the resurrection to establish an intricate link between the sins of some (of everyone, in the case of some sins) and the suffering of others. Although suffering may seem arbitrary, because of its link to sin—and therefore grace—it indirectly leads to a world that is better than any of its alternatives. "The permission of evils," writes Leibniz, "comes from a kind of moral necessity: God is constrained to this by his wisdom and his goodness; *this necessity is happy.*"[19] The term *theodicy* is derived from the Greek words *theós* (god) and *díkē* (justice), which are combined to form the phrase, in English, "the justification of God." Leibniz coined the term in the title of his book, *Theodicy: Essays on the Goodness of God and the Freedom of Man and the Origin of Evil.*[20]

The publication of *Theodicy* was the first time an issue was explicitly made—or had to be made—of defending God against empirical objections that would begin to emerge in the context of a modern, scientific worldview oriented toward gathering evidence and verifying hypotheses.[21] Before Bayle's objection, it had not really occurred to sufferers in the face of evil to question whether God was impotent or indifferent to their plight. The prevailing assumption had been that when things in the world went drastically wrong and good people became victims of injustice, there had to be a reason for it. This assumption was still dominant, but Bayle's *Dictionary* pressed its defender to explain why it should continue to be.

Bayle's rejection in the *Dictionary* of an unchecked faith in the divine was thus novel in that it represented a refusal to accept what used to be a valid explanation for injustice in the world: evil as the mystery that is God's alone to unravel. Bayle, in essence, was calling for God to explain himself. Is pain really necessary for pleasure? Logically necessary? Are sin—and the punishments to which sin is linked—structurally essential components of enlightenment and salvation? At what point does pedagogically useful tribulation constitute abuse? How much pain does the one on trial have to endure before it is reasonable to demand to be shown how suffering leads to its opposite? Before Bayle, God had not been put on trial by the intellectual community.

In *Theodicy*, Leibniz proposed a classical solution to a new problem, appealing to the divine prerogative encapsulated in the biblical tautology of God's unapologetic reply to Moses, "I am that I am." Traditionally, this passage from Exodus was invoked as a display of unsurpassable divine might, not as a defense of God's right not to have to answer for himself. But for Leibniz, it stood as a useful reminder of the unbridgeable gap between finite and infinite. Human beings were cognizant of but a glimpse of God's overall design and thus poorly positioned to evaluate their purpose and destiny, let alone God's means of overseeing their realization. What God saw, but we were incapable of seeing, was that the best possible of all possible worlds entailed evil, albeit the least amount of evil. A world bereft of evil would paradoxically contain more evil precisely because of the occasions for experiencing the good that a world without evil would preclude. Here is a theodicy in which a defense is issued on God's behalf without a single example needing to be furnished to support that defense. Although evil may not be logically necessary, it is causally necessary for the good to exist. God knows, in a way we are precluded from knowing, just how in this, that, and indeed every instance evil, or rather what seems evil, will lead to the greater good. It is beneath the sort of God in whom it makes sense to believe to have to explain himself. An explanation would belie the divine character and wisdom of a being categorically apart from us.

Leibniz's defense of God thus amounts to a claim that God needs no defense, along with an assurance that even were one to be provided, it would be beyond human grasp. Although to the critic this seems a self-protective strategy, constructed deliberately to be impossible to disconfirm, to Leibniz it is a simple clarification of what amounts to an unreasonable demand on the part of the skeptic. The world is designed to involve punishment that sometimes assumes the guise of unwarranted suffering. Calamity is the silent first step to revelation of a grand design, and God is the grand designer. God has his reasons that will be made known on his timeline. All that is necessary by way of explanation now is to understand, to trust really, that what strikes us as inimical to our pursuit of the good is in fact tantamount to the overall good. In this schema, suffering (i.e., natural evil) becomes the legitimate manifestation of sin (i.e., moral evil) because sin warrants suffering. Sin, by extension, becomes a requirement for self-knowledge without which we would be forever lost to God and exiled within ourselves. We would see these connections for ourselves were we infinitely wise. But we are not.

In the end, Leibniz's theodicy comes to a rejection of the idea of evil as evil. Everything we negatively experience has a greater positive outcome, even if such a judgment is afforded only in retrospect. It is beyond human capacity to have a say in the parameters within which God's perfect goodness unfolds:

> For to assert that he knows what is best, that he can do it and that he does it not, is to avow that it is rested with his will only to make the world better than it is; but that is what one calls lacking goodness. It is acting against that axiom already quoted: *Minus bonum habet rationem mali.*[22] If some adduce experience to prove that God could have done better, they set themselves up as ridiculous critics of his works. To such will be given the answer to all those who criticize God's course of action, and who from this assumption, that is, the alleged defects of the world, would infer that there is an evil God, or at least a God neutral between good and evil. . . . [They shall] receive this answer: You have known the world only since the day before yesterday, you see scarce farther than your nose, and you carp at the world. Wait until you know more of the world and consider therein especially the parts which present a complete whole (as do organic bodies); and you will find there a contrivance and a beauty transcending all imagination.[23]

Whether it be a manageable hardship or an urgent crisis with which one has to cope, Leibniz enjoins the skeptic to not be impatient when weighing the impact of a trying experience on our overall evaluation of the amount and quality of goodness in the world. To Bayle's assertion that enough was enough, that God had to answer for the universe he had created, Leibniz replies that empirical assessments of this nature are in principle irrelevant. God transcends all conceivable methods of human verification. Leibniz thus refuses to acknowledge the ground of Bayle's objection, namely, that some threshold of suffering exists beyond which we can no longer take for granted, carte blanche, the remedy of more patience. That point when the defender of God is pressed to make an argument on his behalf never comes. Our capacity to furnish accurate judgments about what resides in overall human interest is precluded by human finitude.

Leibniz's theodicy is, as I call it, *simpliciter*, that is, without qualification, because it presses its adherent to summon whatever faith is necessary to interpret any injustice or instance of seemingly gratuitous suffering—there is no limit to its egregiousness—as an event en route to a larger justice or greater meaning. In earlier times faith had no rival explanatory mechanism for addressing the mystery of suffering. It was the standard. That it was, however, should not be taken to affirm a dichotomy between old and new modes of explanation. Lest he be mistaken as regressive, Leibniz was wont to point out that he allied himself with the harbingers of the modern, scientific worldview. Newton's discoveries confirmed rather than belied all that was beautiful in the grand design, albeit sometimes this design took some time to become manifest.[24]

Leibniz recognizes no calamity that falls outside the purview of God's grand design. We are finite creatures, limited in our wisdom and biologically locked into a brief mortality. These are all the facts one needs to quell any proffered suspicion about the goodness inherent in the world. Human beings are simply ill-equipped to identify an evil that remains evil-only. How could one know this was true? Where would one derive the confidence with which to insist on proof to the contrary? One is here reminded of William James's observation in "The Will to Believe" about the skeptic's request for assurance as a precondition of belief. Over matters in which evidence is not conclusive either way, insistence on the validity of scientific proof is but another instance of faith. As James points out, the cynic backs the field against the specific horse represented by a particular set of beliefs.[25] For Leibniz, as for James, when it comes to one faith pitted against another, it behooves the meaning-seeker to acknowledge with humility the unavailability of evidence with which the cynical case could be made. If this is true for the one on the fence, the one still deciding about the extent of the world's goodness in light of evil, then it is especially true for the one suffering, because surely no evidence suggests that the one suffering who adopts a cynical attitude will be any better off than the one in faith. She or he will just be more alone in her or his suffering, according to the implications of Leibniz's argument.

The problem, of course, is that as finite creatures, we are not simply limited in our knowledge about the world, subject to the constraints of poor understanding befitting our creaturely existence. We are vulnerable beings as well, and though we cannot escape our vulnerability, we can at least take small measures to reduce or increase it, depending on the degree to which we choose to rely on ourselves. A point does come, in other words, when it makes pragmatic sense to pay attention to how well the blind faith approach is working for us. To be forced to accept that suffering is not really suffering—to compel the sufferer to issue a blank check to the source of the suffering—is potentially to exhaust the sufferer's buffer for tolerating the pain the world doles out. For the mere mortal, this arguably amounts to a version of blaming the victim. In the worst of times one is going to need better from one's theodicy. The sufferer will need an explanation, not simply the assurance that an explanation is forthcoming. Theodicy *simpliciter*, as I have characterized it, not only fails to answer the critic from the outside, the skeptic insistent on evidence in support of the consoling theodicy. It also falls short from the perspective of the religious insider, whose suffering is not enough ameliorated when the faith that things will get better is only diffuse. Also needed is a specific roadmap, the details enumerated in the content of one's faith, which shows how they will get better.

The notion that evil really is the good "because we live in the best of both worlds" thus remains intact until we have to experience those sorrowful, heart-crushing moments that shatter our threshold for patience. Theodicy *simpliciter* may work when things go badly, but it does not work for evil. Hence the rhetorical power in Voltaire's *Candide*, in which Dr. Pangloss's advice to Candide to weather any conceivable storm strikes the reader as aloof in the wake of the absurd losses the protagonist has already suffered. Pangloss's stubborn ongoing characterization and recharacterization of the world as the most perfect one imaginable strains any reasonable person's capacity to charitably interpret successively devastating events. At one point, from the believer's perspective, one does not necessarily have to abandon one's faith but is still within one's rights to ask for more details about how God works.

When put to the empirical test in a world post-Eden, Leibniz's theodicy does not fare well. It is a theodicy in harmony with a relatively innocent existence in which one has the luxury of upholding the ethos "one should in all moments

have faith," but it is one that would be hard-pressed to survive broader, cataclysmic events such as the Lisbon Earthquake of 1755 or the various genocides
common to the contemporary world.[26] To claim that "evil exists in service of
the good" more believably in broader contexts, a theodicy must do better than
make theoretical assertions about a greater good that compensates for all imaginable evils. It must make an attempt to show the explicit connection between
suffering and redemption. One example of how this improvement can take
place is by acknowledging evil for what it is rather than denying it. The theodicist need not quarrel with Bayle. She can agree with him that suffering can
strike the sufferer as unmerited and then seek out the pedagogical upside. Evil
is still evil, but it is now seen as an evil that leads to the good. This is the
strategy exemplified in the Book of Job.

The Educative Theodicy: From Job
to Irenaeus and Lactantius

Leibniz's theodicy is thus found wanting on the grounds that a sufferer does
not have an unlimited amount of patience. The wisdom that our understanding
of suffering is to be deferred until we are in a better position to be able to judge
God's ultimate plan, an understanding which will not take place until perhaps
the afterlife, is not persuasive in light of the crushing and meaning-denying
experiences that we must endure in this life. In withholding the right of the
typical sufferer to grasp what is happening now, the theodicy *simpliciter* treats
corporeal misery and psychological exhaustion too lightly.

Job

What more can be offered by way of justification? The book of Job, in many
respects the father of theodicy, offers an answer. Unlike Leibniz's solution in
Theodicy, Job suggests that suffering is not beyond our understanding. To the
contrary, it is educative, that is, something deliberately introduced into the
human situation for the purpose of being understood.[27] In educative theodicies,
once the narrative of a trial is disclosed in full from beginning to end, its lesson
will be clear to its audience. As a result, the ones suffering (as well as we, as
potential sufferers) will get a better sense of the point of their (and our) lives.
The book of Job does not take refuge in abstractions. It presents itself as a
manual for how we should go about assimilating the inevitable lapses in justice
we experience, as well as the feelings of exile that accompany them, into our
meaning-affirming worldview. Various educative moments have been proposed

by theodicists in Job, including instances that identify suffering as a punitive consequence of sin (8:2), and those that serve as the beneficial opportunity for Job to prove his loyalty to God (1:21; 2:10). The most prominent, however, are those in which suffering becomes the occasion in which Job confronts his mortality and discovers he does not have to face it by himself. The linearity of the narrative of Job, which places the protagonist in intimate proximity with the divine at the climactic juncture, ensures that God's goodness is not declared by fiat, as in the case of Leibniz, but rather reflects a goodness that is convincingly shown to be valid. In educative theodicies, God is not so much the focus as we ourselves are. It is not God but the human being who stands on trial.

A few key features of the story of Job suffice to lay the ground for the general blueprint of educative theodicy. Job is a characterized as a morally upright man, beyond reproach (1:1), exemplary of the creature made in God's image, in fact. When God boasts of his perfect specimen, Satan retorts that it is easy for a person to be faithful, to be obedient, and to possess high moral character when things are going well for him (1:11). In response to this a bet is made and a trial organized. Confident that Job's loyalty is independent of his fortune, God allows Satan to strip Job of his wealth, children, and health. Job receives the facile advice of three friends, who suggest he must have done something to deserve it all (because suffering is the result of sin and sin is always punished), as well as the far more bitter judgment of his wife, who, echoing Satan's prediction, recommends that he curse and abandon God. Fighting off these temptations, Job wails to God directly:

> Have I not wept for those in trouble?
> Has not my soul grieved for the poor?
> Yet when I hoped for good, evil came;
> when I looked for light, then came darkness.
> The churning inside me never stops;
> days of suffering confront me.
> I go about blackened, but not by the sun;
> I stand up in the assembly and cry for help.
> I have become a brother of jackals,
> a companion of owls.
> My skin grows black and peels;
> my body burns with fever.
> My harp is tuned to mourning,
> and my flute to the sound of wailing. (30:25–31)[28]

Job is, of course, accurate in his self-assessment, but his appeal before God is daring. By asking what virtues he is lacking, by listing his moral credentials,

Job risks offending God. God would be within his rights to read into Job's query a request for clarity on what the criteria for praiseworthiness and reward must be if a man as good as Job fell short. How does one express justice and compassion better than by seeking out and weeping for the imperiled or by grieving for the poor? For Job, these questions are not rhetorical. In good faith, he is wondering what is expected of him.

In sharp response, God reprimands Job for abandoning humility, his sense of place among the creatures, and an understanding that ought to have been implicit about whom one, in darkness, seeks for guidance (38:1). Importantly, however, God does not stop here. He proceeds to connect Job's feeling of inadequacy to the possibility of his redemption. Because Job is ill-equipped to lift himself out of misfortune, by implication he is urged to look elsewhere to do so (40:9). In other words, what God imparts besides a lesson in creaturely humility is that creatureliness itself is a spur to seek out the creator. In suffering, Job learns two things about himself that within the worldview of the educative theodicy had always been true but not necessarily obvious: that by himself he is not complete and that he is nevertheless fortunately not alone. These truths are not readily apparent to Job when things are going well. They are revealed only under the harshness that characterizes the trial of a lifetime. The divine reprimand thus doubles as an admonishment and as evidence of the protection God offers Job against exile. It is significant that Job prevails on God for understanding without ever blaming him, and also significant that God, in turn, blames Job without condemning him. The connection between God and Job is as a consequence strengthened when it could have been severed. Although Job's disposition is bitter (27:2), his heart is troubled and restless (30:27), and his tone is angry (30:29), he knows all the while that God abides with him (19:25) and that he is therefore justified in having faith in his redeemer's goodness.[29] Thus when God answers Job, the voice that emerges from within the whirlwind is a comfort despite its paternalistic, condemnatory tone, for the alternative is that there is no voice to be heard.

God's presence, expressed in the I-Thou relationship, is the harbinger of Job's forthcoming reward at the end of the story, but the reward itself is never as important as God's simply being there to offer Job a reply. God does not leave the scene. He shelters Job through the worst he has to tolerate. This is why Job memorably concludes—before the Lord returns his possessions twofold, gives him seven sons and three daughters, and allows him to live for a hundred and forty years—"Therefore I will be quiet, comforted that I am dust" (42:6). Comforted in dust, one is redeemed, for it is ironically in dust that one realizes one is not alone and, in turn, that suffering becomes the remedy rather than forbearer of despair. The educative aspect of the theodicy of Job becomes especially clear in chapter 38, when God appears before Job to offer his testimony. God's motivation is not to get Job to submit to brute omniscient force, but rather to rescue him from a life that could have been lived in isolation. This counterintuitive facet of the reprimand is well noted by the classic philosopher of religion, Rudolf Otto. Commenting on the divine defense, Otto observes that "He conducts it to such an effect that Job avows himself to be overpowered, truly and rightly overpowered, not merely silenced by superior strength. Then [Job] confesses: 'Therefore I abhor myself and *repent* in dust and ashes.' That is an admission of inward *convincement* and conviction, not of impotent collapse and submission to merely superior power."[30]

Job's rehabilitation in loss constitutes a turn of events that reinforces the "thesis of containment" discussed earlier in reference to William James's allusion to Reni's painting of the Archangel St. Michael's foot on Satan's neck. The more drastic an overpowering and conspicuous an evil, the more efficacious the containment of that evil and its ensuing conversion into good.

Although historically much earlier, Job represents an advance in sophistication beyond Leibniz's "blank check" defense, because the one struggling for meaning now has a reason not to succumb to despair in that struggle beyond the mere Leibnizian command not to do so. The reason the theodicy offers is that in struggle and suffering the I-Thou relation is revealed. Job's light comes after going through a dark stretch.[31] Suffering, in this sense, becomes the purposeful foil signaling a more lasting and triumphant calm. The good would not be as good without evil because without evil it would be harder to know the good. It is a similar wisdom with which Shakespeare endows one of his most sympathetic characters for whom, due to exigent circumstance, frolic is no longer an option. Assuring the audience that he hasn't taken leave of his senses, the young prince Hal, just coming of age, promises

> I know you all, and will awhile uphold
> The unyoked humour of your idleness.
> Yet herein will I imitate the sun,
> Who doth permit the base contagious clouds
> To smother up his beauty from the world,
> That when he please again to be himself,
> Being wanted, he may be more wondered at
> By breaking through the foul and ugly mists
> Of vapours that did seem to strangle him.
> If all the year were playing holidays,
> To sport would be as tedious as to work;
> But when they seldom come, they wished-for come,

And nothing pleaseth but rare accidents.
So, when this loose behaviour I throw off
And pay the debt I never promised,
By how much better than my word I am,
By so much shall I falsify men's hopes;
And like bright metal on a sullen ground,
My reformation, glitt'ring o'er my fault,
Shall show more goodly and attract more eyes
Than that which hath no foil to set it off.
I'll so offend to make offence a skill,
Redeeming time when men think least I will.[32]

This soliloquy is Shakespeare's educative theodicy. Clouds serve the sun, for beauty is all the more beautiful when it was once "smothered up." Ideals of flourishing conceptually require counterexamples to avoid or overcome. Underscoring this point, the philosopher Eleanor Stump remarks, "a loathing focus on the evils of our world and ourselves prepares us to be the more startled by the taste of true goodness when we find it and the more determined to follow that taste until we see where it leads."[33] Evil, Stump argues, is both an affliction and the mirror that leads back to the good. As long as one manages not to abandon the source of one's ground of meaning during the course of the trial in question—as long as one keeps open the dialogue between oneself and one's redeemer—one stands not only to survive an ordeal but to benefit from it as well. God does not allow Satan to test Job nonchalantly. Job's misfortunes do not just happen. God oversees their happening, and in so doing retains full moral agency. Thus, the evil he might have been thought to perpetrate is, in view of all the facts, if not a moral good in itself, an affliction that represents the doorway through which one finds moral purpose.

Irenaeus

This kernel of the educative theodicy, that evil leads to the good when suffering brings the sufferer closer to the ground of goodness, is unpacked in greater detail in the case of the great church father, Irenaeus (130–201 CE). According to Irenaeus, the world we know is under a process of perfection. God intentionally creates a human existence for us marred by hardship so that we can bridge the distance between ourselves and the creator and develop into the child of God we were essentially intended to be.[34] *Against Heresies*, Irenaeus's main work, is a polemic against Gnostic dualism in the form of a treatise on the unity of the creator and creation, in which evil, too, has its place in the overall schema.[35]

The fall, our subsequent sin, and the various forms of punishment meted out as a result are all part of a broader plan to maximize the conditions for realizing our potential as creatures made in God's image who are eligible for heaven.[36] Irenaeus refers to the process of soul-making as a kind of ethical participation in God's work. Initially a "moist clay," human beings have the opportunity to grow out of their weaknesses and in the next life achieve immortality.[37] Irenaeus's strategy is in this sense not only educative but also eschatological in which we move in two stages from image to likeness of God.[38] The philosopher John Hick, a committed defender of the Irenaean theodicy in the modern era, argues for the eschatological character of the two-part movement, as follows:

> The *imago dei* is man's nature as a rational, personal and moral animal. Thus man in society, man the ethical being, man the creator of culture, exists in the image of God. It has taken many hundreds of millions of years of biological evolution to produce him, and yet even so he is only the raw material for the second stage of the creative process, which is the bringing of man, thus fashioned as a person in the divine image, into finite likeness of God. This latter stage represents the fulfillment of the potentialities of our human nature, the completed humanization of man in a society of mutual love. Whereas the first stage of creation is an exercise of divine power, the second stage is of a different kind; for the creatures who have been brought into existence in God's image are endowed with a real though limited freedom, and their future growth into divine "likeness" has to take place through their own free responses within the world in which they find themselves. Human life as we know it is the sphere in which this second stage of creation is taking place; though it seems clear that if the process is to be completed it must continue in each individual life far beyond our earthly threescore years and ten.[39]

In an existence in which human beings are not bound by their earthly longevity, evil finds a natural place. According to Irenaeus, this life should be understood as a rough draft that prepares us for the next. For example, we endure natural calamities in order to develop critical virtues, such as compassion, that help us achieve a divine likeness. By this logic, there is no way to come closer to God than in death, which is one of the worst of evils. Likening the pedagogical lesson in death to the moral to be gained in the ordeal of Jonah, Irenaeus notes a "strength made perfect in weakness," showing the "kindness and transcendent power of God":

> For as He patiently suffered Jonah to be swallowed by the whale, not that he should be swallowed up and perish altogether, but that, having been cast out again, he might not be the more subject to God, and might glorify Him the

more who had conferred upon him such an unhoped-for deliverance . . . so also, from the beginning, did God permit man to be swallowed up by the great whale, who was the author of transgression, not that he should perish altogether when so engulfed . . . but that man, receiving an un-hoped for salvation from God, might rise from the dead, and glorify God, and repeat that word which was uttered in the prophecy of Jonah: "I cried by reason of mine affliction to the Lord my God and he heard me out of the belly of Hell."[40]

In contrast to Manichean determinism, the Irenaean narrative is theologically optimistic. Suffering is not indicative of but anathema to doom. According to Irenaeus, the possibility of salvation trades on the human being's initial distance from salvation. In any period before being redeemed, one should expect to feel pain, experience suffering, and languish in exile, without, at the same time, resorting to any sort of resignation or despair. The educative theodicy is, as announced, pedagogical and, if necessary, eschatological. Any outstanding balance not cleared in this life will be addressed in the next.

In one form or another, versions of the Irenaean variation on the educative theodicy have appeared in prominent theologians, social activists, and public intellectuals down through to the contemporary era. Martin Luther King Jr. famously remarked that this life is punctuated by a comma rather than a period. He meant both that we have business beyond this life and that suffering is redemptive in the present. We can lament the hateful murder of innocent girls in Birmingham, King taught, while still using the moment of tragic injustice at the 16th Street Baptist Church to illuminate a larger truth that leads to the betterment of human beings in and beyond the segregated South.[41] The rightness of a desegregated society becomes manifest—a whole society comes of age in 1963—not just in anticipation of, but through actually experiencing and witnessing the inherent wrongness of segregation, and the terrorist attack to which segregation led.

In a similar vein, C. S. Lewis argues that we may understandably be tempted to brand God a "cosmic sadist" who toys with us for his amusement, lash out at God as a result, and claim that our indignation over the gratuitous misery we encounter is legitimate, without, at the same time, missing the opportunity to benefit from the anger to which our misery leads.[42] In acute pain following the loss of his wife to cancer, Lewis ultimately recommends we resist despair when we have most cause to embrace it. His refusal to resign follows an argument he makes throughout most of A Grief Observed on behalf of that resignation. When it does arrive, it does so subtly, in the form of the ongoing dialogue that we have expected soon to cease, but which instead endures between him and his maker. The conquering of despair derives not from the intellectual consolation in the typical exhortation, "they say these things are sent to try us." Rather, it stems from the realization that it is in one's actually being tried where one is poised to realize, with full clarity, what is good in the world, for one best knows that goodness once one understands how suddenly it can be taken. Coming to terms with a God who has stripped him of what he loves the most, Lewis cries out, "We have come to the same point; he with his spade, and I, who am not now much good at digging, with my own instrument. But of course one must take 'sent to try us' the right way. God has not been trying an experiment on my faith or love in order to find out their quality. He knew it already. It was I who didn't."[43]

In grief we learn that the good is not an abstraction but an iconoclastic concreteness, one we come to know as good both in the context of how it helps us to function and interpret the world as meaningful, as well as in the context of how difficult it becomes to function and find meaning without it. Whence, as Lewis's title indicates, grief is something properly to observe. It is worthy of our pausing to reflect on the many respects in which we are vulnerable, dependent beings, not in full control of what we need to flourish. Pain is not nothingness but the affirmation of something the deprivation of which hurts us.

Elie Wiesel, coming out of the experience of having survived genocide, concurs. Reflecting on the long dark "night" from which he has emerged, he comments: "Because I remember, I despair. Because I remember, I have the duty to reject despair."[44] In *Night* Wiesel, like Lewis, lashes out at God. At one point in the text he suggests that it is not only the innocent boy whose murder his fellow prisoners were forced to witness that is hanging on the gallows, but God himself.[45] Yet, after writing *Night* Wiesel stayed with his God, searching for increasingly creative ways to maintain the difficult I-Thou relationship. Consider the maturing reflection that appears in *The Gates of the Forest*, written eleven years after *Night:* "God's final victory, my son, lies in man's inability to reject Him. You think you're cursing Him, but your curse is praise; you think you're fighting Him; but all you do is open yourself to Him; you think you're crying out your hatred and rebellion, but all you're doing is telling Him how much you need His support and forgiveness."[46] Protest is the enemy of indifference, not trust.

King, Lewis, and Wiesel, each intimately familiar with a spirit-crushing calamity beyond that of the usual sufferer, accept their respective historical moments as harbingers of a better day. In so doing they connect past to future, and suffering to happiness. These temporal and evaluative links feed into the Irenaean conviction about the unity of all things held together by God and reinforce the complementarity of good and evil revealed in the longer view of the educative theodicy.[47] Irenaeus insists that humanity's imperfection is a necessary step in the process of molding humans to become (more) perfect beings.[48] Perfection is a gradual undertaking through which we are meant to stumble awkwardly, learning along the way what we stand to gain through our experienced loss. Human beings are not compelled to choose the good. They are only exhorted to do so, otherwise "it would come to pass that their being good would be of no consequence, because they were so by nature rather than by will, and are possessors of good spontaneously, not by choice; and for this reason they would not understand this fact, that good is a comely thing, nor would they take pleasure in it."[49] The good, Irenaeus impresses, must be pursued against resistance. It cannot simply be granted.[50] Spiritual betterment, moral development, and becoming happy require patience as well as the ability to see ourselves within a narrative ever unfolding rather than as agents judged to be fortunate or unfortunate in individual snapshots in time.

Lactantius

This observation about the interconnectedness of past and future and the subsequent link between suffering and redemption is brought to a point in the writings of Lucius Caelius Firmianus, the church father better known as Lactantius. Whereas Irenaeus sought to provide a long-term developmental rationale for pain and suffering, his successor extended the appeal of the educative theodicy further by explicitly attributing all of the bad things of this world to a payoff to be made apparent by a purposive, providential deity in the present. To this end, he targets the Epicurean postcreation conception of God as an aloof, if generally kind, deity. In *De Ira Dei* (the Wrath of God) Lactantius polemically sets out to correct the impression that God is not at all times actively engaged in all the good and bad things that happen to human beings. The just and merciful traits of God are inextricably bound up with one another, because, Lactantius reasons, "if God is not angry with the impious and the unjust, then, to be sure, neither does He love the pious and the just. So the error of those who take away both anger and kindness together is a more consistent one. For, in opposite things, it is necessary either to be moved toward each side or toward neither."[51]

A loving God is one who is occasionally necessarily moved to anger. The theodicy can be broadened beyond its theological context. As beneficiaries of moral sentiments such as care, compassion, and so forth, we must at least be able to tolerate the callous, divisive, and sometimes malicious actions in contrast to which these essential virtues become known and graciously felt. In this manner Lactantius expands Irenaeus's thesis about the unity in all things to the crucial faculty of wisdom in consultation with which, *via negativa,* evil reveals the good.[52] Whence the urgency with which he proposes to refute Epicurus:

> When God made man as His image, the creation which was the summation of the divine workmanship, he breathed wisdom into him alone, so that he might subjugate all things to his power and sway and make use of all the advantages of the world. He put before him, however, both good things and evil, because He gave him wisdom, the whole reason of which rests in discerning good and evil. For no one can choose the better and know what is good unless he knows, at the same time, how to reject and avoid what things are evil. Both are mutually connected with each other, so that if one is removed, the other has to be taken away. . . . Unless these had been set before us, we would not be rational animals. And if this reasoning is true, which the Stoics could see in no way, that argument of Epicurus is dissolved also where he says: "God either wishes to take away evils and he cannot, or he can and does not wish to, or he neither wishes to nor is able, or he both wishes to and is able. If he wishes to and is not able, he is feeble, which does not fall in with the notion of God. If he is able to and does not wish to, he is envious, which is equally foreign to God. If he neither wishes to nor is able, he is both envious and feeble and therefore not God. If he both wishes to and is able to, which alone is fitting to God, whence, therefore, are there evils, and why does he not remove them?"[53]

Lactantius's answer to Epicurus's implication that God is a creator but not a preserver, a deity who has stopped caring about his creature, invokes an explicit utilitarian justification. We should trust that God knew what he was doing in creating evil: "since He granted wisdom at the same time . . . and there is more good and pleasure in wisdom than there is annoyance in evils. For wisdom brings it about that we know even God, and, through that knowledge, we seek immortality, which is the greatest good. And so, unless we first recognize the evil, we shall not be able to recognize the good."[54] Evil, in leading to the good, is already part of the good. The unity thesis, moreover, is not just instrumental in this epistemological sense. Our identification of evil as evil can be an immature perspective based on a rushed analysis of what more careful study would prove to be a virtue in disguise. A good parent is capable of temporarily infuriating his child, just as a wise judge cannot cultivate only a compassionate disposition but must also mete out punishment when it is called for.[55] Lactantius commits to a vision of the good according to which the arsenal of the right habits and dispositions do not always manifest themselves in the obvious manner. Unpleasant traits also have their place among the pantheon of the virtues. To the skeptic worried about what this suggests about an all-loving deity, Lactantius replies, "For if God forbade anger entirely, He would have been a reprehender of His own workmanship in a way, since in the beginning He had given anger (its seat, the liver) to man, inasmuch as the cause of this reaction is believed to be contained in the moisture of the bile. Therefore, not entirely does He forbid anger since that emotion has been given as a necessary part of creation, but He forbids the continuation of anger. For the wrath of mortals ought to be mortal, and if it should last, enmities are strengthened into everlasting ruin."[56]

Lactantius's qualification with regard to the toughness of love owes a debt to Aristotelian conceptions of the well-balanced application of the virtues. What he deems key is not the presence or absence of particular traits but their being exhibited in the right measure. Viewed over the long haul, what initially comes across as unchecked wrath might in fact be the corrective an unfolding situation requires, harsh as this might seem at the time. With Lactantius, then, we have a mature rendering of the educative theodicy according to which evil plays a necessary part in our ability to define, appreciate, and finally participate in the good. The wisdom with which we come to know the good, in contrast to what it is not, would be rendered moot were it not for the sometimes extremely painful experiences that teach us good from bad.[57] We are prone to misinterpreting painful experiences in the immediacy of the moment as leading to more pain for us in the long run. This explains the lengths to which Lactantius goes to connect pain to wisdom. With wisdom, we do not rush to a judgment but begin to see a larger picture.

The educative theodicy is improvement on theodicy *simpliciter* to the extent that it does not in principle disallow the sufferer from asking for an explanation for suffering. It offers concrete reasons for why evil is tied to or already the good, not merely as something that is compatible with it but as also tantamount to it. If not in the present, then eschatologically evil will be shown not to be absolute. Consequently, evil does not have the final word but always has something positive behind it. It is armed with such insight that Martin Luther King anticipates a promised land for his fellow marchers that he may never visit, or the bodhisattva returns to attend to "the last blade of grass" knowing that when the final ladder is kicked away there is no longer any tension between karma and nirvana. Even C. S. Lewis, who does not bear his burden quite as gracefully, concedes that the accurate dichotomy is not between good and evil but between a life of pains and pleasures on the one hand, and a life where one acts to avoid pain at all costs on the other. The avoider of pain is the one marooned in a pleasureless grey twilight. Once evil is forced to be examined outside itself, all sorts of maladies from assassination to cancer become more than just the isolated events that affect the individuals who proximately experience them. Indeed, they become transformational instances of what John Hick has identified as the movement from "self-centeredness to Reality-centeredness."[58]

The educative logic is thus that any trial, looked at in the right way, ultimately advances one's well-being. The question is whether this logic can be
applied to every example of evil, or to use Hick's language, whether some terrible occurrences are not so easy to assimilate conceptually into the transformation from self-centeredness to Reality-centeredness. The assassination of
Martin Luther King culminated in a realized civil rights movement, and the
deadly cancer of the American poet Joy Davidman retrospectively led C. S.
Lewis to discover the gift of marital love that had been his to treasure for a few
happy years. Yet, these losses, tragic as they are, are not the worst that can befall
a human being. The question remains, are there pains in this world that are so
life-halting and meaning-defying that afterwards redemption becomes less
rather than more likely, perhaps even impossible? C. S. Lewis connects his
wife's untimely death to the blessing of her life. Does this make him a credible
interpreter of all calamities? Does his insight apply, for instance, to Levinas's
orphan or widow, the abject, destitute other?[59] Does it apply to the concentration camp survivor, whose particular form of suffering can never be anticipated
in advance? Here, Primo Levi's suggestion always to assess the damage of evil
from the victim's point of view seems apt. As Levi exhorts in the poem
"*Shemá*," the one safe and sheltered cannot possibly know what it is like to be
otherwise. From our vantage of shelter, we must nevertheless strain to

> Consider whether this is a man who labours in the mud
> Who knows no peace, who fights for a crust of bread, who dies at a yes or no.[60]

Some things are so terrible that they obstruct a victim's efforts to move
beyond tragedy. Levi inveighs against the project of theodicy, particularly its
educative variety, for, he worries, cost-benefit analyses that measure present
pain suffered against future benefit accrued are undertaken at the expense of
understating a victim's understanding of his or her predicament.

In addition to the concern that the educative theodicy fails to address the
worst sorts of atrocities one might experience, it can be normatively criticized
on the basis of its attribution of personal responsibility to the divine will. Post-
Holocaust theologians worry that for theodicists who look for the lessons in
tragedy, villains such as Hitler become "another Nebuchadnezzar," one of
God's agents effecting the divine grand design.[61] In attempting to stave off
despair, the educative theodicist mischaracterizes immoral individuals as not
acting on their own agency. Moreover, in pursuit of this grand design, the victims are used in a way that does not respect them as an end in themselves.
Could any genocide be justifiable, even one that led to the future consequence
of no genocides? Are there evils from which the good lessons that come fail to

compensate for the terrible set of events that precipitated them? We are back to Ivan's objection.

In the end, the educative theodicy fails to answer complaints raised on behalf of the victim for whom a future good fails to address a current evil. One of the advantages of the final and most serious theodicy we consider—the free will theodicy—is that it accepts as a central premise that human freedom and dignity require tolerance for calamity in the harder sorts of cases. Free will theodicists grant, whereas educative theodicists do not, that in some cases no particular good comes from an experienced evil. For them, evil is to be considered good only in the much larger sense, that without its existence we would cease to be the sorts of beings for whom the good is available to be humanly experienced in the first place.

The Free Will Theodicy

One of the terrible ironies of malicious actions occurs when the willfulness of one or some agents deprives another or others of theirs. When an individual knowingly sets out on a violent course of action, usually the first casualty is the ability of another to retain the same sort of control over his or her agency. People who are attacked lose security, shelter, social stability, and in more drastic instances, normal use of their bodies and their willful agency. Susan Neiman argues that in another sense, however, the agency-depriving intention of malicious activity can turn out to have the opposite effect. Commenting on September 11, she writes, "The terrorists' resolve to make us feel we have no power showed that in fact we do. For they revealed how far evil as well as resistance to it remain in individual human hands. A few men with determination and pocket-knives killed thousands in an instant and set events in motion that threatened the earth as a whole. This would be reason for dismay, or at best reflection, were it not for flight 93."[62]

The horrific propensity of malicious individuals to place the world in jeopardy is the same gift others are allotted to engage in spontaneous and sustained acts of resolve, compassion, and goodness. Although Neiman refuses to call this freedom a theodicy—she is worried that the consequence of invoking free will as a form of consolation will deflect attention from the loss of life incurred in acts of moral evil—precisely such an argument has been made by others.[63] The argument, in a nutshell, is that it is impossible to attribute gestures of decisive goodness to human beings without their also having the unfettered capacity to act otherwise. Divinity, fate, karma, or any other source thought to be responsible for why terrible things happen in this world can not be behind *moral* wrongdoing lest the critical feature of moral agency, our volitional capacity, be rendered moot.

Earlier in this chapter I examined the strong link between moral agency and evil in the thinking of Kant, who argues in *Religion within the Limits of Reason Alone* that if God were to direct human action for the better, then we would essentially become puppets without any real capacity for freedom. Kant characterizes moral evil as the result of the habitual corruption of the will, whereby we ultimately substitute a desire to act on inclination for the imperative we are compelled to obey to do what is right. Kant famously called evil radical because it involves a complete subversion of the will. Although moral conversion was possible for Kant, it required an overwhelming effort on the part of the self, constantly afflicted by evil (selfish) inclination. But this is part of the point: According to Kant, to ensure that our choices for good are free, they must always be tested against the countercurrent of the inclination that leads us astray. "Man *himself* must make or have made himself into whatever, in a moral sense, whether good or evil, he is or is to become. Either condition must be an effect of his free choice; for otherwise he could not be responsible for it and could therefore be *morally* neither good nor evil."[64]

Without the equal possibility of one's deciding to act on evil inclination, in other words, the condition of self-legislation that opens our participation in moral goodness would not be possible. As noted earlier, this is of course not to say that for Kant himself, evil is itself a form of goodness simply because it makes free will possible. That the concepts of moral good and moral evil stand in a formal positive relation to one another does not make evil a form of good, or, according to Kant, provide an adequate consolation to the victim who suffers because of the fortunate existence of free will. Kant was not a defender of theodicy, and he did not believe that we could have the solace of knowing when or how evil was to be overcome. If we did know this, then we would also know how all things are eventually to turn out. There would not be enough space within human agency for our doing things for the right reason alone, that is, without regard for consequences. According to Kant, God does not come in to rescue the world. From the victim's perspective evil is and always remains a mystery.

Nevertheless, an argument within philosophy and theology is to be made on behalf of the view that because free will is a good in itself, and because it is only made possible by the genuine prospect of choosing evil, that evil, by extension, at least moral evil, must therefore be justified—although not, as other theodicists might claim, good per se.[65] The argument rests on a wager that a world with people—created by a divinity or not—who are genuinely free, and thus free to perform any good moral action, is better than a world with people causally determined only to do good. A succinct statement of this wager is expressed by one of its most formidable purveyors, Alvin Plantinga: "A world containing no creatures who freely perform both good and evil action—and do more good than evil—is more valuable than a world containing quasiautomata who always do what is right because they are unable to do otherwise."[66]

In an effort to be as empirically honest as possible, stronger versions of this wager dispense with Plantinga's qualification and stipulate that it may be the case that in a world with free will, more evil—in terms of both number and intensity of deeds—will be performed than good. They also acknowledge that from the perspective of the victim it is often true that nothing retrospectively justifies a suffered harm. Such defenders of the free will defense nevertheless remain convicted that any other world in which the evil we caused was limited by something (e.g., God) that intervened in the process of self-determination would be worse than the one which we in fact inhabit.[67] In such a world, they reason, we would not be human beings with a full measure of dignity, rendering moot all the other goods that are tantamount to but not as centrally constitutive of human flourishing as our freedom is. Even a world in which God only rarely intervened on behalf of humans to prevent the worst sorts of genocides or malicious catastrophes would be marred by an irretrievable impingement on human freedom: After that calculation a (no doubt compelling) argument for exemption could be made on behalf of the victim of a slightly less drastic evil, and soon every evil would be called into question by the same logic.[68] According to the free will defense, then, God's allowing the actuality of evil is the consequence of his having given us the ability to choose good or evil. Those who in this process get a raw deal are on this account interpreted as justifiable collateral damage in the grand scheme of things.[69] In *Is There a God?*, Richard Swinburne takes the argument a step further by suggesting that only full self-determination gives us a share in the creative activity of the divine.[70] This point can be made bereft of its theological context: Had we no free will, we would cease to be human, at which point the concepts of good and evil would be unintelligible.

In this respect, the idea of free will alludes to the nature of our mortality. Moral evil consists of the humanly caused psychological sorrow and physical pain that sometimes leads to death. Is a life without these experiences, perhaps even a life without death (or at least death for which other human beings are responsible), preferable to one in which we do not die, or even suffer, or have the ability to cause others to suffer? Reflections about a universe lacking moral evil compel us to examine the wisdom of leading the kind of life befitting an immortal. Martha Nussbaum seriously considers the value of a hypothetical existence of one who is immune to the threats of others when everything comes easily in Homer's *Odysseus*. Reflecting on the goddess Calypso's offer of a life of immortality and ease alongside her, she weighs in favor of Odysseus's refusal: "We don't quite know what it would be for this hero, known for his courage, craft, resourcefulness, and loyal love to enter into a life in which courage would atrophy, in which cunning and resourcefulness would have little point, since the risks with which they grapple would be removed, and in which love, insofar as it appears at all, would be very different in shape from the love that connects man to wife and child in the human world of poem."[71] An enabling condition of human flourishing entails living life within limits, including the often painfully constraining limits of our mortality.[72] Conversely, the circumvention of pain would turn out to be "disaster and emptiness," because it would deprive us of participating fully in our most valued activities, such as the activities of loving and giving to others, which involve risk, vulnerability, and the ongoing threat of failure.[73] We are not vulnerable if our susceptibility to pain is not real. Having free will necessarily means entering into a lottery in which one could very well turn out to be a victim of a horrific crime, but who by virtue of this risk is eligible for all of the goods relevant to human flourishing.

One might take away from Nussbaum's Aristotelian argument in favor of human mortality that moral evil is integral to the human experience not simply because it is logically necessitated by the existence of beings such as ourselves who have free will (Plantinga), or because our possibility of participating in it represents the best set of circumstances under which we can hone our creative capacities and approximate divine likeness (Swinburne and Hick). It is integral instead because of the value of fragility in the first place, both as a state that is intrinsically good in itself as part of human flourishing, and as a state that is instrumentally tied to the acquisition of virtue and maintenance of human dignity. To suggest as much is not to claim evil is something other than evil. It is, however, to argue for the natural place of evil in accounts of the best sort of life, that is, the sort of life most conducive to flourishing.

Is free will worth the price of the sort of unspeakable misery that does not merely ruin the lives of unlucky individuals, but often degrades or destroys entire communities in acts of egregious neglect (e.g., Hurricane Katrina) or willful malice (e.g., the Holocaust)? The free will defense, in its various versions, is an improvement even over educative theodicies to the extent it regards the victims of evil as at most the foreseen but unintended side consequence of a gift without which we could not humanly flourish. Instances of evil are now not in themselves part of God's grand design (really to be interpreted as good). To the contrary, they are the upshot of the measure of accountability, self-determination, and autonomy with which we have been graced. Evil is "the presence of goodness" merely in the second-order sense that it is the necessary residue of the best imaginable good. Is this enough consolation to the victim of evil? Does the model of evil as the necessary residue of free will adequately capture the extent to which evil is destructive? Is evil by virtue of free will morally defensible?

In its favor, the classic free will defense does not explicitly equate evil with good. It therefore retains its empirically honest flavor, for it in no way plays down the terrible suffering evil causes by equating it with the good in disguise. It is important to distinguish among claims. Plantinga maintains that evil is justifiable on the basis of its making possible freedom, and thereby creating the best sort of world for human beings to inhabit. The stronger claim asserts that evil is, strictly speaking, necessary for the good and therefore good itself, more broadly construed. In this sense, it needs to be pointed out in fairness, the most sophisticated form of theodicy—free will—is not the neatest fit for the title of this chapter. Evil, for the majority of the free-willists, results from freedom's misuse in the world, actually, but not necessarily.[74] This distinction is important because it credits the advocate of the free will defense with espousing not a cavalierly Panglossian portrayal of the universe, too dismissive of the victim's pain and suffering, but rather a tragic view of it according to which evil becomes the unintended, foreseeable by-product of the good. Still, this disclaimer does not go all the way toward absolving the free will defense, for in the final analysis Ivan's objection remains unanswered. A victim's suffering remains justified on the consequentialist's balance sheet, allowing the philosopher to explain away evil on the basis of broader speculative considerations.

A number of issues in fact arise in consideration of the viability of the free will defense. First is that it ignores the devastating effects of nonmoral evil, often just as community-crushing and faith-shattering as instances of moral evil. The ability to choose to harm rather than do good may be necessary to be human beings who are ultimately the best sorts of creatures, but goes no distance toward comparably interpreting hurricanes, tsunamis, and other natural disasters as goods without which we would be worse off (acknowledging that the cause of many natural disasters is culpable inaction, not natural evil per se). It seems the theodicist sympathetic to the free will defense has the right to reason that the world would be better if it only allowed for the possibility of moral and not natural evil. After all, certain imaginable natural disasters are enough to destroy the world—and the very notion of goodness along with it—which though not yet encountered could well be on the horizon. It would appear that though no limit can be placed on the sorts of harms that might ensue from a world in which humans are free to make their own choices, the same is not true for harms in general.

Second, one could seriously challenge the fundamental assumption that the good of the will outweighs the good of a world bereft of terrible suffering.

Granting Plantinga's assumption that we would become quasiautomatons without unfettered free will, who is to say that this would be a worse existence? Additionally, as the philosopher of religion Philip Bennett asks, who is to say that the answer is the same for everyone?

> The world is more valuable if it has a certain feature—but more valuable for whom? For God or the poor souls who inhabit it? For us, perhaps: "Surely you'd rather be a free person than a quasiautomaton." Well, I don't know, for I don't know what it is like to be a quasiautomaton. "Well, surely you'd rather be free than not." Yes, but when I and others prize freedom, we do so by contrast to slavery, domination, manipulation, and control. And is being enslaved, dominated, manipulated, and controlled—is that what it is to be a quasiautomaton?[75]

If the condition of freedom implies the suppression of certain concrete freedoms, potentially in disproportion to what is gained, we ought not to be so quick to assume that it is an equally good thing for all affected. At the very least, one has to roll up one's sleeves and take a hard look at slavery and the like to make that argument. The extent to which a little free will goes a long way—in the wrong direction—is something we cannot neglect to consider. On top of this, some of the most horrible evils, those that are simultaneously gratuitous and maximally harmful, occur for no reason other than the momentary impulse of the psychopath or opportunist who causes them. Too many instances of these "unabsorbed" evils abound to justify their presence in the context of an outweighing greater good.[76]

Last, and perhaps most serious, is the moral argument introduced by Kenneth Surin and others, an amplification of Ivan Karamazov's objection: Some atrocities are so cruel and imagination defying that, if we are a theist, we have no choice but to conclude that if God exists he must also be seen to be behind the terrible thing in question, and that for this reason God is not only not good but quite probably monstrous.[77] The Augustinian-Kantian solution of noninterference—in which God, in deference to having created creatures with autonomy, is imagined to be totally on the sidelines with regard to the perpetration of such occurrences—will not do. One need only consider the especially graphic examples of throwing babies up in the air and catching them on bayonets, or of using daggers to cut them out of their mothers wombs, to reject the idea that the gift of human autonomy serves as a justification for moral atrocity.[78] Certain "artistically cruel" acts simply have no justification.[79] As Plantinga advocates, it may both be that God exists and is the author of free will and that our ability to decide for ourselves precludes divine intervention even in the worst scenarios.

However, these stipulations do not legitimately excuse or provide sufficient moral warrant for God having created us in this fashion. For God is still, at the very least, indirectly responsible for the events that take place in the name of free will, having created us as he did, knowing the consequences for his having done so.[80]

Ultimately, Ivan Karamazov's objection on behalf of the innocent child remains unaddressed. To be sure, the historically true and gruesome examples mentioned give pause to a logic according to which any individual is eligible to be subjected to unbearable pain for the sake of preserving a broader human dignity.[81] As Surin rightly notes, Ivan's protest atheism is less about propositions that pertain to believing or disbelieving in the existence of the divine and more about his conviction that such a God must be morally reprehensible. In light of the multitude of horrific examples from history, it is repugnant that "God should (seem to) expect such a terrible price to be paid," either for the dignity with which he endows us now, or for our salvation later on.[82] A circumstance in which actual people must suffer unspeakable atrocities for the sake of preserving even a beneficent principle fails the test of proportionality. To the critic— and the victim—free will does not let God off the hook.

Theodicy under Scrutiny: Some Broader Issues

At this point in thinking about the relation of evil to goodness, the point at which even the most logically sensible kinds of arguments on behalf of theodicy fail to grip the victims of horrific suffering on the basis of their relevance or emotional power, philosophical sophistication gives way to a kind of theological anticipation. The defender of theodicy concedes that some victims are left with a residual mystery following even the best rational explanation for their ordeal, but, out of a good faith refusal to despair, turn back to a Leibniz-like refuge in the ineffable largeness and impenetrability of divine intent. God's ways are beyond our comprehension (Exodus 3:14), although God himself ensures a moral order. In ways we likely do not see, suffering is due punishment for sinful behavior, or as a test that prepares us for redemption, or as a brief even if seemingly extended state of affairs bound to give way to a future bereft of misery and hardship. In view of God's impenetrability, the right way to approach the problem of evil is not through recourse to the intellectual virtues of wisdom and understanding, but rather through the more spiritual virtues of patience and humility. God's presence and goodness are biblically if not historically affirmed in a manner beyond human control and understanding. In this respect the hopeful wails of the prophets serve as "last lines of defense," for example, as when God avers, "I revealed myself to those who did not ask for me. I was found by those who did not seek me. To a nation that did not call my name, I said 'Here am I, here am I," (Isaiah 65:1–2). What is to be made of this strategy, the turn from philosophy to theology, as a viable defense against hopelessness and despair? Thessalonians exhorts those who submit to Jesus Christ not to grieve in anticipation of being with the Lord forever (1 Thessalonians 4:13–17). Is this sort of scriptural refuge, one that at times exhorts a blind trust, to be regarded as a legitimate source of comfort to those in mourning? Is it, alternatively, a refuge that constitutes what critics allege amounts to a self-protective strategy, nonfalsifiable because, given that God defies comprehension, divine exhortations cannot be tested in any meaningful way?

In answering, one cannot ignore the recent wave of thinkers insisting on a standard of fairness and consistency with regard to the elevation of scripture as an authoritative source for providing comfort and solace to the sufferer who has abandoned attempts to seek such solace through reason. What does scripture actually have to say? This is the question that the critics of the theological strategy, who include both "recovering" Catholics and Protestants and the new atheists, would like us to ask with more persistence than we usually do when we quote a passage that affirms that God works in mysterious ways.[83] A comprehensive analysis of the Bible, they argue, will reveal that not only does Scripture fail to insulate God from the critique that he is not all-loving, but also that the Bible actually does say that we have no choice but to come to the conclusion that did God exist he would have to be found guilty of sponsoring human misery in its worst forms. Bart Ehrman, a once-committed Christian who still writes as an insider to his faith, argues that on the basis of earnest scriptural excavation, we fare worse rather than better than we would were we to leave the effort of consolation to purely secular mechanisms.[84] Ehrman calls attention to what he names the "smorgasbord approach" to Scripture, in which many believers pick and choose what suits them and their views without acknowledging that the Bible is not only an "intricate concatenation of views, perspectives, and ideas," but at times the very source of the condemnation of the innocent whose interests it is meant to protect in the context of a theodicy. As an example, he cites the millions of people around the world who are socially ostracized for their sexual orientation because of a disproportional reliance on some scriptural passages over neglected others that, for example, require stoning disobedient children to death, or executing those who curse their parents, touch pig skin, or work on the Sabbath (Leviticus 20).[85] Ehrman insists that whatever the Bible says, it has to be analyzed honestly and in its totality, neither according to a believer's arbitrary wishes nor on the basis of a blind faith attribution to the wisdom in some of its passages that suggest that in the end everything will turn out well.

The problem of the inconsistent pining of Scripture is exacerbated by some biblical passages that in any reasonable analysis are unambiguously cruel. One example on which Ehrman focuses is the story of Lot, the one righteous citizen of Sodom who nevertheless countenances the gang-rape of his two virgin daughters in a gesture curiously intended to display altruism toward the other townspeople (Genesis 19:7–8). Ehrman, for whom Genesis 19 can be understood as reflecting antiquated, chauvinistic codes of hospitality, wonders how the literalist unlike himself could possibly interpret Lot's actions as anything other than barbaric, or see the God who would put Lot in a position of defending Sodom in this way as anything short of vindictive.[86] Lot need not be singled out. Ehrman, Richard Dawkins, and others allude to Genesis 6 (the story of Noah), Genesis 21 and 22 (Abraham's sacrifice of Isaac), Deuteronomy 28 (in which Moses warns of the consequences for disobedience), and from the New Testament the book of Revelation, to drive home a similar point. If one, through unassailable trust in the divine, has not taken leave of one's critical faculties altogether then one must conclude that to look to the Bible for solace is to make matters worse, not better. An even greater theodicy is needed after reading Scripture.[87] Ehrman and Dawkins are surely advocates for a skepticism in line with their atheistic ambitions. My point in bringing up passages like Lot, however, is not to insist that it is disingenuous not to read the Bible literally, without picking and choosing, and then avoid damning God on this basis. (I maintain that it is perfectly reasonable to relate to the Bible mythologically or metaphorically and in turn conceive of a redeemer, mysterious and ineffable.) Rather, it is to call attention to the fact that when philosophical theodicies, such as the free will defense, are found to be inadequately responsive to the concrete experience of the victim, alternative faith-acts that have us turn to Scripture or other signposts will not fare much better.

What then do we make of demagogues like Pat Robertson and the late Jerry Falwell, well known for linking suffering to sin on the basis of condemnations enumerated in Leviticus 20 and elsewhere, who attribute episodes like September 11 and Hurricane Katrina to gays, abortionists, or the ACLU?[88] My answer interprets their faith claims through a sociological lens. Were there some way to free them from the powerful effects of their own cognitive dissonance, Robertson and Falwell, like the rest of us, would be compelled to see that unmerited suffering ceases to be sustainably understood as an instance of divine wisdom but is more plausibly the reflection of the whim of a God who is notoriously vindictive, jealous, or egotistically obsessed with his own might. In any case, the cause and effect analyses of a Robertson and Falwell ring hollow to the victim of this world for whom life is a cesspool of misery and suffering most of the time, not a positive experience with a silver lining, but a profoundly dehumanizing and tortuous one that at best leaves us scratching for answers.[89] In the final analysis, neither philosophy's aloof God described in the best free will arguments nor the deliberate God of retributive, biblical theodicy addresses the concrete suffering of real victims. In an effort to render the senseless sensible, the defenders of both sorts of theodicies serve to complicate rather than resolve the mystery of suffering.

What about the solution that suffering remains a mystery? This solution is readily available to the sufferer as a last line of defense when the more explicitly explanatory and sanguine ones fail. The afflicted are meant to accept, in humility, that what will happen, will happen. It is not within our purview to divine God's intentions, or even to assert in the first place that his intentions are ours to be able to appreciate. Although not as ambitious as the solutions of speculative philosophy (God leaves us to choose our own ends) or purposive theology (God knows and acts for our best even though it may not seem so to us at the time), which manage to make suffering make sense, the solution of "suffering is a mystery" is more believable. It does not shoulder the burden, as the others do, of linking meaning to understanding, and therefore of selling credible, tangible explanations for why bad things so often happen to good people. In the suffering remains a mystery solution, consolation is in the recognition that something terrible has transpired. In lieu of an explanation that makes any sense, all emphasis is placed on after-the-fact recovery and a spirit of hope that governs one's attitude toward the future. Sometimes such hope takes the meager form of the company or sympathy of others who walk through the darkness alongside us. Is this enough? The question bears asking. To what extent can the adage "God's ways remain mysterious to us" provide comfort and solace to the afflicted? Ehrman, for his part, parts company with Dawkins and the new atheists in offering his own biblical answer:

> As it turns out, it is the view put forth in the book of Ecclesiastes. There is a lot we can't know about this world. A lot of this world that doesn't make sense. Sometimes there is no justice. Things don't go as planned or as they should. A lot of bad things happen. But life also brings good things. The solution to life is to enjoy it while we can, because it is fleeting. This world, and everything in it, is temporary, transient, and soon to be over. And so we should enjoy life to the fullest, as much as we can, as long as we can. That's what the author of Ecclesiastes thinks, and I agree.[90]

Amidst tragedies over which we have no control, things are to be enjoyed in this life, particularly if we manage our expectations and embrace with humility the fact that anything could be taken from us at any second. In the wreckage of the worst that happens to us, furthermore, we still have each other, and with this, the possibility of showing compassion, making new connections, and rebuilding communities.

This rather humanistic solution is fine to the extent that we take God out of the picture, but from a theological point of view the conundrum remains. If the solution entails a world in which understanding and recovery is truly up to us then either God becomes unacceptably marginalized in the process of redemption or remains still very much present and in control of matters, just at a further remove. At first glance, the first of these options seems a likely interpretation; the solution of mystery seems patently secular. Ehrman's Ecclesiastical solution is curiously similar to Camus's Sisyphean one. Both characterize happiness as precious but ephemeral, and, most important, neither within divine control nor really our own. Perhaps, however, the solution that suffering will remain a mystery alternatively expresses the experiential theological view that God is in all respects ineffable, our relative smallness in relation to the divine excusing us from requiring any understanding for redemption. In this case, belief in God is all that is required for solace, no matter what happens. Everything, even the most gruesome, pales in comparison to the comfort of one's faith and the peace one's faith promises to deliver in the afterlife.

We have already raised a serious problem with this solution from a nontheological point of view: It inappropriately dismisses the pain of the victim in this life in deference to eschatological assumptions about the next. From a theological perspective, however, there are also good reasons to find the solution wanting, for it is a solution that trades a sensible life in the present for the promise of a future reward that negates all prior discontents. Consider, in this light, Susan Neiman's exposition of Kant's denunciation of the weak theodicy that consoles merely with the cryptic adage "God has his reasons."

> For Kant, even this much knowledge is too much knowledge. To say that God has purposes, though we don't know them, is to say that God has purposes. That's precisely what was in doubt. To assert it a priori is to trade recognition of the reality of suffering for a consolation so abstract it cannot really comfort. . . . For Kant [this] is blasphemy. The problem with [this sort of] superstition is less what it does to us—turning what should be autonomous adults into self-made, foolish children—than what it does to God. Every superstition is an act of idolatry, the attempt to appease or flatter a powerful being in the hope that he'll reward us, on earth or elsewhere. . . . To defend God by insisting a priori that He always rewards happiness with virtue is to fly so directly in the face of experience that one who does it can only have one of two base

motives. If he isn't hoping that God is eavesdropping and will reward his flattery—a hope that debases the Creator no less than created—he must be out to convert or console. But to win friends for God by pointing out the fruits of His friendship is to give instrumental reasons for being holy—a clear contradiction, and a vile one at that. No wonder Kant held the biblical prohibition on God's image to be central and sublime. To break our tendency toward idolatry, our idea of God must be so exalted that we cannot even represent it.[91]

On religious grounds, grave problems are implicit in the hermeneutical endeavor to convert evil into something other than evil. Such an effort not only assumes that a defense of God is something that is needed to begin with, it prioritizes, without license, divine prerogatives. Why should God be constrained to make human benefit a highest priority? Such an ordering of hierarchies, this objection runs, does not square with an insistence on an absolute difference between creature and creator.[92] When we force evil to be good in this way, we safeguard our loyalty to God at the expense of undoing creation. Not only is the price too much to pay, this is not a loyalty for which a God worth praying to should be in the position of having to bargain.

Defenders of theodicy—in all of its versions—will have to deal with another sort of criticism, more historical than theological. Namely, in its tendency to subsume particular evils within a general theory about evil, theodicy becomes a remedy for an intellectual problem instead of an actual one. To offer academic solutions to historical realities, and in turn to provide a faux comfort for a problem that remains unsolved, is to add insult to injury. Moreover, it is to betray a naïve confidence in the independence of theory from practice. The scholar of religion and social theorist Kenneth Surin is the thinker best known for voicing this objection. To refer to the issue as a mental conundrum of reconciling the problem of evil with providential goodness, is

> to provide—albeit unwittingly—a tacit sanction of the myriad of evils that exist on this planet. Crucial to this argument is the tenet that *all* philosophical and theological reflection, no matter how abstract such reflection may be, inevitably mediates a certain social and political praxis. All significant intellectual visions have a socially-mediated purchase on reality. Thus they have the capacity to determine the way(s) in which a certain segment of reality is either to be transformed or else maintained in its existing form. The philosopher and the theologian do not reflect and discourse *in vacuo*: it is their responsibility, therefore, to ask themselves, continually, what particular praxis their work mediates. For it is only by such self-scrutiny that they can avoid being implicated in a rarified discourse which legitimizes and mystifies the social processes that block the transformation of life and reality.[93]

Theodicy, in its ahistoricity, is impotent in dealing with victims of institutions that allow systematic oppression, and it may even accidentally sanction the perpetuation of these institutions.[94] In this respect, theodicy's "success may be worse than its failure."[95] It is disingenuous to expect any power besides ourselves to undo an institution that we have erected. A real theodicy would issue forth from victims and is directed at their human oppressors, because, as Surin notes, any other sort of justification for suffering would "succumb inevitably to what Paul Ricoeur called 'the bad faith of theodicy': 'it does not triumph over real evil but only over its aesthetic phantom.' "[96] The test of a good theodicy is according to this line of reasoning that it tangibly changes the experienced reality of sufferers by, for instance, modifying the oppressive practices or relaxing the systemic pressures of institutions that dehumanize the powerless. Of course, when this is the sort of change in perspective that occurs, when there is a palpable reduction of suffering in this life as a result of the things we do, the need for theodicy as it is traditionally conceived is rendered defunct by just that degree of improvement. What is in question with Surin's objection, it appears, is the material effectiveness and impact of any sort of abstract, intellectual, or even theologically speculative enterprise.

This consideration leads to another related one that pertains to the relevance of theodicies to the sufferers they are meant to comfort. Theodicy is so concerned with ultimate meaning that it misses what is, on a day-to-day basis, actually meaningful in life: relationships, opportunities to help the one in need, and the intermittent moments of enlightenment that bring a sense of wonderment and satisfaction to the often frustratingly indifferent and apparently arbitrary world we inhabit. According to this criticism, in theodicy our faith is misplaced. It pertains to something inaccessible and grandiose rather than to smaller, more manageable occasions of affirmation. "What once was cuddled must learn to kiss the cold worm's mouth. That's all the mystery." So utters Mr. Nickels, the elderly circus vendor in Archibald MacLeish's award-winning *J.B.*, a modern, demythologized retelling of the story of Job.[97] MacLeish, writing in the 1950s, was informed chiefly by the recent experiences of the Great Depression and the Holocaust and the wave of meaninglessness that he felt swept over those most directly affected by them. The story stays roughly true to its biblical rendering, but the possibility of faith in any source outside humanity or the human spirit to bring about redemption is not presented as a live option. Rather, like Camus, MacLeish maintains that we are thrust into a universe indifferent to our concerns, whose rules we are at loss to understand, and whose occasional revelations, when they come from the proverbial whirlwind, offer us little help. What this means in terms of the suffering we cause is that we are also its solution. The traditional I-Thou relationship conceived in Job is

no longer one to which modern man and woman, who have had modern experiences, can relate. In *J.B.*, MacLeish argues in essence that we must grow up.
As J.B.'s wife Sarah realizes by the play's close, we must not cling to ideals of
universal justice at the expense of getting along in the world. Why there is not
enough justice and too much death is, as Mr. Nickels observes, a mystery. It is
a mystery, not merely a complexity. Suffering can neither be fully understood
nor appropriated within our "sacred canopy" despite our best spiritual efforts.
Nevertheless, that evil cannot be converted to good does not imply the abandonment of meaning altogether. Good is experienced simply in continuing to
live life.

This conclusion is consistent with Sartre's characterization of evil as unredeemed, by which he means evil is something that we have to be taught better
to take seriously:

> It is neither our fault nor our merit if we lived in a time when torture has been
> a daily fact. Chateaubriant, Oradour, the Rue des Saussaies, Tulle, Dachau,
> and Auschwitz have all demonstrated to us that Evil is not an appearance, that
> knowing its causes does not dispel it, that it is not opposed to Good as a
> confused idea is to a clear one, that it is not the effect of passions which might
> be cured, of a fear which might be overcome, of a passing aberration which
> might be excused, of an ignorance which might be enlightened, that it can in
> no way be turned, brought back, reduced, and incorporated into idealistic
> humanism. . . . We heard whole blocks screaming and we understood that
> Evil, fruit of a free and sovereign will, is, like Good, absolute. . . . In spite of
> ourselves, we came to this conclusion, which will seem shocking to lofty souls:
> Evil cannot be redeemed.[98]

In its denial of the reality of evil, Sartre argues, theodicy is simply too optimistic. Sometimes evil may be a blessing in disguise, but not nearly on the bulk
of occasions on which we experience it. This is not to close off the possibility
of salvation, or even of seeing evil as an opportunity for good. But it is, along
with the Manichean approach, to resist explanations of evil that subsume it
within the good.

A deeper critique of the theodicy project, also raised by Kenneth Surin, sees
attempts to provide solutions to the problem of evil in a historical light, as part
of the intellectual legacy of the Enlightenment. This is essentially an ethnocentric critique. The theodicist assumes that God is the providential architect
responsible for everything that goes on in the universe, thereby, in pragmatic
terms, attempting to get a prospective sufferer to buy into a truth about a meaning he or she has not grasped.[99] Naturally, a number of questions arise when

one does not make Western assumptions about suffering and divinity. What is the nature of the relationship between evil and rebirth? Is there a self that suffers, or is suffering a by-product of attachment to an incorrect notion of self-hood according to which the self is imagined to be both fixed and desiring of various objects? If the latter is so, then might the very problem of evil, as it is traditionally construed, be a pretext for reifying culturally and historically specific worldviews? That is, might evil be a perspective, presented objectively as a way of masking power structures and protecting people in power who benefit from the definitions of good and evil in standard use? According to the logic of this criticism, the *problem* of evil is one organized around terms favorable to purveyors of an eschatology and salvation scheme that homogenizes the "other." Is theodicy as such ineluctably attached to a specific sort of theology? And if it is, what does this say about the presumed reality of evil, suffering, and victimhood?

The historicist critique, which bears the imprint of Nietzsche and Foucault, comes close to denying the reality of evil. If it does not deny this reality, it certainly insists on maintaining an attitude of skepticism about the objectivity with which theodicies identify an evil to be interpreted as good in a broader sense. Surin and other theorists who engage in the hermeneutics of suspicion are no doubt on to something when they point out the potential for discourse about evil to serve as a pretext for leaving structures of power intact. Nevertheless, it seems that the observations of Jonathan Glover, Richard Rubenstein, Primo Levi, Jean-Paul Sartre, and many others regarding suffering to which this chapter has exposed us convincingly demonstrate that victims' suffering is real, and may well be one of the few common denominators of a human condition that features disparate cultures and religious traditions. Viewed in a charitable light, the idea of theodicy is merely to preserve the possibility of meaning for anyone who doubts it following a traumatic experience. There is a difference between posing general arguments for how to interpret suffering and providing tradition-specific narratives that serve as therapies for coping. At the same time, as discussed earlier, to the extent that proffered remedies are presented and remain in the abstract, they fail to comfort actual victims.

Finally, a model that sees evil—particularly moral evil—as tantamount to the good faces an Augustinian sort of objection that maintains that in a rush to find a hidden goodness in everything one fails to acknowledge the sin and finitude endemic in human nature. Theodicy's optimism, its complete faith in the overcoming of despair, unrealistically exempts human subjects from the inevitable stain of human history. This has the undesirable normative consequence of morally excusing the perpetrators of evil of grave wrongdoing, because in the model of theodicy they ultimately serve the good. According to the alternative

Augustinian model, privation, evil is characterized as the absence of goodness. This implies, among other things, that one begins in one's moral life from the default position of denying the good. By extension, one must act to compensate for one's fallen nature (which in Augustine's theocentric worldview necessitates nothing short of a radical turn toward God). Theodicy is too passive. It concedes too much descriptively to a greater good thought to be capable of justifying everything that has led up to it. Additionally, it unduly lets responsible moral agents off the hook for failing to know themselves as sinners and to act accordingly.[100] Privation gets right, in a way theodicy does not, that suffering is not a positive experience but a radically destructive one. In this sense, it importantly puts human beings on notice: Evil lurks within the self and when it becomes manifest it causes catastrophe that it is nearly impossible to undo. In this case of natural evil, this is unavoidable. In the case of moral evil, however, an informed self-knowledge can translate into gains in human flourishing.

These criticisms notwithstanding, in defense of theodicy, it is plausible that some of what is evil can be explained away through good. Sometimes, for a door to open two others need to slam shut. Martha Nussbaum is persuasive on a phenomenological level that a life bereft of pain and mortality would not be a recognizably human one. This said, theodicy is not a comprehensive theory of evil. Following even the most sophisticated justification, a residual, elusive component of many evils, the worst sorts of evils, haunts victims in particular and humanity in general.[101] It is fatuous from both religious and secular perspectives to think that despair could be overcome entirely. Or is it? It is time to turn our attention to the third model of evil to be discussed, the perspectival model, which in its denial of the reality of evil welcomes an attitude in comparison with which theodicists seem pessimistic.

Notes

1. Russell, *The Sparrow*, 394. The first quoted passage is on page 400.
2. Wiesel, *First Person Singular*.
3. James, *Varieties of Religious Experience*, 32.
4. Kant, *Religion within the Limits of Reason*, 23.
5. Ibid., 38.
6. The crucial narrative between Ivan and his younger brother Alyosha is reprinted in a stand-alone volume. See Dostoevsky, *Grand Inquisitor*.
7. Jonathan Glover makes the case that our most recent century is also the morally worst on record, devoting nearly the entirety of his volume *Humanity* to chronicling instance after instance of brutality, unprecedented both in cruelty and havoc wrought.
8. For the different senses of understanding theodicy, see Laato and de Moor, "Introduction," x. The theodicy project has a rich history as well as many defenders the

lion's share of whom are more sophisticated than Voltaire's fictional Dr. Pangloss, the representative straw man among theodicists for whom the world could be not anything other than perfect (see Voltaire, *Candide*). Serious theodicists acknowledge that evil is for real and that our world is marred by the inexplicable agonies of its inhabitants. They understand that with regard to even the best proposed solutions to the problem of evil, the nagging question of "why" still lingers, leaving the suffering victim with a residual sense of inadequacy. Yet, in one way or another, they resolve the problem of evil such that it is finally integrated into the good, finding a place for pain and loss in a meaningful world.

9. Max Weber was the first to apply the notion of theodicy in a broad, nontheological sense, as referring to any effort undertaken to "render suffering and evil intelligible." See Laato and de Moor, "Introduction" to *Theodicy in the World of the Bible*, x. In this Weberian spirit, Wendy Doniger O'Flaherty observes: "not only is theodicy not confined to monotheism, but it is the touchstone of all religions, an existential rather than a theological problem." See O'Flaherty, *Origins of Evil*, 1–2, quoted in Laato and de Moor, "Introduction," xi. I would even go further than O'Flaherty, extending the notion of theodicy to include all meaning-affirming worldviews, religious and nonreligious, so long as they include the existential element that Doniger specifies.

10. Some language skeptics and moral relativists for different reasons would of course object to the assertion that there is any "great conundrum." Their dismissal is based on a belief that good and evil are illusory notions to begin with. For them, the problem of theodicy is a red herring caused by a confusion of what we perceive to be real or objective with what is real or objective. They do not necessarily acknowledge the latter. I reserve my treatment of this group of thinkers for chapter 3.

11. Rubenstein, *After Auschwitz*, 298.

12. McFague, *Models of God*.

13. For more on this deity, see Isichei, *Voices of the Poor*, 72.

14. As in Camus and Rubenstein. See Camus, *Myth of Sisyphus*.

15. See Nussbaum, "Non-Relative Virtues."

16. Both Lactantius and David Hume attribute the first version of what I have called the "Great Conundrum" to Epicurus, although there is some speculation that Lactantius's attribution (the accuracy of which Hume may well have taken for granted) was presumptuous and likely motivated by the church father's critique of Epicurus's supposed atheism. See Larrimore, *Problem of Evil*, xix–xxi.

17. Bayle, *Historical and Critical Dictionary*, 176.

18. Leibniz, *Theodicy*, 129–30.

19. Ibid., 201.

20. Interestingly, Leibniz includes the term *theodicy* in his title without ever using, much less specifying, what the term means within the book. See Sarot, "Theodicy and Modernity," 2.

21. Ibid., 3.

22. "As a lesser evil is relatively good, so a lesser good is relatively evil."

23. Leibniz, *Theodicy*, 248.

24. Neiman, *Evil in Modern Thought*, 28. Shortcomings in the design represent for Leibniz the exception that proves the rule. He alludes to the assuring adage of St. Bernard "*Ordinatissium est, minus interdum ordinate fieri aliquid*" (It belongs to the great order

that there should be some small disorder). We should rejoice all the more for lovable flaws that upon greater acquaintance turn out to be strengths. See Leibniz, *Theodicy*, 277.

25. James, *Will to Believe*, 24.

26. Hence the claim of many theologians living in the aftermath of World War II that "now any reasonable theology must be post-Holocaust theology."

27. Ron Green is responsible for what is still the most frequently utilized contemporary typology of theodicy. He introduces five categories: free will, educative, eschatological, deferred, and communion. In this chapter I touch on all of these, spending the bulk of my time with the first two. See Green, "Theodicy."

28. All citations from the book of Job come from the website BibleGateway: www.biblegateway.com.

29. Kellenberger, "God's Goodness and God's Evil," 25.

30. Otto, *Idea of the Holy*, 78. In the continuation of this passage, Otto takes aim at more traditional interpretations, advanced by St. Paul and others, that see God's reprimand of Job as a display of divine might and omnipotence. In Otto's alternative account, "convincement" pertains to the soteriological event of the creature's complete immersion in the divine "wholly other," as a self subsumed within the divine relation. Otto, it should be noted, has been criticized by some scholars for placing too much emphasis on religious experience within the broader discipline of religious studies. Otto admittedly does view Job's God as an overwhelming, ineffable, and sui generis other who is compelling strictly on the basis of His nonrational core essence. Such an emphasis might seem to work against the objectives of the educative theodicy, which are to make sense to the religious insider what God's reasons are for introducing suffering into the human situation.

31. Lonely as it must have been for Abraham to travel up Mount Moriah for three and half days and ponder what he was about to do to his beloved son, Isaac, it was on the mount where he, like Job, is "redeemed in dust." In Genesis 21–22, the threat of losing what he treasures the most is revealed in context to be Abraham's "greater goodness." Soren Kierkegaard notes the existential element in this "religious" moment of realization. See Kierkegaard, *Fear and Trembling*.

32. Shakespeare, *Henry IV, Part 1*, act 1, scene 2, 195–217.

33. Stump, "Mirror of Evil," 242. Quoted in Kellenberger, "God's Goodness and God's Evil," 31–32.

34. Irenaeus, "Against Heresies," 4.37.1: 518–19. In arguing on behalf of the necessity of hardship in the process of spiritual development, Irenaeus considers the case of the divine restoration of a fallen city. It may be objected, could not God have chosen to keep the city intact in the first place? Indeed he could have; that he did not, argues Irenaeus, is an indicative demonstration of what God allows because of what he also knows ultimately to be in our best interests.

35. For an elaboration of this point, see Osborn, *Irenaeus of Lyons*, 219–20.

36. Irenaeus, "Against Heresies," 5.24.1: 552. John Hick, who has offered the most well-known Irenaean theology of the modern era, calls this process a "vale of soul-making," a phrase he took from the poet John Keats. See Hick, *Evil and the God of Love*, 295.

37. Irenaeus, "Against Heresies," 4.39.2: 522, 5:3:1–3: 529–30.

38. Even though Ronald Green treats them separately, there is an argument to be made that the eschatological theodicy exists in service of the educative one. I treat the two categories in complementary fashion here.

39. Hick, *Death and Eternal Life*, 47–48.

40. Irenaeus, "Against Heresies," 3.20.1: 449–50.

41. King, "Eulogy for the Martyred Children," in *Testament of Hope*, 221–23.

42. Lewis, *A Grief Observed*, 30. Along these lines, see Milhaven, *Good Anger*.

43. Lewis, *A Grief Observed*, 51–52. This somewhat ambiguous passage and could be interpreted to be considerably more pessimistic than I have interpreted it. I read Lewis as presenting the case for the "protest atheist." It is a stage in grief to be superseded by a subsequent one that better comes to terms with pain and suffering.

44. Elie Wiesel said this in his Nobel Acceptance Speech, which he delivered in Oslo on December 10, 1986. See http://nobelprize.org/nobel_prizes/peace/laureates/1986/wiesel-lecture.html.

45. Wiesel, *Night*, 62.

46. Wiesel, *Gates of the Forest*, 33.

47. Irenaeus, "Against Heresies," 359.

48. Ibid., 3.22.4: 452.

49. Ibid. 4.37.6: 520.

50. Elsewhere, Irenaeus supplements his pedagogical argument with a practical one: if God had offered perfection to humanity, humanity would have been unable to accept it. See "Against Heresies," 4.38.1: 521.

51. Lactantius, *Wrath of God*, 69.

52. Although I happen mostly to be concerned here with *The Wrath of God*, Lactantius also speaks at length about the problem of evil in his major work, *The Divine Institutes*, particularly about the necessity of evil for good. In book 5 of this work he asks, "how can a commander prove the valor of his soldiers unless he have an enemy?" Stress and strife, argues Lactantius, bring us closer to God. This line of reasoning is consistent with Green's communion theodicy. See Lactantius, *Divine Institutes*, 388. Like Leibniz and others who subscribe to the theodicy *simpliciter*, Lactantius believes that the righteous are ultimately rewarded and the wicked punished. See *Divine Institutes*, 390.

53. Lactantius, *Wrath of God*, 91–92.

54. Ibid., 91.

55. See Zagzebski, *Virtues of the Mind*, 101.

56. Lactantius, *Wrath of God*, 108–9.

57. This is also a classic communion theodicy in Green's sense, according to which suffering brings us closer to God. The prophetic character of Lactantius's line of argument seems to rely here on the book of Isaiah, especially 52:13–53:12.

58. Hick, *Interpretation of Religion*, 36, 236–37, 248, 300.

59. Levinas, *Totality and Infinity*, 215.

60. See http://famouspoetsandpoems.com/poets/primo_levi/poems/3719.

61. Rubenstein, *After Auschwitz*, 54.

62. Neiman, *Evil in Modern Thought*, 287.

63. Ibid., 288.

64. Ibid., 40.

65. The number of citations one could furnish just on free will theodicy is stagger-ing. One of the best resources for listing these is still Whitney, *Theodicy*. After a very good summary of the arguments of the key defenders and detractors of the free will theodicy, Whitney mentions no fewer than 349 entries (articles and books) on the topic. Obviously, I will barely be able to scratch the surface here. As Whitney notes, the free will defense has been around since at least the fourth century (during the time of Augustine). For more on the history of this theodicy, see Kondoleon, "Free Will Defense."

66. Plantinga, *God and Other Minds*, 132.

67. Even though Plantinga has clarified the distinction between a free will defense (a refutation of the supposed logical problem that pertains to the contradiction between the existence of evil and an all-loving, all-powerful God) and a free will theodicy (a justification for God's actions), the majority of those who write on the topic use the terms interchangeably. For more on the distinction, see Plantinga, "Free Will Defense"; Whitney, *Theodicy*, 15.

In one noteworthy theocentric version of this argument, Alasdair MacIntyre develops the thesis that God deliberately suppresses divine power in order to allow humans genu-ine free will (see *Difficulties in Christian Belief*). In two classic articles, J. L. Mackie and Antony Flew have argued for the compatibilist view that an omnipotent God could have created a world in which human beings act freely but always (or at least are much more likely to) choose the good. They both criticize the free will defense on the grounds that we ought not to accept the contradiction such as the one for which Plantinga argues, between compulsively good choosing and free agency, because it could have been that were we created with sufficient virtue we would always choose (moral) goodness of our own accord. See Mackie, "Evil and Omnipotence" and Flew, "Divine Omnipotence and Human Freedom." A possible objection to this sort of compatibilism is that it is the nature of virtue to be acquired over time, with moral training. That is, it is the nature of a virtuous disposition that we are not simply endowed with it, but rather that we morally develop into it by cultivating a resistance to acting on selfishness and vice. This is an empirical objection that suggests that it is unlikely that we can be virtuous, and thus be able to freely choose the good on a consistent basis, without also having had the ability to not be virtuous. John Hick argues along these lines in "Irenaean Theodicy," 44.

68. See Hick, *Evil and the God of Love*, 8.

69. Swinburne, "Does Theism Need a Theodicy," 288.

70. Swinburne, *Is There a God?*

71. Nussbaum, *Love's Knowledge*, 366.

72. I discuss the connection between mortality and flourishing at length in *Heroes, Saints*, 116.

73. Nussbaum, *Love's Knowledge*, 381. Also see Nussbaum at length on the concepts of limits in "Aristotle on Human Nature," 96.

74. I am indebted to Ron Green for helping me to think through this distinction.

75. Bennet, "Evil, God, and the Free Will Defense," 40.

76. Mackie, *Miracle of Theism*, 154.

77. Surin, *Theology and the Problem of Evil*, 96.

78. Glover, *Humanity*, 2.

79. Ibid.

80. In this regard there is an interesting reference to the biblical passages (Exodus 9:12; 10:20) in which the question arises as to how the Pharaoh after each successive plague could have been so daft to continue to defy Moses's admonition to release the Jews. Both citations contain the divine assertion: "And I will harden Pharaoh's heart." With this admission does God not undermine his own objectives? It would seem that on the one hand, God intends to make an example out of the one who violates a divine decree while on the other God, in exerting influence over the Pharaoh's disposition, essentially exonerates him from the charge of malice. A traditional way out of this conundrum is to see God as acting pedagogically, i.e., as permitting (without explicitly directing) an iniquitous creature to act defiantly and then make an example of him through divine punishment. The issue with this solution, of course, is that it cuts against the idea that the "evildoer" acts with unfettered free will, for at the very least God foresees and allows the evil to occur. For more on the argument that God is at the very least indirectly responsible for creatures who act with free will, see Russell, "Davis's Free Will Defense."

81. Surin, *Theology and the Problem of Evil*, 98.

82. Ibid., 97.

83. The three new atheists with the most notoriety and who have made the most impact, often referred to as the unholy trinity, are Richard Dawkins, Sam Harris, and Christopher Hitchens. See especially Dawkins, *God Delusion*; Harris, *End of Faith*; Hitchens, *God Is Not Great*.

84. Ehrman, *God's Problem*, 13.

85. Ibid., 16–17.

86. Ibid., 66. Also see Richard Dawkins' especially poignant and polemical analysis of Genesis in *God Delusion*, 239.

87. On this score one might consult the recent rendering of the entire book of Genesis offered by the comic artist R. Crumb. Crumb's depiction of the many "plot-thick," description specific scenes in Genesis is bereft of artistic satire—indeed it is conspicuously deadpan in its literalism—because Crumb felt Genesis needed no embellishment. Crumb's motivation was not to editorialize but simply to educate, letting the graphic representation of the biblical words make their own impression on the reader. See Crumb, *Book of Genesis*.

88. Read Robertson's own words: http://mediamatters.org/research/200509130004.

89. Ehrman, *God's Problem*, 3.

90. Ibid., 276.

91. Neiman, *Evil in Modern Thought*, 69–70.

92. See also Otto, *Idea of the Holy*, 75.

93. Surin, *Theology and the Problem of Evil*, 50.

94. For a good example of the kind of historically sensitive approach to the problem of evil of which Surin would be in favor (expounded by a philosopher), see Card, *Atrocity Paradigm*, especially 6, where Card highlights the respects in which philosophical and empirical inquiries inevitably overlap.

95. Wetzel, "Can Theodicy Be Avoided?" 2.

96. Surin, *Theology and the Problem of Evil*, 52.

97. MacLeish, *J. B.*, 49.

98. Sartre, "Literature in Our Time," 635. Also quoted by Surin, *Theology and the Problem of Evil*, 51.

99. Surin, *Theology and the Problem of Evil*, 39.

100. It bears noting that although in this book I establish them as two alternative models, the Augustinian model of privation, which insists on human accountability, is very similar to the free will theodicy discussed earlier in the chapter, according to which evil occurs by our hand, not God's. Indeed, as I have already noted, one of the earliest versions of the free will defense occurs with Augustine. Augustinian cosmogony held that at the time of creation, God created the world good but it became less than good when angels turned their back on God, abused their free will, and transmitted their grave sin to Adam and Eve who they tempted to follow suit (Genesis 3).

101. As Claudia Card explains, some evils are worse than others. *Atrocity Paradigm*, 13.

CHAPTER THREE

Evil as "Evil"

Perspectivalism and the Construction of Evil

Guido: You've never ridden on a train, have you? They're
fantastic! Everybody stands up, close together, and there are
no seats!
Giosué Orefice: There aren't any seats?
Guido: Seats? On a train? It's obvious you've never ridden one
before! No, everybody's packed in, standing up. Look at this
line to get on! Hey, we've got tickets, save room for us!

—*Life Is Beautiful*

Beyond Convention

JUST BEFORE BEING SHIPPED to a concentration camp, a father attempts to pass
off the sentence as a novelty worthy of anticipation. By generating his son's
enthusiasm for the trek, Guido protects him from all the implications of their
forthcoming doom. Roberto Benigni's Oscar-winning film about a condemned
man's determination to shield his son from the worst life brings shows the creative force of the will triumphing over genocide. By adopting the right attitude,
the film argues, we have the capacity to transform the gloomiest reality into
something tolerable. Shortly after *Life Is Beautiful* was released it met with great
controversy. Critics wondered: Can the Holocaust really be willed away? How
far can an optimist disposition go towards alleviating human suffering? Is evil
something whose destructive vortex is linked to one's chosen orientation to the
universe, or is it something more, something that cannot simply be fixed by a
revised attitude? Chapter 3 examines the figures and thinkers, all of whom, if
not straightforward subjectivists who fall into the former camp of this divide, at
least see evil as a point of view, that is, something we designate rather than
discover in the world.

According to the third model, evil in essence is an illusion, a function of psychological reactions. As such, it is a perspective from which we can wrest ourselves with the right sort of self-reinvention. The problem of evil is a problem of adjustment, of looking at old situations in new, unconventional ways. Disaster, physical pain, even death constitute calamities because of the meaning we give these events, meanings that take form in culture and, as such, are irretrievably linked to the context of their advent. In other words, the word *evil*, as with other rhetorically powerful designations, is something to be understood genealogically. The definitions we give evil have a history, and their introductions in history serve directed psychological, social, and political purposes. A genealogical account of evil grants neither that evil is ontologically necessary nor that universal norms exist the violation of which could ever be described, in any universal sense, as evil. Rather, discussions about evil are used as a way of foisting an agenda. By identifying something as good or evil, we betray our allegiances. We do not yet make a valid argument for the legitimacy of some ethos.

What constitutes what we call evil is therefore more likely an indication of where power resides and which entities have successfully emerged in society. As a perspective, evil can also sometimes become saddled with ideological baggage and in this sense become a rhetorical tool in a struggle among vying powers. Whereas evil in the third model is a moniker that poorly characterizes individuals, institutions are something of which we should generally be wary. Thinkers such as Friedrich Nietzsche, Hermann Hesse, and Michel Foucault have an underlying skepticism about the moralism of assigning characterizations that are intended to be indicative of praiseworthiness or blameworthiness, as if consensus on what these judgments amount to could be possible. There is thus a contrast between the third model considered in this book and the first two. In both Manicheanism and theodicy, the person threatened by evil enjoys metaphysical security under the canopy of a sanctioned worldview. Evil plays a constant role and has a place within this worldview. One knows where one stands vis-à-vis evil, by virtue of which one becomes informed of what, eschatologically speaking, lies in store once life has run its course.

The questioner of convention and institution enjoys no such resting place.[1] Evil indicates an absence, not of the good (i.e., privation), but of any objective standard of good or bad that can be trusted. At the same time, the term evil is an instrument of reification, a concept that reinforces our confidence in existing norms and mores, which in itself has no meaning independent of its usage in some context.

The upshot of this view of evil is that tradition only haunts us if we let it. We establish our "metaphysical comfort" by deceiving ourselves into believing that our moral sensibilities have foundations, doing so at the expense of developing our self.[2] Instead of uncritically accepting the values we inherit, we ought to aspire to a life beyond the trappings of convention and to engage in the possibly terrifying but rewarding project of determining for ourselves what is to be valued. Thus Nietzsche draws a "contrast between the real truth of nature and the lie of culture that poses as if it were the only reality."[3] At issue here is human agency. Notions of evil, however instrumental they are at securing a stable society or at keeping individual anxieties at bay, stifle the will and in turn prevent us from being ourselves. Their seductiveness traps us and locks us into recognizable patterns. Nietzsche warns us

> Not to remain stuck to a person—not even the most loved—every person is a prison, also a nook. Not to remain stuck to a fatherland—not even if it suffers most and needs help most—it is less difficult to sever one's heart from a victorious fatherland. Not to remain stuck to some pity—not even for higher men into whose rare torture and helplessness some accident allowed us to look. Not to remain stuck to a science—even if it should lure us with the most precious finds that seem to have been saved up precisely for us. Not to remain stuck to one's own detachment, to that voluptuous remoteness and strangeness of the bird who flees even higher to see ever more below him—the danger of the flier. Not to remain stuck to our own virtues and become as a whole victim of some detail in us, such as our hospitality. . . . One must know how to *conserve oneself*: the hardest test of independence.[4]

"Conserving oneself," protecting oneself from dissolution, entails questioning, doubting, bucking, and ultimately rejecting that without which society's foundations become shaky. It is not an activity that is comfortable, codifiable, or transferable. It is a life event, one of perennial severing and re-severing. To become free of the shackles of the past, the past must be undone.

Can the past be undone? Do we have the capacity to reinvent ourselves? In 2006, a phenomenon swept over the American psyche in the form of a best-selling book, *The Secret*, to which the Oprah Winfrey Show devoted two full episodes. Rhonda Byrne, the author and self-help guru, explains "the secret" as a kind of law of attraction: "Nothing [good or bad] can come into your experience unless you summon it with persistent thoughts."[5] The message is as clear as it is immodest: With sufficient positivity we can think our way clear of any calamity, presumably freeing us up to beckon the fortunes our imagination deigns to conjure. Byrne, according to some of her critics an Australian scam artist with a knack for preying upon American greed, surely lacks the gravitas of Nietzsche. The principle that resounds throughout her book, however, is quintessentially Nietzschean: Although it is not necessarily obvious to us, we have the capacity to create our own situations ex nihilo. With a hubris that would make even Prometheus blush, Byrne urges her readers to avail them-selves of the power to which they gain access by learning the secret: "You are God in a physical body. You are Spirit in the flesh. You are Eternal Life express-ing itself as You. You are a cosmic being. You are all power. You are all wisdom. You are all intelligence. You are perfection. You are magnificence. You are the creator, and you are creating the creation of You on this planet."[6] What was yesterday is the result of yesterday's attitude: We can remake ourselves today. Benigni's Giosué Orefice might be boarding an overpacked train headed with his father to a concentration camp, but this is only one among several possible descriptions of what he is doing. His reality is not a settled matter.

In the worldview of the self-reinventor, the projected others of the Mani-chean tradition are false externalisms. Likewise, the various narratives of theod-icy, alleged to reveal hidden goodnesses, serve a political purpose rather than a salvific one. In both is an abdication of agency, an escapism in the form of determinism in the former, and the illusion of volition in the latter. They are two sides of the same enslavement: a Manichean resignation that denies the self its role in shaping reality, and a theodicist's submission to an eschatological script that releases the self from the burden of self-determination. Evil, corre-spondingly, is understood as suppression of the good in the former and as an uncritical affirmation of the good in the latter. Both models are primitive, fueled by the fear of embracing authentic selfhood. To understand better how this is so, it is helpful to examine the tradition of subjectivism—the strongest version of perspectivalism (and many contemporary Nietzscheans would say a view stronger than Nietzsche's own)—as well as the intellectual movement toward overcoming categories it spawned.

Subjectivism

Unlike the models of evil examined in chapters 1 and 2, the tradition that sees the problem of evil as too bound in politics, language, and power to have inher-ent independent meaning is, at least in the West, decisively modern. Subjectiv-ism, the view that the existence of every describable thing depends on an individual's awareness and filtering of that thing through language and culture, implies that no objective underlying reality exists, including any reality thought to correspond to the ontological existence of superhuman evil forces, as such. Whenever a word, phenomenon, experience, or event is imbued with some meaning, it is given that meaning by virtue of the attitudes at the time of partic-ular people. Evil, in this definition, cannot mean anything more than what

someone says is evil at a certain time. Charles Mathewes, addressing the current
challenge such a view poses to traditional claims about evil's reality and threat
to the good life defines subjectivism as "an account of human existence which
gives priority to the human intellect, and/or the brute fact of human action,
over against some mute and inert reality, material or otherwise."[7] Mathewes, an
Augustinian, is forced to grapple seriously with subjectivism because, if true, it
ultimately implies that the idea of inherited sin is a fraud: At no point could
any particular individual rise above him or herself to pronounce that a transgression against humanity has taken place. No thing that has meaning in the world
is ever discovered; it is always created. Thus, Mathewes goes on to explain,
"The human agent has the capacity for self-determination (strictly speaking, *is*
this capacity), and is an originating principle for events in the world, one influenced by the world's causal patterns. This is, by and large, how we think about
ourselves: we typically assume the subject's independence from outside influence or formation, and thus take human knowing to be a matter of matching
subjective mental constructs with the outside world, and human freedom to be
a matter of subjective 'spontaneity,' acting *ex nihilo* into an essentially exterior
world, or intervening upon a world to which *we* are external."[8]

We are what is primary, not the world. Contra Manicheanism, there are no
forces outside ourselves for which we have to be on the lookout that use human
beings as instrumental agents in an unfolding cosmic drama. Contra theodicy,
there is no larger purpose, either hypothesized or experienced, according to
which we, in time and with sufficient wisdom, find our place in the universe.
Both of these options, according to the subjectivist account, fail to acknowledge
the enormous role we take in constructing a world we later interpret, whether
we are aware of it or not. If true, subjectivism implies that our involvement with
the world, with the people we meet in the world, and with pursuing the things
that matter is, literally, voluntary. Once we realize that we are the creators of
what we think we discover, it quickly becomes apparent that life is, in fact, not
bigger than we are.[9] Enslavements, betrayals, violence—these are episodes best
not described in morally judgmental terms but instead as a description of winners and losers of contests into which we are thrust (and thrust ourselves) in
various human dramas.

Where did such a tradition—a tradition of antitradition—come from? Is the
use of words such as *good* and *evil* a scam? Are the authorities that have sanctioned the standard meanings of these terms in a position to speak for humanity,
of a "human condition," or not? If not, what do we make of human suffering in
lieu of any plausible means of referring to an inherent evil in the world?

The idea that tradition is not to be unconditionally trusted goes at least as
far back as David Hume, who in the eighteenth century maintained that it is

imperative to move beyond metaphysical principles to understand a thing itself. Hume argued that capturing the essence of suffering precludes providing an account of it.[10] Evil, if it can be said to exist, is not a consistently knowable or identifiable phenomenon; it is a sensory experience or string of experiences. If no principle is beyond doubt, then no narrative about a feature of human experience, including what we have named evil, can reliably be used to explain the human condition or, for that matter, how we should or should not behave. No philosophy or account of the good is neutral or objective; each philosophy reifies, if in sometimes subtle ways, the worldview that gives it birth. Any philosophical interpretation of an event intended to connote something in advance of the human experiencing of it is a phantom, a blunt attempt to promote an agenda without revealing any of the relevantly interested parties. Principles, ideas, states, foundations—these are but stand-ins for the dogma behind them. This is true of institutions and individuals alike. Thus Hume writes,

> Take any action allowed to be vicious: Willful murder, for instance. Examine it in all lights, and see if you can find that matter of fact, or real existence, which you call vice. In whichever way you take it, you find only certain passions, motives, volitions and thoughts. There is no other matter of fact in the case. The vice entirely escapes you, as long as you consider the object. You never can find it, till you turn your reflection into your own breast, and find a sentiment of disapprobation, which arises in you, towards this action. Here is a matter of fact, but it is the object of feeling, not of reason. It lies in yourself, not in the object. So that when you pronounce any action or character to be vicious, you mean nothing, but that from the constitution of your nature you have a feeling or sentiment of blame from the contemplation of it.[11]

Our sentiments, our preferences and passions, are at the heart of what tells us what we should and should not do, what our actions mean, and whether we have, at the end of the day, committed some transgression. Because only we can be in possession of our sentiments, we should be skeptical of declarations about what constitutes evil qua evil, even as a thing whose role is to be instrumental to the good. Hume's observation is a comment about the limitations of philosophy. Reasons for choosing one way of life and avoiding another can exist; they can even be used in the service of an argument. They are only reasons, however, not assertions that become more compelling by virtue of the fact that they have been announced with apparent authority. As reasons, they are fallible and subject to revision, and, perhaps most important, applicable only in historical context. Ultimately what we do we are persuaded to do because we have become convinced. We feel we ought to so act. William James, a Humean in his own right, makes this point on behalf of the real nature of philosophical argumentation, despite what philosophy sometimes claims itself to be:

> The history of philosophy is to a great extent that of a certain clash of human temperaments. Undignified as such a treatment may seem to some of my colleagues, I shall have to take account of this clash and explain a good many of the divergences of philosophers by it. Of whatever temperament a professional philosopher is, he tries, when philosophizing, to sink the fact of his temperament. Temperament is no conventionally recognized reason, so he urges impersonal reasons only for his conclusions. Yet temperament really gives him a stronger bias than any of his more strictly objective premises.[12]

The passions govern everything of import regardless of the extent to which we think they do. What remains in abeyance is but the process of becoming pragmatic about truth.

Hume's and James's subjectivism should not be mistaken for nihilism. The idea that nothing is right or wrong is not quite nihilism. Although Hume was clear about reason's impotence and James unrelenting about the passional nature of decision making, neither thinker denies the existence of a moral good itself, that we ought to strain ourselves to pursue this good, and that people suffer when they fail to attain it or are deprived of its more significant components.[13] They are skeptical merely of ubiquitous or apodictic uses of good and evil as principles from which further philosophical principles then follow. Richard Rorty summarized this distinction well when he famously denounced the existence of all alleged Truths (capital *T*) while proclaiming that it is perfectly within our rights not only to pursue the truths (small *t*) that work for us, but also unflinchingly to back the vision of the good that reflects those truths. Rorty defines "democracy" as the worthwhile endeavor of persuasion in hopes of achieving consensus on what is true. In such an understanding there are no substantive, "philosophical" principles of democracy.[14] Rather, Rorty's sense of democracy implies a relativism that favors local rather than global sources and sanctions for adopting norms. Better to be honest about the local nature of our purchase on the truth than to posit a facile Manicheanism that structurally reverts to name calling, or commit the theodicist's error of Procrustes by imposing the same soteriologies on people who come from incommensurably different places. For Hume, James, and Rorty, evil is a meaningful concept—indeed, for Hume it represented a powerful reason to think twice about religion. At the same time, these three thinkers remind us that philosophers interested in making sweeping claims about human nature, or, more modestly, about the human condition, run the risk of overplaying their hand by becoming ethnocentric about even the most seemingly obvious violations against humanity. Moral transgressions go "all the way down." There is no universal language for articulating them and thus ultimately no getting through to the torturer who does not share our fundamental suppositions about civility, justice, and flourishing. Victims are not victims everywhere.[15] Cross-cultural consensus is contingently possible, but translation between cultures is not something we can expect, much less count on.[16]

Nietzsche

For Hume and his intellectual descendants, then, evil acquires a more local flavor, but we are not "beyond" good or evil. To say that a norm is motivated by the passions is for Hume not a slight, but an empirical observation that, once acknowledged, frees us to experience the world with less pretense and intellectual colonialism. Nietzsche, on the other hand, hones in on the passions as a way of exposing the fraud of rational discourse, at the bottom of which, if one looks hard enough, one will always discover some struggle for power. With Nietzsche, cross-cultural consensus turns out to be a myth. There cannot realistically be temporal agreement beyond ephemeral alliances because at the base of what is motivating every idea, movement, maxim, or norm on which to agree is a self-interested struggle for power that, despite appearances, is at all times inherently unstable. No abstract, rational, impersonal, or impartial guides to action are possible. Every great philosophy put forward as a potential avenue for bringing parties together is, as Nietzsche says in *Beyond Good and Evil*, "the personal confession of its author."[17] Philosophy might be aesthetically interesting, but it cannot do our work for us by telling us what sort of person we should become. Each of us has to determine this individually and then strive to become that person.

In fact, argues Nietzsche, no standard or norm with pretensions of universality ought to get a pass. Every value has a history. As for those who are resistant to the idea that there exist no foundational norms, Nietzsche has a thought experiment he wishes us to consider:

> Let us articulate this *new demand:* we need a *critique* of moral values, *the value of these values themselves must first be called in question*—and for that there is needed a knowledge of the conditions and circumstances in which they grew, under which they evolved and changed (morality as a consequence, as symptom, as mask, as tartufferie, as illness, as misunderstanding; but also morality as cause, as remedy, as stimulant, as restraint, as poison), a knowledge of a kind that has never yet existed or even been desired. One has taken the *value*

of these "values" as given, as factual, as beyond all question; one has hitherto never doubted or hesitated in the slightest degree in supposing the "good man" to be greater value than the "evil man," of greater value in the sense of furthering the advancement and prosperity of man in general (the future of man included). But what if the reverse were true? What if a symptom of regression were inherent in the "good," likewise a danger, a seduction, a poison, a narcotic, through which the present was possibly living *at the expense of the future?* Perhaps more comfortably, less dangerously, but at the same time in a meaner style, more beastly?—So that precisely morality would be to blame if the *highest power and splendor* actually possible to the type of man was never in fact attained? So that precisely morality was the danger of dangers?[18]

What if the virtues we most prized, for all of their presumed inherent goodness, in the broader view turned out to lead to the dissolution of civility? This is the equivalent of asking a committed Christian whether he would still be a believer if an archaeological expedition were suddenly to discover bones that could be decisively carbon-dated back to the man Jesus of Nazareth. Probably, that Christian would remain a Christian, but continue to do so, as he has all along, by virtue of his unshakable faith, not the compelling force of scientific evidence. Nietzsche's point is that our dedicated support of the moral norms to which we ascribe universally binding force is no different. These norms reflect a strong preference of ours, matched by our strong faith in them. This faith is affirmed and reaffirmed to the degree that preferences get us somewhere in the world. In undertaking his thought experiment, Nietzsche questions whether, at the very bottom, the virtues we value are valued not because they are their own reward, intrinsically valuable, but because of where their being regarded as their own reward gets us, or more precisely, gets the ones who are responsible for assigning their value.

To take one of Nietzsche's favorite examples, were we convincingly to be shown that by pitying the helpless and weaker among us, we weaken the foundations on which society rests by creating communities of freeloaders and dependents, pity might not be regarded with the nobility that it currently is. Disabusing us of our errant understanding of pity is Nietzsche's objective in discussing the emotion in *The Antichrist*. Although pity is a large part of Christianity's raison d'être, when we look at just its effect on normal people, and extract it from its institutional context, we see that it intensifies our suffering, makes that suffering contagious, and gives an undue disadvantage to those— that is, the pitiers—whom nature otherwise favors.[19] Where pity works for the Church—it is one of the currencies by which the Church purports to absolve its flock of sins in return for renewable support—unmasked, it is revealed as an inducement to depression and stagnation. It turns out, then, that pity is a virtue for some and a vice for others. Or, it is a virtue in one context but a vice in another. For, as Nietzsche observes, pity, in conventional Christianity's promotion of a neighbor-love as the summum bonum of the moral life, is endorsed in such a way so as to also induce an individual's "bad love of himself."[20] If we flee to the neighbor by fleeing from ourselves, Nietzsche worries, we create a society of dependence, and fail to cultivate a more mature friendship that simultaneously helps develop authentic selfhood.[21] Pity can be a virtue.[22] However, as with all states, it all depends on context, the end for whose sake the character trait in question is cultivated, other side-consequences of its cultivation, and so forth. Nothing is a virtue by definition. This is true for all of the subsets of good and evil: it is not clear until the context is spelled out how any particular trait ought to be morally characterized.

Moreover, once such a particular determination has been made, the issue remains of the extent to which vice remains useful for virtue. On this score, Nietzsche challenges the foundation on which any moral system can legitimately be built:

> I deny morality as I deny alchemy, that is, I deny their premises: but I do *not* deny that there have been alchemists who believed in these premises and acted in accordance with them.—I also deny immorality: *not* that countless people *feel* themselves to be immoral, but that there is any *true* reason so to feel. It goes without saying that I do not deny—unless I am a fool—that many actions called immoral ought to be avoided and resisted, or that many called moral ought to be done and encouraged—but I think the one should be encouraged and the other avoided *for other reasons than hitherto.*[23]

Actions are to be avoided because of their potential impact on our goals and self-maturation, but not because of anything intrinsic about them. Nietzsche unequivocally denies the project of morality per se, even if he can be read as favoring a new morality of authenticity or resistance.[24] Is there any difference between Nietzsche's skepticism about moral foundations and moral nihilism, the view that there can be no moral truths and therefore no genuine sense in which morality can be practiced? This is a tricky question. On the one hand, Nietzsche claims that any imaginable value ought to be subject to revaluation; no norm can be defined as good or bad. On the other hand, when Nietzsche offers examples of our tendency to unduly attach a timeless quality to what we morally value, he seems to do so consistently in the service of a particular norm: the norm that we ought to cultivate authentic selves.[25] The question is further complicated by the varying senses in which Nietzsche himself uses the word *nihilism.* He invokes it sometimes to indicate that modern man can no longer believe in what he values, ushering in an age of rudderlessness that is presumably undesirable, and sometimes to suggest that it is something to favor in order to rescue "value" from the misleading language of moral judgment with which it has unfortunately become intertwined.[26] In the first sense, the word "nihilism" is used descriptively, as a characterization of a movement sweeping over the West; in the second, it is understood normatively, as a "sign of strength" used to critique those who assign metaphysical status to values that should be understood purely in terms of their historicity.[27]

What is important for our purposes is to elucidate that, in either case, Nietzsche is strongly perspectivalist, not merely asserting that our passions are what determine the strength of our norms, but also that our norms themselves become unintelligible when divorced from the historical circumstances of their advent. Everything posited to be true, Nietzsche claims, is "necessarily false."[28] By invoking nihilism, in other words, Nietzsche signals the advent of an era in which everything cherished would crumble before our eyes, leaving the strongest among us to rise up from the ashes and create meaning anew. According to this view of meaning, never quite articulated before Nietzsche, there is a massive resetting of what is to be valued, and even an ongoing critique of the activity of valuing. The moral conflicts we experience are ones we impose. In actuality, we are conflict-free. We are in our essence formless individuals always capable of reforming, our degree of success tied to our persistence, aptitude for persuasion, and capacity to sustain our will through our strength and the formation of the right sorts of alliances. What Nietzsche proposes is radical. It is not the ethos advocated by Milton's Satan ("evil be thou my good"), for there is no deliberate inversion where an antagonist affixes his intentions to malicious ones, as if the standard for what is benevolent or malicious need not be questioned. According to Nietzsche, there are no concepts of good and evil to be meaningfully switched. Nor is this the undoing of a polarization in favor of a unity such as that posited in theodicies. Nietzsche's alternative to Manichean dualism represents a different overcoming of fear, namely, the unchecked experimentation with all untested *ethoi,* even those conventionally denounced as abominations. Thus, in contrast to substituting a scripted dualism with a static monism, Nietzsche set out to preserve the creative impulse that is our birthright by doing away with categories altogether.

Nihilism at least implies, then, the continued undoing of any given understanding of good and evil, or whether a thing is to be valued or avoided. Does it also imply that human suffering is subject to interpretation? How about the sort of suffering that entails brutal harm to the physical body? Or the sort of sorrow one experiences when one loses something one has rightly come to love?

That is, how does the revaluation of values bear on the experience of the victim? Is it that to deny evil is to deny that people, when deprived of the fundamental components that go into human flourishing, languish? Are there not recognizable, cross-cultural ways of characterizing pain, loss, emptiness, and the like? If we grant Nietzsche's point that judgments about evil are inevitably polluted with the manipulations of individuals or groups, and that we should likely become suspicious when evil is given a meaning distinct from the good, we are at the very least committed to treading cautiously on attempting to identify victims in our midst, or, for that matter, to pausing before speaking of any sort of universal suffering or predicament that pertains to human nature or the human condition. This, again, is what makes Nietzsche's proposal so radical. It permits no intelligible discussion of a human condition that suffers from a common, existential angst caused by our imperfection as finite beings.

Here, we are at the heart of what makes the third model in this book—which I have identified as evil as the absence of badness—so distinctive. What the one who wants to move beyond good and evil eschews is not merely the demonization of an enemy, but any traditional understanding of philosophy and, for that matter, morality. Along with the departure of philosophy's nonchalant use of the rhetoric of right and wrong goes any entity, external or internal, that would check the will's will to rise to power. On such an account the weak fall prey to the strong. History is written by its winners. Moreover, we must ask ourselves in earnest whether objections we might have to this fact are based on anything more durable than an antiquated slave morality. In the balance lies the dissolution of any stable assignation of normativity, a reduction of every "should" to an aesthetic choice.[29] There can be no real culpability or moral progress, only ressentiment, that is, a hostility redirected by the oppressed back to the oppressor. With the dissolution of normativity is an infinite regression of righteous indignation. Whence Nietzsche's emphasis on the will to power epitomized in his paradigmatic antihero, Zarathustra.

Interpreting Nietzsche and establishing in particular whether, in the end, his view is tantamount to thoroughgoing subjectivism in the form of moral nihilism has become its own academic subspecialty. Perhaps anticipating that such a debate about his thinking would take place posthumously, Nietzsche was clever and opaque enough to avoid attributing anything definitive to him, either way. Although he deliberately (indeed, mockingly) equivocates about abstractions such as "good," "evil," and "virtue," he writes with relatively little ambiguity about concrete concepts such as "hate" and "courage." Nevertheless, the Nietzschean project of the revaluation of values, independent of Nietzsche's own views, is a Pandora's box begging to be opened, even if it never was by Nietzsche himself. Because of Nietzsche, discussions about the tenability of moral nihilism and the ubiquitous although faintly recognized role of power underlying supposedly binding norms reverberated throughout the intellectual West by the turn of the twentieth century.

The Intellectual Legacy of Nietzsche

By the early twentieth century, there were at least two directions in which to take Nietzsche's genealogical method of understanding tradition and authority. The first was a new trend in the modern approach to ethics to downplay the normative in favor of the aesthetic. This approach, whereby the value of the values was called into question, naturally led to the view that underlying everything we hold dear are our preferences. A flurry of thinkers began to develop the idea that we ought to pursue the good, but that the good entails the cultivation of what we individually identify to be those traits latent in us, which, when developed, mark us for distinction among our peers. In this revised *eudaemonia*, the beautiful takes center stage over the moral law, the morally right, or the universal good. In this vision, the self is a work of art that needs to be allowed to blossom into whatever it is destined to become. Impositions on the self for the sake of other-regard are unnatural. Morality is a yoke, no justification. Bonds can form between individuals and we can care about one another, but nothing metaphysical warrants these connections. They form contingently and voluntarily, in history. We ought to gravitate toward people who will help develop our characters and whose characters we can influence in a positive way while having little to do with everyone else.

The second direction is to ask what, if not the binding force inherent in the norms that we live by, is at work when such norms come to assume their timeless quality. The short answer, say some who have been influenced by Nietzsche's thought, is power. They assert a link between power and knowledge. When we or the institutions of which we are a part create a norm, the norm quickly becomes internalized in society, creating the impression that the norm has always existed. This, in turn, leads to a constructed system of legal and moral judgment, that in no way bears the appearance of being constructed, in which determinations are made about whether people are normal or deviant. Thus, a society's general knowledge of right and wrong, assessments that determine what actions warrant discipline or punishment, is really a reflection of what those in power have themselves constructed and introduced into society. It is our role as responsible activists to uncover the various links that de facto exist between knowledge and power—for purposes of giving voice to the hitherto silenced.

Herein is a key difference between the two sorts of Nietzscheans described. In the first are no moral imperatives. Underlying everything is preference, that is, aesthetics. In the second is at least a concerted effort that represents a kind of procedural, if not substantive, norm that would be right to characterize as cross-culturally binding, namely, the norm that everyone—including those whom society deems deviant and worthy of punishment—ought to have the right to be heard.[30] These two strands—the triumph of the aesthetic over the normative, and the empowerment of the previously disempowered—bear exploration.

Hermann Hesse and Michel Foucault are two thinkers in the Nietzschean tradition committed to moving beyond good and evil in these two alternative ways. For both, evil is not what we think it is. For Hesse, it either plainly does not exist, or what we call evil might be so wrapped up in the larger good that it cannot be meaningfully distinguished from the good (in a sense that is very different than theodicy). For Foucault, the use of the term ought to signal warning bells that likely indicate atrocities or certainly injustices attributable to the ones who invoke the term. This is not necessarily to deny that such a thing as evil exists. Evil, however, is for Foucault institutional, part of the societal machine to which we succumb without our full awareness. Foucault enjoins us to reflect critically on how power surfaces and subtly unfolds in all of our interpersonal interactions so as to be able to harness an ability, as a society, to become more evenhanded about how we deal with those who apparently violate the norm.

Hermann Hesse and the Triumph of the Aesthetic over the Normative

In an early climactic moment in one of the great coming-of-age narratives in literature, Hermann Hesse's *Demian*, a frequently bullied schoolboy, Emil Sinclair, encounters the charismatic Max Demian, who exhorts him to throw off the chains of his self-imprisonment and to stop seeking the approbation of others. To drive home this point, Demian invokes the archetype of all biblical villains:

"The story of Cain who has that mark on his forehead. Do you like it?"

No I didn't. It was rare for me to like anything we had to learn. Yet I didn't dare confess it, for I felt I was being addressed by an adult. I said I didn't mind much the story.

Demian slapped me on the back.

"You don't have to put on an act for me. But in fact the story is quite remarkable. It's far more remarkable than most stories taught in school. Your teacher didn't go into it at great length. He just mentioned the usual things about God and sin and so forth. But I believe—" He interrupted himself and asked with a smile: "Does this interest you at all?

"Well I think," he went on, "one can give this story about Cain quite a different interpretation. Most of the things we're taught I'm sure are quite right and true, but one can view all of them from quite a different angle than the teachers do—and most of the time they then make better sense. . . .

"Here was a man with something in his face that frightened others. They didn't dare lay hands on him; he impressed them, he and his children. We can guess—no, we can be quite certain—that it was not a mark on his forehead like a postmark—life is hardly ever as clear and straightforward as that. It is much more likely that he struck people as faintly sinister, perhaps a little more intellect and boldness in his look than people were used to. This man was powerful: you would approach him only with awe. He had a 'sign.' You could explain this any way you wished. And people always want what is agreeable to them and puts them in the right. They were afraid of Cain's children: they bore a 'sign.' So they did not interpret the sign for what it was—a mark of distinction—but its opposite. They said: 'Those fellows with the sign, they're a strange lot'—and indeed they were. People with courage and character always seem sinister to the rest. It was a scandal that a breed of fearless and sinister people ran about freely, so they attracted a nickname and myth to these people to get even with them, to make up for the many times they had felt afraid—don't you get it?"

"Yes—that is—in that case Cain wouldn't have been evil at all? And the whole story of the Bible is actually not authentic?"[31]

When Sinclair further presses Demian to explain the murder of Abel, the response is, again, not one of denial but provocative reinterpretation: "Oh, that's certainly true. The strong man slew a weaker one. It's doubtful whether it was really his brother. But it isn't important. Ultimately all men are brothers. So, a strong man slew a weaker one: perhaps it was truly a valiant act, perhaps it wasn't."[32]

Hesse's young overman does not mince words. On his account we should not be so quick to saddle the sinister with bad reputations. Murder can be valiant. Cain is the hero and Abel the coward. The conventional story taught in school that claims the reverse, that calls Cain evil, can be "untaught," or taught better, or taught differently in different places.[33] Cain can be beautiful. This, in any case, is what Sinclair realizes on further exploring his friendship with Demian: "my conscious self lived within the familiar and sanctioned world, it denied the new world that dawned within me."[34]

The new world is that developed by Hesse through the deity Abraxas, the ageless, androgynous god of both love and the devil, transcending morality, but immanent in the world. Demian describes the deity's revelation as the result of the bird who claws its way out of an egg, destroying a prior world to make possible its own new one, and who, on hatching, flies directly to its god, Abraxas.[35] Leaving aside, for the moment, allusions in this description to Taoist themes pertaining to the unity of all things, what is clearly being suggested is that the path to true selfhood, not an easy one, entails the suspension of the traditional distinctions by which we order the world. Abraxas is a symbol for all that is both good and evil in the world. In another of Hesse's works, *Siddhartha*, the protagonist tells his friend upon enlightenment, "if time is not real, then the dividing line that seems to lie between this world and eternity, between suffering and bliss, between good and evil, is also an illusion."[36] Hesse hardly means to convey the point negatively. A case can be made for the allure of anything. The path to oneself can lead anywhere. In the service of taking that path, one has the right to avail oneself of what one needs in order to travel. No taboo, prescription, proscription, habit, valued or cherished thing has a monopoly over any other. In Hesse's vision, traditional roles dissolve and binaries lose tenability. One death signifies another rebirth; one person's justice is another's injustice.

One implication of the perspectivalist attitude such as the one Hesse optimistically embraces is that no one has a monopoly on our sympathy. Terrorists in context become freedom fighters.[37] Everything can be beautiful if it is looked at in the right way.[38] Indeed, to every *yes* is a rationale for *no*. Hesse writes,

> Everything is true, "Yes" can be said to anything. To bring order into the world, to attain goals, to make possible law, society, organization, culture, morality, "No" must be added to the "Yes," the world must be separated into opposites, into good and evil. However arbitrary the first establishment of each "No," each prohibition, may be, it becomes sacrosanct the instant it becomes law, produces results, becomes the foundation for a point of view and system of order.[39]

Rules and boundaries are practical requirements to organize society, but on some basis, somewhere, any one of those rules could be challenged. Rules are always somewhat of an upshot of historical accident. We can imagine that if one rule had turned out to be less historically foundational than it in fact had been in our organizing of society, then society would look quite different. The oppositions with which Hesse here is seemingly obsessed are really a reflection on how things ever come to be regarded as forbidden in the first place. A *no* becomes impermissible by virtue of an historical decision that can be undone, or it can be synthesized with an opposite decision. In dualism's place Hesse offers the syncretist view advocating the unity in all things, according to which, to be an authentic seeker of truth, one must never swallow one version of the truth whole, but rather be open to glimpses of different truths that opaquely characterize a common reality to which they are all ultimately reducible. The syncretist point is concretely made through Gore Vidal's unlikely defense of one of our country's most notorious villains. Timothy McVeigh, a homegrown terrorist, Vidal construes as a patriot whose defense of the constitution we should be wont to emulate. His description is notably not without an evaluative component:

> He was a dedicated student of the American way, of the Constitution itself. . . . You should read his writings—they're very good. Particularly on the Posse Comitatus Act of 1876, which forbids the Federal government ever to use its troops against the American people—but which they proceeded to do at Waco. . . . They killed more people than he managed to kill when he blew up that building in Oklahoma City. He was a noble boy.[40]

Noble? A murderer of 168 people? The primary culprit of the largest terrorist attack on American soil undertaken by an American citizen? This is a "dedicated student of the American way," the actions of one who safeguards the Constitution? How easy it would be, prods Vidal, not to think so.

No doubt the full stories of McVeigh and that of every other publicized villain, to say nothing of the heroes we prize, have yet to be written. Gandhi was reputed as an adult to have slept naked with his teenage cousin in order to establish his own capacity for self-discipline.[41] One need not dig very deep to discover Martin Luther King's penchant for plagiarizing and womanizing.[42] If one looks hard enough, a case can be made that all the good and bad things in the world are wrapped up together in one big messy ball. It is only through perspective, our chosen interpretive lens, through which we are equipped to understand our given realities. And once we are engaged in interpreting our world, then we can reinterpret it.

Hesse and Vidal make a compelling case for adopting an attitude of humility before adopting the conventional take on the heroes we place on the pedestal. The things we are most sure of become things about which we have a little less confidence when we look at them more closely. With enough analysis and open-mindedness, a case could be made that everything looks like everything else. It may be logistically necessary to erect moral categories to make judgments, but it behooves us at all times to recognize the historicity of the construction of these categories, lest our judgments acquire a vacuous, dogmatic quality. According to the model of perspectivalism, categories can never be more than a temporary, if stable, heuristic device.

Michel Foucault, Power and Judgment

Like Hermann Hesse, and in keeping with Nietzsche's legacy, Michel Foucault raises serious questions about the history of moral judgments, a history which, when acknowledged, reveals the organizational purpose for which specific norms have been created. Like Hesse, Foucault exhorts us to be wary of the overwhelming institution:

> This indeed is the diabolical aspect. . . . One doesn't have here a power which is wholly in the hands of one person who can exercise it alone and totally over the others. It's a machine in which everyone is caught, those who exercise power just as much as those over whom it is exercised. . . . So much so that one has the vertiginous sense of being in the presence of an invention that even its inventor is incapable of controlling.[43]

The standards by which we judge good and bad, suggests Foucault, are irretrievably caught up in the process by which norms are introduced out of a formless chaos and then reinforced tacitly but grippingly by the very people most subject to the law under these norms. No one is directly responsible for but everyone is responsible to the rules of a system that, once in play, become resistant to being supplanted or rendered defunct. It would seem, under the sway of such situational pressures, an idea of evil can never be divorced from all of the other constructions of the machine. Foucault departs company from Hesse, however, in calling our attention to a social evil that, if nameless, is nonetheless a persisting reality responsible for and behind the institutional concepts we come to idolize. Indeed, what is evil, for Foucault, is precisely our system's resistance to being remodeled or refashioned in any way, despite the unequal distribution of power among the parties within it. Thus, in spite of the fact that Foucault writes that "nothing is fundamental" or metaphysically necessary about which "foundations of power in a society" historically endure, he does, nevertheless, retrieve a sense of ethical transgression that transcends subjective context.[44] As the political theorist William Connolly observes, Foucault, after all, "finds a covert problem of evil to be lodged within the conventional politics of good and evil. Evil not as actions by immoral agents who freely transgress the moral law but evil as arbitrary cruelty installed in regular institutional arrangements taken to embody the Law, the Good, or the Normal."[45]

The relentless subjection to conventional institutions issues in a real and palpable cruelty every bit worthy of a polemical, dare one say "ethical," response.

According to Foucault, we are both the producers and the products of the institutions in which we are embedded. The moral subject imagined by Enlightenment philosophers that is thought to be free to act in conformity with the moral law is in actuality not autonomous, for it is powerless to assert its independence from the underlying grid of social structures which, to a very large extent, also determines its options. As both the agents and products of power, we are incapable of grasping or acting on an uncontaminated truth; the truth is always already corrupted by one form of a political regime or another. Understood, the real fight against evil becomes a piecemeal endeavor to expose these variously influential regimes for what they are, one by one. Hence, Foucault characterizes his project as "archaeological:" It uncovers the way in which power relations form and are maintained on a subconscious level and, as a result, breaks down institutional legitimacy to attempt to rebuild a more distributively just and historically self-conscious world order.[46] Removing power from truth is an impossible futility. But we can pursue more modest ambitions. We can, for example, work harder to identify where power resides and, once we have done this much, dampen some of the more pernicious aspects of the way in which politics gets infused in truth. In this respect, one might interpret Foucault to be saying that we are not entirely powerless if we can expose injustice.

According to Foucault, then, at least in a meta respect, a meaningful evil to avoid exists, if not an explicit good to pursue. This is the evil of treating history as if it were out of history, of seeing the way things are as if, upon discovery, they always had to be this way, of mistaking power for legitimacy. Foucault takes up a normative stance, namely, that of expelling the myth of the necessity of truths and judgments. To acknowledge contingency is to "contribute to changing people's ways of perceiving and doing things, to participate in this difficult displacement of forms of sensibilities and thresholds of tolerance."[47] When we come to terms with the historicity of norm construction we also cannot fail to acknowledge that norms serve interests of power, depriving the evaluator of the usual excuses for lack of sensitivity and even intolerance. Blasphemous exegeses, deviant criminality, abnormal sexuality, indeed any and all alternatives to the dominant reading—these aberrations all veer from the norm by hegemony that postures as objectivity. Not only the terms *normal* and *objective*, but also *legal, proper, permissible, impermissible,* and *acceptable* ought immediately to invoke the suspicion of the one who hears them uttered. Each implies the beginning of the transcendentalization of an identity that should instead be recognized as a political manifestation, conceived in history.[48] Ethics can exist, but only modestly, bereft of such monopolies, that is, as a corrective to hegemonic dominance, not as ontology.

Foucault thus retains what Fredric Jameson calls the "archaic categories of good and evil" while dispensing with the false sense of security of some stable philosophy favored at the expense of the ones who lose out when such a philosophy is imposed in the form of discipline and punishment.[49] There is evil, but ironically in the intentions of those who with the air of authority set up oppositions between good and evil. As David Frankfurter notes, "real evil happens when people speak of evil."[50] Evil is not the act of being chauvinistic in our constructions. In this, as the subjects of power, we have no choice. It is instead the act of confusing our chauvinism for an evenhandedness that, in turn, justifies the enterprise of distinguishing the normal from the deviant. Power is not evil, in other words, domination is.[51] Power is a life force; domination is an insidious conservatism with respect to this force, one that has a freedom-denying effect. Therefore, whereas Foucault eventually does arrive at a specific understanding of evil, he unequivocally shares Nietzsche's skepticism about foundations and human nature. Intellectual honesty demands the resort to perspectives. The good, by default, becomes a process of dereification, the dismantling of privilege, and finally, inclusion.

With such inclusion slowly comes the loss of good and evil as referents. Nevertheless, there is for Foucault an ethics, a normative view. Accusation, domination, and punishment—in which the authorities who use their privilege to accuse, dominate, and punish remain unchecked—are to be avoided. We can also, with due care, referencing the archaeological and genealogical methods of investigating truth, avoid them. This normative view, however, is radically antiauthoritarian, cynical about tradition, and, in the end, inconsistent with any posited vision of the good. It outright denies the possibility of a human nature, despite the universal ineluctability of power relations in the human situation in connection with our search for the truth.

In the summer of 1978, in the process of assembling a cadre of journalists and activists to make sense of a populist uprising in connection with the overthrow of the Shah in Iran, Foucault observed,

> There are more ideas on earth than intellectuals imagine. And these ideas are more active, stronger, more resistant, more passionate than "politicians" think. We have to be there at the birth of ideas, the bursting outward of their force: not in books expressing them, but in events manifesting this force, in struggles carried on around ideas, for or against them. Ideas do not rule the world. But it is because the world has ideas (and because it constantly produces them) that it is not passively ruled by those who are its leaders or those who would like to teach it, once and for all, what it must think.[52]

Herein lies a clue to what, if anything, constitutes a Foucauldian vision of the good. We should, when possible, safeguard, if not pursue, conditions that allow for the unexpected emergence in history of fresh ideas, events, movements, or, especially, challenges to the established order. Some of these ideas will be benign, some revolutionary. They are all necessary, according to Foucault, to ensure that power not lapse too frequently into domination (it will inevitably do so enough of the time). When we require recognized intellectuals to sanction the "new" ideas, power becomes calcified, signaling the passivity of humanity. Philosophy, the codification of any particular good, is inimical to human *eudaemonia*. Perspectives that come into view refracted by the "specter of relativism" represent the alternative to totalizing narratives that serve to materially suppress the underrepresented as well as suffocate the human spirit. What metaphysical assurances we lose in this vision are compensated for by whatever reduction there is in the systemic cruelty we experience in unchecked conventionality. Welcoming and not merely tolerating historical vicissitudes, we de-anesthetize ourselves to the comforts otherwise provided by the stagnant authorities who have become accustomed to scripting our future. By taking this risk, power is ironically managed.

Along with Nietzsche and Hesse, Foucault stands in sharp contrast to the disparately redemptive accounts depicted in Manicheanism and theodicy. Unlike the two earlier models, the perspectivalist model is resistant to being assimilated within a religious setting. Neither the Manichean condemnation of end-times, for example, nor the salvific rosiness of the eschatological fate in most theodicies allows for a flexibility with the truth required in the genealogical method. This raises a natural question that pertains to the tenability of describing a tradition of antitradition. What status can a critique of tradition, after all, have? How could such a tradition in the first place be named without undermining itself?

I do not think any of the thinkers discussed in this chapter would feel troubled by their critics' likely charge of "anti-theory." The method of genealogy is about the disruption of theory and universalities, and through that disruption afflicting us in our "metaphysical comfort." Anticipating the objection that his approach to philosophizing was itself too unstable to enter the philosophical canon, Nietzsche insisted that the revaluation of values is ongoing, without respite, never affording the luxury of theoretical stasis enforceable by trustworthy authorities. But, he pressed, the restlessness associated with the "flight from authority" is only a problem for the intellectual revolutionary if its being given a historical label is a priority, and it is not. By self-consciously not pressing any association with tradition, whether subjectivist or deconstructivist or postmodern or poststructuralist, the question of what authorities are at work and on what basis when we engage in a hermeneutic of suspicion is rendered academic. Nevertheless, the question of a tradition of antitradition remains in principle. Could a religious worldview entertain a vision of the good skeptical toward norms, meaning, and truth? If so, what might that tradition look like? I now turn to some Eastern figures and texts to sketch one possible response.

Taoism, Zen Buddhism, and Perspectivalism

Does the somewhat self-referential understanding of evil presented earlier— evil happens when we affix ourselves to a specific meaning of evil—necessarily imply nihilism? Could such an understanding be consistent with a specific vision of the good? What might that tradition of antitradition look like? How does an insistence on perspectives square with a coherent worldview and corresponding ethos of perpectivalism?

Chuang-Tzu, Dōgen, and Objective Good without Objective Meaning

In the *Inner Chapters*, the expert describer of the elusive Taoist exemplar, Chuang-Tzu, could have been channeling Nietzsche, who lived two thousand years later, when he wrote the following passage, one of the most famous in all Taoist literature:

> Everything has its "that," everything has its "this." From the point of view of "that" you cannot see it, but through understanding you can know it. So I say, "that" comes out of "this' and "this" depends on "that"—which is to say that "this" and "that" give birth to each other. But where there is birth there must be death; where there is death there must be birth. Where there is acceptability there must be unacceptability; where there is unacceptability there must be acceptability. Where there is recognition of the right there must be wrong; where there is recognition of the wrong there must be right. . . . A state in which "this" and "that" no longer find their opposites is called the hinge of the Way. When the hinge is fitted into the socket, it can respond endlessly. Its right then is a single endlessness and its wrong too is a single endlessness. So I say, the best thing to use is clarity.[53]

There is a way, a right way, but it is not this way or that way. The way (tao) is inaccessible through recourse to acceptable means. It is linguistically corruptible and propositionally unknowable, a wispy, scarcely available referent for the virtue-seeker but one we should nevertheless strive to emulate. In the Taoist vision, all distinction is transcended, the words *good* and *evil* distractions that preclude connection to the ineffable Tao. Exemplars are "skilled beyond skillfulness," life's worthwhile dishes bereft of any recipe. One approaches Enlightenment with *wu-wei*, an inactive state of mind, indicating not laziness but an absence of purposive or tendentious goal-directedness, with *hsu*, a mind emptied of conventional advice and prudential objectives. The goal of overcoming evil in Taoism is to overcome all binaries, including the binary of good and evil.

In such a worldview, good and evil are never quite identifiable, but they do exist. Evil is a reality, but not a concept that is distinguishable from the good. Thus, we read in the *Te-Tao Ching*, "When everyone in the world knows the beautiful as beautiful, ugliness comes into being; When everyone knows the good, then the not good comes to be. . . . Therefore the Sage dwells in non-active affairs and practices the *wordless* teaching."[54] One stays in harmony with the universe when one does not impose one's way on the world. This is the way to becoming a virtuous exemplar, to produce in one's own way, on one's own terms, without having copied another or having served as a template for future followers. Conversely, evil is that which—by overemphasizing words, concepts, and distinctions—keeps us from successfully striving to achieve the tao. It is, literally, an absence of badness, where badness, like goodness, is something we are reliably capable of predicting in advance. The ethos toward which this understanding of the tao leads, then, is linguistically and conceptually subjectivist, but ethically objectivist in terms of its recommendation of how to go about pursuing the good. It behooves us to conceive of evil as an absence of badness, for to identify something explicitly as bad, or evil, is precisely to ignore the extent to which we are prevented—in language or concepts—from articulating, philosophically or theoretically, the good life.

The Taoist scholar P. J. Ivanhoe clarifies that though it is in this sense appropriate to think of Chuang-Tzu as a language skeptic, he is not necessarily a moral relativist.[55] Although the virtuous exemplars of which Chuang-Tzu speaks offer no ethical guidance about how someone else ought to pursue the good life, the tao itself refers to the way the world naturally is in its ideal state, and to which, by virtue of this, we ought to return.[56] Chuang-Tzu, in other words, does not merely acknowledge the way, he endorses it, even if it seems at times we ought to call into question whether our perceptions about reality are in fact real. The tension between intelligibly rendering what is and ought to be the case, and the reality we ought to positively regard, comes to the fore in Taoism's twin Cartesian anecdotes:

> He who dreams of drinking wine may weep when morning comes; he who
> dreams of weeping may in the morning go off to hunt. While he is dreaming

he does not know it is a dream, and in his dream he may even try to interpret a dream. Only after he wakes does he know it was a dream. And someday there will be a great awakening when we know that this is all a great dream. Yet the stupid believe they are awake, busily and brightly assuming they understand things, calling this man ruler, that one herdsman—how dense! Confucius and you are both dreaming! And when I say you are dreaming, I am dreaming, too.[57]

Once Chuang Chou dreamt he was a butterfly, a butterfly flitting and fluttering around, happy with himself and doing as he pleased. He didn't know he was Chuang Chou. Suddenly he woke up and there he, solid and unmistakable Chuang Chou. But he didn't know if he was Chuang Chou who had dreamt he was a butterfly, or a butterfly dreaming he was Chuang Chou.[58]

What is being rejected in these two anecdotes is the authority with which reality is sometimes interpreted, not that there is an ultimate reality.[59] Knowledge can be reached by no surrogate. We are each capable of wakefulness, but only if we pursue it by taking control of our spiritual therapy. There is no shortage of the skillful exemplars to whom Chuang-Tzu introduces us in the *Inner Chapters*, such as master chef Cook Ding, who demonstrate that they are at home with their points of view. As with Nietzsche and Foucault, we ought to be skeptical about the conventional methods by which truth is said to be accessible. With Chuang-Tzu, however, the undoing of our various social realities ushers in the affirmation of a deeper, underlying reality. As Ivanhoe points out, Chuang-Tzu's "*use* of perspectivism is quite different: unlike Nietzsche, [he] believes there is something behind or beneath traditional social norms . . . [and] is not out to build a new world upon the rubble of the old. He believes that the process of dismantling of tradition itself allows an inherently existing pattern— the *Dao*—to emerge."[60] For this to happen, we must all assume the burden of cultivating our own spontaneous energy (chi), something no one else can do for us.[61]

In a tradition in which one never parades one's talents or speaks about what one knows, in which the sage is fameless, in which an authentic reality is signaled by the absence of interpreting reality, the staying power of values and norms exists in inverse relation to their explication, dissemination, and elevation in status. There is, as Emmanuel Levinas might have noted, an emphasis on infinity over totality, on the irreducibility of the sincere and uncontaminated experience between the individual and the world of others that that individual encounters to the ontologically closed assimilation of that experience into all prior experiences.[62] So construed, there can be no fixed meaning of evil without the consequence of succumbing to a greater, totalizing evil. Just as the tao cannot be learned, nor can we resort to any set of proscriptions or prescriptions to reliably protect us from losing our way.[63]

Dōgen and Morality-Transcendence

Similar to Taoism and its emphasis on overcoming convention and formal prescription, Zen Buddhism, as interpreted through the thirteenth-century Japanese mystic, Dōgen Kigen, construes morality as part of the fleeting phenomenal world, something to be conceptually transcended, though this is not to say that there is not a way we ought to live. For the enlightened Zen practitioner, the concept of evil is nondualistic, that is, does not depend on contrasts to acknowledge what ought to be avoided:

> Evil is not nonexistent, but simply of "not committing"; evil is not existent, but only of "not-committing." Neither is evil formless but it is of "not-committing," nor is it form but it is of "not-committing." Ultimately speaking, evil is not so much something that "thou shalt not commit" as it is something that resides in [the primordial reality of] "not committing." . . . Such an understanding of the problem [of evil] constitutes the kōan realized—the kōan realizing itself. The problem is examined from the standpoint of subject as well as from the standpoint of object. Such being the case, even if you feel remorse for having committed what ought not to have been committed, you are never alienated [from the primordial reality of "non-committing"], for this very feeling is unmistakably the striving power of "not-committing."[64]

Evil, as for Chuang-Tzu, is not any specific set of things to be avoided, but rather a state of becoming attached to things, precluding our realizing the ultimate reality of emptiness. *The Gengokoan*, which introduces Dōgen's great work, *The Shobogenzo*, expresses the author's commitment to unmasking a nondual awareness and thinking. *Gengo* means becoming manifest, or immediately manifesting, that is, uncovering the presence of things as they are in themselves, untouched by our conscious strivings.[65] Thus we cannot get caught up in external *dharmas* that get in the way of forgetting our attachments to things, ideas, and even ourselves, and that keep us locked into a misleading contrast between "fullness and lack."[66] For the *dharmas* to teach effectively, they must, as Nietzsche claimed of God, die.

Like Nietzsche, Dōgen emphasizes the crucial role of unlearning en route to enlightenment: "To learn the Buddha Way is to learn one's own self. To learn one's self is to forget one's self. To forget one's self is to be confirmed by all dharmas. To be confirmed by all dharmas is to effect the casting off of one's own body and mind and the bodies and minds of others as well. All traces of enlightenment [then] disappear, and this traceless enlightenment is continued on and on endlessly."[67]

Nothing is worth cherishing or hating, no happiness worth algorithmically seeking, no calamity we should go out of our way to avoid. Freedom occurs in a state of presence in which everything is at once synchronous with everything else. In practicing the right way of looking at evil, as a grand absence of badness, in the same way that good is an absence of goods, we make ourselves eligible to experience an equality, or sameness, that transcends inequality, distinction, and by extension attachment. Awakening, *satori*, corresponds to an emptiness of mind in which "no-thing" is valued above any other. If this happens, we can begin to see how states that are troubling in various ethical theories, such as egoism, now evaporate by default rather than through effort. Conversely, the ego will surface immediately on any return to goal-directedness, including one's intentional attempts to overcome it. Things cannot be forced, and there are no signs of expertise. *Shoshin* (beginner's mind) refers simultaneously to the mind-set of the novice practitioner and the bodhisattva. As with Nietzsche, emphasis is on beginnings, rebirths, and the breaking away from the yoke of inherited custom and belief. Unlike Nietzsche and as with the Taoists, however, *shoshin* corresponds to a wakefulness embedded in a spiritual practice—in Dōgen's Zen it is the meditative posture of *zazen*—that ultimately signals a coherent tradition.

Indeed, although the Zen practitioner would be hard-pressed to describe a particular notion of good or evil at work when (forgetfully) aspiring to achieve *shoshin*, we can explanatorily identify a specific notion of the good that the Zen tradition endorses, namely, simplicity and nonsectarianism bereft of hierarchy and division. The notion of evil consistent with such a view is tied to an ethos of democratic humility, equanimity, and omnipresent awakening. It involves an unbroken connection to others of which we are always a constitutive part. There are not things we ought to do or not do, there is simply silent illumination reflected in the freedom from attachment to all things and all oughts.

So conceived, evil becomes a lingering attachment to the goods of the world whose loss we wish not to bear. Disease, injustice, loneliness are material and existential states that, to dwell on in any substantive fashion, lock us into attachment and the craving for permanence in a world of streaming inconstancy. We must therefore learn to look at these things in a different way, that is, as part of the process of something whose negation they signify. (We are back to the anecdote from *Life Is Beautiful* with which we began the chapter.)

We have, then, an ethos of transcendence. An empty mind is no longer subject to the constraints of traditional loss. With the right spiritual training, we are free to overcome the sort of loss and threats to attachment that thrust human beings captive to conventional assumptions into despair. What this in essence means is that with the right kind of thinking, through the achievement of mind-only in meditation, we can conquer any particular trouble (although we cannot think of ourselves as doing this). The individual assumes an unexpected and unusually important role in overcoming misery. Every imaginable thing can fall away if understood as it is, as transitory, as something whose affirmation or negation has no real bearing on languishing or flourishing. Self-transcendence calls for overcoming reasons and affectations, both of which are susceptible to being propped up as static dogma at the expense of the mindful awareness of the subject. Liberation from suffering involves the cessation of any sort of emotional attachment or belief structure compelled by rationality. With such cessation we become attuned to everything around us and its indistinguishableness from everything else, and acquire a dispassionate, preference-free disposition that obtains in selfless other-regard, not by intention, but by default. Good and evil are concepts attention to which prevents the pure consciousness experience that makes dispassionate equanimity possible. This does not mean that in Zen Buddhism good or evil do not exist. It means that talking about them gets us no closer to one or farther away from the other.

Thus, to refer to good or evil meaningfully, the terms must be divested of linguistic content. Goodness is the upshot of cultivating, through spiritual practice, an empty and mindful mental attitude. Evil is the upshot of remaining trapped in the morass of distinction. The point is put beautifully by the Zen scholar and founder of the Kyoto school of philosophy, Kitarō Nishida. Nishida attributes the undesirable consequence of poor living to an errant subject-object dichotomy according to which we make improper divisions between the external world and our internal appropriation of it.

> Subjective consciousness and the objective world are the same thing viewed from different angles, so concretely there is only one fact. As stated before, the world is established by the self's unity of consciousness, and the self is one small system of reality. As emphasized in basic Buddhist thought, the self and the universe share the same foundation; or rather, they are the same thing. . . . To know reality is not to know something external to the self but to know the self itself. The truth, beauty, and good of reality are the truth, beauty, and good of the self. Doubts may arise as to why if this is so we encounter falsehood, ugliness, and evil in the world. When we consider this problem deeply, however, we see that in the world there is neither absolute truth, beauty, and

good, nor absolute falsehood, ugliness, and evil. Falsehood, ugliness, and evil always arise in our viewing abstractly just one aspect of things while we are unaware of the world, and in being partial to just one facet of reality and thereby going against the whole.[68]

Where distinctions and partial realities roam, the ego, selfishness, and evil are not far behind. In the nondualistic worldview of Zen, evil is a misrepresentation: It is neither the same thing as it was before, nor something that can reliably be avoided or set apart. Evil is an absence, but not in the Augustinian sense as privation of the good, that is, the null set of human flourishing, which is very much real. Rather, in Zen, like the good, the referent of evil is a red herring, a shard, something we think helps us organize our world but in fact further distorts reality.

If Dōgen and Kitarō Nishida are right, if the subject envelopes the externally objective, and vice versa, then it is a mistake to think of suffering as referring to specific instances of loss, pain, or grief in life. Suffering is instead the upshot of a misconception in which any one of these instances is assigned undue importance, for in reality such instances, as with everything, are shared. Victims do not own their suffering; rather, they fail to see the interdependence of all things and, as a result, fail to live intersubjectively. It follows that no experienced calamity really changes anything. It is wrong to think of victims in a traditional sense.

What tremendous influence we potentially wield over our well-being. By harnessing the right state of mind, we acquire an immunity over the events that devastate and paralyze us in conventional frameworks. What is at issue with the problem of evil, we are being told, is not the coping preoccupations of theodicy according to which sorrow and suffering present grave challenges to the very idea of meaning. Indeed, the problem of evil is a problem of orienting one's mind, forgetting oneself as a distinct self, with distinct problems, and realizing that one's nature is ultimately impermanent. If there is no I, there is no suffering of an I.

If this is so, then, wonderfully, the problem of evil can be solved. Evil slows us down when we let it. Correspondingly, the remedy for evil is a change in attitude, a putting perspective in perspective. In the Zen tradition such a change, it of course bears noting, is not an easy thing to do. Right-mindedness requires unyielding resolve, which includes overcoming distractions and cravings. The degree of self-mastery required to loosen the grip of traditional distinctions is rare and entails a whole new way of experiencing life. With that new way of experiencing, nevertheless, the crippling effects of calamity and loss, sorrow and despair, dissolve into the seamless stream of all worldly experiences and, eventually, insignificance. Ultimately, albeit not easily, evil can be solved. Suffering, by implication, is of our own making.

Positive Psychology

The Taoist-Buddhist determination that our suffering and sorrow are our decision, as we have seen, is circumstantially supported by the almost Pelagian confidence asserted by Nietzsche and his successors in our ability, through the will, to remake ourselves once freed from the shackles of convention. Both worldviews entail a radical revisioning of self and postulate an avenue away from constraining external realities that are thought to become psychologically hampering if we allow them to be. These traditions' faith in the will's capacity for self-reinvention resonates enough with a separate contemporary attitude, increasing in popularity in this country, that it behooves me to devote some consideration to that tradition here.

The movement to which I am referring is positive psychology, pioneered by Martin Seligman and colleagues in the late 1990s, which expanded the discipline of psychology to focus not just on mental illness or pathology, but also on normal, positive human experience. Its main tenet is that we have the ability to pattern future experience on that which is working successfully, in the present. A quick Internet search of the phrase "positive psychology" yields an association with specific virtues that appear with a frequency worth noting, such as "mindfulness," "flow and forgetfulness," "spiritual awakening," each of which, in their own way, invoke an Eastern exhortation to release oneself from stressful distraction and hone in on harmonious, happy, union with one's larger environment. The home page of Positivepsychology.net reads, "there is an alternative to thinking about people and the world as needing to be fixed." As the site goes on to point out, positive psychologists do not endorse a Pollyannaish denial of evil. They do, however, welcome a shift of emphasis in the disciplines of philosophy and psychology on what is wrong with the world to the "science and anatomy" of "happiness, positive experiences, hope, optimism and altruism." Too much attention in philosophy and the other disciplines is paid to what is wrong with us.[69] According to positive psychologists, optimism can be learned by virtue, of which—following William James's principle of overbelief that belief in a fact can help to create that fact—we have a good measure of control over ensuring good outcomes in the future.[70] In what is arguably the most authoritative manifesto of the movement, Martin Seligman's "Positive Psychology: An Introduction" (co-authored with Mihaly Csikszentmihalyi), the authors state, "A science of positive subjective experience, positive individual traits, and positive institutions promises to improve quality of life and prevent pathologies that arise when life is barren and meaningless."[71] The optimism laden in this statement is striking: a one-size-fits-all remedy to ubiquitous despair in the form of identifying moments of happiness and flourishing, and subsequently focusing one's energies on replicating these experiences.

What does positive psychology have to say about the problem of evil? Seligman, in his introduction, relates a telling anecdote involving his daughter Nikki when she was five and he was weeding in his garden: "Daddy, I want to talk to you." "Yes, Nikki?" "Daddy, do you remember before my fifth birthday? From the time I was three to the time I was five, I was a whiner. I whined every day. When I turned five, I decided not to whine anymore. That was the hardest thing I've ever done. And if I can stop whining, you can stop being such a grouch."[72]

There are legitimate things to whine about in life, but, difficult as it is, if a five-year-old can decide to stop, so can we, and in stopping, have a positive effect on others too. This story is not intended merely to present the transformation of a petulant toddler into a life-affirming little girl; it is, in a much larger sense, about the capacity for deliberate, positive living to counter whatever in life seems beyond our control.

In *The Varieties of Religious Experience*, William James sets up a contrast between those who suffer from a sick soul, who he believes overemphasize the universal problem of evil, and healthy-minded individuals who believe that evil is not a necessary or even essential element of the world.[73] By reinterpreting bad experiences as good, the healthy-minded transform their world and make the rest of us eligible to follow suit. Walt Whitman, one of James's heroes, was, in James's view, unable to feel evil because of his thoroughgoing investment in everything beautiful around him.[74] Whitman was able to deal with "the more evil aspects of the universe by systematically declining to lay them to heart or make much of them by ignoring them in his reflective calculations, or even, on occasion, by denying outright that they exist."[75] A little later in the lecture on the "sick soul" from which this passage comes, James summarizes that in Whitmanism (a Jamesian term that may well have been code for *positive psychology* long before that term was officially coined), evil "is a disease; and worry over disease is itself an additional form of disease, which only adds to the original complaint. Even repentance and remorse, affections which come in the character of ministers of good, may be but sickly and relaxing impulses. The best repentance is to up and act for righteousness, and forget that you ever had relations with sin."[76]

However bad the universe is, we make it worse by dwelling on its fallen state. Again, what we have here is not an overtly Nietzschean denial of evil, but rather an Eastern confidence that right-mindedness is equal to the challenge of staying its execution. In the spirit of James, Seligman suggests not only that positive emotions promote health, a thesis no longer in dispute, but also that through evoking such emotions, the universe itself is altered.[77]

We are back, full circle, to Hume and the passions, and the idea that our passions govern what we interpret reality to be. We have certain innate strengths and virtues that, once identified, can be developed on an individual and societal basis such that the overall quotient of (moral and other) goodness in the universe increases. Not all, but most positive psychologists have signed onto a list of core, cross-culturally identifiable, traits developed in the Character Strengths and Virtues handbook.[78] These six classes of core virtues, which in turn consist of twenty-four measurable character strengths, collectively give the optimistic implication that we are biologically hardwired to add to the level of wisdom, courage, human identification, justice, temperance, and spirituality that currently exist in the universe. We need only also adopt a positive orientation and exert effort. We can, in other words, avail ourselves of what we are already biologically furnished with and amplify it by occupying a productive, creative, positive state of mind. This goes beyond what Aristotle suggested in the *Nicomachean Ethics* when he talked about the centrality of habituation of virtue—requiring some very hard work—for moral development. Success, as it is with regard to the two Eastern traditions just examined, is now defined to be within the immediate grasp of positive psychology's practitioner. Evil is a deterrent to this process only if we let it become that, and even then it is not akin to the ubiquitous metaphysical dread as characterized in, for example, *No Country for Old Men*. Evil is, by contrast, a choice, a looking at the glass half empty for which the person who so looks bears some responsibility. We live, positive psychologists posit, in a culture of fear in which the media and other outlets for disseminating information focus too heavily on our collective human penchant both to do others harm and, as a result, to adopt an unduly pessimistic attitude. Reality, if we choose to see it for what it is, involves a much happier set of circumstances. The philosophers who have spilled so much ink on the problem of evil have gotten it wrong.

Is Evil Illusory? Model Three under Scrutiny

The Nietzschean critique of moralistic convention—intended to keep in check the intellectual, the theologian, or the representative of an institution who wants to impose the constraints of tradition on the individual, and whose lust for condemnation or cooption stifles individual character development—is well taken. As we have seen in the first two chapters, there is a temptation in thinking about evil to essentialize, either by erecting facile categories that demarcate *us* from *them*, or by subsuming the experience of individuals, including victims of horrific atrocity, within a larger narrative about why bad things happen. In both cases, what is evil is predetermined by a governing institution legitimized in history despite the suprahistorical justifications such an institution, perhaps unaware of itself, is wont to proffer. The upshot is sadly too often a witch hunt or whitewashing the experience of those whose victimization does not cohere with the story of which that experience is meant to be an instrumental part. Descriptively, it seems, the perspectivalist critique is a much needed corrective to an oversimplified account of the experience of individuals who are living life, not fulfilling roles in a drama. Nietzsche, Hesse, Foucault, and the Eastern figures we have studied each warn against the temptation to color a reality in advance of living it.

Normatively, perspectivalism also beckons us to make the most of the notion of the will, the distinctively human capacity that enables us to rethink a situation that seems hopeless. It refuses to accept excuses that arrive under the pretext of a Manichean abdication of agency (Satan either acts through us or he doesn't) or the quietism of theodicy (nothing, in the final analysis, has escaped God's watchful eye, nor, because God has been watching all along, should we have wished things turned out any differently). We do not simply inherit the realities through which we then live. How we look at things tailors our experience of these realities. According to Chuang-Tzu and Dōgen, the phenomenological experience of loss is almost always amplified by one's dwelling on it. This is a complication caused by our inability to deemphasize ourselves in attempting to understand the world. The problem, however, can be resolved through reorientation. Positive psychologists, likewise, challenge the rush to pathologize people as problems to be worked on. Hypothesizing instead that we are first and foremost creative forces whose natural affinity for virtue can be replicated by healthy-mindedness and good modeling, we can refocus our attention on the difference we stand to make in our lives and those of others. The third model of evil discussed in this chapter is, to be sure, hopeful. By denying the ubiquity and even consistency of evil, the model challenges assumptions once deemed beyond questioning, thereby daring the human spirit to rise above its familiar failures and roadblocks. Seeking to construe as oppressive a resignation to which we might have once become accustomed, the figures we have examined in this chapter throw the existential ball, as it were, back in our court, insisting that we face a future that is, correctly understood, radically underdetermined.

This said, the extent to which this model gets evil remains to be seen. Just how free are we to flourish in a world replete with material lack, unchecked cruelty, intractable injustice, and a rampant callousness that all too frequently seems to be the response to these forms of misery? The third model unveils the way those that rise to power take on a status as ontological givens. But it is a big leap from this historical-genealogical assessment to a different ontological claim, namely, the denial of evil. Although the unmasking of power to which Foucault, for example, dedicated his scholarly attention is indispensable for holding Manichean self-righteousness at bay, and although the ways in which we define socially deviant behavior or mental illness tend to say as much about us as they do those we objectify, criminally unreachable psychopaths do exist in our world. What is to be said in a Foucauldian analysis about this particular assertion, that psychopaths, perhaps to be understood as Satan's minions, exist? Is there irreducible evil in the world? Terry Eagleton, for one, has his doubts. Commenting on a recent famous case in northern England involving the torture and subsequent murder of a toddler at the hand of two ten-year-old boys, Eagleton observes,

> A police officer involved in the case . . . declared that the moment he clapped eyes on one of the culprits, he knew that he was evil. This is the kind of thing that gives evil a bad name. The point of literally demonising the boy in this way was to wrong-foot the softhearted liberals. It was a preemptive strike against those who might appeal to social conditions in seeking to understand why they did what they did. And such an understanding can always bring forgiveness in its wake. Calling the action evil meant that it was beyond comprehension.[79]

Rightly responding to the tendency of some in a position of authority to sidestep the hard work of getting into the particulars of a case, Eagleton nevertheless avails himself of his own conversation-stopper: We ought always to resist giving evil a bad name lest we forgo an opportunity to understand better and maybe revise our view of an evildoer's self-understanding. Granting this police officer's rush to judgment, is it not still fair to assert that, like pornography, evil, hard as it is to define, is often recognizable when we encounter it? As Charles Mathewes rightly notes, a misuse of language does not necessarily amount to condemnation of language's proper use.[80] By habitually straw-manning the acknowledgers of evil as "othering" Manicheanists, one dismisses out of hand the scores of incomprehensible examples of willful torturing, often state-sanctioned, for which human history ought to answer. Eagleton therefore engages in his own shortcut with commentary: "An English Evangelical bishop wrote in 1991 that clear signs of Satanic possession included inappropriate laughter, inexplicable knowledge, a false smile, Scottish ancestry, relatives who have been coal miners, and the habitual choice of black for dress or car color.

None of this makes any sense, but then that is how it is with evil. The less sense it makes, the more evil it is. Evil has no relations to anything beyond itself, such as a cause."[81]

Is this really how it is with evil, or for that matter, a fair way of characterizing Eagleton's critics? Eagleton correctly contends that many in the established order are self-servingly bent on becoming the megaphones through which the menace of evil is declared to the world. However, granting as much should not imply, ipso facto, that all harsh characterizations of evil and evildoers are oversimplifications because events that defy meaning are inflicted by one party and suffered by another. We must seriously ask whether such a characterization is a lazy romanticizing of evil, as Eagleton would suggest it is.

At least four issues must be addressed to render a verdict. The first is descriptive. Is evil something in our heads only or does it exist as an external reality? The second is theoretical and normative and addresses the ethical tenability of ethical subjectivism and even nihilism. Is it true that there are no objective standards for right or wrong, no objective good for human beings? If not, why not? Third, there is some question about whether physical suffering or psychological sorrow is as reinterpretable as the perspectivalist suggests. The optimism inherent in the judgment that healthy-mindedness can trump despair seems unrealistic and perhaps not attentive to the victim's experience. Critics are likely to allege that Eastern reconstruals of selfhood fundamentally sidestep, and maybe even provide false hope for, the ability to avoid an impending or already occurring loss. Finally, the perspectivalist must withstand the Augustinian charge that the view is too Pelagian, ascribing more power and wherewithal to the will than could actually ever be present in the face of unexpected and calamitous upheaval. Finitude, the Augustinian points out, requires due appreciation of our mortality and vulnerability, which are fundamentally beyond rather than within our control. This final critique is principally theological and invokes theocentric notions such as humility and sinfulness.

First is the question of description: is evil only in our heads or also in the world? Does evil, to adopt Eagleton's parlance, have relations to anything beyond itself? If not, if it is primarily a construct of our making, then evil is, at the very least, not intrinsically or absolutely bad. It would instead be a reflection of our own hermeneutic exercise, independent of what is happening in the world, and moral agency no longer implies a subjective conforming to an objective law, as Kant thought. On this account, we are morally bound only to the degree we let ourselves be. Does this description accurately reflect the moral agent's experience? Or, for that matter, a victim's experience? Is it an adequate reflection of victims' control over their experiences? In short, does the perspectivalist view represent a plausible solution to the problem of evil? Do we buy—do we have the luxury of buying—the descriptive premise of *Life Is Beautiful* in which a father finds a way to make the Holocaust palatable for his son?

Nietzsche happily announces that the problem of evil is a red herring from which a mature self is liberated. A proclamation alone, however, does nothing to deliver us from our loneliness. It does not resolve the philosophical paralysis to which Camus thinks we are subject when we consider what he calls the absurdity of life: a universe indifferent to our concerns.[82] Thinkers in the tradition of Freud and Nietzsche, who in the contemporary era see themselves as having grown up about the problem of evil, like Richard Rorty, in the end offer us neither a strategy to deal with the harmful elements of society, most distant from the good, nor a therapy to help us overcome the malaise that overtakes us in the solipsism of their proposed universe.[83] At best, he and those in his school offer ad hoc measures to cope with the unpleasant. We can adjust our focus such that our time behind bars in this life becomes more tolerable, but in prison we remain. In the final analysis, this criticism asserts, perspectivalism, and in particular its criticism of the rhetoric of evildoing, amount to mythologized evil. In saying that evil is not really evil but rather the psychological handicap of our decision to buy into one among many optional ways of looking at the world, we end up repressing a truth we would be better off confronting.[84]

Moreover, as Claudia Card points out, the paradigmatic authoritative voice in speaking to the reality of evil is that of the victim, the one to whom evil happens, not the subject, the prospective evil-causer. Pointing out a distorting bias in the Nietzschean rebellion against the standard modes of valuation, Card elucidates:

> In his critique, Nietzsche appears to identify with the perspectives of conquerors in that he sees their victims as one might expect conquerors to see them, referring, for example, to conquered peoples with the derogatory terms "herd," "rabble," and "masses," rather than, say, "the folk" (which would be more respectful). Even in his characterizations of the perspectives of the dominated, Nietzsche seems to be looking through the eyes of the powerful and imagining from that vantage point what their subordinates must be seeing. The result is an arrogant distortion of the character and experience of common folk.[85]

It is as if, Card suggests, slaves have bought into their own slave-morality, a choice they have made to negotiate power strata, a survival strategy to deflect the threat of abuse.[86] Although those in society who are stripped of power sometimes play the roles assigned to them, such an account does not begin to exhaust the number of scenarios in which the powerless are subject to unspeakable harm and humiliation. Card alludes to a couple of poignant examples that a Nietzschean analysis of the slave's experience fails to appreciate:

> Consider Harriet Jacobs, who in 1861 published her memoirs of slavery under the pseudonym Linda Brent. Describing thoughts that she had while still a slave, she wrote, "When I lay down beside my child, I felt how much easier it would be to see her die than to see her master beat her about, as I daily saw him beat other little ones." Harriet Jacobs refused a Northern white woman's offer to purchase her from her master (in order to free her), on the ground that this would be too much like being passed from one master to another. (The white woman did it anyway.) Toni Morrison's novel *Beloved* tells the story of a mother who acted on the same values as Harriet Jacobs, choosing death for her children rather than allowing them to be recaptured. The history of Masada in 73 C.E. is an instance in which a Jewish community is said to have chosen death by their own hands over enslavement by Romans. These do not sound like the Jewish values of which Nietzsche complains in the *Genealogy*.[87]

Nietzsche simply fails to give attention to the intolerable wrongdoing and injury victims often suffer at the hands of their oppressors. Nietzsche aptly identifies the abuse with which a calcified concept like that of evil can be used to legitimate historically contingent occupiers of power. In his campaign, however, he neglects to appreciate the destructive content of evil acts, acts about which we need a sufferer's account to fully understand. As Emmanuel Levinas reminds us, the experience of the victim can never be theorized in advance of the face-to-face encounter.[88] We must, in light of Levinas's observation, seriously ask ourselves whether an outpouring of sentimental expression following a genocidal world event like the Holocaust is the result of self-conscious victimhood of the sort Nietzsche thinks it is time to outgrow or, rather, part of a genuine grieving process that calls our attention to what would otherwise be unthinkable. Evil, in other words, motivates a response that goes beyond mere role fulfillment. The basic goods tantamount to human flourishing that it denies its victims preclude our characterizing it simply as a perspective.

The second issue with which the perspectivalist must contend pertains to the belief that underlying notions of right and wrong are nothing more than preferences. This is a normative critique of the third model. Nietzsche and especially Hesse argue that what we should do in this world is what we would do unconstrained in the state of nature. We lose our way, in their view, when we succumb to burdens brought on by convention and society; we have the ability to find our way if we return to what strikes us as more natural. Hence, we ought neither to believe the institutionalized narratives that direct us in

ways that thwart our self-development nor trust that the standard dichtomiz-
ations, such as Abel and Cain, correspond to what is bad or good for us, regardless of our idiosyncratic needs and context. The concern is whether the
preferencing of preferences, the triumph of the aesthetic over the normative,
leads to a version of ethical naturalism according to which moral properties are
never reducible to anything beyond what is manifest in the natural world. Can
instinct and natural impulse lead us in the wrong moral direction? If so, it seems
sensible not to travel there. To follow Hesse's Demian out of the morass of
adolescence is to deny vociferously that sources of ethics bear down on us from
the outside, even if that outside is merely an outside that is outside ourselves,
such as the welfare and well-being of another. Thus, it is in essence tantamount
to a denial of other-regard in general, unless other-regard turns out to be an
upshot of the certain path of self-development down which we choose to walk.
The problem is that ethical naturalists announce the denial of moral imperatives; they do not necessarily show that they do not exist. It may be the case
that we are not quite so free to determine for ourselves our own moral good. If
we were, there would be good reasons to feel guilt, remorse, contrition; these
states wouldn't be interpreted as the residue of some fraudulent ideology we
have swallowed whole.

The ethical issue with perspectivalism is similar to that raised against the
Manichean view of evil discussed in chapter 1: In each case we are, as moral
agents, absolved of responsibility to become certain sorts of persons and not
others. In perspectivalism's glorification of the aesthetic, in which beauty can
potentially be found in anything if we look at it the right way, our ability to
make use of significant normative concepts like praiseworthiness and blameworthiness, and to engage in crucial forms of moral judgment, such as approval
and critique, atrophies. An adequate conception of evil should have a conceptual apparatus that equips us to condemn, for example, callousness as a trait, to
say nothing of callous persons. Malicious conduct ought not to be explained
away as a lifestyle choice. The inadequacy of a perspectivalism that moves
beyond good and evil is revealed in even a rudimentary self-examination, as,
for example, in those instances when we are aware of the extent to which we
are being selfish by betraying someone we love, or by neglecting someone in
need. Regardless of whether the word *guilt* does justice to the sense of dismay
or alarm we experience when we perceive such feelings arise within us, it is
disingenuous to dismiss the feelings as ersatz psychological baggage we can
shed with the right sort of reinvention. We affect the world, but the world
affects us as well. As limited beings subject to finitude, we do not have the
wherewithal to redescribe our way out of the many ways we are hardwired to
be deficient. Whether known by sin or something else, the wound with which

we live daily that causes us to hurt ourselves and to hurt others surfaces of its own accord. Any consolation that fails to acknowledge this experience, which we do not fully control, will not stick.

What is at issue here is Nietzsche's claim in *The Birth of Tragedy* that morality is a fraud:

> For confronted with morality (especially Christian or unconditional morality) life *must* continually and inevitably be in the wrong, because life *is* something essentially amoral—and eventually, crushed by the weight of contempt and eternal No, life *must* then be felt to be unworthy of desire and altogether worthless. Morality itself—how now? Might not morality be a will to negate life; a secret instinct of annihilation, a principle of decay, diminution, and slander—the beginning of the end? Hence, the danger of dangers?[89]

To accept that the aesthetic trumps ethics, to regard morality as a "danger of dangers," one must accept that self-exploitation is the upshot of all instances of other-regard and that the alleviation of suffering others is never in itself an enterprise that warrants our unconditional and morally binding attention. Such a view flies in the face not only of the insights of moral theorists from a wide variety of backgrounds and traditions, but also the firsthand experiences of moral heroes and saints who report with compelling and consistent frequency the fulfilling nature of their heroic and saintly sacrificial acts.[90] The meaning of life, for such individuals, does not occur in the denial of suffering but in our attention to it. Why should we take Nietzsche's word for it when he asserts that when heroes and saints claim they are fulfilled in service to needy others, they are really fooling themselves? We could invoke countless testimonials on the part of such individuals claiming that human dignity accrues in proportion to our willingness to go out of our way to heal the world.[91] The last ten years have witnessed an explosion of research testifying to the health benefits associated with altruistic living, adding scientific credence to the long-standing assertion on the part of the world's saints that human fulfillment is inexorably linked to the performance of saintly deeds.[92]

More to the point, however, even if this did not turn out to be the case—even if no evidence linked human flourishing to other-regard—Nietzsche does little more than to announce that what we ought to do is what is most accessible to us in terms of self-interest. Nietzsche, Hesse, and others arguably commit the naturalist fallacy: They derive from facts of nature the set of principles on which to construct any prospective viable ethical theory. It is far from clear, however, that this is a justified basis for imperatives for living. Although *ought* implies *is* (i.e., what lies within the realm of possibility), *is* does not indicate what *ought* should be. Nietzsche's suggestion that the oft-heard moral claim "shun evil" is tantamount to an ascetic denial of human development is at most offered as a playful hypothesis rather than an actual argument meant successfully to dismantle an objective theory of the good. As such, it does not go very far toward undoing existential arguments for human solidarity (e.g., Camus), neo-Aristotelian accounts of societal virtues it behooves us always to strive to preserve (e.g., Nussbaum), a radical ethics of alterity that places the moral imperative squarely in the face and passionate gaze of the other (e.g., Levinas), or—Nietzsche's primary targets—traditional religious groundings of a commandment to love the neighbor in a prior divine commandment to love God. That the latter is subject to corruption, as Nietzsche genealogically demonstrates, is not enough to show that the central Christian virtues of charity and love of the neighbor are themselves falsehoods. A hermeneutic of suspicion at best raises questions about the commitments of established worldviews. The hypothesis of amorality is a provocative challenge to ethics preached in the name of morality, but it is not a convincing argument against morality itself.

The third issue that warrants our attention is with regard to the optimism inherent in the claim that evil is a merely a viewpoint that can be willed away with a new and better attitude. This claim can arguably be read into the Taoist and Buddhist literature examined in this chapter as well as into positive psychology. How far will a positive attitude take us in the face of unspeakable horror? Our world contains no shortage of such examples. In *Humanity: A Moral History of the Twentieth Century*, the historian Jonathan Glover describes with uncharacteristic accuracy and comprehensiveness the worldwide commission of crimes against humanity perpetrated in the last century, by far our bloodiest on record. The total impression of these examples is to leave the reader dumbfounded, grasping for meaning in a world that is so arbitrarily "artfully cruel" (Ivan Karamazov's phrase). Here is but one of many graphic examples to which Glover alludes in response to any philosophical or theological optimism that forecasts harmonious recovery from what our universe will sometimes have us experience:

[Consider] what the Turks did in Bulgaria, where they burnt, killed and raped women and children. They hanged prisoners after first making them spend their last night nailed by the ear to a fence. ("No animal could ever be so cruel as a man, so artfully, so artistically cruel.") They used daggers to cut babies out of women's wombs. They tossed nursing infants in the air, catching them on bayonets: "the main delight comes from doing it before their mothers' eyes."[93]

What are our prospects for hoping for harmonious reconciliation and faith in the goodness of the universe following such instances of cruelty? We need not go to the extreme flank of immorality to ask the same question. A mundane example from the normal life cycle is enough. For example, what, if any, are the limits of hope in the face of a terminal cancer diagnosis? The surgeon Bernie Siegel argues in *Love, Medicine, and Miracles* that cancer is something that arises from negative feelings.[94] The well-known author and sociologist Barbara Ehrenreich recounts her encounter with Siegel and company after she was diagnosed with breast cancer. Seeking online support among fellow sufferers, Ehrenreich discovered to her dismay a surprising percentage of victims, inspired by Siegel's writings, that had come to develop a love of their illness ("If I had to do it over, would I want breast cancer? Absolutely," said one. "I am happier now than I have ever been in my life," said another).[95] The implication is that if one fails to hope, one brings about one's disease. By extension, one has the power, through hope, to undo what one has brought on oneself. The logic of such an analysis quickly becomes a version of blaming the victim. In such a view, the evil of cancer is understated, the subjective capacity to will cancer away is overstated, and in the meantime the precious time one has left is in danger of being squandered due to both false impressions. Clearly, hope ought not to replace criticism, sober reflection, and a realism that protects rather than spoils the resources one still has at one's disposal.

This is not to say that hope has no role in the face of calamity. However bad things get, it behooves us to grant, with positive psychologists, that the right attitude can make them better. To steel oneself to cope with the aftermath of a traumatic occurrence, to avail oneself of the resources with which one becomes equipped to face the future, to try to find meaning among the ashes—these are all life-affirming activities that can make a terrible situation a little less terrible. None of them, it nevertheless needs to be pointed out, imply that the precipitating crisis was illusory. A wonderful fable from Taoist lore tells of a farmer who was skilled at interpreting events:

> One day, for no reason, his son's horse ran away to the nomads across the border. Everyone tried to console the son, but his father said, "What makes you so sure this isn't a blessing?" Some months later the horse returned, bringing a splendid nomad stallion. Everyone congratulated the son, but his father said, "What makes you so sure this isn't a disaster?" Their household was richer by a fine horse, which his son loved to ride. One day he fell and broke his hip. Everyone tried to console him, but his father said, "What makes you so sure this isn't a blessing?" A year later the nomads came in force across the border, and every able-bodied man took his bow and went

into battle. The Chinese frontiersmen lost nine of every ten men. Only because the son was lame did the father and son survive to take care of each other. Truly, blessing turns to disaster, and disaster to blessing: the changes have no end, nor can the mystery be fathomed.[96]

Reminiscent of Chuang-Tzu's observation that "a state in which 'this' and 'that' no longer find their opposites is called the hinge of the Way," the anonymous author of this Chinese folktale cautions the sufferer prone to a dour disposition not to have too much confidence in his or her description of the events that have transpired. Here is a thought experiment: apply this wisdom not to the mysterious disappearance or return of a favored horse, but rather to the concrete, simple, and horrifying occurrence of a baby being caught on a bayonet. Suddenly, the Janus-faced account of how disasters are blessings and vice versa seems a tad misplaced. To reinterpret some events as the opposite of what they seem is to do them a descriptive injustice and leave the victim without redress as well.

In addition, it is not clear that erasing the memory of a loss (e.g., by no longer understanding loss as loss), rather than grieving that loss, is desirable. Here theodicists have an objection to raise against perspectivalism. By removing suffering from human experience, we lose an invaluable teaching moment, namely, the pedagogically redemptive moment of suffering, a moment tantamount to bringing about a larger good. It is in our existential best interests, this argument runs, to go through darkness to get to the light. In is in the victim's best interest to approach evil first by identifying it as such and then by dealing with it. This, I think, captures the gist of the offense Barbara Ehrenreich took at Bernie Siegel's disciples when she looked for a community of fellow cancer copers. As beings of finitude we are delicate, vulnerable, and fragile, privy at best to the ephemeral enjoyment of all things human and prone to decay, suffering, loss, and ultimately death.[97] We would lose something dear were we to be deprived of any of the key aspects of the human life cycle, including the painful ones. This is not to deny the significant respects in which right-mindfulness has the capacity to improve the existential malaise and resignation that ensues when we despair over dreadful things that happen to us—just as long as the attitude adjustment supplements rather than supplants the reality it is intended to ameliorate.

This observation leads to a final issue about perspectivalism, reminiscent of the Augustinian criticism of Pelagianism, which faults the doctrine for forecasting the possibility of human redemption without divine assistance. The perspectivalist account overemphasizes the role of human freedom in the face of moral turpitude, crisis, loss, and death. According to the Augustinian worldview, the inevitability of sin and the fall taint human nature to such an extent that we are prone to hurting one another in significant ways, repeating our mistakes despite this self-awareness, and ultimately lacking the ability to act responsibly in lieu of God's grace. The Pelagian doctrine, by contrast, posits a confidence in our ability to choose to do the right thing and, in effect, imbue life with meaning and moral purpose on our own. What is at stake here, for our purposes, is not so much the debate over the lasting impact of original sin, as the appropriateness of conceiving of voluntary choice as a viable solution to the problem of evil. Theological commitments aside, how free are we in this world to choose to do the right thing, or to recover when we become victims? How much control do we have? Are we fallen, and if so, what are our prospects for rising? What, exactly, does it mean to suggest that as human beings we are creatures who are free?

The Augustinian answer to this question is, "yes, we are free, but our freedom is not easy." Finitude, a condition without which we cannot know what it is to be human, carries the price of never being able to lift ourselves out of history and transcend the vulnerability we have both to hurting others and to being hurt. Too often life puts us in a situation in which we have no option but to choose between relatively tragic options. At such times, committing or enduring a lesser of evils is the best we can do. Denying that we suffer or cause others to suffer does little to undo the existential reality of suffering. Rather, it puts that reality on hold until a time we are ready to face it. Part of that reality, in the Augustinian account, involves a responsibility for having ushered evil into the world; to deny it when it becomes psychologically inconvenient would be both delusional and irresponsible.

To say as much is not a concession to Manichean determinism. We do, both in Augustinian and secular worldviews, for example, have the ability to acquire self-knowledge, and, in turn, submit in humility to what is beyond our control. In Augustinian theocentrism, such knowledge will propel us to condition ourselves to receive God's grace, a precondition for redemption. In secular worldviews, self-knowledge staves off the self-righteousness that accompanies reinventing oneself. Realizing our propensity to succumb to a life bereft of virtue, we at the very least can begin to recognize the ease with which our participation in the world can lapse into inhumanity. Both cases call for an indefatigable vigilance. Thus, unlike Manicheanism, our unwilling and potentially malicious participation in a destructive drama that unfolds is something we can—with difficulty—do something about. This said, something is not everything. The struggle to do the right thing and find meaning when we have done or suffered wrongs is ongoing. Staving off resignation and despair is piecemeal, comes in spurts, and is often hard-won.

For Augustine, the source of goodness is not within human beings; only God can perform the creative act of goodness. Hence the health of the world is outside the control of human beings. Again, momentarily bracketing Augustine's theocentric approach to conceiving of good and evil, the question arises on the extent to which humans have control over their potential to flourish as well as to enable others, across the globe, to do the same. Let us for the moment be particularly interested in the second part: the flourishing of others suffering under enormous disadvantage. Do the optimism and right-mindedness recommended in various respects by the figures we have examined in this chapter have the ability to repair a world that, in Augustine's words, entertains a ubiquitous "wretchedness?"[98] As with some versions of theodicy, it seems at the very least reminiscent of quietism, and maybe even a little escapist, to invoke a prerogative to opt out of history and write our own story. To the extent we, by adjusting our expectations and overcoming our disparate attachments in the world, transcend wretchedness, it seems that the flight from distinctions and the corresponding unwillingness to engage in the language game of good and evil does little to change a sick world we have inherited under circumstances not of our own choosing, but for which we are no less responsible. Radically subjective engagement with the world perhaps obtains in successful self-transcendence, but at the expense of leaving the world behind. We must seriously ask whether this sort of freedom is worth its price in the enduring enslavement of others. What good is a solution to the problem of evil that abandons the world to its problems?

In the end, perspectivalism, and in particular its emphasis on the human subject as the locus of all created reality, is inimical to our efforts to absorb, appreciate, and do something about evil because it deflects our attention from the many ways in which we are already implicated in its advent. In short, it is to be found wanting because it is not a sufficiently responsible answer either to our unwitting participation in wrongdoing, or to our or others' suffering. Perspectivalism unilaterally announces our invulnerability to evil but leaves us no less vulnerable. A better response must address both the internal and external components of immorality and suffering.

Notes

1. Mary Midgley makes this claim on behalf of Nietzsche. See *Wickedness*, 32. To treat Nietzsche in any other fashion, Midgley suggests, is to strip from him one of the things that makes him of most value, namely, the pedagogical corrective that emerges in his perennial stance of standing against.

2. Nietzsche, *The Birth of Tragedy*, 59.

3. Ibid., 62.

4. Nietzsche, *Beyond Good and Evil*, 52.

5. Byrne, *The Secret*, 28.

6. Ibid., 164.

7. Mathewes, *Evil and the Augustinian Tradition*, 52.

8. Ibid.

9. What Mathewes describes is reminiscent of Peter Berger's classic theory about our search of a stable *nomos* according to which we incorrectly believe we discover the norms that we actually create. Motivated by a desire to avoid *anomie* in the form of (for example) the absence of organized religion, we project the content of this organization out onto the cosmos. Through three stages by which we so project—externalization, objectification, and internalization—Berger outlines the process by which the norms we introduce ultimately become legitimized. See *The Sacred Canopy*. The anthropologist Clifford Geertz presents a similar theory in *The Interpretation of Cultures*, see especially chapter 4, "Religion as a Cultural System."

10. See Hume, *A Treatise of Human Nature* and Hume, *Enquiries Concerning Human Understanding*, especially sections 7 and 10. Susan Neiman characterizes Hume's account of evil in a similar manner. See Neiman, *Evil in Modern Thought*, 42.

11. Hume, *Treatise of Human Nature*, book III, 468–69.

12. James, *Pragmatism*, 6–7.

13. Hume, *Treatise on Human Nature*, 457–58; James, "The Will to Believe," 11.

14. Rorty, "The Priority of Democracy to Philosophy."

15. A beautiful example of this occurs in Mary Doria Russell's *The Sparrow*, discussed in chapter 2, which portrays a specific act as a violent rape through the interpretive lens of one party that is seen as a socially sanctioned ritual from the point of view of another. Russell's novel, among other things, represents an instance of nontranslatability.

16. MacIntyre has made this claim at several points in his work. See, for example, *Whose Justice? Which Rationality?*, especially chapter 14, "Tradition and Translation." MacIntyre says we can "translate" by learning a second first language and by practicing hermeneutical innovation on our own. "Justification," according to MacIntyre, occurs at a local and not a global level, but he does allow a role for first principles, making possible universally applicable truth claims.

17. Nietzsche, *Beyond Good and Evil*, 13.

18. Nietzsche, *On the Genealogy of Morals*, 456.

19. Nietzsche, *The Antichrist*, 572–73.

20. Nietzsche, *Thus Spoke Zarathustra*, quoted in Kaufmann, *Nietzsche*, 367. This is not to say that Nietzsche is not in favor of a type of measured neighbor love construed as a mature friendship bereft of a manipulative rhetoric of pity. Such a friendship presumably entails that right symbiotic environment for the promotion of virtue.

21. Kaufmann, *Nietzsche*, 367.

22. As Kaufmann notes, it is hard to establish the extent to which Nietzsche intended to distinguish pity from, for example, sympathy and compassion, arguably deeper and more defensible virtues that, unlike pity, can be better divorced from connotations of weakness.

23. Nietzsche, *Daybreak*, 60.

24. See, in particular, the third essay of *On the Genealogy of Morals*, 538.

25. Kaufmann, *Nietzsche*, 109–10.

26. Nietzsche, *Will to Power*, 17–18.

27. Ibid.

28. Ibid., 160–63.

29. This, again, represents one of the tricky instances of how one should read Nietzsche. Although the revaluation of values implies that jettisoning of any fixed sense of normativity in the respect I describe, it does not necessarily imply the getting rid of normativity as such, for judgment itself is an enabling condition of a new value coming to replace or modify a former value. Not surprisingly, the extent to which Nietzsche is therefore to be understood as a normative thinker is vigorously debated.

30. An almost Habermasian strain of Nietzsche's intellectual legacy, attributable to Foucault, emphasizes procedural over substantive norms, but, with more emphasis on power and less on communicability than Habermas would have found comfortable.

31. Hesse, *Demian*, 23–24.

32. Ibid.

33. Ibid., 95.

34. Ibid., 40–41.

35. Ibid., 78.

36. Hesse, *Siddhartha*, 115.

37. See, for example, Lincoln, *Holy Terrors*, for a close comparison of the rhetoric of George W. Bush and Osama bin Laden as well as Vidal, *Perpetual War*, for a rare instance of apologetics on behalf of Timothy McVeigh. Vidal construes McVeigh as a destructive but misunderstood patriot with substantial grievances against his nation that deserve a hearing. Vidal, as I read him, goes a good distance toward excusing McVeigh for the Oklahoma City bombings that killed 168 people and wounded hundreds more. Vidal argues that once McVeigh's actions are appropriately evaluated in light of the context of the thoroughly corrupt government in which he hatched his plot, we will come to see just how relative a term *terrorist* is.

38. This is the thesis of the popular and critically acclaimed film, *American Beauty*, rife with Nietzschean themes. In the vein of Hesse's Damien, the sympathetic character Ricky argues that literally everything in life can be seen as beautiful once properly appreciated. Ricky puts his theory into practice near the end of the film when, upon discovering the murdered body of his girlfriend's father, Lester, he appears to absorb the scene with a gleeful, knowing, glint in his eye. This sad moment arguably represents the triumph of the aesthetic over the normative.

39. Hesse, "Thoughts on 'The Idiot.'" The book in which the essay appears is out of print but the essay, written in 1919, can be found online at www.gss.ucsb.edu/projects/hesse/works/idiot.pdf.

40. Hari, "Gore Vidal's United States of Fury."

41. See Rudolph and Rudolph, *Gandhi*, 56; Caplan, *Cultural Construction*, 278.

42. Dyson, *I Might Not Get There*, 139–51 (on King's plagiarism) and 216–21 (on his womanizing).

43. Foucault, *Power/Knowledge*, 156.

44. Foucault, "Space, Knowledge and Power," 247.

45. Connolly, "Beyond Good and Evil," 366.

46. Baynes, Bohman, and McCarthy, *After Philosophy*, 95.

47. Foucault, *Power/Knowledge*, 131, quoted by Baynes, Bohman, and McCarthy, *After Philosophy*, 97.

48. Connolly, "Beyond Good and Evil," 366.

49. Jameson, *Fables of Aggression*, 56.

50. Frankfurter, *Evil Incarnate*, 12.

51. Foucault, *The Essential Works*, 298–99.

52. Eribon, *Michel Foucault*, 282.

53. Chuang-Tzu, *Basic Writings*, 34–35.

54. Lao-Tzu, *Te-Tao Ching*, 54. Emphasis added.

55. Ivanhoe, "Zhuangzi on Skepticism;" Ivanhoe, "Was Zhuangzi a Relativist?"

56. Ivanhoe, "Was Zhuangzi a Relativist?" 201.

57. Chuang Tzu, *Basic Writings*, 43.

58. Ibid., 45.

59. Ivanhoe, "Zhuangzi on Skepticism," 642–43.

60. Ibid., 645.

61. Lee, "Finely Aware and Richly Responsible," 531.

62. Levinas, *Totality and Infinity*, 93. Of course, for Levinas there is the additional qualification that the infinite embracing of the Other also represents the precondition of all moral consciousness. See p. 84.

63. Chuang Tzu, *Basic Writings*, 78. This is not to say that Taoism is ideologically open to any action. One could not be a good (i.e., skillful) Taoist murderer or self-interested deceiver, for example, because such activities are inherently reliant first, on the positing of a distinction between self and other, and second, on a betrayal of a concerted effort to act on behalf of the former.

64. Dōgen, quoted by Kim, *Dōgen Kigen*, 216.

65. Waddell and Abe, "Introduction to the Shobogenzo Genjokoan," 130.

66. Kigen, "Shobogenzo Genjokoan," 33.

67. Ibid., 134–35.

68. Nishida, "An Inquiry into the Good," 143.

69. Positive psychologists would certainly take issue, for example, with Susan Neiman's claim that the problem of evil is the primary issue around which philosophy and intellectual thought since the beginning of the modern era ought to be organized. See Neiman, *Evil in Modern Thought*, 3–8.

70. James, *The Will to Believe*, 25.

71. Seligman and Csikszentmihalyi, "Positive Psychology," 5.

72. Ibid., 6.

73. James, *The Varieties of Religious Experience*, 88.

74. Ibid., 79.

75. Ibid., 88.

76. Ibid.

77. Seligman and Csikszentmihalyi, "Positive Psychology," 10.

78. The six classes of virtues and strengths enumerated in the CSV are wisdom and knowledge, courage, humanity, justice, temperance, and transcendence. It should be

pointed out that this list has been both debated internally, among positive psychologists themselves, and contested externally, particularly with regard to the sixth, transcendence, which signals an appreciation of spirituality.

79. Eagleton, *On Evil*, 2.

80. Mathewes, *Evil and the Augustinian Tradition*, 50.

81. Eagleton, *On Evil*, 3.

82. Camus, *Myth of Sisyphus*, 40.

83. Mathewes, *Evil and the Augustinian Tradition*, 21.

84. Ibid., 23, 51.

85. Card, *Atrocity Paradigm*, 34.

86. Ibid., 42.

87. Ibid., 43–44.

88. See Levinas, *Otherwise than Being*.

89. Nietzsche, *Birth of Tragedy*, 23.

90. Flescher, *Heroes, Saints*.

91. A great example is Martin Luther King's speech, "I've Been to the Mountaintop," in which King states his preference to live in the second half of the twentieth century, when, as he put it, "the world was all messed up," so as to have the opportunity to attend to it. See King, *Testament of Hope*, 279.

92. See Post, *Altruism and Health*.

93. Glover, *Humanity*, 2.

94. Siegel, *Love, Medicine, and Miracles*.

95. Ehrenreich, "Welcome to Cancerland," www.barbaraehrenreich.com/cancerland.htm.

96. Langer, *Power of Mindful Learning*, 99–100.

97. See especially Nussbaum, *Fragility of Goodness*.

98. St. Augustine, *City of God*, book XIX.6, 860. In this passage, Augustine explains the inherent imperfection of meting out justice in the world. In the case of torturing innocents, Augustine explains the ease with which those in a position to judge inevitably lapse into self-righteousness upon rendering their judgments. This is a situation that stems from ignorance on the part of the punisher and leads to unwarranted condemnation on the part of the accused, and yet it is inescapable in such a world as ours of "darkness that attends to the life of human society." Hence Augustine's pessimistic diagnosis: "All these serious evils our philosopher does not reckon as sins; for the wise judge does not act in this way through a will to do harm, but because ignorance is unavoidable—and yet the exigencies of human society make judgment also unavoidable. Here we have what I call the wretchedness of man's situation."

CHAPTER FOUR

Evil as the Absence of Goodness

Privation and the Ubiquity of Wickedness

"People hasten to judge in order not to be judged themselves. What do you expect? The idea that comes most naturally to man, as if from his very nature, is the idea of his innocence. From this point of view, we are all like that little Frenchman at Buchenwald who insisted on registering a complaint with the clerk, himself a prisoner, who was recording his arrival. A complaint? The clerk and his comrades laughed: 'Useless old man. You don't lodge a complaint here.' 'But you see, sir,' said the little Frenchman, 'my case is exceptional. I am innocent!'

We are all exceptional cases. We all want to appeal against something! Each of us insists on being innocent at all cost, even if he has to accuse the whole human race and heaven itself."

—JEAN-BAPTISTE CLÉMENT, of Albert Camus's *The Fall*

Evil and Character

JEAN-BAPTISTE, CAMUS'S UPSTANDING CITIZEN who slowly unravels in the wake of a decisive moment of moral paralysis, laments a lost innocence whose recovery is eternally beyond him, and, from his perspective, beyond each of us. In the quoted passage Jean-Baptiste describes the avocation he has taken up, that of a judge-penitent: one who judges others as a way of deflecting introspection and self-diagnosis in service of real reform. Innocence here assumes an almost mythical sense: It pertains not just to freedom from responsibility but also to freedom from the condition of having to be responsible. In lieu of innocence, life becomes very hard work, a chore to live well given that we are in the first instance so prone to self-absorption. To face our inadequacies is to surrender to them, realize we are not self-sufficient beings, and admit that our failings and struggles are not entirely external. In the portrayal of the spectacularly self-evasive Jean-Baptiste, Camus suggests that we are our own biggest problems. Evil will overtake us by default if we do not go out of our way to build the good into our lives. As human beings, we have quite the ability to rationalize, procrastinate, and offer any number of justifications for our missed opportunities to help others. We could rationalize our indifference indefinitely and not violate any law. As we miss these opportunities to interact compassionately, though, we propel our descent into sin. To be proactive—to pursue compassion—is the work of a lifetime.

Although both how and to what extent we are positioned to do this work is a matter of great dispute—thoroughgoing Augustinians unrelentingly insist that it is impossible to do it without God's help—we have, reflected in Jean-Baptiste's sentiment, a fourth model of evil before us to consider. Evil is both real and irreducible to the good, but, in contrast to the Manichean view that also subscribes to these two descriptors, evil in the Augustinian model pertains not to some external referent but rather to an internal defect. Specifically, evil pertains to an indication of something that is missing inside us and therefore in need of replenishment. There are no exceptions in this understanding. If we are a human being, evil is the state to which we have been susceptible since the beginning of our existence. We risk hypocrisy if we accuse others of wrongdoing without implying our participation in it (Manicheanism) and, perhaps worse, play the fool if we too easily justify evil's existence (theodicy) or deny it altogether (perspectivalism). In other words, in the fourth model, evil represents a permanent limitation of human nature, or at least the human condition.[1]

In both theological and nontheological systems of thought, St. Augustine's response to the existence of evil is the traditional and still probably most widespread one. This response is, in a nutshell, the view of privation: Evil is nothing substantive in itself. It is the state when a precious good goes missing. For Augustine, this good is and could be no other than God, the only constant by which human flourishing on any level can be preserved or by which faith in a good future can be assured. It is thus wrong in the model of privation to think of evil as one thing among each of the (good) things that God has created. Evil is, rather, the absence of something that should be present. Evil is a result, a state reached once something has gone terribly wrong. The privation thesis is notably comprehensive. It includes acts of commission and omission. Evil pertains both to what we do and what we do not do: It is both a stepping into and a turning away. Indeed, it is an acknowledgment of our shared, flawed humanity: a proclivity toward uncaring and selfish behavior to which all human beings, not merely monstrous others, are inevitably prone. Thus characterized, evil is something to which everyone is in danger of succumbing, but also something which, through the grace of free will, we have the ability to resist.

In locating evil within the sphere of human responsibility—evil is ultimately the doing neither of God nor impersonal (mis)fortune—privation theorists do not seek to change the facts of reality. That evil pertains strictly to an absence rather than something substantive nevertheless remains strongly indicative of a world rife with injustice, pain, and at times unspeakable brutality. For Augustine, these outcomes flow from original sin, the archetypical turning away. As described in Genesis 3, a constitutive biblical text for Augustine, moral evil initially stemmed from the disobedience of the angels coupled with Adam and Eve's fall, the punishment for which was natural evil.[2] According to Augustine, we inherit the stain of original sin that inclines us toward damnation. The only remedy for this is the union with God. However, although God foresees who is to be saved and who is to be damned, it is essentially our choice, through inculcating a humility that will make us eligible for grace, as to which of these outcomes comes to pass. Thus, to avoid evil, we must work to avoid the loss of the profound good that is ours to claim.[3] In other words, evil is in its essence a corruption of the initial good with which God has graced the world, and it is this corruption—a diminution of a prior good—for which we are responsible. Whence Augustine's famous metaphor of evil as blindness, the absence of sight indicative of a thing, perfectly good in itself, that no longer functions as it should.[4]

For Augustine, moral evil is therefore the result of the misuse of the will. Evil ensues when we assert undue independence from God's dominion, which would naturally have led to the damnation of everyone were it not for the gift of redemption made possible through Jesus Christ. Those who choose to "turn back toward" can still be saved. Still, the gesture must be undertaken under the harsh circumstance of the ubiquitous condition of human suffering, a suffering that all too often manifests itself in the random affliction of seeming innocents. Augustinian theological anthropology thereby reveals itself to be outright democratic in its application. The distinction between garden variety moral agents and moral monsters is not hard and fast: We all have the potential to succumb to the temptation that threatens each of us in the context of our lived experience. Likewise, suffering is to be built into our psychological expectations for the world simply because of the kinds of flawed creatures we are.

Augustine thereby powerfully flattens the distinctions pertaining to disparate flaws that exist among human beings by emphasizing the obvious: We are each creatures of finitude for whom living is synonymous with the experience of erring, and for whom, as a result, we subsist in profound vulnerability. We lack the self-sufficiency to flourish on our own. Herein Augustine issues a personal indictment against all of humanity that is inherent in the thesis of privation: We are bound to spoil the good that has been ours to receive unspoiled and thereby bound to an existence beset by a culpability it behooves us to overcome. Correspondingly, we are pressed to acknowledge that just to exist is to shoulder the responsibility of exemplifying certain sorts of goods gracefully made available to us.[5] Although what we have control over is very limited—no matter who we are we have to contend with evil—whether we nevertheless acknowledge our participation with evil in order to hold it at bay is exclusively of our choice. That is, our success in this world, restricted as it inevitably will be, is to a certain extent up to us. Our potential to be redeemed is in the Augustinian account primarily a matter of God's grace. But it is, as Kant would have said, also up to us to look in the mirror and recognize the "dear self" staring us back in the face.[6] According to this understanding, evil is the waning away of an initial goodness that is easily overtaken in the context of the totality of the bad habits we develop, habits the acquisition of which also ironically provide an occasion for our virtuous overcoming of them. If Augustine is right, then acknowledging the absence of goodness is an opportunity for the replenishment of goodness. Privation structurally entails that what has eroded can be restored.

So construed, evil represents not only the commission of wrongdoing, but also the failure to act in a proactively virtuous and other-regarding manner. Evil is no mere act or label. It is a reflection of the bad character formed by the consistent abandonment of better things.[7] Evil is not a fiction (perspectivalism), nor goodness realized or enabled (theodicy), nor opposed to goodness (Manicheanism). It is the misapplication of good. There are no naturally evil things per se. On the contrary, evil is the chain of events of things gone and yet to go wrong. Because it is a function of events linked to one another, events that transpire in history, evil is not a necessity, even when it is foreseeable. Evil is instead inevitable, with the caveat that in the wake of its destruction people retain the ongoing opportunity to undo, slowly and piecemeal, the intensity of its quality and the enormity of its degree. Evil is, as the secular neo-Augustinian Hannah Arendt would come to say, banal, the daily upshot of not thinking hard or often enough about what one ought to do in any given circumstance. Because it is a function of laziness of character, evil is something we all legitimately have to contend with. The alternative to evil is the demanding and often exhausting process of adopting the perspective of and being sensitive to the other person. It requires us to strain ourselves to not simply accept our inherited situations. This said, an evil character also possesses, as Rowan Williams notes, "a power of initiative," a harmful but coherent design for which the one committing evil lusts in furtherance of selfish ends.[8] This is consistent with the aspect of banality in which, in contrast to Manichean determinism, we are not destined for badness or goodness. Evil, in other words, is not a trait that becomes manifest by some individuals and not others who play out the roles assigned to them in a cosmic script. We determine the degree to which we will fall prey to the temptation to form an evil character.

This is the heartbreaking component of evil on the privation account: Evil did and does not have to be. The corruption to which the one doing evil has willingly assented thwarts a good or a beauty that otherwise might have flourished. As the classic lamentation *corruptio optimi pessima* goes, it is the ones with the most moral potential we need to be concerned about, the ones who disappoint us because of, not despite, their promise.[9] Scoundrels are easy enough to identify, but evil has much do with the righteous. Just as the angels were corrupted, seduced from their loyalties in heaven, we too defect from ones who in our own assessment we should stick by and love. It is not necessarily the harmful act, identified at a singular event in a snapshot in time, that is evil, but the lapsing yet forming evil will that brings the context for the harmful act. Such abandonment, writes Augustine in *The City of God*, is a perverse sort of pride that casts away the search for a better life in favor of static self-satisfaction. This much was clear with Adam and Eve. The will exalts or infects one's actions, as the case may be. The latter

> happens when a man is too pleased with himself: and a man is self-complacent when he deserts that changeless Good in which, rather than in himself, he ought to have found his satisfaction. This desertion is voluntary, for if the will had remained unshaken in its love of the higher changeless Good, which shed on it light to see and kindled in it fire to love, it would not have been diverted from this love to follow its own pleasure; and the will would not have been so darkened and chilled in consequence as to let the woman believe that the serpent had spoken the truth."[10]

Evil is thus the process of corruption that takes place both in the critical moment of the fall with which Augustine is preoccupied as well as over several moments that link together over the course of a lifetime. Corruption typically does not occur instantaneously. The Augustinian preoccupation with the desertion of one's better character is reflected in the observation of C. S. Lewis's consummate tempter, Screwtape, according to whom wickedness subsumes the one it occupies slowly, and not in a way that requires the proverbial hard sell:

> The Christians describe the Enemy as one "without whom Nothing is strong." And Nothing is very strong: strong enough to steal away a man's best years not in sweet sins but in a dreary flickering of the mind over it knows not what and knows not why, in the gratification of curiosities so feeble that the

man is only half aware of them, in drumming of fingers and kicking of heels, in whistling tunes that he does not like, or in the long, dim labyrinth of reveries that have not even lust or ambition to give them a relish, but which, once chance association has started them, the creature is too weak and fuddled to shake off.

You will say that these are very small sins; and doubtless, like all young tempters, you are anxious to be able to report spectacular wickedness. But do remember, the only thing that matters is the extent to which you separate the man from the Enemy. It does not matter how small the sins are provided that their cumulative effect is to edge the man away from the Light and out into the Nothing. Murder is no better than cards if cards can do the trick. Indeed the safest road to Hell is the gradual one—the gentle slope, soft underfoot, without sudden turnings, without milestones, without signposts.[11]

Screwtape advises his apprentice nephew Wormwood that in beckoning evil the best recipe is patiently to induce the waning away of virtue. No need to affect any dramatic sin; the key is to "separate the man from the Enemy." The Augustinian turning away is, in effect, a string of missed opportunities to do something better than that which one is in fact doing. To be sure, evil is neither a label to be uncritically affixed to a recognizable referent (Manicheanism), nor a label to be mistrusted (perspectivalism), nor a philosophical conundrum to be unraveled (theodicy). On the contrary, a shift takes place with the model of privation to conceiving of evil as an issue of character. The Augustinian approach, despite its radical dependence on God, is intolerant of any sort of passivity as a response to the human encounter with evil.

How the dynamics of agency affect the relationship between the will and the aspects of human nature that are beyond our control to marginalize remains to be seen. It will be challenging, for example, to square the account of privation so far offered with a characterization of Augustine that is sufficiently non-Pelagian. What the will can do is limited. I explore in more detail Augustine's unrelentingly theocentric account of the problem of evil and then contemporize it by examining both religious and secular proponents of the privation thesis, including Reinhold Niebuhr, Albert Camus, Hannah Arendt, as well as others. Each of these thinkers retains Augustine's insight that evil is somehow a misuse, missed opportunity, or failure to think and act, despite that it often can and does involve the deliberate formation of harmful or pernicious motives. This is to say, evil points to a problem intrinsic to the human species, the locus of which is in the self. Evil is not the externality it is in the first and arguably the second models in this book, but rather a nagging and deafening inscrutability the unraveling of which demands a turn inward.

Evil in the Mind of Augustine:
The Will and Difficult Freedom

Ambivalent about whether to commit fully to Christianity and saturated with the spiritual opinions of others to the point of paralysis, Augustine recounts in book 8 of *The Confessions* the moment of internal crisis that brought him to the brink of worldly renunciation and surrender. Admiring Victorinus, a Roman rhetorician and pagan who accepted Christianity late in life, Augustine explains the cause of his inability to have so far followed suit:

> For this very thing did I sigh, bound as I was, not by another's irons but by my iron will. The enemy had control of my will, and out of it he fashioned a chain and fettered me with it. For in truth lust is made out of a perverse will, and where lust is severed, it becomes habit, and when habit is not resisted, it becomes necessity. By such links, joined one to another, as it were—for this reason I have called it a chain—a harsh bondage held me fast. A new will, which had begun within me, to wish freely to worship you and find joy in you, O God, the sole sure delight, was not yet able to overcome that prior will, grown strong with age. Thus did my two wills, the one old, the other new, the first carnal, and the second spiritual, contend with one another, and by their conflict they laid waste to my soul.[12]

What is interesting about this passage is that the enemy Augustine refers to is not a force opposing him from the outside but the self in error. Specifically, the reference to the enemy, footnoted *The Confessions*, is to 1 Corinthians 5:7, "Cleanse out the old leaven that you may be a new lump, as you are really unleavened." In naked self-reproach, Augustine reveals that he captained both sides of a battle that remained stalled in a "wretched" stalemate due to the lag between what he knew in his heart he had to do and the capacity he held to act on this knowledge.[13] Acting would involve not only forgoing worldly pleasures but also changing habits hard to break, and thereby replacing the slavish familiarity of bondage with the exhausting oppression of freedom. So marred is the self following original sin, so recalcitrant are habits to changing in its wake, that ultimately the human actor is, bereft of grace, able only to sin despite that it is much more commonplace to know oneself as a sinner.

Thus, in book 8 of *The Confessions*, Augustine conveys that there is a gap between knowing and acting, the awareness of which justifies a new emphasis on the will as that human power that could, if rightly oriented, fundamentally alter the quality of one's life. Here, even before his conversion, Augustine breaks with his Manichean past, because the will represents a possible (though hard-won) exercise of freedom intolerable within the worldview of dualistic determinism. The two wills that Augustine identifies in the passage as existing within the self call attention to an indecisiveness in which the self is trapped between a conception of what, due to formed addictions, it wants to do but cannot. Whence his anguish and resulting disgust at his inability to act on what he knew:

> In the shifting tides of my indecision, I made many bodily movements, such as men sometimes will to make but cannot, whether because they lack certain members or because those members are bound with chains, weakened by illness, or hindered in one way or another. If I tore my hair, and beat my forehead, if I locked my fingers together and clasped my knees, I did so because I willed it. But I could have willed this and yet not done it, if the motive power of my limbs had not made its response. Therefore I did many things in which to will was not the same as the ability to act. Yet I did not do that which I wanted to do with an incomparably greater desire, and could have done as soon as I willed to act, for immediately, when I made that act of the will, I would have willed with efficacy. In such an act the power to act and the will itself are the same, and the very act of willing is actually to do the deed. Yet it was not done: it was easier for the body to obey the soul's most feeble command, so that its members were moved at pleasure, than for the soul to obey itself and to accomplish its own high will wholly within the will.[14]

Interestingly, Augustine admits to not doing what he wished to have been able to do, and that is to have acted on his deepest, rather than most pressing, urges. In other words, he had formed the right sorts of desires, but it was easier to obey the self's "most feeble command." Evil is an "illness," a "hindrance." It is the wrong sort of desire combined with a failure of the right desire to overpower the wrong one. It is the inability of the soul to obey itself. The vices of pride and lust are in essence surrogates for the will's ability to do what one knows one ought to do but does not because of the hard work required. Pride and lust are therefore absences, abandonments. As Augustine notes, "For when the will leaves the higher and turns to the lower, it becomes bad not because the thing to which it turns is bad, but because the turning itself is perverse."[15] We are the authors, the first causes, of evil. We are the ones to be blamed for the formation of an evil will, or rather, for the failure to form a good will, or rather still, for the failure to produce a will in which goodness prevails over its lack. For Augustine, evil is the indecision (which is in fact an important kind of decision) of defaulting one's way to the lesser good or no good at all. Moreover, the decision of indecision is encapsulated in the culpable and volitional commitment to turn away from God, but this too, despite God's all-knowing ability to foresee what we will do, is a decisive action the commission or noncommission of which falls on our, and nobody else's, shoulders.

Understanding evil as the upshot of the decision to turn away from God, it becomes easy to see how Augustine had moved away from Manicheanism by the time he worked out the relationship between sin and the will. Nevertheless, something needs to be said about his initial attraction to the heresy. Like many sophisticated thinkers of the classical and contemporary world, Augustine began his philosophical foray into thinking about evil with his reflections in *The Confessions* about the Great Conundrum: If evil really does exist, then either God is unable to rid the world of evil, in which case he is not all-powerful, or he is unwilling to do so, in which case he is not all good. Augustine ultimately ended up making neither concession, retaining the idea of God as all-powerful and all-loving and seeing evil as the corruptible result of his good creation.[16] He did, however, understand the attraction of descriptive economy provided by the Manichean solution, which in its honest acknowledgment of the jeopardy in which evil put human beings captured our fallen nature in its all of its rich, dark starkness.

In dualism, evil is explained not as a rejection of the existence of terrible suffering and wrongdoing but as a God with limited capacity interminably locked in a battle with some independent force. (The ultimate goodness of God is something that was never questioned by Augustine.) The problem with such a solution, for Augustine, was that such a God was one in whom it did not make rational sense to have faith or to whom it did not make intuitive sense to pray, for limited by a counterforce of equal magnitude, God would be subject to the same material parameters of the evil entity opposing it. Thus Augustine writes in his *Confessions* that he could not answer questions posed to him such as "Whence is evil?" or "Is God confined within a corporeal form?" or "Does he have hair and nails?" affirmatively as a Manichean, although neither did he know yet "that God is a spirit in whom there are no members having length and breadth and in whom there is no mass."[17] Eventually committing to a conception of a deity as spirit, immutable and incorruptible, opened the door for concluding that God never creates imperfectly or stands deterred by an imperfect entity. Every creature, to the extent that it exists, is good.[18]

Evil is thus the measure of the distance one has traveled from goodness. This is how evil can exist: It is a process of going bad, a state characterized by the erosion of a better state. No creature is in itself evil, only worse than others.[19] Evil, as Augustine writes, is nothing itself but the choice to use a good evilly, totally the fault of the creature, not of God.[20] In his strongest repudiation of Manicheanism, in *On Continence*, Augustine places the responsibility on the misuser's sinful consent, in which consent entails the action that leads away from the good, or at least the failure to form the desire that would keep one there.[21] Evil can supersede God's will no more than God bears any responsibility for evil. Manicheanism, with its claim about a substantively formidable force capable of rivaling God's goodness, thus not only fails to do God justice, it also fundamentally misses the original, immaculate, if variously corruptible state in which God's creatures are given their first chance. That is, it does not allow for a process in which human beings can distinguish themselves as better or worse, notwithstanding the same initial circumstances.

As Aaron Stalnaker shows, it is thus pedagogically important to Augustine to make evil parasitic on, if disrupting of, the good: "In Augustine's famous formulation, the field of evil is completely exhausted by sin and its penalty, that is, by love that disorders God's ordering of nature, the hierarchy of being, and God's justly imposed penalty for such wrong loving."[22] Stalnaker's emphasis draws connections between Augustine and the classical Confucian figure Xunzi, also preoccupied with the centrality of evil for created beings, to call attention to a human nature that is inherently corruptible, in the case of Augustine a corruptibility that indicates a veering from a once pristine template. So understood, evil becomes a reality that is nevertheless an internal problem of self. Augustine's analysis has a significant egalitarian spirit, despite our being differently corruptible and thus better and worse individuals. This egalitarianism is simply that we are each subject to a defecting evil will, of wanting when we should not to see darkness or hear silence.[23] Our oneness with Adam establishes our fallen nature, but it also lays at our heels a common project, namely, by the grace of divine help, to reunite with God and restore what had gone awry.[24] No one can simultaneously exercise responsibility and claim an exemption from this undertaking. The Augustinian picture of evil rejects outright the passive, spectatorial unfolding of a drama between good and evil in which individuals come to assume their cosmic roles. God, all-knowing, foresees who will become better and worse, and, all-powerful, determines upon whom his grace will be dispensed, but we alone are responsible for correcting the formation of the evil will.

Thinking about this feature of Augustine's moral anthropology, in which we are all in it together, the temptation seems to be to interpret Augustine in a Pelagian light. Augustine's insistence on the relationship between evil and the consenting will responsible for the erosion and even perversion of the good seems to imply that evil, our failure, is a breach of thinking and acting, somehow a lapse in effort on our part. Is this characterization of Augustine too Pelagian? This concern becomes pressing in considering some explicit passages from *On Free Choice of the Will*, where Augustine's conversation with Evodius reveals, over and over again, the author's obsession with the will's flight from things higher to things lower. Consider the following exchanges:

> E: How is it then that man does evil, if evil is not learned?
>
> A: Perhaps because he avoids and turns from education, by which I mean the act of learning. But whether this or something else is true, the following is clear: since education is good and "education" is derived from "learning," evil cannot be learned. For if evil is learned, then evil is part of education and education will not be something good. However, as you yourself grant, it is good. Therefore evil is not learned and it is useless to ask from whom we learn evil. Or, if we learn evil, we learn so as to avoid it, not to do it. From this reasoning we may say that to do evil is to turn from education.[25]

> A: Perhaps then lust [*libido*] is the evil element in adultery. As long as you look for evil in the overt act itself, which can be seen, you are in difficulty. To help you understand that the evil element in adultery is lust, consider the case of a man who does not have the opportunity to lie with another's wife; but nevertheless, if it is somehow obvious that he would like to do so and would do so had he the opportunity, he is no less guilty than the man taken in the very act.
>
> E: Nothing is more obvious, and I now see that there is no need for a long discussion to show me how homicide and sacrilege and all the other sins are evil. Now it is clear that lust is dominant in every kind of evildoing.[26]

> A: For the present, we can be certain that whatever be that nature which, by right, is superior to the mind strong in virtue, it cannot be unjust. Therefore, even though it may have the power to do so, it will not force the mind to serve lust.
>
> E: No one would hesitate to admit this.
>
> A: Since, because of justice, whatever is equal or superior to the mind that possesses virtue and is in control does not make the mind a slave to lust; and since, because of its weakness, whatever is inferior to the mind cannot do this (as the things we have established prove)—therefore it follows that nothing can make the mind a companion of desire except its own will and free choice [*voluntas et liberum arbitirum*].[27]

Finally, to drive home the point that evil is not an event to be endured, an innate trait one must cope with, or a necessary affliction, Augustine says this to his interlocutor about poor prioritizing and improper loving:

A: Thus some men make evil use of these things, and others make good use. And the man who makes evil use clings to them with love and is entangled by them (that is, he becomes subject to those things which ought to be subject to him, and creates for himself goods whose right and proper use require that he himself be good); but the man who uses these rightly proves that they are indeed goods, though not for him (for they do not make him good or better, but become better because of him). Therefore he is not attached to them by love, lest he make them limbs, as it were, of his spirit (which happens if he loves them), and lest they weaken him with pain and wasting when they begin to be cut off from him. Instead, let him be above temporal things completely. He must be ready to possess and control them, and even more ready to lose and not to possess them. . . .

E: This is most true. The things themselves are not to be blamed, but rather the men who make evil use of them.[28]

The combined impression of these assertions leads to a robust account of moral responsibility in which we are enjoined not merely to avoid wrongdoing but also to pursue the good (i.e., God), to take the right steps to form virtuous intentions, and to order goods in view of the freedom with which we have been happily created.

In particular, four traits can be gleaned that indicate the importance of freedom in coming to resist the formation of an evil will. From the first passage we see that Augustine clearly argues in favor of the proactivity of learning the good to stave off evil; this is construed as a decision to become educated. In the second passage evil is seen as a matter of forming the wrong dispositions, or of failing to exert the effort to form the right ones—"lust" is so pernicious because it represents the poisoning of the tree that bears bad fruit. In the third passage Augustine equates poor desires with free choice. In the fourth he assigns responsibility to the human will for exercising self-control to choose eternal over temporal things; evil is never, Augustine states, a matter of any particular thing, but rather one of our use or misuse of that thing. These four observations from *On Free Choice of the Will*, which could easily be supplemented by others, affirm the importance in Augustine's thought of pursuing the good beyond merely avoiding the bad, of loving in the right way by intentionally forming the right sorts of desires, and of acquiring a virtuous character through forming the right sorts of habits. Thus, for example, evil does not paradigmatically occur merely when one follows the example of Satan or is overtaken by him on this or that occasion, as it is presupposed to have taken place in the Manichean model.

Learning and knowledge are, by definition, always good, and so measuring evil or our distance from evil, in this respect, becomes a function of measuring our amount of learning and accumulation of knowledge. On this point, G. R. Evans's analysis is instructive:

> Can a man's will be compelled to evil? No, says Augustine, for nothing is more excellent in man than a wise, rational and virtuous mind . . . [leading him to] define wrongdoing as neglect of eternal things (which we cannot lose if we give them our love), or pursuit of temporal things (which it is easy to lose). It is, in other words, misdirection of energy, perverted desire, misplaced zeal; where energy, desire, and zeal are good in themselves, but given up to an end God does not intend. Why do we do wrong then? Through free choice of the will. Why does God give us free choice of the will, if we can abuse it? That is the question with which Book I ends. Augustine tries to answer it by looking at that which is undoubtedly good: the will itself and its freedom.[29]

Here we have, according to Evans, an unmistakably theocentric characterization of evil and ethics according to which, by virtue of God's grace, we are given the free choice to pursue the good, but in which it is also our burden to engage in that pursuit. We are culpable when we stray from the good and participate in evil. This is obviously not the Manichean account of evil.

Is this picture of the Augustinian view of evil and ethics, however, too Pelagian? We have gone some distance in distinguishing the fourth model of evil from the first, but perhaps not enough from the third. The normative view so far attributed to Augustine is incomplete, because the account of evil so far has not made clear the set of theological commitments that make Augustine's ethical ones possible. Augustine, unlike Pelagius, decisively holds that human beings cannot on their own make themselves good. To be a human being is to be constrained by finitude, which specifically means to be subject to corruption at the hand of sin.[30] What this implies is that only grace can restore human beings to their natural state of created goodness. Ought implies can, but only with God's help. Augustine's earlier work, including *On Free Choice of the Will*, was intended primarily to be a polemic against Manicheanism. Worried that Pelagius was using these texts to claim Augustine as a supporter, Augustine turned his attention in his more mature writings, notably *Nature and Grace* and his *Retractions*, to refute the Pelagian heresy. In these texts it becomes clear that Augustine does not really acknowledge distinctions between grace and agency, human freedom and divine action, and finally, therefore, between theology and ethics.

We have the capacity to choose in a moral fashion because of the way in which we have been created. Human freedom is in every way ancillary to the divine will. Our initially inherited sin, which morally blinds us, also causes us to stumble and sin more. Left to our own devices, we stray further not move closer to the good.[31] Thus, unlike Pelagius, for whom prayer is not really needed to ask for forgiveness, with Augustine prayer is nonnegotiable in light of our sinful existence.[32] For Augustine, the will is still critical in the process of reversing the "turning away," but the will depends on a grace that can undo the ubiquitous consequences of Adam's initial error.

This initial disobedience, which would be passed on to Adam and Eve's descendants, forever spoiled God's having created humans aright. Augustine takes the narrative of the Fall in Genesis as the literal account of how things went wrong, an account lent credence by the manifold respects in which we engage in unjustified self-love on a daily basis all of the time. In fact, such self-love bears the imprint of the original mold. In *City of God* Augustine writes,

> The soul, in fact, rejoiced in its own freedom to act perversely and disdained to be God's servant; and so it was deprived of the obedient service which its body had first rendered. At its own pleasure the soul deserted its superior and master; and so it no longer retained its inferior and servant obedient to its will. It did not keep its own flesh subject to it in all respects, as it could have kept it for ever if it had itself continued in subjection to God. This then was the time when the flesh began to 'lust in opposition to the spirit,' which is the conflict that attends us from birth. We bring with us, at our birth, the beginning of our death, and with the vitiation of our nature our body is the scene of death's assault, or rather of his victory, as the result of that first disobedience.[33]

Human disobedience, which is solely our doing, commits us to a situation in which we depend on God to return to an essential goodness. Augustine characterizes Adam's sin, which we have inherited, as a fantastic hubris in our idolatrous propensity to assign a set of goods to be valued independently of the divine being who gives us our creative capacity. Pride is central here. It causes us to ignore what ultimately would secure a stable happiness and infects us with a misery revealed in the disappointment attendant to withering ephemera.[34] Augustine defines pride as "a perverse kind of longing for a perverse kind of exaltation," that is, unjustified self-sufficiency, as if human beings by themselves could know what to love and value.[35]

Against the backdrop of the sin of pride is the psychological reality of privation, paradigmatically located in the absence Adam and Eve first brought upon themselves, which provides the raison d'être for the drama of grace and salvation. Adam and Eve were initially free not to sin, but did. We, on the other hand, through inheritance, bear the consequences of their decision. "In fact," writes Augustine, "because of the magnitude of that offence, the condemnation changed human nature for the worse; so that what first happened as a matter of punishment in the case of the first human beings, continued in their posterity as something natural and congenital." Human beings are irretrievably marred, "tossed about by violent and conflicting emotions," consigned to endure the bodily withering and death that is the punishment for Adam and Eve's disobedience, and now, especially prone to sinning more.[36] This is to suggest that, in contrast to the impression given in *On Free Choice of the Will*, Augustine acknowledges that we are free, but not so free as to escape inherited but debilitating givens. We are thus not only vitiated metaphysically so that we stand at the mercy of God to recreate what has been spoiled through Adam and Eve's primal deficiency, but we are also physically condemned to pass along to our offspring a propensity to perpetuate sins.[37] It is a cycle that, more than repeating itself, worsens with each iteration. God is the singular constant that can break into this replenishing negativity. Despite the fall, we retain the essence of God's created goodness, which, among an elect few, can be restored to those who receive God's grace.[38] Unlike the Pelagians, Augustine believed that sin was the result not of unwisely imitating Adam and Eve, but of something inherited through natural descent. As such, more than human effort is required to undo our sinful nature. In terms of our orientation (but made possible through God's grace), this is reflected in the cultivation of an undiluted loving disposition toward God, movements of the soul in the direction of God. Again, this is primarily a matter of God's doing, not ours. We can dispose ourselves to his grace, but it is God's grace to give. Salvation is thus a matter of deliverance from our sinful nature and a release from our bodily enslavement to the proclivity to sin received through human reproduction. It is a gift from God, who releases a goodness previously held captive. We are made righteous. Righteousness is not conferred upon us. At the same time, it is up to us not to be negligent. We have an existential duty to participate individually in the City of God.

I have provided a rough account of Augustine's tenuous and pained understanding of the connection between the will and grace, indicating what is up to us and what is not in terms of our potential deliverance from sin. The path Augustine steers between Manichean determinism and Pelagian overconfidence presents a restrictedly free human nature. The condition of finitude is such that evil, and in particular the moral evil that is the unavoidable consequence of the sinning creatures we are born, is a perennial predicament always in need of overcoming. We are evil, prone to more evil, and must deal with evil, whether we like it or not. Contrary to the Pelagians, who believed all sins were individual, and thus atonable on an individual basis, Augustine democratically adhered to what we all have in common: a damaged nature badly in need of restoration.[39] A certain indistinguishability is thus forged in Augustine's theology and ethics. With Dostoevsky, Augustine maintained that though few may be guilty of this or that particular crime, all are responsible. As corporeal creatures who have come into being through a direct link that leads back to Adam and Eve, we all have the same handicap to overcome: a putrid self-love beset by the first turning away. Our prescription for this is governed by the beings we are. Only God's grace, manifest in the replacement of self-love with divine love, constitutes a remedy sufficient to attend to our fallenness. In Augustine's view, we are to be judged as better or worse based on our degree of success in this transformation, but none of us is existentially better or worse with regard to the whole. We must all leave the City of Man in search of the City of God.

Augustine's theocentric ethics sheds a new light on one strong version of the perspectival model of evil explored in the last chapter, namely, subjectivism, the view of human existence that lays all creative credit with human intellect and action above and against some independent superseding reality.[40] According to the subjectivist view, evil is not a reality in itself but a reflection of our created values. Precisely this attitude is, for Augustine, sin. Augustine insists that the perverse will disregards the objective good that is known to be best and desires instead to endorse a self-created and therefore arbitrarily upheld set of goods. In this respect, we might again indirectly identify the virtue of humility at work in the Augustinian view of evil. As finite beings, we lack the ability either to determine that objective good it is our essential nature to share or, unto ourselves, to occupy it. Although in pride we think otherwise, when we do think otherwise our perverse will makes us lustful and we end up perpetuating our desire for the wrong things. What this means is that without God, regardless of our attitude, we will cause others to suffer and we will suffer ourselves, whether we think we are doing these things or not. We can never fully erase the gap between the perfected goodness with which we were originally endowed and the flawed existence with which we have to cope. "No one is certain and secure of his own predestination and salvation," Augustine writes in *On Rebuke and Grace*.[41]

In practical terms, the account of privation implies that evil remains a constitutive problematic of the human situation. There is both a world of nothing and nothing to do about this predicament. We have, by definition, been made unworthy despite that we were once worthy. This means that we have neither the luxury of resigning ourselves to a Manichean quietism or a theodicist's overconfidence in the necessity of eventual evil or good. We have little, but something, to say about where we end up. Despite predestination, merit, although it comes from God's grace, is indicative, if not determinative, of our salvation. Thus, to do nothing, or to count on the fact that everything will have been done, or that everything is for the best, is to our detriment and too easily lets us off the hook. Evil has both an external and internal component. Original sin refers to something that is historically real, with real consequences, and stands as a justification for our punishment and continued human suffering. By the same token, whether we ultimately end up in the City of Man or City of God depends on our love of God, and in turn right love of self and others, which is a task of internal transformation of rightly imitating God. Of the understandings of evil so far examined in this book, Augustine's is the most demanding and exhausting. Evil stays with us, but we are for this reason no less accountable for replacing the unacceptable absence to which it refers with a love that can refashion us in God's image.

Broadening Augustine's Account of Evil

Augustine's conception of evil differs from the others we have so far considered. First, he postulates a difference between our created essence and lived existence. The former is pristine and not in need of improvement; the latter calls attention to major shortcomings for which we are culpable. The tension between the two states of affairs is palpable. The one we are living is decisively inadequate, implying a certain moral pressure we ought to feel to make things right. As corrupted beings, we have proclivities to inconstancy and self-service, which we are never fully able to fix by ourselves. Already, at the start of our existence, something crucial is missing, the work of a lifetime to recover.

Second, the Augustinian account emphasizes self-awareness, knowing oneself as defective in our default existence. That Augustine's understanding of evil contains both external and internal components is what locks in place a soteriological *telos* that also entails moral reformation. In Manicheanism, we may be enjoined to be active, but only to participate in a predetermined cosmic drama. There is no impetus to change. Similarly, theodicies construe us as the beings we should be, even if we are not aware of it at the time. Perspectivalism characterizes us as free from the pressure to self-transform: We are to know ourselves as we make ourselves. Gone in most versions of this account, save those in Eastern traditions (like Taoism), is any sense of an objective good toward which we must subjectively orient ourselves. Of the four we have seen, only the Augustinian model understands knowledge of our defective condition as the impetus that helps to motivate us to repair our complacent, self-centered dispositions, battle our pride, and acquire dignity. Attending to our fallen selves, and thereby bridging the gap between ourselves without and with God (or ourselves without and with the good) is the quintessential task of the well-lived life. Evil, it logically follows, is failing to be responsible to this self-transformation.

Third, the Augustinian picture is unsettling in its insistence on an "inward turn" and the negotiation that remains ongoing between the inner and outer worlds of the self. It entertains the hypothesis that every one of us is deeply sinful and in need of a good dose of contrition as the minimum prerequisite to prepare the way for a redemptive future. The privation model calls our attention, in a way that its rivals do not, to the small sins we commit, "little by little," en route to habits that fortify our sinful nature. That we do not necessarily do something readily identifiable as monstrous is to Augustine no concession. Without turning inward, our descent into moral lapse is virtually guaranteed. It is not only moral monsters who are capable of morally monstrous things. The subscriber to the thesis of privation has the least flattering view of self of the available options. At the same time, he or she is served by self-reproach, for with self-reproach comes the virtues of patience, sensitivity, humility, and resistance to moral and spiritual complacency.

Can these basic observations survive their extraction from the sin, grace, and redemption to which they are linked in Augustine's view? Can there be a non-Augustinian Augustinianism, a moral tradition that retains the virtues and reparative tasks implied in Augustine's privation account but does not commit its adherent to the biblical drama of the fall and salvation, which, for Augustine, gives these virtues and tasks their justification?[42]

Albert Camus

The idea that Augustine could be used in service of an attempt to lay the grounds for a this-worldly ethic is anathema to Augustinian scholars, for whom grace, finitude, and the constancy of God cannot be overemphasized. Any commitment to the improvement of self or society in this life that one would attribute to Augustine, these thinkers maintain, is to miss the point of the climactic Book XIX of *The City of God*, where all such endeavors are announced to be not only futile, but also destructive to the priority of orienting oneself toward God and away from the human situation bereft of God.[43] John Milbank, a primary representative of the Radical Orthodoxy movement, insists on the non-overlapping magisteria of theology and secular theory, vogue attempts to read into Augustine anything akin to liberal values or virtue notwithstanding.[44] With regard to nontheological retrievals of Augustine, Milbank has this to say:

> Augustine does not endorse, indeed utterly condemns, every tendency towards personhood as a view of self-ownership itself as unrestricted freedom

within one's own domain. . . . There can be no doubt that Augustine contributes here to the invention of liberalism, though in a negative manner, by
insisting that in the economy of things there remains a place for a kind of
political rule which is not really justice, indeed whose presumption is of the
essence of sin.[45]

Attempts to cope in the world are, on Milbank's reading of Augustine, necessary and require a dirtying of hands, but this is to be associated with our wicked
rather than our virtuous nature. That we have the wherewithal to improve our
lot in this life in any genuine way is, for Milbank's Augustine, a fatuous and
proud aspiration that, taken seriously, simply reifies the distance from God originally established in the fall. A just or charitable society can only be in the City
of God, no other city. Sympathetic but resistant to the conservatism inherent in
the traditional reading of Augustine, Eric Gregory affirms that

Augustinians, with all of their eschatological longings, are right to expose lazy
claims to have satisfied the demands of justice even as they search for a just
ordering of society. They are also right to recognize tensions and fault lines
between the goals of a good citizen and the good person. For theological reasons, they neither expect nor want the state to become a confessing religious
community. But I want to push this tradition in a new direction in order to
reconstruct a kind of *Augustinian civic virtue* that might in turn encourage a
more ambitious political practice. By more "ambitious" political practice, I
mean the promotion of an actual society that is more just, more egalitarian,
and more charitable.[46]

Gregory goes on to defend a virtue-oriented liberalism based on Augustinian
promotions of a communally fueled polity and a correctly ordered love in service
of human flourishing. In doing so, however, he must take a stand that bears on
how to interpret the critical book 19 of *City of God*, namely, on whether Augustine's two cities exist in entirely different universes. According to Gregory,
divinely inspired loving, resulting in love of the neighbor, can and should, on
Augustinian grounds, be cultivated in this life despite the correct intuitions of
theologians such as Milbank to remain dissatisfied with rationalist, individualist,
or justice-oriented ways of breaking into the eternal. Against the mainstream,
Gregory puts less emphasis on sin and our irretrievably sinful nature than is
usually emphasized in Augustinian scholarship and more than the usual emphasis on love.[47] One critical upshot of this move, in contrast to the wishes of those
who want to keep Augustine strictly theological, is to present an argument for
an Augustinian ethic teleologically directed toward our flourishing on earth

based on the democratic supposition that love, the linchpin of all virtue, is in principle and practice available to all.

In the vein of Gregory, I am attracted to drawing connections between caritas and a this-worldly ethic of human flourishing, and to seeing Augustine as an inspiration to repair our fallen world, to think about ameliorating, in Gregory's characterization, our "disordered, misdirected, and disproportionate" loves that in the human situation lead us into conflict with one another.[48] Augustine normatively advocates equality in fellowship, in contrast to the notion of human beings as ultimately vying nomads, competing among one another for political position and the fruition of ephemeral ambition. To Augustine, such competition is tantamount to idolatry, the abandonment of what is better for what is worse. To Camus, likewise, it reveals a presently broken but possibly reparable connection among human beings, all of whom are to some degree laboring to recover from undeserved damage.

Camus, like Augustine, sees people as facing a collective predicament. Whereas Augustine speaks of the fallenness warranted by sin with which we all have to contend, Camus identifies a human condition we have no choice but to confront together. Our condition is rife with struggle after new struggle and faces the challenge of making sense of gratuitous suffering that amounts to an absurdity at the bottom of which lies a universe indifferent to human concerns. Camus thus replaces Augustinian despair in lieu of grace with a comparably harsh depiction of our post-innocence world in which salvation, if any is to be had, surfaces as a remote, if hopeful, possibility. For Augustine, salvation depends on a God through whom love is made manifest in forgiveness and mercy. Camus reaches the same conclusion in his description of a human connection forged out of the ashes of collective calamitous encounter. Camus imagines a solidarity without which meaninglessness and injustice reign unchecked. In both instances, human beings revolt against what they inherit and must suffer by default. Camus's rebel, propelled by "a strange form of love," is "condemned to live for those who, like themselves, cannot live; in fact, for the humiliated."[49]

The condemned are those, like Camus, who cannot help but reject theological solutions to the seemingly cruel injustice everywhere in the human condition. Yet Camus's atheism, just like Augustine's grace-fueled redemption, entails a vocal *no* to that condition we inherit. In both cases, rebellion implies a unity in response. Camus is Augustinian in the broad sense that privation serves as a spur to overcome our initial state of affairs.[50] Consider Camus's list, in order, of the components of the self-transformative movement from initial resignation to a life of affirmation and purpose: "I derive from the absurd three consequences: my revolt, my freedom, and my passion. By the sheer activity of consciousness, I transform in a rule of life what was an invitation to death—and I refuse suicide."[51] Ironically, absurdity is what precipitates a meaningful life. Wounded by the world that batters us daily, we can share our experiences, bond, and find a genuine cause behind which to rally. Whether it is sin that gives us cause to despair over our predicament or an emptiness created by the conditions of the absurd, we discover in the human experience the phenomenon that we are all in it together, an insight that, once absorbed, gets us beyond ourselves. This is how we can "imagine Sisyphus happy," through rebuilding an inherited broken world.[52] Admittedly, the language of rebuilding is to the Augustinian too Pelagian. Still, Camus and Augustine share an understanding of evil as a resignation, an absence of the constructive impulse (at the behest of either God's grace or our own) to move past the despair that ensues when we fail to become restless with our initial predicament.

In *The Fall*, Camus develops a contrast between the uncritical individual before self-transformation, who subsists bereft of any real connection to others, and the one after, who exercises freedom by surrendering to a life beyond solipsistic existence. Jean-Baptiste, Camus's upstanding defense attorney, fills the former bill. He adopts a performative existence. His professional persona exempts him from having to engage in introspection. The adulation he receives from onlookers in the public eye is, he thinks, enough to get him by. "My profession," he writes, "set me above the judge whom I judged in turn, above the defendant whom I forced to gratitude. Just weigh this, *cher monsieur*, I lived with impunity. I was concerned in no judgment."[53] Even with all of its social benefits, however, Jean-Baptiste's life of luxury and good reputation could not bring him any happiness or infuse his life with meaning. In the wake of a missed opportunity to help someone who needed him, all of the carefully garnered approbation in the world was not enough to spare him the taunting reminder of his hollow existence. His failure to jump in after a woman who had fallen in the Seine to her apparent death was the result of a moral character that, over time, simply lacked the resources to act. Jean-Baptiste spent his life paying attention to how he was being perceived by others: "I lacked practice. For more than thirty years I had been in love exclusively with myself. What hope was there of losing such a habit?"[54] Here privation is characterized concretely. The prospect of a meaningful life is squandered because it is missing the authenticity cultivated by those who are sensitive to their "responsible" proximity to others. Despite the differences in particulars, we come to share the same fate. As the woman Jean-Baptiste does not save meets her fate in the water, Jean-Baptiste learns that his failure to act has consigned him to a future in which "nothing remained but to grow older." He realizes

> calmly as you resign yourself to an idea the truth of which you have long known, that that cry which had sounded over the Seine behind me years

before had never ceased, carried by the river to the waters of the Channel, to travel throughout the world, across the limitless expanse of the ocean, and that it had waited for me there until the day I had encountered it. I realized likewise that it would continue to await me on seas and rivers, everywhere, in short, where lies the bitter water of my baptism.[55]

We each testify to the shortcomings of one another. No one, regardless of circumstances, can claim innocence.[56] That this is the case is beyond our control. It is the extent to which we acknowledge our guilt that varies, as does whether, in solidarity, we take this acknowledgment as an indication of our responsibility for one another.

Camus's protagonist contrasts palpable despair with its admittedly exhausting alternative, freedom. It is difficult to resist one's long, slow decline, particularly when it becomes exposed by the resignation that one accepts as one's fate. In Camus's version, the model of privation calls our attention to something in the form of an absence that does not yet exist but we very much ought to build into our experience. This is the fundamental sensitivity to others who are just as tainted and in need as we are. In this case, however, the world opens up and makes several demands. Freedom requires real commitment:

Without slavery, as a matter of fact, there is no definitive solution. I very soon realized that. Once upon a time, I was always talking of freedom. At breakfast I used to spread it on my toast, I used to chew it all day long, and in company my breath was delightfully redolent of freedom. With that key word I would bludgeon whoever contradicted me; I made it serve my desires and my power. I used to whisper it in bed in the ear of my sleeping mates and it helped me to drop them. I would slip it . . . Tchk! Tchk! I am getting excited and losing all sense of proportion. After all, I did on occasion make a more disinterested use of freedom and even—just imagine my naïveté—defended it two or three times without of course going so far as to die for it, but nevertheless taking a few risks. I must be forgiven such rash acts; I didn't know what I was doing. I didn't know that freedom is not a reward or a decoration that is celebrated with champagne. Nor yet a gift, a box of dainties designed to make you lick your chops. Oh, no! It's a chore, on the contrary, and a long-distance race, quite solitary and very exhausting. No champagne, no friends raising their glasses as they look at you affectionately. Alone in a forbidding room, alone in the prisoner's box before the judges, and alone to decide in face of oneself or in the face of others' judgment. At the end of all freedom is a court sentence; that's why freedom is too heavy to bear, especially when you're down with a fever, or are distressed, or love nobody.[57]

Our decision to be free is ours alone to make. If we decide to be free, we can immediately expect the world and other people to make demands that exceed any standard to which we have become accustomed. Slavery is much easier than freedom. But if we do make the decision to be free, a decision Camus calls a "solitary chore," it becomes a collective act of communal resistance, and life again retains a larger purpose.[58] We then stop playing the universe's game. This is the answer to absurdity: to replace, piecemeal, the emptiness of a harsh, indifferent universe with real human connections, sometimes found in the unlikeliest of places.

Evil is in this way expanded by Camus as an absence of meaning, and simultaneously indicative of a good that thankfully has at least the improbable chance of being established through human engagement, resistance, and moral action. The fight against evil, by extension, is represented by the articulation of a decisive *no!* to the dainty passivity to which Camus refers. Evil must be resisted through fortitude of character and an unwillingness to accept what the universe hands down. This is so whether the crisis comes in the form of a calamitous hurricane caused by culpable indifference or a Gestapo that comes to power via power-hungry tyrants abetted by self-absorbed bystanders.

Hannah Arendt

Hannah Arendt, like Camus, and in keeping with the model of privation, locates the phenomenon of evil in a critical activity not undertaken. In Arendt's case, this is the activity of thinking. In her study of Adolf Eichmann, one of the consummate technicians responsible for executing Hitler's meticulously fashioned genocidal plans, Arendt remarks,

> Whether writing his memoirs in Argentina or in Jerusalem, whether speaking to the police examiner or to the court, what he said was always the same, expressed in the same words. The longer one listened to him, the more obvious it became that his inability to speak was closely connected with an inability to *think*, namely, to think from the standpoint of somebody else. No communication was possible with him, not because he lied but because he was surrounded by the most reliable of all safeguards against the words and the presence of others, and hence against reality as such.[59]

Thus characterized, Eichmann is evil because of a profound absence, the failure to relate to others, rather than an overt or proactive commission of the crimes of which he was rightly accused. The underlying feature that makes him evil, in other words, is an inescapability from self-absorption, one that, though leaving intact his ability to be a good father and employee, prevented him from involving himself in the flourishing of others. Eichmann, the exemplary cog in the Gestapo machinery, could have been anyone who failed to put the effort into thinking about one's place in the world alongside others. With the series of *New Yorker* articles she published chronicling the Nuremburg trials, Arendt thereby arrived at the chilling hypothesis for which she became famous: evil is banal, the altogether ordinary, the result of the everyday erosion of virtue and compassion that takes place when we stop thinking about others. Evildoers are not recognizable monsters. They are society's vacuum-oil salesmen, as Adolf Eichmann once was.

Arendt's metaphor for evil is that of a life form that grows unchecked, in the dark. "Evil possesses neither depth nor any demonic dimension. It can overgrow and lay waste the whole world precisely because it spreads like a fungus on the surface."[60] The descriptive innovation here, Augustinian in inception, pertains to evil's conceptual accessibility. As Susan Neiman notes, the fungus metaphor "signals evil that can be comprehended. It also indicates an object that has no intention whatsoever. . . . Here . . . is an attempt not to avoid responsibility but to develop new idioms for assuming it. Arendt was convinced that evil could be overcome only if we acknowledge that it overwhelms us in ways that are minute."[61] With Arendt the contrast between the Manichean and Augustinian models of evil comes to the fore. Contemporary dangers, she points out, do not come with a neon beware sign but are instead within the seemingly small temptations to not respond to the world around us. The smallest steps down the road leading away from virtue can result in disastrous outcomes that could not have been foreseen.[62] Attracted to Augustine's notion of the corruptibility of the soul, Arendt nevertheless secularizes the emphasis in theological privation on sin to construe moral straying as an exile of our own making. Worldly seduction that eclipses us from the City of God on the Augustinian account becomes for Arendt a political seduction that precludes the good. Fungus signifies a complacent passivity, an evil that is not radically fringe, but within civilization, part and parcel of its sanctioned mechanisms for institutional decision making. This is why Arendt calls it a sad truth that most evil is done by "people who never make up their minds to be good or evil."[63] Fungus, no less than entropy, is pervasive. Its prevention requires a measure of organization and careful vigilance. We are at home when we commit evil, in surroundings we often recognize, and availing ourselves of familiar strategies to get ahead in our careers, secure our social standing, and the like. Arendt reiterates this point about our need to be on alert in the epilogue of *Eichmann in Jerusalem:*

> The trouble with Eichmann was precisely that so many were like him, and
> that the many were neither perverted nor sadistic, that they were, and still

are, terribly and terrifyingly normal. From the viewpoint of our legal institutions and of our moral standards of judgment, this normality was much more terrifying than all the atrocities put together, for it implied—as had been said at Nuremberg over and over again by the defendants and their counsels—that this new type of criminal, who is in actual fact *hostis generis humani*, commits his crimes under circumstances that make it well-nigh impossible for him to know or to feel that he is doing wrong.[64]

Again, as with Augustine, one may claim no plausible exemption to the silent threat one faces simply by doing nothing.

What, in the face of evil, can one do? According to Arendt, one ought to act, and do so publicly. Arendt invokes free and creative activity as the inspiration behind the moral philosophy she develops in part 3 of *The Origins of Totalitarianism*. Elaborating her notion of the will, which is to resist, always, passivity in the public realm, she writes, "Beginning, before it becomes a historical event, is the supreme capacity of man; politically it is identical with man's freedom. *Initium ut esset homo creatus est*—'that a beginning be made man was created' said Augustine. The beginning is guaranteed by new birth; it is indeed every man."[65] In this passage, Arendt explicitly transposes into secular concepts Augustine's reference in *City of God* (book 12, chapter 20), which alludes to God's capacity to introduce into the world, ex nihilo, goodness in the form of new beings created afresh. Redemption, for Arendt, is a matter of our proclivity for novelty, through social action. Arendt subverts the contrast Augustine wishes to establish in *City of God* between this world and the next but retains his observation about what, in our default mode, is fundamentally missing in the human situation, namely, a focus beyond self, the restoration of which spurs reflection about our alienation from one another. The activity of attending to one another for the other's sake is for Augustine and Arendt a crucial virtue for creating a novel situation for human beings, independent of the postulated source of this creativity. For this creation to take place, some measure of interior examination is critical. Whereas for Augustine this attendance is in fact a love that is fueled by, and culminates in, a heavenly, Godward orientation, for Arendt it is just attention, narrowly directed at the world, where individuals ultimately are to reside naturally. Augustine and Arendt are both interested in our deliverance from exile in spite of the different places they see human beings as properly ending up afterward. As Gregory notes,

> Augustine holds that our true home is in God, not in any worldly thing or set of worldly things. But this portrayal of Augustine as lingering Manichee is problematic if it does not recognize the extent to which Augustine also holds

that we are estranged from God's good creation (and our own creatureliness) as well. Creation is itself a revelation of God's love. Arendt seems to operate with a philosophical notion of eschatology without Christology, or at least without a Christology that ensures love of God is correlative with love of neighbor such that to love God is to love the whole of creation that exists in God.[66]

The essential eschatological components proper to both Augustine and Arendt's understanding of human purpose have to do with the self-knowledge of inward examination. For Augustine, the motivation for self-transformation is prompted by an other-worldly love manifest in the shepherding of souls whose existence in this precarious world hangs in the balance. For Arendt, the inward turn is precipitated by, and in turn furnishes, an other-regarding responsibility that propels the isolated self into the public realm. For Augustine, the alternative to the passivity that characterizes a state of evil is grace in the form of love, whereas for Arendt, grace is a matter of human action.

The larger point here is that evil, for both figures, is a matter of uncritically accepting the current state of affairs rather than acting—through one form of grace or another—to bridge our existence and essence. Evil is utter negativity. Augustine proposes that the vacuum be filled through attention to our relatedness to God in this life for the sake of the heavenly city to come. Arendt recommends undoing the "unworlding" of those who stifle public discourse and disrupt the creative process of strengthening communities.[67] For both, the inaction of a bystander amid genocide is unacceptable, because the bystander's prospective defense—that he or she has encountered a formidable evil externally, an evil that gained momentum before he or she ever entered the scene—misses the attitude of maladjustment we are supposed to cultivate toward our inherited world, on which both Augustine and Arendt insist at all costs. There is a lesson in this essentially descriptive observation about where evil's real threat lies, namely, in any uncritical acceptance of the inadequate world we inherit. Such acceptance, doing nothing, perpetuates more evil. As with Camus, Arendt's secularized appropriation of the privation account of evil leads to an ethos of vigilance, introspection, and possibly self-reproach, states that, seriously inhabited, also turn out to be useful spurs in the fight against evil.

In seeing evil as an absence in the present moment that does not have to be, Augustine, Camus, and Arendt distinguish themselves from purveyors of the three examined models of evil. In deference to the Manichean view, pure psychopaths do exist in this world. No amount of self-introspection can prevent the eventual encounter with, for example, a Hitler. However, Hitler did not and could not have acted alone. Bystanders faced a myriad of options delineating the extent to which they would be involved in the perpetuation of the Final Solution, or, alternatively, in the resistance to it.[68] The privation account characterizes inaction in the face of a great threat as more horrifying than the perpetuation of those given evils of the world, like Hitler, about which we can do nothing. In a telling passage from *Eichmann in Jerusalem*, Arendt captures the havoc wrought by Hitler's "willing executioners" who were importantly not psychopaths.[69] The "murderers," she writes,

> were not sadists or killers by nature; on the contrary, a systematic effort was made to weed out all those who derived physical pleasure from what they did. The troops of the *Einsatzgruppen* had been drafted from the Armed S.S., a military unit with hardly more crimes in its record than any ordinary unit of the German Army, and their commanders had been chosen by Heydrich from the S.S. élite with academic degrees. Hence the problem was how to overcome not so much their conscience as the animal pity by which all normal men are affected in the presence of physical suffering. The trick used by Himmler—who apparently was rather strongly afflicted with these instinctive reactions himself—was very simple and probably very effective; it consisted in turning these instincts around, as it were, in directing them toward the self. So that instead of saying, "What horrible things I did to people," the murderers would be able to say, "What horrible things I had to watch in the pursuance of my duties, how heavenly the task weighed upon my shoulders!"[70]

Such a justification in the context of everyday life, free of genocide, seems preposterous. In the context of Himmler's encroachment, nevertheless, a rationale becomes a reason, and finally a burden for which the one shouldering it sees oneself as doing his or her part in a national campaign. What seems to be the strangest kind of self-understanding in one context becomes, in another, the common perception. The model of privation provides an explanation for this mystery. With the erosion of thought, action, and sensitivity to others, the dastardly and morally horrific become commonplace. What Arendt describes is an erosion of character on a massive scale. This phenomenon is simply not capable of being adequately accounted for in the Manichean model.

Similarly, the model of privation, with its emphasis on what is presently absent, is more complex and encompassing than theodicy, which construes evil as a present goodness (and thus not in need of any fundamental modification), or perspectivalism, which sees evil as historical circumstance that has no real ontological purchase. We have already discussed the problem of quietism in theodicy. If the world is as it should be, where is the impetus to find the present state of affairs inadequate, or, for that matter, to feel the compulsion to turn inward in constructive pedagogical self-criticism? In the theodicy model, bystanders have the luxury of seeing Hitler and Himmler as agents symbolic of an ultimate goodness that cannot be seen in the present. They were sadists and murders, yes, but more important, they were God's agents.[71] Even sophisticated theodicies, such as free will defenses, require examples like Hitler to put into sharper focus the contrast to the good—evil—that is ultimately to be avoided and defeated, but which sometimes must be endured to enunciate the real possibility of free choice.

We are again reminded of William James's discussion of Reni's painting of St. Michael with his foot on Satan's neck: We are better off in the world with evil in it, as long as that evil is eventually contained. Evil is, by this logic, a form of good. Neither Augustine nor Camus nor Arendt is so quick to let us off the hook. For them, opting to interpret evil through the lens of theodicy is a complacency that permits the self to accept what the world brings. They enjoin us to be dissatisfied with the world as it presents itself. They reject the perspectivalist attitude that evil is a prop used by the one doing the propping. To be sure, something is objectively terrible about genocide, gratuitous bloodshed, and so forth, and no less terrible is our potentially uncaring response to these phenomena. With all three figures, staving off evil entails specific habit formations and actions.

Finally, the model of privation, in both its theological and secular forms, has something to recommend it as a descriptively apropos understanding of contemporary evil. Technology makes our participation in evil easier than ever before. As the socio-psychologists Stanley Milgram and Philip Zimbardo, and more recently the historian Jonathan Glover, have each shown, much of the terrible behavior human beings cause has to do with the situations into which they are thrown, under circumstances that almost assuredly they did not anticipate. Today technology facilitates the easy killing of many people at a distance. This reduces both the sympathy for the victims of conflict as well as the feeling of responsibility for the forces that put them in harm's way.[72] Such a development, along with others (e.g., totalizing institutions within the global arena that efficiently exert control over their respective domains; the sophisticated means we now have to market and sell wars; the new technologies that enable us to fight them without feeling the costs), become malignancies when powerful people of weak to average moral character have to choose between doing their jobs and bucking the system that has until then supported them.

More than ever it has become easy to do nothing and yet find oneself doing harm. Depending on the confluence of givens beyond one's control, givens that are ever on the rise, it requires unusual effort and strength of character not to cause others harm. Here is where the privation model, again, becomes descriptively apt. Of the four models presented, it seems best equipped to capture the phenomenon by which otherwise normal individuals come to participate in the perpetuation of horrors and wrongdoing they might never have thought possible. The majority of instances in which we encounter evildoing do not involve psychopaths but instead individuals whose normal capacities for sympathy, fellow-feeling, and solidarity have eroded in response to both situational pressures and character devolvement. If this is so, the remedy for evildoing becomes, in turn, the burden of self-awareness by which one goes out of one's way to become more familiar with the kinds of dangerous situations whereby one becomes susceptible to dehumanization, as well as the burden of character development whereby one cultivates the wherewithal to resist the path of least resistance that so often is evildoing. On this last point, many of Augustine's theological descendants have a good deal to say.

Neo-Augustinians

When the wolf lies down with the lamb, the concern is not that the wolf will gobble up the lamb, but that the lamb will, through a process of toughening and resignation, become a wolf. Commenting on the prospects for redemption in an imperfect world, Reinhold Niebuhr worries that retributive justice, indeed all attempts to redress evil, face the perennial threat of lapsing into vindictiveness and tyranny themselves. Nevertheless, he posits one possible way out of the quandary: "It is possible to transcend a conflict while standing in it. Forgiveness is such a possibility. But forgiveness . . . is possible only if I know myself to be a sinner—that is, if I do not have some cheap or easy sense of moral transcendence over the sinful reality of claims and counterclaims which is the very stuff of history."[73]

Niebuhr's overt repudiation of theodicy, in which he attempts to expose as fatuous the belief that any of us can ever escape the stain of human history unscathed, nevertheless presents a hopeful prognosis in the face of evil. Although we can never be completely purged of vindictiveness, which Niebuhr defines as "an egoistic corruption of justice," true justice can be approximated in the context of conflict depending "upon the degree to which a 'Kingdom of God' perspective can be brought upon the situation. It is this higher imagination rather than some unspoiled rational definition of retributive justice that pulls justice out of the realm of vindictiveness."[74] Sin thus can be stabilized but not obviated through humility, whereas an appeal to conscience, though substantially reined in by history, nevertheless borrows in the present against the returns of an eternal future to prevent us from becoming the tyrannies we are trying to defend ourselves against. Niebuhr's characterization of evil is descriptively plausible by virtue of his resistance against any move to water down suffering, calamity, and moral atrocity.[75] However, like Augustine, whose theological example he retrieves, freedom is a notion that exists in its pure state in the kingdom to come that at present is at best "both here and not yet." Niebuhr in this sense is neither too optimistic nor Manichean. He is, as Robert MacAfee Brown once called him, a "pessimistic optimist."[76] That is, for Niebuhr freedom breaks into sin in piecemeal, sometimes small, and always hard-won victories during which compassion prevails where it did not need to do so.

Evil, correspondingly, is absence of virtue. Niebuhr characteristically describes this in theological terms. Seeming very similar to Augustine, he writes that moral evil "is the consequence of man's abortive effort to overcome his insecurity by his own power, to hide the finiteness of his intelligence by pretensions of omniscience and to seek for emancipation from his ambiguous position by his own resources." Sin, on the other hand, a mixture of vanity and pride, amounts to a person's penchant to think "more highly of himself than he ought to think."[77] Niebuhr thereby construes evil specifically as a failure to exhibit humility or the capacity to get outside oneself. Love fully realized is an "impossible possibility."[78] Freedom, though difficult, exists at least insofar as it remains within our ability to perceive the ways in which we are fundamentally not free. Mathewes notes that according to Niebuhr we cannot simply will to remake ourselves de novo,

> for our freedom is constrained by our nature, and particularly our finitude, in ineliminable ways. Freedom is not any simple exercise of human will which can overcome all constraints, for our freedom bears within itself vexations and limitations which make it always dangerously "partial." We are only partly free and hence remain partly governed by forces outside our own intentional control; and even our limited exercises of freedom always favor some faction or fraction of the relevant truth to the detriment of other, equally valid, perspectives. Given this, we become most free by realizing our freedom's limits and our sinfulness—in the paradoxical idea, extending at least as far back as St. Paul, that our freedom is found under the form of bondage.[79]

The contrast between the understanding of freedom in the model of privation and the other models in this book becomes clear in Niebuhr's formulation. We are tragic beings, or at least beings consigned to choose between relatively tragic options, because of our inability to fully understand, let alone remedy, our insufficiency, both as perpetrators and as victims. Manicheanism and perspectivalism take two easy ways out by positing, respectively, an ineluctably hopeless or fatuously hope-free circumvention around the pressure that ought to fall on our shoulders to acquire self-awareness. Manichean despair and a sub-jectivist denial of what would plausibly cause us to despair amount to a char-acter laziness that causes us to ignore who we are, and thereby make us susceptible to forms of complacency that, as time transpires, become pernicious. For example, in the case of repelling the armed enemy we become unthinking oppressors ourselves when we believe, on resisting oppression, that we do not dirty our hands at the same time. Justice is never a substitute for love, only an approximation. Meanwhile, it is also a contradiction.

Given Niebuhr's emphasis on human finitude, theodicy is also to be found wanting on the grounds that it fails to emphasize the residual mystery that is always to be associated with experienced evil as well as the evil we cause. This is an observation, again, attention to which is heightened in a world wherein it is increasingly easier to participate in oppression and widespread campaigns that cause others to suffer. The utmost vigilance is required to ensure that we do not contribute in subtle ways to forms of oppression and violence which, were they exposed, would most likely evoke our outrage. Daily, without realiz-ing it, plenty of us support slave labor, side with governments that resort to violence to secure an international advantage, and harm the environment with the wasteful habits of a consumerist culture. It is our ignorance, our seeing ourselves as outside these practices, that contributes to our participation in them. Sometimes such insults to human flourishing are unavoidable. What we might control, however, is our awareness of the human encounter with subtle and institutional wrongdoing. Although awareness of my participation in evil does not remove my evildoing, it does make a tangible difference. Moral evil is, therefore, a function of the absence of self-awareness, including the aware-ness that evil does not exist outside human life. We are evil, but the extent to which we are is within our control.

Whereas for Niebuhr the absence of a theological virtue finds its expression in pride, for Karl Barth the sin of sloth signals the occasions on which we over-estimate our self-sufficiency and ability to steer clear of participation in wrong-doing. As with Niebuhr and Arendt, Barth identifies the culpable (and godless) decision in that of remaining idle rather than being explicitly monstrous: "At every point, as we shall see, this is the strange inactive action of the slothful man. It may be that this action often assumes the disguise of a tolerant indiffer-ence in relation to God. But in fact it is the action of the hate which wants to be free of God, which would prefer that there were no God, that God were not the One. He is—at least for him, the slothful man."[80]

According to Barth evil is, literally, nothingness. In *Church Dogmatics*, Barth speaks of evil as wholly other than God, the lie of self-sufficiency we tell our-selves that manifests itself as a foreign, disruptive disturbance in creation with which God has nothing to do.[81] In other words, evil is our own accomplishment. It is bereft of God's grace, leading to entropy and negation of meaning. It is the by-product of time that is wasted, and, particularly given how that time could have been creatively spent, destructively so. Evil, for Barth, cannot be domesticated or theorized away. Evil is a stark departure from our essential purpose, a self-alienation.[82] It is conceptually derivative of reality but in no way to be identified with reality. In practical terms it is the denial of creation, community, and any sense of human flourishing. Thus in Barth we have perhaps the most emphatic expression of the privation account: Nothingness has no justification, no raison d'etre, yet it exists as a threat to God's created splendor. "Its existence, significance, and reality are not distinguished by any value nor positive strength. The nature underlying its existence and activity is perversion. Its right to be and simply to express itself is simply that of wrong. In this sense it is nothingness."[83]

Barth wrote *Church Dogmatics* in the wake of World War II, and the polemical interest in the work's attempting to make sense of fascist order within a larger context of disorder ought not to be lost on his reader. This said, the Nazis are a concrete example of an absurd and inexplicable yet potentially commonplace abdication of humility, and with it dignity and moral agency.[84] For Barth, the moral is ancillary to the theological: It is God's creative gift that makes sensible acting possible. Murderous Nazism epitomizes rogue acting on one's own. Arrogance dovetails sloth. Without God, we betray an "unhallowed lust" for what is not our own, engendering a "falsehood, hatred and pride in which [we] are enmeshed in relation to [our] neighbor, the stupidity to which [we] are self-condemned, and a life which follows the course thereby determined on the basis of the necessity thus imposed."[85] Evil is that denial of reality that we have no choice but to live through (because of the self-fulfilling prophesy just described), but for which at the same time we are culpable (because it is we who have in the first place turned our backs on God). Evil is the denial of the well-lived life, the life lived in favor of a flourishing. With Barth, the content of ethics is filled out in consultation with God's command: "Knowledge of the good is the self-knowledge in which we see that in our reflection on the good which precedes decision we are *not ourselves judges* and are in no position, through a choice of this or that act preceding our decision, to pronounce judgment on ourselves or to bring about our own determination for salvation or perdition."[86]

Thus, for Barth we are free, though our freedom is limited to reflection to become responsible to a higher judge and respectful of our place in relation to that judge. Spiritual and thereby ethical flourishing requires life lived in the example of Jesus Christ whose grace makes the deliverance from suffering possible. This said, the vacuum created by inaction is present in Barth and Niebuhr no less than in Arendt and Camus. Evil, the participation with which we are all metaphysically susceptible to, is to be associated with an abandoning of creaturely self-awareness. So understood, sin, the embodiment of evil, becomes the turning away from God, for "in sin [evil] becomes man's own act, achievement, and guilt."[87]

We can now draw some conclusions about subscribers to the privation model. The nontheological and theological descendants of Augustine agree, first, that evil is not something attributable to a distinct few, monstrous human beings, but rather an ascription applicable to all of us. Indeed, it is part of the human condition, if not human nature, and woven into the conditions of our existential predicament. From the moment we are born, evil is something with which we have to contend. By doing nothing, our proximity to evil increases. This finding leads to the second observation the figures we have examined in this chapter commonly note about evil. Whether construed as sin, nothingness, abandonment, or the failure to think or form human connections, evil is the upshot of inaction just as much as if not more than it is the upshot of action. It is the *is not* for which human beings are distinctively accountable. We are not self-sufficient. We either need God's grace or have to work on ourselves, but the status quo, inertia, will impel us to get washed away in, and eventually contribute to the momentum of, evil's tide. To be a human being is to be a problem. This conclusion in turn leads to a third observation. Countering evil is centrally about acquiring the self-awareness that indicates we should resist our default predicament to realign our existence (problematic) with our essence (good). That is, even for the theological accounts that require grace for ethical action, self-awareness is the spur for building the good into our lives, a process without which we remain most susceptible to evil. Self-awareness, if it is to be genuine, requires ongoing vigilance. This involves adopting perspectives through which we see how the wrongdoing of others implicates our own participation. Self-awareness goes hand in hand with cultivating a remorseful attitude that enjoins us to consider with Dostoevsky that though "few are guilty, all are responsible."

A virtue of privation is therefore the way in which it connects lesser and greater evils and exposes subtle injustices. Augustine reminds us that in fighting evil, we risk perpetuating it. To solve our problems is to become more problematic, often in ways it is easy for us to not fully grasp. Genocide, ecological neglect, institutional dehumanization, discrimination on the basis of class, gender, race, sexual orientation, and so forth, are always our problems, so it behooves us to become involved in addressing these wrongs. In this respect, a descriptive strength of the privation model becomes a normative challenge to it, for such careful and ongoing inquiry into the self is exhausting. One rightly wonders if it is sustainable for the good life. If Augustine and his descendants are correct, then to do nothing, or too little, when we could otherwise strain to do a better job knowing ourselves as finite, sinning, and all too often indifferent selves, is to actually do something evil.

The Privation Account under Critical Scrutiny

To synthesize the four models that make up the typology I have introduced, imagine what defenders of the first three models would say about the fourth. Supporters of the Manichean view are inclined to point out to the Augustinian critic that the bid to construe evil more inclusively overlooks the raw, maleficent nature characteristic of psychopaths, whose evildoing surely goes beyond culpable negligence. This raises the issue of whether the privation account is adequate to address the motives of the perpetrator as well as the horrific experience of the victim. Is wrongdoing merely the absence of going out of one's way to do right? Are pain and suffering merely the absence of pleasure and flourishing? Or is there something specifically insidious about evil that distinguishes it from the kind of participation in sin which the Manichean might be inclined to acknowledge? This is all to ask whether the privation account is strong enough to descriptively capture evildoing in its most extreme manifestations. It is also a criticism that challenges the supposed universality of evil, pressing the observer to distinguish wrongdoing for which the possibility of redemption exists from instances that are incorrigible. The Manichean wonders whether the characterization of evil as a vacuum or an absence goes far enough in doing justice to the culpability of the evildoer or to the lived reality of that individual's victims.

Second, theodicists, who share with Augustinians presuppositions about the universality of evil, question whether the construal of evil as absence of goodness might yet qualify as one more theodicy. Consider St. Augustine's solution, which preserves free will and grace. People have an inevitable propensity for, but not a necessity to commit, evil. We are responsible for our fallen nature but not so much so that despair remains our only option. In such an account not only is God off the hook for creating evil, but his grace remains a legitimate option for our redemption. Evil, in other words, ought to be seen as the gateway to good, via the process of grace and redemption—a theodicy. To be sure, what I have just described is sometimes referred to as the "Augustinian theodicy." This leads to the speculation that privation is really a species of the larger genus of theodicy, in which case there is no need to distinguish it as a separate model.

If one of the normative objectives of privation is to bridge the gap between our existence and essence, then the supposition at work is that our essence is, in fact, good to begin and end with. It therefore remains to be shown that the privation account is sufficiently distinct from that of theodicy to warrant a separate treatment. As we saw in chapter 2, sophisticated theodicies make extensive use of the notion of free will in theological systems that characterize free will as a gift from God.

Third, perspectivalists perhaps issue the most serious criticism against the privation model, which, whether theological or secular, posits a human condition or, more strongly, a human nature alleged to govern the limiting and enabling conditions within which human beings have the ability to flourish. Privation theorists see our prospective participation with evil as a function of the ever-present vacuum that afflicts all of us variously, depending on the degree to which we are successful, with God's help or on our own, filling it with the good. Thus in their view there is an explicit account of the objective good at work. But, wonder perspectivalists, on what grounds can one establish such an account? What mechanism is at work that helps us identify the biases and influence of the various institutional powers through which what is good comes to be known? How can we confidently know that use of the language of sin, for example, is not undertaken on behalf of the one uttering the judgment rhetorically to affirm the balance of power relations as they currently exist in society? How can a human condition, much less human nature, be defended? On what grounds should these phrases not be subject to a Nietzschean or Foucaultian hermeneutic of suspicion? Whereas privation theorists focus on finitude, humility, and submission to prompt spiritual or character development, perspectivalists construe these traits as suppressions that stunt personal growth. In whose historical and current interests, they wonder, do we labor under the handicap of "difficult freedom?" Whose good does our humility serve? Augustine's way of understanding the connection between natural and moral evil relies on a role for retributive justice in which human suffering corresponds to legitimate punishment. Nietzsche, in response, asks us to "mistrust all in whom the impulse to punish is powerful."[88] It seems at least fair to require the defender of the privation account to distinguish legitimate pronouncements on humanity, the purpose of which is to bring helpful clarity regardless of circumstances, from the sorts of condemnation motivated by political or other self-interested factors. I will briefly say a word about these three general criticisms that emerge from the voice of the Manichean, theodicist, and perspectivalist.

The Manichean critique questions the comprehensiveness and descriptive power of a theory of moral evil that fails to distinguish between the sin in which we all engage—plausibly explained by the absence of traits that are tantamount to moral flourishing—and the sort of pernicious evil, capable of being perpetrated by a psychopathic few who go out of their way to harm others. According to the Augustinian view, evil, in its very many forms, accrues from the pursuit of transient or false or, worse, destructive ends, a result, as Rowan Williams puts it, of a "mistaking of the unreal and groundless for the real."[89] Selfishness, in all its many guises, is the upshot of an ambition substituted for what should have been prioritized, a concrete reality (in the case of Augustine, God) that directs the loving subject outward.

The question is whether the evildoer and the ordinary sinner represent non-overlapping magisteria. Granting that habitual failure to cultivate other-regarding virtues can often lead to evil, is there no special category for some of history's most insidious villains, such as Hitler, Stalin, and Pol Pot? In the case of such figures evidence is abundant that they had the will and means to commit sustained crimes against humanity. Bracketing the question of whether it is Satan acting in the world in the imagined evildoer, it surely at least stands to reason that when we encounter fictional characters such as Shakespeare's Iago, Flannery O'Connor's Misfit, or Cormac McCarthy's Anton Chigurh, or historical individuals like Joseph Goebbels, Hitler's intellectual visionary behind the final solution, something creatively evil is at work. To construe such figures as the passive participants in Arendtian unworlding somehow misses their destructive contribution to the worlds they undo. These figures do not participate in evil by default. They introduce it into the world by carefully orchestrated destructive means. What is defective in these individuals is not merely that they do not think, as Eichmann did not, but that they are committed to undoing human connection and community. There is something invasive and not merely internally defective in such individuals.

We have already seen the debate between Manichean and privation theorists at the end of chapter 1, when the defender of the Manichean view was under examination, and the debate ultimately hinged on which model was most effectively able to capture the full range of evil under a general descriptive heading. Whereas we concluded then that privation scores points for accommodating most instances of evil, perhaps it behooves us here to recognize that the Manichean model attends to the worst instances. Is this true? What does one who defines evil as absence of good have to say to the critic who wishes to do descriptive justice to what is distinctive about the worst sort of moral monster? Rowan Williams contends that such a challenge underestimates the destructive power inherent in the wicked, human will:

> the more power, dignity and liberty adhere naturally to a created being, the more energy there will be for the pursuit of false or destructive goals, illusory

goods. The corruption of a human will is a more far-reaching disaster than the corruption of an animal will, because the latter has a severely limited range of possibilities for innovation on the basis of reflection. . . . The disposition and habits of intelligent beings have a wide range of effects, because intelligences exist in conscious and creative interaction and interdependence: that is why they can do more damage; and it is one reason for the disproportion between the experience of evil and the level of moral culpability in any individual's life. An Augustinian would have to say that this and this alone does justice to moral personality.[90]

Evil, in the privation model, is fully capable of being and indeed is often enough introduced into the world as a horrific novelty. That mothers and fathers, and not merely conspicuous psychopaths, have the capacity to be creatively and skillfully malicious in no way diminishes the destruction of their evil. The privation account, it seems, could plausibly furnish us with an added understanding of a more recent momentous horrific event, that of the suicide bombers who flew or attempted to fly American planes into American buildings on September 11, 2001. By all accounts, these men were well-adjusted members of society, had real connections to other people in their lives, including family and other loved ones, and formed connections with others in the normal sorts of ways. Something was both brilliant and chilling in the way in which they imagined and coordinated their plot, thinking outside the box simply by, as Williams puts it, "innovating" and "reflecting" in the process of directing their will to a destructive end. Their activities were by no means simply those of a psychopath. A corrupt will needs only determination and some measure of intelligence to put an entire society on guard.

Thus evil is arguably just as if not more harmful when willed by capable moral agents as when it is to be expected according to a deterministic model. The criticism that the privation account fails to distinguish sufficiently between kinds of evil agents, thereby letting supposedly truly evil evildoers off the hook, underestimates how terrible the otherwise normal individual, who for specific reasons goes out of the way to harm others, can be. The privation model is more descriptively comprehensive than the Manichean critic realizes.

The second critique speaks to the supposed need to create a fourth model that can clarify the second model, theodicy. Does privation, albeit in a more roundabout way, not affirm theodicy? In the *Enchiridion* Augustine writes that there can be no doubt "that the only cause of any good that we enjoy is the goodness of God, and that the only cause of evil is the falling away from the unchangeable good of being made good but changeable, first in the case of an angel, and afterwards in the case of man."[91] Evil, as we have noted in this chapter, pertains to a turning away from God, the acknowledgment of which is an inducement to participate more fully in the good life for which we are intended. Despair is averted as long as suffering contains meaning, or serves as a signpost to ultimate meaning.[92] Privation becomes a temporary existential stage poised to give way to a permanent, essential one in keeping with God's good creation. Adam and Eve introduced into the human situation the sinful dishar-mony that causes us to betray our relationship to God and others. Nevertheless, through grace, (fallen) existence can give way to (redeemed) essence. For the sake of free will, God opts not to intervene in human affairs, but moral evil, our own doing or lack thereof, does not have the final word. God's perfectly created world has not gone wrong. We have. And, by virtue of grace, we can be righted. Is there something more being suggested in the privation thesis that makes it sufficiently distinct from the type of theodicy just explained?

It is important that though both theodicy and the privation thesis signal an ultimate good, the latter does so any way but simply. The emphasis on interior-ity in the model of privation is tremendous. Internal exile of the sort suggested in the Augustinian narrative implies a moral and existential pressure to be other-wise diametric to the potentially quietistic worldviews in many theodicies, according to which a world already perfect requires no modification. That is, in theodicy God's grace has already been rendered, reducing the significance of self-vigilance and contrition, both impetuses for genuine reform. The privation thesis, in calling attention to what is not present, awakens us to the spectacular variability of human experience. Daily opportunities present themselves to us as ways to build more good into the world, access our better angels, and, with rich creativity, have an influence on others. Conversely, if we do not do these things, and furthermore do not reflect on not doing them, our inaction leads to further inaction and even negative action, in short, an affirmation of the initial privation that worsens by doubling back on itself. Defenders of privation insist that we not remain static in relation to our world. The condition of variability, in turn, means the burden falls on our shoulders either to make ourselves eligi-ble for grace (Augustinian) or to repair our broken worlds ourselves (secular privation). In theodicy, there is not quite this rush to remake the world. In contrast to privation, theodicy enjoins us to discover the world, as it already stands, better than we have before.

Finally, the third critique, leveled by perspectivalists who question whether we can reliably point to human nature or even a human condition in the first place, raises the issue of the existence of a good thought to have been lost. Does such a good really exist? What are the descriptive and normative implications if it does not? No doubt, Nietzsche and his intellectual descendants rightly alert us to the many ways in which seemingly universal norms are foisted on society to the advantage of a ruling few. Reinhold Niebuhr points out the degree to which Gandhi and Martin Luther King Jr. both understood that an ethic like "turn the other cheek" followed with consistent purity would lead to the exploitation of its adherents.[93] Not just tyrants, but also moral freeloaders, roam among us in abundance. In light of this, the supposed virtuous nobility of other-regard becomes another example of something part of the moral good of which we should be, if not skeptical, at least genealogical.

Granting this point, however, does not mean that we need to dispense with the idea of the good as such. That the notions of virtue and vice have been used tendentiously by those in power does not in and of itself imply that we are not still each flawed (or sinful) in some way or other. Nor does it suggest that our flaws are comprehensibly measurable in terms of a flourishing good in which we should otherwise be partaking. One need not commit the error of the strong epistemological foundationalist, often criticized for eliding the perspective of history from one's philosophical or theological methodology, to claim that human beings share certain grounding experiences that are cross-culturally native to our species. As human beings, we experience pain in roughly the same way. We learn how to love others within the confines of family and community, wherein are systems of mutual support and interdependence. We enjoy the same kinds of benefits from play and sociality, and we are wounded in the same sorts of ways when we are betrayed or abandoned by the ones we care about. These experiences furnish us with knowledge about the kinds of things we wish to enjoy or avoid that others would wish to enjoy or avoid. The decision to provide the right and prevent the wrong sorts of things is a kind of balancing act that depends on correct insights and actions, that is, virtuous insights and actions. Rightness acquires a universality because of our awareness of the degree to which we commonly experience happiness and sorrow across cultures. Thus there can be said to be some "non-relative virtues" the noncultivation of which indicates a fundamental abdication of moral agency.[94] When we fail to support certain grounding human experiences we reveal a betrayal of character. The good, in this sense, flows from common experiences, while evil pertains to ignoring, denying, or subverting these experiences. Such an understanding is consistent with the suppositions of the privation model. By failing to act to bring about flourishing for ourselves and others, or by failing to act to prevent ourselves and others from experiencing physical pain and psychological sorrow, we display an absence of virtue and invite evil into the sphere of human experience.

Notes

1. *Human nature*, on which Augustine himself would insist, is considerably stronger than *human condition*. Human nature implies that we are hardwired to share certain feelings, motivations, experiences, that we are subject to certain physical and psychological shortcomings and moral failings, and finally, that we have certain sentiments and obligations simply by virtue of our biological status as human beings qua human beings. Human condition hints at these suppositions but grounds them in our lived experience rooted in history. Thus, when one uses the phrase human condition one is referring to a shared existential predicament, revealed to us collectively through the process of living, rather than to what necessarily constrains or drives us because of our membership in the human species.

2. See *City of God*, XIV:11, where Augustine writes, "They were alone together, two human beings, a married pair; and we cannot believe that the man was led astray to transgress God's law because he believed that the woman spoke the truth, but that he fell in with her suggestions because they were so closely bound in partnership. In fact, the Apostle was not off the mark when he said, 'It was not Adam, but Eve, who was seduced', (I Tim 2:14) for what he meant was that Eve accepted the serpent's statement as the truth, while Adam refused to be separated from his only companion, even if it involved sharing her sin. That does not mean that he was less guilty, if he sinned knowingly and deliberately. Hence the Apostle does not say, 'He did not sin,' but, 'He was not seduced'. For he certainly refers to the man when he says, 'It was through one man that sin came into the world', and when he says more explicitly, a little later, 'by reproducing the transgression of Adam' (Rom 5:12)." See Augustine, *City of God*, 570. Augustine also discusses the relationship between original sin and the connection between moral and natural evil in his anti-Pelagian writings, especially *Against Two Letters of the Pelagians*. See Augustine, *Anti-Pelagian Writings*, especially chapters 29–35.

3. Augustine, *The Confessions*, VII:3–7, 160; Augustine, *City of God*, XI:9, 353.

4. See Aristotle, "Categories," 31–32.

5. Williams, "Insubstantial Evil," 106.

6. Kant, *The Groundwork*, 23.

7. Williams, "Insubstantial Evil," 109. Also see Augustine, "On the Nature of the Good," 338. See also Mann, "Augustine on Evil and Original Sin," 45.

8. Williams, "Insubstantial Evil," 112.

9. "Corruption of the best is the worst."

10. Augustine, *City of God*, XIII:14, 571–72.

11. Lewis, *The Screwtape Letters*, 60.

12. Augustine, *The Confessions*, VIII:5, 188–89.

13. Ibid., VIII:7, 193.

14. Ibid., VIII:8, 196.

15. Augustine, *City of God*, XII:6, 478.

16. Augustine, *The Confessions*, XII:12, 172.

17. Ibid., III:7, 85.

18. Augustine, "On the Nature of the Good," 326; *The Confessions*, VII:12, 172.

19. Augustine, "On the Nature of the Good," 330; *City of God*, XI:22, 453–56. See Mann's discussion, "Augustine on Evil and Original Sin," 44.

20. Augustine, "On the Nature of Good," 338.

21. Also discussed in Mann, "Augustine on Evil and Original Sin," 45.

22. Stalnaker, *Overcoming Our Evil*, 88. I thank Stalnaker for pointing me to the relevant passages in *On True Religion* (23, 38–39, 44) and *City of God* (XII:2–3) that demonstrate sin's subsuming evil.

23. Stalnaker, 88.

24. Rist, *Augustine*, 121. I became aware of Rist through reading Stalnaker.

25. Augustine, *On Free Choice*, I:1, 4.

26. Ibid., I:3, 7–8.

27. Ibid., I:11, 21–22.

28. Ibid., I:15, 32–33.

29. Evans, *Augustine on Evil*, 115–16.

30. St. Augustine, *On Nature and Grace*, XIV (www.newadvent.org/fathers/1503.htm).

31. Evans, 121. Evans points out that this is the meaning of Romans 1:21, "their foolish heart was darkened," which Augustine took to heart.

32. Augustine, *On Nature and Grace*, XVIII, discussed by Evans, 121.

33. Augustine, *City of God*, XIII:13, 522–23.

34. Ibid., XII:6, 477.

35. Ibid., XIV:13, 571.

36. Ibid., XIII:3, 512; XIV:12, 571; see especially books XII–XIV. Stalnaker, again, is helpful here. See especially *Overcoming Our Evil*, 94–95.

37. Stalnaker, 95.

38. St. Augustine, *On Free Choice of the Will*, 152.

39. Kent, "Augustine's Ethics," 226.

40. It is important that subjectivism, the idea that good and bad pertain to what each individual subject says is good or bad, and Pelagianism, the idea that we are subjectively free to overcome evil and partake in an objective good, are not terms that are confused. The latter, and not the former, acknowledges an objective account of evil.

41. See the subtitle of chapter 40 in *On Rebuke and Grace*, www.ewtn.com/library/PATRISTC/PNI5–11.HTM.

42. I am here acknowledging, with, for example, Eric Gregory, that while he himself was no "political liberal," Augustine could certainly be used for politically liberal purposes, one of which is to explore a possible secular Augustinianism. For a discussion of the legitimacy of taking this tack, as well as a consideration of the precedents for doing so, see Eric Gregory's introduction to *Politics and the Order of Love*, 1–29.

43. Ibid., 8. See also Mathewes, *Evil and the Augustinian Tradition*, 220.

44. See Gregory's discussion in *Politics and the Order of Love*, 17–19.

45. Milbank, *Theology and Social Theory*, 405–6.

46. Gregory, *Politics and the Order of Love*, 8.

47. Ibid., 14.

48. Ibid., 21.

49. Camus, *The Rebel*, 304.

50. Very little work exists on connecting Augustine to Camus, much less on construing Camus as an Augustinian. However, perhaps my move to do so should not be quite so surprising given (the relatively little known fact) that Camus did his dissertation on

Augustine. For more, see the best insider account of Camus I have come across, Hawes, *Camus, A Romance.* I thank Lloyd Steffen for turning me on to Hawes's volume.

51. Camus, *The Myth of Sisyphus*, 64.

52. Ibid., 123.

53. Camus, *The Fall*, 25.

54. Ibid., 100.

55. Ibid., 107–8.

56. Ibid., 110.

57. Ibid., 132–33.

58. See Camus on "Natural Community," in *The Rebel*, 249.

59. Arendt, *Eichmann in Jerusalem: A Report*, 49.

60. Arendt, "Eichmann in Jerusalem: An Exchange," 51–56.

61. Neiman, *Evil in Modern Thought*, 301.

62. Ibid., 301.

63. Arendt, *Life of the Mind*, 3.

64. Arendt, *Eichmann in Jerusalem: A Report*, 276.

65. Arendt, *Origins of Totalitarianism*, 177.

66. Gregory, *Politics and the Order of Love*, 206.

67. Mathewes, *Evil and the Augustinian Tradition*, 190.

68. For an extensive discussion of the question of whether, and to what extent, bystanders similarly and differently circumstanced ought to be found culpable for their inaction during the Holocaust, see Flescher, *Heroes, Saints*, 127–57.

69. This is Daniel Jonah Goldhagen's controversial phrase. See *Hitler's Willing Executioners.*

70. Arendt, *Eichmann in Jerusalem*, 105–6.

71. This view is considered and criticized by Richard Rubenstein in *After Auschwitz.* See especially Rubenstein's introduction.

72. Glover, *Humanity*, 100.

73. Niebuhr, *Love and Justice*, 53–54.

74. Ibid., 54.

75. See Mathewes's discussion of this, *Evil and the Augustinian Tradition*, 107.

76. Brown, "Introduction," xi., cited by Mathewes, *Evil and the Augustinian Tradition*, 109.

77. Niebuhr, *Faith and History*, 121.

78. Niebuhr, *An Interpretation*, 80.

79. Mathewes, *Evil and the Augustinian Tradition*, 115–16. See also Niebuhr, *Nature and Destiny of Man*, 260.

80. Barth, *Church Dogmatics*, IV:2, 405.

81. Ibid., III:3, 289.

82. Barth, *Christian Life*, 213.

83. Barth, *Church Dogmatics*, IV:3, 178.

84. Ibid., III:3, 354.

85. Ibid., 305.

86. Barth, *Ethics*, 74.

87. Barth, *Church Dogmatics*, III:3, 310.

88. Nietzsche, *Thus Spoke Zarathustra*, 100.

89. Williams, "Insubstantial Evil," 111.

90. Ibid., 111–12.

91. Augustine, *On Holy Trinity*, 245.

92. The Holocaust survivor, theologian, and psychologist Victor Frankl says something similar. See www.youtube.com/watch?v = 9EIxGrIc_6g.

93. See Niebuhr, *Moral Man and Immoral Society*.

94. Martha Nussbaum, "Non-Relative Virtues," 32–53.

CHAPTER FIVE

Evil as Inaction

Augustine, Aristotle, and Connecting the Thesis of Privation to Virtue Ethics

"Quite often even the most important step in a man's life, his choice of vocation, is taken quite frivolously. He does not bother to find out enough about the basis and the various aspects of that vocation. Once he has chosen it, he is inclined to switch off his critical awareness and to fit himself wholly into the predetermined career."

—ALBERT SPEER, *Inside the Third Reich*

Overcoming Evil Situations

DISHEARTENING STORIES of forsaken opportunity mar today's headlines. Just as Hurricane Sandy bore down on the New York metropolitan area in late October 2012, a mother drove across Staten Island to find shelter for her two sons, aged four and two. Battling winds of nearly 100 miles an hour, her Ford Explorer hit a ditch, and the woman carried her boys to a tree in hopes of anchoring them with the support of its branches. The futility of this strategy evident, the mother banged on the door of a nearby residence and begged the occupant for shelter. Her request was abruptly denied, and very shortly afterward her boys were swept to their death by the rising waters. Their bodies were found four days later a quarter of a mile from where the mother had relinquished her final grip. Just over a month later, an argument broke out at a Times Square subway station in Manhattan as a result of which a thirty-year-old man threw a fifty-eight-year-old man onto the tracks. As the victim struggled to lift himself up to the platform, he was run over by an oncoming train to an untimely death. The aggressor was arrested shortly afterward, but the feature of this story that brought it special notoriety was the inaction of a freelance photographer who witnessed the incident up close and opted to capture it on film rather than attempt to offer the victim a helping hand. Affixed next to his image picturing the doomed man about to be caught between the train and the edge of the platform, the tag in the *New York Post* read, "Pushed on the subway track this man is about to die."

Neither the resident who refused a desperate mother safe haven for her sons nor the photographer at the Times Square subway station did anything illegal. One might say they acted well short of, even offensively below, the line of duty. Still, in terms of causing the tragedies in question, they retained deniability. Hurricane Sandy and a madman were the ones directly responsible. In both cases the bystanders had reasons of which they could avail themselves to appeal to common sense notions of that for which we are to be held minimally responsible in society. Charitably, one could argue that the Staten Island resident who denied shelter to strangers might have been thinking about the safety of his or her family, and the photographer perhaps desired not to risk his own safety in a low probability rescue attempt. After the incident he repeatedly claimed he was not close enough to the fallen man to have made a difference. Nevertheless, something is terribly disappointing about the self-absorption of these two bystanders. Although neither intended harm, their priorities were tied exclusively to their needs, and in these two cases this was enough to make both complicit in the unfolding of potentially avoidable tragedies.

Is being complicit in this fashion something for which human beings should be found morally culpable or, for that matter, something that belongs in a book about evil? In the real world, one must look after oneself, and perhaps it is too much to expect that an altruistic impulse should override self-preservation, especially when the stakes are high. The temptation to be for oneself is powerful, and this consideration provides some natural sympathy for these bystanders when we think about how we would behave if we were in similar circumstances. In life, simply by waking up in the morning, we can find ourselves in a situation in which, starting out doing something good, or neutral, we end up doing something bad. On the other hand, this does not have to be the outcome, and it is conceivable that the episodes described are ones of a good character that has either devolved or never developed. Our attitude toward others, I suggest, is determined by the situations we inherit as well as the success with which we oversee the progress of our developing character. Complicating the matter is the ever-present human temptation to rationalize one's nonvirtuous actions with self-deception.

One horrific example of moral evil in which self-deception played a role in lessening the pressure one might otherwise have felt to act on behalf of the other in need is that of Albert Speer, one of the twenty-one leaders of Nazi Germany tried and found guilty of war crimes and crimes against humanity in Nuremberg in 1945 and 1946. Speer, minister of Armaments and War Production for the Third Reich and ultimately Hitler's chief architect, is famous both for his unique apology at the Nuremberg trials and for his memoirs, the thrust of the first of which, *Inside the Third Reich*, was to assume a general responsibility for genocide by virtue of a willful ignorance that at the same time did not amount, in his view, to any particular culpability on his part. The precise degree to which Speer was aware of the extermination of the Jews is in dispute.[1] It at least seems clear, however, that the construction of the armament facilities he supervised, some of which used slave labor from concentration camps where many workers died due to deplorable conditions, furnished him with some sense of Hitler's Final Solution.[2] The nearest Speer comes in his memoirs to betraying explicit awareness of genocide occurs in discussing an exchange with his former supervisor and close friend Karl Hanke, who implored him never to accept an invitation to inspect one of the concentration camps:

> I did not query him, I did not query Himmler, I did not query Hitler, I did not speak with personal friends. I did not investigate—for I did not want to know what was happening there. Hanke must have been speaking of Auschwitz. During those few seconds, while Hanke was warning me, the whole responsibility had become a reality again. Those seconds were uppermost in my mind when I stated to the international court at the Nuremberg Trial that as an important member of the leadership of the Reich, I had to share total responsibility for all that had happened. From that moment on, I was inescapably contaminated morally; from fear of discovering something which might have made me turn my course, I had closed my eyes. This deliberate blindness outweighs whatever good I may have done or tried to do in the last period of the war. Those activities shrink to nothing in the face of it. Because I failed at that time, I still feel, to this day, responsible for Auschwitz in a wholly personal sense.[3]

Speer's confession of being too afraid to become informed and take responsibility for dissuading Hitler's genocidal policies ironically can be read to serve as an attempt to exonerate himself from the even worse crime of orchestrating the efficient mechanisms within which murder could take place. Thus, even if he believed it himself, one must ask, with David Burrell and Stanley Hauerwas, "whether Speer's admission is not an extremely clever way of reclaiming his place in decent society."[4] As David Jones notes, Speer's confessions were likely "carefully limited" assumptions of culpability for the purpose of reducing his criminal liability and also for creating the deliberately misleading impression that he did not know that the concentration camps he helped build existed alongside death camps.[5]

Such observations about the tactical nature of Speer's admissions are supported by passages in *Inside the Third Reich*, in which the author discusses his ambitions as an architect. In one appeal to the reader, Speer contends that to have had any chance of professional success in Germany in the 1930s and early 1940s, one's loyalty could not be questioned. Thus, one had to be willing to abide Hitler's magnetic hold over the turning wheels of bureaucracy at every level.[6] Under such pressure it is not hard to see how self-deception becomes a coping mechanism: To thrive but also live with oneself, one might sometimes have to be creative in redescribing to oneself the situation in which one is trapped. Speer implies that this habit, widely adopted among his contemporaries in leadership positions, in turn led to an unchecked culture of absurdity:

> The departure from reality, which was visibly spreading like a contagion, was no peculiarity of the National Socialist regime. But in normal circumstances people who turn their backs on reality are soon set straight by the mockery and criticism of those around them, which makes them aware they have lost their credibility. In the Third Reich there were no such correctives, especially for those who belonged to the upper stratum. On the contrary, every self-deception was multiplied as in a hall of distorting mirrors, becoming a repeatedly confirmed picture of a fantastical dream world which no longer bore any relationship to the grim outside world.[7]

In this remarkable account, it is the very acknowledgment of self-deception that furthers the acknowledger's habit of self-deceiving. Speer assumes responsibility for his willful ignorance but manages also to construe himself as a victim of circumstance, one who ought not to be judged too quickly, lest anyone not in his shoes fail to grasp the full nature of his motives and the obstacles with which he had to contend. Like the bystanders discussed earlier, Speer asserts reasonable grounds to maintain that he of course would never prefer his own regard to come at the expense of the well-being of others. Under unusual duress he acted in favor of his survival, certainly blameworthy, he admits, but perhaps not criminally so.

Does Speer's observation that his were not normal circumstances really make a morally mitigating difference to his decision to turn a blind eye to sustained massacre? Specifically, were the bulk of his limitations merely a result of the situation he inherited coupled with the self-deception he admits he adopted as a coping mechanism, or did they have to do with something more essential about Speer? Burrell and Hauerwas provide an alternative explanation to

Speer's account of his motives. They argue that the problem in this case has to do with a lack of clarity, a not-thinking, as it were, which in the first place led to Speer's susceptibility to falling prey to his society's culture of self-deception. Self-deception alone, they suggest, is neither a compelling mark of distinction nor that uncommon:

> Contrary to our dominant presumptions, we are seldom conscious of what we are doing or who we are. We choose to stay ignorant of certain engagements with the world, for to put them all together often asks too much of us, and sometimes threatens the more enjoyable engagements. We profess sincerity and normally try to abide that profession, yet we neglect to acquire the very skills which will test that profession of sincerity against our current performance. On the contrary, we deliberately allow certain engagements to go unexamined, quite aware that areas left unaccountable tend to cater to self-interest. As a result of that inertial policy, the condition of self-deception becomes the rule rather than the exception to our lives.[8]

The lesson to draw from Speer's autobiography, in other words, is that the critical variable in the fight against evil is not one's experience of self-deception, or even one's sincere attempt to overcome self-deception, but rather the extent of one's commitment to undertaking those painstaking and hard-fought attempts throughout one's life to acquire the right skills, and eventually traits, that enable one to overcome selfishness and adopt the other's perspective. The death of others in our midst may sometimes be explained as a not uncommon turn of events, worthy of examination in context. This does not make it an unavoidable or, for that matter, morally excusable turn of events. Were Albert Speer an individual who had before the rise of Hitler been more vigilant and worked harder on maintaining his good character, he might have been more resistant to that character lapsing when he inherited a situation that made perspective-taking difficult.

This judgment is not entirely consistent with the conclusions of both Milgram and Zimbardo, who argue that disadvantageous situations are what make individuals whose instincts are humane under normal circumstances become callous and sadistic under stressed ones.[9] Milgram's and Zimbardo's subjects were made to believe that the disobedient over whom they had control could be punished through either painful electric shock or severe discipline in a prison setting, respectively, and, to the surprise of even Milgram and Zimbardo, the majority of their subjects in fact availed themselves of these options.[10] From these findings they concluded that ordinary people who display morally praiseworthy traits can nevertheless act maliciously under specific, and not necessarily out of the ordinary, environmental pressures. We are not above the situations in which we find ourselves. Milgram and Zimbardo, to their credit, were each interested in these findings as a way of recalling our attention to larger institutions of oppression, such as the war machine of the state, as a way of protecting ourselves against our darker demons, which, when placed under stress, are too easily released on one another. Their experiments are of value because they make us self-aware and alert us to the sorts of things in which anyone unwittingly can come to participate in civil society. Yet, to draw from such social experimentation the conclusion that human beings are ineluctably prone to participate in evil under the right set of circumstances and understand evil as banal in this respect, it seems to me, is to fail to recognize a critical feature of how otherwise normal individuals come to participate in evil, a feature quite distinct from situational circumstance. It is true that ordinary people have been known to do extraordinarily rotten things, but they are not required do them. Thirty to 35 percent of Milgram's subjects reached a point at which they refused to torture fellow human beings.[11] Why? What makes some individuals more resistant to situational pressures than the majority? Milgram's thesis about our susceptibility to norms of obedience that arise under the canopy of systemic totalities, even norms that appear weakly in the form of verbal orders, does not account for the differences among human beings.

We are not all equidistant from the good. Milgram's experiments are intended to simulate real-world, top-down oppressions. However, in the sort of crisis situations Milgram has in mind, not only are some actors clearly culpable, but also some witnesses become villains and still others become heroes, and still others do not act at all. We might conclude that our religious and moral traditions—and our developing character within these traditions—explain the differences between how we process and respond to an evil that presents itself, at least initially, as beyond our control. Milgram, by contrast, could be characterized as a situational determinist. He maintains that submission to authority is a "powerful and prepotent condition in man," claiming that once ensconced in social organizations, which are hierarchical, human beings undergo an "agentic shift" whereby they lose their autonomy.[12]

> Specifically, the person entering an authority system no longer views himself as acting out of his own purposes but rather comes to see himself as an agent for executing the wishes of another person. Once an individual conceives action in this light, profound alterations occur in his behavior and internal functioning. These are so pronounced that one may say that this altered attitude places the individual in a different *state* from the one he was in prior to integration into the hierarchy. I shall term this the *agentic state*, by which I

mean the condition a person is in when he sees himself as an agent for carrying out another person's wishes. This term will be used in opposition to that of *autonomy*—that is, when a person sees himself as acting on his own.[13]

Milgram accounts for the person who bucks the system, the dissenter, not in terms of his or her objection to the immorality of the proposed cruel act of obedience, but rather in terms of one's distance to the totalizing system that induces the actor's resistance. He asserts that the disposition of anyone having undergone the agentic shift will be to appease the systemic pressures to which that person is now subject. He characterizes as strain any opposition to those pressures, oppositions that arise, for example, from the discomfort one feels when one causes pain in others, fears retaliation for the pain one causes, or desires to see oneself as someone who does not cause others pain.[14] In other words, what is key for Milgram is the relation between subject and authority. The subject is always most susceptible to the pressures endemic to hierarchical totalities that reward compliance with a system and punish disobedience. However, this susceptibility is tempered by lesser self-interested pressures, "strains," that count against one's succumbing to the totality. Thus, Milgram accounts for the 30 to 35 percent of those who refused to administer shocks by calling attention to the redefinition of their assigned role within the social order. For this minority, the strains that afford the defecting group of individuals distance from the system prevail over the gravitational pull of the system. Compliance with immoral obedience, for Milgram, is always a function of an ongoing negotiation between the self and the various influences to which it is subject at any given time. Obedience and disobedience can be measured in terms of toleration of experienced conflict about subverting competing authorities. French Protestants, according to Milgram's theory, sheltered hunted Jews not because of a communal understanding of what represented virtuous versus inhumane behavior toward vulnerable others, but because their historical experience as Huguenots provided them with too much cognitive dissonance to be able to comply with the Gestapo's objectives in Vichy France. Protestants resisting the Gestapo is explained as the result of one authority superseding another, not the trump card of communal conscience.

The problem with Milgram's explanation is not only that it fails to account for what the descendants of Huguenots have to say about what they did in their own words.[15] It also places everyone on a continuum relative to an individual's susceptibility to the totalizing system in question. The implication is that if obedience to the oppressive regime is to be overridden, it must be overridden by an even greater locus of influence, or combination of influences. Milgram does not consider an alternative explanation, namely, that one is not obedient to a cruel end, despite the self-interested pressures that mount in favor of that outcome, because one's character, informed by acquisition of virtue, helps one resist being obedient in this circumstance. Such an explanation, though, is in fact both the most consistent with how dissenters characterize their actions and allows for the descriptive flexibility to account for how bystanders could call attention to a conscience that trumps authority.[16] In the epilogue to *Obedience to Authority*, Milgram rightly claims that the example of immoral obedience that occurred with Nazism ought not to be dismissed easily by those in democratic societies as apropos only to fascist regimes. Even when legitimately elected, our leaders assume the authority bestowed upon them and begin to exert the influence of their office, which can become easily corruptible.[17] A tremendous value of Milgram's work is its role in putting citizens of a free society on notice that we too will find ourselves in situations in which we feel coerced to participate in oppressions simply because of the nature of authority.

However, Milgram becomes a reductivist when he attributes instances of moral disobedience as exclusively a function of actors successfully overcoming their cognitive dissonance to resisting a totalizing system. Indeed, some of these "defectors" resist the immorally obedient thing but have no sense of cognitive dissonance whatsoever. They are able to see an encroaching evil clearly for what it is, and know immediately what their response to it must be. A good example of one such dissenter is that of the Lutheran pastor, Dietrich Bonhoeffer, who paid with his life for the plot in which he participated to murder Hitler. Unlike Albert Speer, Bonhoeffer went out of his way, in conjunction with the German Military Intelligence Office (*Abwehr*), to pose as one working within the system in order to undo it.[18] His conviction came from a sense of self robust enough to not accept the dominant wave of sentiment overtaking persons in positions of leadership in his country, and to respond proactively, resolutely, and daringly. No doubt Bonhoeffer's conviction was fueled by his religious beliefs and role in the "Confessing Church." Like the French Protestants, Bonhoeffer's character and corresponding conscience did not appear ex nihilo from within but in the social context of a faith-community. Nevertheless, resistance to an evil tide in his case is not merely explainable in terms of overcoming the pressure to be swept away by that tide. Resistance also had something to do with a positive act in favor of contributing to an overall good.

Obedience to Authority is in many respects a period piece that reflects the innovative thinking in the 1960s, when the consciousness of the world was grappling with the question of how the Holocaust could have come to take place in a society of caring fathers and mothers, of citizens quite capable of interacting civilly with one another. Milgram was a seminal figure in a new school of thinkers committed to making the world understand that evil is more ubiquitous than presumed, more the upshot of reactively fearful sheep than proactively malicious wolves. However, characterizing those sheep as incapable of being other than sheep, which Milgram also seems to do, is dangerous. About the soldier who pays a dear consequence for questioning, much less disobeying orders, Milgram remarks that he is "locked into a structure of authority, and those who charge that he is doing the devil's work threaten the very psychological adjustments that make life tolerable."[19] This characterization, though, overlooks the arguably much greater psychological benefit one accrues from having developed a moral character based on the desire to occupy goodness and attend to others in need for their sake, a good which our moral and religious traditions help us define and refine. By placing so much of the explanatory burden for immoral behavior on situational pressures, Milgram lets us off the hook despite that his motivation is to put us on the hook (by alerting us to our propensity to unwittingly participate in evil). We can drift into the danger zone when hierarchical structures of authority impel us to go with the flow. But when this happens, neither are we completely helpless nor are our prospects for resisting unjust authority simply a function of our ability to overcome the cognitive dissonance such a situation is prone to induce. Situational pressures do impinge on our autonomy in ways that are sometimes not so apparent. However, this is a reason self-awareness is crucial to flourishing and reducing our participation with evil. If we train ourselves to expect to run into situations that make our concern for others less than optimal, then we will (we hope) have attended in advance to developing the sorts of moral insights and virtuous skills that prepare us for identifying and staving off the temptation to let fear or reward get the best of us when we become morally vulnerable.

In light of this objection to Milgram's situational determinism, let us return to the example of Albert Speer. We may grant that it is not Speer's fault that he had professional ambitions as an architect that, as it turned out, would be served by the Third Reich as well as immediately ended if he opposed that regime. To the extent that he engaged in willful ignorance about the extermination of innocents perpetrated by the Third Reich, however, he also bears responsibility for his participation in it, whether willing or unwilling. Whether we are talking about the sort of "agentic shifts" caused by systems of authority that preoccupy Milgram or about the commonplace temptations that dilute understandable self-serving motives, the opportunities to become accidentally callous or cruel in this world are everywhere. Our encounters with these opportunities, though irremovable from the human experience, however, do not determine it.

Evil is a constant. There will be a certain frequency with which we are tempted to participate in evil about which we can do nothing. Nevertheless, our response to evil, the success with which we stave off this participation, is a variable. Keeping in mind the model of privation described in the last chapter, there might be said to be a macro and a micro aspect to evil. The macro aspect pertains to the inherited component of evil that is bigger than we are, the component that remains beyond our control because we are finite creatures. These are limiting conditions to being human. We are, as Milgram suggests, not entirely self-aware creatures, and thus are ever susceptible to institutions that take over our social worlds exerting influence in ways that are not apparent. Moreover, we are flawed. We are too often proud and slothful, prone to remain eclipsed from the good regardless of whether this is because of original sin, as Augustine thinks, or because we are always already enmeshed in existing unjust systems of subjugation where simply to be is to be at another's expense.

Yet, a micro aspect of evil also pertains to the responsibility we bear for what we lack, namely, our level of virtue, which in turn determines our distance from the good. According to the privation model of evil, our freedom is "difficult," which means that though we are not totally free to release our better angels at will, nor are we so constrained that we are precluded from doing anything to listen and respond to, connect with, and help out others. As creatures created good, or who, bereft of this cosmological account, find ourselves endowed with a measure of goodness, we are never helpless over long strings of time. Like Camus's Sisyphus, who spends a lifetime rolling a boulder up a mountain only to have it roll down again, but who still finds dignity in the fifteen minutes it takes him to get to the bottom, we each daily have opportunities to make a difference for the better in this world. Although we should perhaps resist both the macro and the micro aspects of evil when we encounter them, we can often do nothing about the macro aspects because their impact on human flourishing is so ubiquitous. We can, however, do something about evil's micro aspect. We can, for example, internalize and take seriously the ubiquity of evil, accept that to be human is to exist under the threat or temptation of evil, and, equipped with this self-knowledge, use it to ready ourselves for evil's approach by becoming the sorts of persons who have virtues in the arsenal of our character to marshal a response to it, taking into account that that response will inevitably be incomplete.

The macro aspect of evil, therefore, we can do little about, but we have some measure of control and autonomy with regard to the micro aspect. We have the ability, for example, to anticipate disasters and moral atrocities to come our way, some of which we are in peril of participating in, including calamities of nature that lay waste to communities, hierarchical totalities that sweep away our autonomous agency, and our own innate tendencies to act selfishly and sometimes cause others harm. If we anticipate these evils, we can almost always do something about them, that is, we can introduce goodness in some way. It is this micro aspect within the model of privation that ensures that free will, despite the extent to which it is sometimes overstated, is not illusion.

One way to spell out the respect in which free will is real is by connecting an Augustinian understanding of evil as absence, by virtue of which we can come to a frank realization of what flawed and vulnerable beings we are, to Aristotle, who has much to say about the acquisition of good habits, and in particular other-regarding habits. Virtue theory is a legitimate and potent, if incomplete, response to the problem of evil. The connection between Augustine and Aristotle may not seem obvious. Augustine is usually associated with an ethos of incessant self-examination that can be interpreted as obsessive self-reproach, whereas Aristotle is associated with finding the appropriate mean, that is, with cultivating habits to procure the balance that is a eudaemonic existence. I nevertheless think a case can be made that these traditional renderings of Augustine and Aristotle underemphasize some key points of compatibility between the two.

Augustine, as I argued in chapter 4, does not merely suggest a dour, resigned attitude toward life. He can also be interpreted both in his anti-Manichean and his anti-Pelagian polemical works, as well as in his own positive thinking, to argue for urging us to embrace an identity as finite, humble creatures capable of the sort of self-knowledge that in turn serves as a spur to be graced with caritas. In this way knowledge of privation, the solipsistical condition of being unto ourselves, can lead to redemption and meaningful communal connection in the face of adversity. Similarly, Aristotle, despite the view of some Aristotelians that eudaemonia implies striking the right compromise between morality and the other nonmoral virtues, can be interpreted as advocating a morally demanding ethic built around the acquisition of virtue, and particularly other-regarding virtue, as the linchpin to attaining the well-lived life. This neo-Aristotelian interpretation of Aristotle is amenable to an ethos of anxious revolt in which, to borrow a phrase from Martin Luther King, we choose to remain "maladjusted" to the overwhelming tide of complacency that always threatens to overtake us.[20] Recognizing a starting point of absence invites a discussion of what should be present. What good presents itself as an alternative to the seductions produced by fame and fortune? What good provides us with the resources to oppose the institutional machines that scare us into conforming to unjust, dehumanizing norms? In lieu of eradicating evil, how may we cope with it, not by removing it from the human experience, which is impossible, but by reducing it with the proactive commission of actions that reveal a commitment to the building and rebuilding of human community and connection?

Aristotle, Self-Deception, and the Will

One feature of virtue ethics on which scholars of Aristotle agree is that the acquisition of virtue produces a steady and reliable state of character. That is, we inculcate virtue through working at it and becoming, over time and through effort and repetition, skilled exemplars with regard to the inhabiting of some critical traits, the combination of which identify as virtuous.[21] Character is key. Who we are is a judgment about our identity, made not in isolated snapshots, but over stretches of time. Goodness is not a matter of happening to do this or that good thing, but becoming and then enduringly being the sort of person who does good things when the situations to do them arise, as they inevitably frequently will if one is paying attention to one's surroundings in this world.[22]

As we have established, the threat of evil, which includes our susceptibility to falling in line with powerful and corrupting systems and institutions, is simply too great to think that we will somehow be exempt from these influences when they find our way to us. We will either be prepared when they arrive or we will not. One must develop a sense of oneself strong enough to combat inertia. In this respect, becoming a good person depends on our learning things about flourishing over the long haul that we do not already know from people who know better about what it means to flourish than we do.[23] What this means is that, to live the good life, several conditions must be present.

First, one must be part of a community in which the virtues find ample expression, and in which one can locate authoritative and trustworthy express-ers of virtue. In this sense, flourishing entails our acknowledging that we depend on others. Second, that one stays connected to one's community, invests in and outside it, and imparts the virtue one acquires to those who are, relatively speaking, less experienced than oneself, are each critical in terms of maintaining a social world that can potentially counter rival, dehumanizing ones. To flourish, one must both build one's social capital and give back to one's community. Third, with regard to the many respects in which one can lose sight of one's connection to and concern with others, one must keep oneself in check. One must always keep a watchful eye towards the inducements one encounters that serve to blunt, and sometimes numb, one's responsibility to others. Because order is more difficult to maintain than entropy, the world is consti-tuted to give the evil the upper hand. A presence requires more effort than an absence. If, as the privation thesis suggests, evil really is an absence, then stav-ing off our participation with evil is going to be hard work. Fourth, and finally, becoming a good person entails a vivid awareness of one's humanity, specifi-cally, one's inescapable need for others' help and to help others, one's irreduc-ible vulnerability to being deprived of either of these two things, and one's inability to become a different kind of being than one in fact is. This is impor-tant. One can become a worse or a better person, but cannot require oneself to need anything other than the fundamental things one does need. Evil, in this respect, takes us away from who we are. It takes us out of our environment. It severs connections that ought to remain intact and anesthetizes us to those breaches in humane response to which we ought to remain acutely sensitive. This is because we are particular sorts of beings. We cannot be without the social connections for which we were intended or become bereft of the compassion that nurtures us as we nurture it without also becoming estranged. In this respect, Augustine's emphasis on privation pertains not just to absence, but to the absence of an objective good that must be pursued and protected for beings like us to be who we are meant to be.

Many Aristotelian scholars, as well as philosophers who write about evil, contend that Aristotle has no concept or even cognate of evil.[24] It may seem odd to talk about evil in the context of a thinker who emphasizes to such a degree aiming for the good. Furthermore, in dividing agents into continent individuals, who overcome their selfish appetites, and incontinent, akratic individuals, who fail to do so, Aristotle affirms his characterizing wrongdoing as a failure to act on behalf of the good rather than a proactive pursuit of the bad. However, he does, in fact, call some people vicious (*kakos*): those who deliberately depart from the norms of those striving to be virtuous by adopting a cynical attitude about justice, generosity, and the like. Such individuals violate the tenets of distributive justice, freeload in society, and seek every prudential advantage for themselves out of greed and shortsighted calculations about well-being.[25] Interestingly, according to Aristotle, in doing so, they do not merely harm others. They also harm themselves. He contends that at the same time vicious individuals desire more for themselves (*pleonexia*), they are undoing the prospects for their future happiness. In a telling passage from *The Nicomachean Ethics*, Aristotle teases out this irony. The vicious, he explains,

> are at odds with themselves, and, like incontinent people, have an appetite for one thing and wish for another. For they do not choose things that seem to be good for them, but instead choose pleasant things that are actually harmful. And cowardice or laziness causes others to shrink from doing what they think best for themselves. Those who have done many terrible actions hate and shun life because of their vice, and destroy themselves. Besides, vicious people seek others to pass their days with, and shun themselves. For when they are by themselves they remember many disagreeable actions, and expect to do others in the future; but they manage to forget these in other people's company. These people have nothing lovable about them, and so have no friendly feelings for themselves. Hence such a person does not share his own enjoyments and distresses. For his soul is in conflict, and because he is vicious one part is distressed at being restrained and another is pleased [by the intended action]; and so each part pulls in a different direction, as though

they were tearing him apart. Even if he cannot be distressed and pleased at the same time, still he is soon distressed because he was pleased, and wishes these things had not become pleasant to him; for base people are full of regret.[26]

This is a fascinating passage, both because of its sensitivity to the phenomenology of how self-regard and other-regard stand in direct relationship to one another, as well as because of its prescience. Aristotle was a man before his time. His claim about the importance of the critical relationship between the acquisition of virtue (particularly in the context of fostering other-regarding social connection) and self-love is just in the last ten years acquiring substantial support in research being conducted in the fields of medicine, neuropsychology, social psychology, and neuroscience.[27] Helping behaviors in a variety of settings, it turns out, are significant in promoting health, helping reduce chronic morbidities, mortality, and psychological well-being. Aristotle turned out to be right that to love oneself in the right sorts of ways, to have friendly feelings for oneself, depends highly on authentic, not merely utilitarian or tendentious, connections to other people. Those who act out of *pleonexia*, or greed, to gain a short-term advantage hurt themselves by obscuring their prospects for a flourishing future and by dividing themselves in a way that strands them internally within the prison of self-reproach. This is how avarice and covetousness cause a "soul in conflict."

This point is crucial on the heels of our discussion of the privation model, because the inability of one driven by vicious motives to benefit in any real way from that viciousness drives home that model's emphasis on the relevance of finitude to human flourishing. The specific constraints within which we can flourish are not up to us, whether we are aware of it or not. We come to hate ourselves when we divest ourselves of the good in which we are meant to participate. We swim upstream when we sever connections that might seem on their surface difficult to nourish and maintain. We isolate ourselves when we forgo opportunities to stand in the way of harm to others. An Augustinian anthropology based on finitude is the conceptual basis for an Aristotelian teleology of eudaemonia. We sometimes choose to be expedient out of an initial and selfish sense of how to get where we want to be faster, but when we do this we embrace "pleasant things that are actually harmful," as Aristotle writes. Virtue is its own reward and vice destroys. This is not necessarily obvious because of the nature of the immediacy of vices such as greed, laziness, covetousness, and so forth. The actions that lead from these states of mind do momentarily seem to resolve certain pressing problems of utility in the present. As the actions that ensue from viciousness make life more expedient, however, they also establish a state of character that thwarts real connection to other people, blocks one's identity from taking shape in a community, and disallows the formation of real friendships (i.e., friendships beyond utility).[28] The absence of virtue in turn, reifies one's propensity to be attracted to the shortcuts one has become accustomed to taking. As this happens, one's worsening character becomes more stably bad.

Another key connection between Aristotle and Augustine is in the percentage of people to whom Aristotle thinks the tendency toward *pleonexia* applies. Immediately before the passage just quoted, Aristotle avers that it is the "many" who are base. Like Augustine, Aristotle recognizes the great democracy in and ordinariness of our temptation to form bad characters. Augustine's theological anthropology traces our fallenness back to Adam's sin. Aristotle establishes a more direct link between the formation of bad characters, through the seduction of vicious impulses, and our failure to know ourselves better and, in service of that self-knowledge, act on behalf of our larger good. For both Augustine and Aristotle, it is not within our control to choose the kinds of beings we biologically are, but for both of them it is the frank acknowledgment that the will can be exercised for the good, albeit in a limited sense. Indeed, Aristotle no less than Augustine would deny that we have the ability to reinvent ourselves to opt for a different sort of good than the one we in fact require. To secure the "best good," Aristotle avers, we have to be mindful of the "function of a human being" and act always to attune what is "good in itself" to one's being.[29] We cannot bracket our humanity. It is always a constraint and the enabling condition of flourishing. Although rarely overlooked in Augustinian scholarship, readers of Aristotle often fail to emphasize the degree to which Aristotle insists that while the highest good is the most choice-worthy, what that good is is not a matter of choice, precisely because of the beings we are. We can deceive ourselves about this fact or we can face it, but a fact it remains.

On the matter of self-deception something else is worth noticing with regard to the commission of self-serving behavior that connects Augustine to Aristotle. This pertains to the tendency to cloak one's vicious actions from the world, either by explaining them as something other than vicious, or by freeloading in society by pretending one is other-regarding when one is not. When we do so, Augustine and Aristotle both suggest, we live in hiding and reify the division already taking place within ourselves because of our initial step away from the good. Self-hatred ensues when we do not act as ourselves. According to Augustine, we desire to discover the truth about ourselves, but to the extent that we seek and delight in the truth to enlighten us, we recoil when it reveals us to be self-deceiving.[30] Hence, Augustine claims that the pride that causes a transgression is worse than the transgression because pride manifests itself in the ultimately futile and self-denying process of searching for an excuse for what we already know to be wrong.[31] Sinning comes at a cost to oneself. When pride causes us to make excuses that deflect our selfishness or evasion of responsibility, asserts Augustine, we are still beings who very much need to be selfless and responsible. This follows from the fact that we are created good. Self-deception is ultimately no real option.

Thus, to act against this goodness is to treat oneself as the enemy. Deception of others is self-deception. Aristotle, in kind, argues that the vicious person, beyond even the incontinent person who knows what is right but acts on appetite instead, acts indulgently often enough that the prospects for reform become dim, so much so that that person becomes eclipsed from experiencing genuine, healthy self-love. An incontinent person is temporarily at odds with himself or herself when he or she commits a deed knowing it is wrong.[32] But the proud, indulgent, vicious person consigns his or her future to a permanent state of contradiction by habituating and repeating vices in willful ignorance. Self-deception is dangerous in the sense that those who veer from the good become more and more accustomed to their vice and occupy a vicious state. Another way of putting the contrast is that one passes through incontinence en route to a vicious character. At first, one is at least clear-headed about doing the wrong thing, but this clarity devolves into self-righteousness. This is how stably bad characters are formed. Thus, an initial commitment to cloaking our self-serving ways, over time, perniciously gives way to a much more insidious, intractable self-deception that makes the prospects for self-flourishing and participation in eudaemonia more and more remote. Whereas for Augustine we are, post–fall, in this place already and consequently in need of God's grace, for Aristotle we bring ourselves there through the habitual failure to overcome our natural propensity to act against our better judgment (*akrasia*). This is the process by which we *become* bad.

It is at this stage of the analysis that we must again refocus our attention on the will. If akrasia devolves, by default, to a less reversible viciousness, then it follows that not to always be becoming good is to become bad. The akratic moral agent acts in knowledge, but akrasia as a reason for a moral agent failing to do the virtuous thing varies depending on the amount of time during which the agent has gotten used to the failure and during which, correspondingly, the will has atrophied. The chronically akratic individual lapses into a persistently blameworthy state that precludes a morally developing character.[33] Thus Aristotle contends that "incontinence is curable, but intemperance is not." The difference is that the latter is not prone to remorse, because the intemperate one has gotten used to no longer questioning the thing that once upon a time struck him or her as wrong. In the real world, in which we are constantly hectored by deadlines, cranky personalities bearing down on us from everywhere, and pressures that new calamities and misfortunes bring with them, it is all too easy to become less and less rigorous about keeping in the forefront of our minds that we are doing the thing we ought not to be doing. Overarching situations, like the ones with which Milgram and Zimbardo are preoccupied, turn distraction into indefinite neglect. Whereas incontinence is by Aristotle's definition "prone to regret," vice is a "continuous bad condition." In short order, the vicious person no longer notices that he or she is vicious.[34]

It is through the will that we have the opportunity to avoid intemperance, specifically by thinking and acting in concert, and by anticipating that we are poised to do that thing we should not. By virtue of the will, moral insight translates into moral action.[35] This does not necessarily mean that we will successfully avoid acting on appetite. Sometimes the will is too weak to counter appetite, and sometimes appetite is exacerbated by outside pressures that leave us few volitional reserves. When we do not have the strength to refrain from doing the tempting, self-interested thing, however, the will can still operate on the self by making sure that the self remembers that it did not do what it should have done. If one is in a rush to get to work, potentially late for a meeting it is in one's best interests to attend, and as a result one does not stop to help an elderly neighbor shovel his driveway after a heavy snowfall (when one believes one really ought to have done so), then it matters that on the rest of one's drive in it bothers one that one didn't do what one might have done. Living with this sort of angst is morally beneficial. It is, to be sure, preferable to simply resigning oneself to moral weakness, or to having no compunction about one's failures. When one struggles but fails, one still has very much in mind the good from which one has strayed. Again, the difference is self-awareness, and the will does considerable work even to keep this much alive in the self. Good living, in turn, amounts to the totality of decisions made in the positive direction of virtue, alongside the equally important decisions to not succumb to the bad habits one always stands in danger of forming.

Like all good decision making in Aristotle's account, to choose in favor of virtue entails practice and repetition. It means living deliberately and watching oneself at all times to make sure that one follows through on one's commitment to becoming better than one currently is. Like steeling oneself for the sacrifices one must make if one is to follow a healthy diet, the only way the good becomes a natural, regular impulse is to do it over and over.[36] To choose in favor of goodness also implies a willingness to keep oneself on the outer edge of the circle that encompasses the private space into which would like to let oneself retreat. To be responsible in the world is to be out of our own world, where we might miss opportunities to become positively involved in the well-being of others. This is a hard commitment to sustain. We need to replenish ourselves by taking a break from the exhausting activity of putting the needs of others first. Sometimes, during hard times, becoming better is a matter of not becoming worse. However, for Aristotle, as for Augustine, becoming better always entails a kind of self-awareness whereby one does not afford oneself the luxury of excusing one's neglect of others, even if temporarily justified, as something else. Among the plenty of limitations we can do nothing about, such as our need to address our immediate needs, we must also keep in mind what is within our control: the ability, if not to act on behalf the good in this or that particular moment, to remind ourselves that we have tried and failed, and to look forward to the opportunity to pursue the good when we are again able to do so.

Finally, common ground between Augustine and Aristotle can be gleaned by looking narrowly at how the concept of the will (*prohairesis*) implies an imperative to prepare for the future. Just as Augustine invokes the concept as a spur (in concert with God's grace) to bridge our lapsed existence with our intended essence, Aristotle characterizes it as a deliberate attempt on the part of a self threatened by the vicissitudes of circumstance to control the character it can develop. *Prohairesis*, Aristotle explains, is the commitment on the part of the self to do something, now, to achieve a good end, anticipating that one will have to confront obstacles along the way that are not conducive to that good. In a revealing passage from the *Nicomachean Ethics*, Aristotle clarifies how the virtuous individual shows his or her character by acting during moments of crises that specifically preclude extended deliberative reasoning. Such an individual, knowing the importance of moral preparation, is able to acquire key virtues such as courage in advance of an emergency.

> Indeed, that is why someone who is unafraid and unperturbed in a sudden alarm seems braver than [someone who is unafraid only] in dangers that are obvious in advance; for what he does is more the result of his state of character, since it is less the outcome of preparation. If an action is foreseen, we might decide to do it [not only because of our state of character, but] also by reason and rational calculation; but when we have no warning, [our decision to act] expresses our state of character.[37]

One displays human dignity by doing what one can to dispose oneself to respond courageously when the time comes that courage is called for, knowing during one's preparation that when that time does come, one will, being human, face limitations. The will is always operating within the confines of a human context, but such self-acknowledgment propels proactive living.

If one is proactive enough, one will not find oneself in the position of Albert Speer, in which one becomes unwittingly seduced by the prospect of one's own flourishing, even at the expense of abiding, and perhaps inducing, the suffering of others. Rather, the one working on becoming more virtuous, by repeating habits that make one more sensitive to the situations of others, will have anticipated the possibility that such a seduction could take place. A wicked person, by contrast, is trapped by his or her nature. We are all potentially wicked, but we can defend against becoming numb to our temptations, and thereby developing a stably bad character, by first going out of our way to keep in mind how that unhappy potential can become a reality, and, second, by taking steps, "little by little," to secure a different outcome, if not in the present then in the future.[38] In this respect the overlap between Kant and Aristotle, as some scholars of virtue have noticed, is important. Both anticipate various contingent, external inducements in this world to take our eye off the ball. For Kant, human dignity lies in exerting the will to conform one's maxim to one's duty. For Aristotle, the notion of *prohairesis* that anticipates, so as to defend against, certain appetites and expedient emotions ensures that one will retain a decent measure of autonomy in a world always seeming to undermine it.[39] Neither Kant nor Aristotle, nor Augustine for that matter, is a determinist. We act for the sake of specific ends, and, even in the face of difficult odds, retain our identity as choosing, responsible beings.

Having connected an Aristotelian pursuit of the good to Augustine's privation thesis, a positive case can now be made for choosing the virtue ethic to which that thesis leads. If we are, as Augustine and Aristotle both suggest, "difficultly" free, that is, able to anticipate evil and therefore prepare for its inevitable advent to a restricted degree (despite the large residual portion of evil about which we are helpless to do anything), then this means that our sometimes Sisyphean existence *is* ultimately laden with meaning. To think about whether one is winning or losing the battle against evil is to ask the wrong question because human dignity lies more modestly and realistically in taking the problem of evil seriously, cultivating a stable mindfulness of the risk of participation one always runs with evil, and countering evil where one can by making connections with other people. Virtue, a measure of "excellent human (social) functioning," pertains to those states that impel us to interact with others and respond compassionately to others' adversity by cultivating the appropriate emotions and the carefully considered actions that correspond to these emotions.[40]

Virtue ethics is in this respect a proactive approach to solving human problems. In its attention to character rather than performance of specific moral acts, virtue ethics flexibly accommodates the reality that human beings will labor under conditions of adversity for a large portion of their lives. Virtue ethics suggest that every individual, regardless of current level of moral development, is always in a position to work on his or her character to better harness traits such as generosity, courage, modesty, compassion, and so forth, as well as to become better attuned to the welfare and well-being of others. It proceeds from the Augustinian premise that no matter where we presently are, we are incomplete with regard to where we want to be. In contrast to an ethic of strict rule-following, in which to be morally in the clear we merely have to avoid the thing that has been labeled bad, in virtue ethics we are always to be found wanting relative to our potential. According to the ethics of virtue I have proposed, we assume responsibility for our inevitable role in all that does go wrong, and has the potential to go wrong, in the world. We neither see ourselves as off the hook in respect to the wicked things that come our way (as aloof bystanders might who justify their spectatorship on the grounds that they didn't cause the evil they are witnessing) nor interpret opportunities to address wickedness as a futility that has no bearing on the future. Virtue is commendable insofar as it discourages one from construing oneself as an innocent bystander. If we look at ourselves and the world in the right way, we will realize that there is always work to do on ourselves as well as a variety of ways we can get more involved in attending to an imperfect world. If evil is such that its tendency to spill over makes us responsible for others when we are in its midst, then we should search for ways to fulfill this responsibility rather than succumb to a defeatist attitude that we will never be able to meet its demands. Is evil in fact this way? How responsible are we for the problems we do not seem to have caused? It may be helpful to consider a concrete example from recent history.

The Privation Thesis, Virtue Ethics, and the Case of Fukushima

In March 2011, a sudden and massive tsunami hit the northern coast of Japan in response to an earthquake that registered at a magnitude of 9.0. The encroaching tide that engulfed hundreds of towns and villages in the affected areas took over nearly sixteen thousand lives, displaced hundreds of thousands of individuals from their homes, and by most estimates cost between $230 and $300 billion dollars, two and a half times the cost of Hurricane Katrina.[41] Communities were permanently destroyed and families tragically ripped apart. Many Buddhist funerals in Japan, typically rite-centered and cremations, were held en masse with little available resources to say good-bye to the dead according to tradition. What made this tsunami especially worrisome, however, as the world now knows, was the devastation it caused to a nuclear plant in the city of Fukushima, comprised of six boiling water reactors maintained by the Tokyo

Electric Power Company (TEPCO). The flooding the tsunami caused resulted in the meltdown of three of the six reactors at the site and partial meltdowns or significant radiation leaks in the other three. To date only Chernobyl has ranked as highly among the world's worst nuclear accidents. Several experts have claimed that besides Chernobyl, Fukushima is the most serious and far-reaching industrial catastrophe in history.[42] Farmers throughout the northern half of Japan lost their livelihoods. The way in which information about the crisis was handled by the Japanese government strained its credibility with the United States and other countries, and fear about radiation poisoning extended well beyond the shores of Japan. Faith in the safety of nuclear energy in general, despite its effectiveness, further put Japan, a land not rich in natural resources to begin with, in an unprecedented economic crisis and challenged the stability of the country as well as the well-being of its citizens in a manner not experienced since World War II. We are decades away from the clean-up. The journalist Victor Kotsev, covering the disaster for the *Asia Times*, said that because of what happened in Fukushima we are all living in unprecedented times:

> Add to this that increased global interdependence comes with increased global vulnerability to crises in distant parts of the world, and we have a situation where our sense of security is not guaranteed any more.
>
> The concept of the state, in a sense, offers a counter-balance to all these powerful and often blind forces, a regulatory mechanism that we like to believe works well and in the public interest.
>
> This is part of why the scale of the Fukushima disaster is so hard to grasp, both for experts and for lay people. In the face of the increased vulnerability of modern societies, we desperately need something that gives us a sense of security. What better safeguards than progress, technology, and order, exemplified by the spectacular ability of nation states, separately and in concert, to mobilize unprecedented resources to achieve an urgent goal? And where a more safe expectation for all these forces to produce the desired effect than in Japan, one of the top industrialized world economies and a paradigm of social cohesion and discipline?
>
> In many ways, Fukushima is the perfect paradigm for the failure of our source of security at its finest. The confusion and panic of the government and industry officials in the wake of the disaster should humble us all. So should our face to face encounter with our limitations, and the contrast with how we like to imagine ourselves.
>
> In some of our most popular science-fiction narratives, the best astronauts of the leading world powers destroy asteroids that threaten the Earth with nuclear weapons (*Armageddon* grossed over half a billion dollars, attesting to our eagerness to consume the images; suffice it to mention that early on in

the Fukushima crisis, some observers suggested nuking the reactors). Yet in reality, we can't deal with a sizeable pile of radioactive waste, even long after the chain reaction has stopped.

Gundersen's conclusions speak loudly: "Somehow, robotically, they will have to go in there and manage to put it in a container and store it for infinity, and that technology doesn't exist. Nobody knows how to pick up the molten core from the floor, there is no solution available now for picking that up from the floor."

So do those of Dr. Sawada, another scientist interviewed by Dahr Jamail: "Until we know how to safely dispose of the radioactive materials generated by nuclear plants, we should postpone these activities so as not to cause further harm to future generations."[43]

We are still sorting out the distress unleashed on so many unfortunate victims of the catastrophe, but Fukushima reaches beyond the immediate cost to those affected by radiation released into the atmosphere. It raises questions about the psychological health of generations of populations increasingly reliant on waning energy sources, a dependence exacerbated in an era in which mega-tragedies are captured in their stark graphic detail by the media as they are happening. As then New York mayor Rudy Guiliani said of the events of September 11, 2001, such tragedies always seem to be "too much for any of us to bear." Perhaps it is not so fruitful to distinguish the clear moral evil of September 11 from the apparent natural disaster of Fukushima, or from the Lisbon earthquake of 1755 for that matter. They are all in their own way examples of an evil triggered by a specific event but whose triggering was made possible by more factors than immediately meet the eye, an evil that, as Kotsev additionally notes of Fukushima, is "the perfect paradigm for the failure of our source of security." If this is true, then should we not as a rule build at the outset into our psychological budgets the expectation that humanity from time to time will have to deal with catastrophic events born of numerous indirect causes which have direct and far-reaching effects on many innocent parties?

This line of thinking challenges the basis on which calamities are often interpreted as someone else's problem. Specifically, it calls into question the way in which devastating calamities that are multifactorial are sometimes passed off as merely natural disasters. To see Fukushima as a natural disaster is to apply a clean and simple descriptor to a broad phenomenon that ought to be assessed in the context of our changing, global world. To blame the tsunami for the devastation of the livelihood of farmers in northeastern Japan, for example, is arguably not plausible in light of the relatively little representation Japanese farmers had in voicing their concerns at the time the nuclear plants were built and developed.

How can we get to the root cause of Fukushima without also discussing risks some people knew they were taking (and that are still being taken at nuclear plants elsewhere in the world) but took anyway to procure a favorable cost basis for the product (nuclear energy) they distributed? Predictions of a potential catastrophe were ignored. Is this relevant to our analysis? And can we reasonably discuss Fukushima without acknowledging the enormous dependence on energy exhibited by many more societies than just Japan? Very quickly, our analysis has the potential to implicate thousands and thousands of culprits in light of which it becomes both an empirical leap and a normative evasion to assume that we are innocent bystanders in the Fukushima disaster.

Indeed, the statement I want to go on to defend with respect to Fukushima and the vast majority of calamities, including those that appear to be natural disasters, is that there are no such things as bystanders. We are all responsible, to a degree, for these kinds of disasters. At some level, if we look hard and honestly enough, we will be able to locate our fingerprints, if faintly, in what happened at Fukushima and what could have happened. This is a strong statement, but in one sense it is no more than an affirmation of the Augustinian thesis about the ubiquity of our participation with evil and (therefore) our inherent responsibility for what is ultimately our own doing. Augustine has a theological anthropology based primarily on his interpretation of the book of Genesis, which grounds his view about our involvement with what goes wrong in the world, but the theological claim can also be supported on independent empirical grounds the more one looks at specific catastrophes that, on first glance, seem to present themselves as arbitrary afflictions of nature. Let us look a bit more closely at the case of Fukushima.

If one were to blame human beings for the disaster at the nuclear plants, then one might turn first to those responsible for failing to anticipate problems that we knew in advance would arise if anything were to preclude access to electricity from a sustained period. The designers at Fukushima-Daiichi knew that if anything were to occur to affect the power source in the reactors that prevented pressure for rising in the core, pumps would be unable to circulate hot fluid from the reactor to the wetwell where it would be condensed and heat removed.[44] The Tokyo Electric Power Company, which had to have the ability to estimate what magnitude of earthquake could knock out electricity for the critical duration, made a self-conscious decision based on cost-benefit analysis that the risk was worth it, given what the company stood to lose if it covered the cost of revamping the plant's entire cooling system. This does not mean TEPCO is solely to blame for the meltdowns, however. Even if one were to be able to definitively establish that the company knew the risk it was taking, it is still a stretch to conclude that the greed lies only with one party, for new questions immediately come to mind. What kind of pressure was TEPCO under from its government to meet its energy demands for its citizens? Did the Japanese government indirectly induce this disaster by letting corporations monopolize the legal debate over how much leeway TEPCO ought to have had in constructing nuclear power plants (to the detriment of local farmers nearby)? What kind of pressure is the government itself under to provide for its country's consumer demands, a country that lacks natural resources and could not have sustained its population's energy needs without nuclear power?[45] Japan is a first-world industrialized nation because of nuclear power. Should we restrict which countries are to become first-world nations on the basis of which of them fare the best without nuclear energy? To some, it might seem arbitrary to force Japan to cap its reliance on nuclear power to a safe level, if that level turns out to ensure that Japan will incur a tremendous global competitive disadvantage. Yet, to not force Japan to restrict itself in this way is to implicate all of us in the disaster that ended up taking place.

This line of questioning goes some distance toward explaining the move on the part of the Japanese government in the days following the disaster to indemnify TEPCO against some of the liability claims issued against it nationally and globally. In Japan, the 1961 Act on Compensation for Nuclear Damage specifies the extent of liability for which a company like TEPCO can ever be responsible in the case of an accident. That TEPCO's indemnification from liability was anticipated around the time plants were being constructed testifies to the plausibility of a widespread assumption of responsibility in this case. The United States has 104 reactors at sixty-five sites, the most in the world, and, not surprisingly, has a similar stipulation to protect the companies that create nuclear power plants and distribute nuclear energy.[46] These compromises were a matter of public debate at the time they were being settled.

Further questions therefore arise. What pressure do we put on our governments to secure a competitive advantage in global trade and production? How has our consumerist dependence on energy, in a country vastly out of proportion with our population relative to the rest of the world, led our government to provide incentives to power companies to supply energy as efficiently as possible? At some point in the analysis it must occur that, just as the radiation released over there is finding its way over here, the causal sequence that fully explains the meltdowns in Fukushima contains the mark of our influence. If we are to be honest brokers in the debate over nuclear energy, we do not have the luxury of not playing an active role in discussions about how much we consume individually and as a society, or of failing to consider what kinds of risks are necessary and unnecessary in the bid to sustain our existing levels of consumption.

Analyses similar to the one just undertaken could be conducted on other far-reaching ills, not necessarily those in which nature played a major role, such as the phenomenon of terrorism and crime in some inner cities.[47] Do we really have nothing to do with the suicide bomber who attacks an oil refinery off the coast of his homeland, a refinery the existence of which simultaneously leads to the replenishment of our energy needs and to the waning of his country's prospects for economic autonomy? Do we think we have nothing to do with crime when we vote for a proposition that prevents our state from collecting revenues that come from property taxes in order to fund the education of our children? What role does the luck of our circumstances and upbringing play in our proximity to the immediate costs that must be borne when these social ills take place? What might we have participated or not participated in if we were born there rather than here?

Although it is possible to make the argument that there are in principle incidental bystanders, when we begin to look at evil situations comprehensively, none of us plausibly retains the identity of a bystander. I learned last week that someone was driving to meet a close friend of mine for dinner when she hit and killed a pedestrian who happened into her driving lane. Neither alcohol nor cell phones were involved. My friend feels terrible for having prevailed on her friend to meet her, which, if she had not done, would not have resulted in a loss of life. As I pointed out to her, we have all been in the situation of asking someone to meet us for a bite to eat. We could just as easily have been her, or the driver for that matter. I didn't mention this to excuse my friend from her role in the chain of events, or to suggest that she should not feel any guilt at all. I meant, rather, to settle her to a degree—or at least forge a solidarity of sorts—by reflecting on the collective responsibility we all bear at all times for the multitude of things that can and so easily do go wrong in this world. As Augustine might say in this and in so many circumstances, "but for the grace of God go we."

Both the privation thesis and an Aristotelian ethics of virtue resist the clear separation between innocent and guilty parties.[48] An Augustinian ethic to tackling evil begins with a notion of collective responsibility in which one asks oneself what part one might have played in the advent of a particular social ill. This is a descriptively advantageous approach in that it accounts for the likely multifactorial explanation of that ill and retains the normative advantage of keeping us honest about our own, not necessarily apparent, involvement in things that happen at some geographical or emotional distance from us. According to the fourth model of evil, we not only have a duty to go out of our way to become better acquainted with the events happening in the world that make people suffer, but also to inquire as to what our responsibility for their advent might have been as well as imagine what kinds of things we can be doing to alleviate their harmful effects. This can be done in a variety of ways, depending on what resources we have at our disposal, what skills we have harnessed the best, and what our interests are. What is not morally optional once we assume that the vast majority of suffered evils are collectively produced, however, is the imperative to do something constructive about the evil we are witness to, particularly when that constructive thing is to become the sort of person who has more internal resources and skills and interest level to help than he or she did before.

The realization that the explanations for some of the worst global calamities we have had to endure can be traced, however faintly, back to us commits us to becoming better people so that we will be better equipped to reduce their effects and recurrence. This is true of ills with which we seemingly have nothing to do. If we look hard enough, we will likely discover that the explanatory causal sequence that led to them is not as simple as we thought it was. I have elsewhere characterized the ought from which this realization comes as an "aretaic meta-duty" of character.[49] The thrust of this duty is, throughout the course of our moral lives, to take us beyond minimal moral requirement and increasingly do what the fully virtuous person would do. Such a duty, for which we can argue on Aristotelian grounds, also has an Augustinian justification. As we increasingly come to see ourselves as indirectly involved with all the things that can cause others to feel pain and sorrow—as we get to know ourselves better as sinners—we understand more fully our responsibility for the evils with which others cope.

The Connection between Augustine and Aristotle under Scrutiny

Herein arises the debate within the Aristotelian camp, because there is more than one way to understand the aretaic duty to become a better person. A non-Augustinian interpretation of Aristotle's recommendation holds that the virtuous life we are to pursue is, at once, the balanced life. According to this view, we are in the first instance not primarily sinful, but rather healthy, functioning, and potentially flourishing individuals whose primary objective ought to be to further develop ourselves in this way. As such, the telos of a virtue ethic should be associated with balance, and human happiness is something to be distinguished and perhaps even preferred over moral betterment. Involving oneself in the plight of others may be considered as a legitimate expression of the good. What is of essence to eudaemonia, however, is the cultivation of those traits with which we are already amply endowed, the idiosyncratic features of our personality and set of interests that presumably bring us pleasure, and the adequate weighing of these features of our developing character against more general ones that are focused on the improved welfare and well-being of others. Thus Aristotelians such as Susan Wolf think we ought not to forgo personal ambitions for the sake of "bland do-gooding." Wolf explicitly says that "moral ideals do not, and need not, make the best personal ideals."[50] Others similarly disposed, such as Jean Hampton, contend that an emphasis on personal relations that is tantamount to human flourishing arguably precludes a "cosmopolitan altruism" that enjoins us to become cognizant and subsequently involved in the plight of everyone, everywhere.[51]

These thinkers raise an interesting point. Can we be efficient flourishers if we are concerned with evil everywhere? Central to the Aristotelian view of achieving fulfillment is the idea that we must first know ourselves as the beings we actually are and then strive to become these beings in the best way. If Augustine is wrong that despite our created good essence we are fundamentally defective, finite beings, then a pivotal basis on which our connectedness to others is established comes under suspicion, and the claimed overlap between self-regard and other-regard is more difficult to sustain. In this case, flourishing at most becomes a communal venture in local settings. Sentiments such as nourishment, love, security and success occur within a broader setting of competition between individuals and groups. And evaluative moral notions such as praiseworthiness and blameworthiness, far from universally identifiable as predicates that apply to how we meet or shirk duty, come to be understood as internal markers that measure our personal success against our potential growth. Such a hypothesis is reminiscent of Nietzsche's emphasis on self-actualization, and in fact many neo-Aristotelians embrace virtue theory in service of a perspectivalist worldview and radically antideterminist ethos. By linking Augustine and Aristotle, have I unduly saddled virtue ethics with the unwelcome baggage of moral ideals such as self-reproach, solidarity, humility, and repentance?

The question of whether the Nietzschean or Augustinian picture of the human being is more accurate will not be fully settled here. However, evidence can be brought to bear on the discussion to link Aristotle more explicitly to Augustine than those neo-Aristotelians who focus on balance, contentment, and the accomplishment of personal or aesthetic ambition would be inclined to do. Aristotle does suggest that regardless of what our existing strengths or interests happen to be, we should always "strain" ourselves to the greatest extent to perform "the finest actions." By this he means we ought to attempt to change

our character in the direction of acquiring the moral virtues that are both universally recognizable and in principle accessible and, for this reason, "welcomed
and praised by everyone." He argues for a nonstatic existence, according to
which flourishing and contentment are explicitly opposed to one another: "We
ought not to follow the proverb-writers, and 'think human, since you are
human,' or 'think mortal, since you are mortal.' Rather, as far as we can, we
ought to be pro-immortal, and go to all lengths to live a life that expresses our
supreme element; for however much this element may lack in bulk, by much
more it surpasses everything in power and value."[52]

It is not enough to perfect those strengths and traits I already recognize in
myself as a noteworthy propensity. If I take the pursuit of virtue seriously, I
must also make a concerted effort to get outside myself and pay special attention to those virtues that will affect others in a positive way. As the neo-
Aristotelian David Norton observes, the acquisition of moral virtue is not only
conterminous with human flourishing, it also encompasses it.[53] That is, without
moral virtue, without assuming responsibility for others, we cannot realize the
good.

Flourishing, if it is legitimate, will therefore take one onto new terrain. The
acquisition of virtue, as Aristotle understands it, is not predictable or strictly
prescribed but always a process of development. As the neo-Aristotelian Julia
Annas explains, Aristotelian ethics places

> an initial stress on one's life as a whole. When I wonder about where my life
> is going and whether I can change it, I am asking if my life as a whole might
> change direction. And when I ask whether I could acquire one of the virtues,
> I am not asking whether I could become generous *now*. Perhaps I could not
> bring myself to act generously, given the way my feelings and reactions have
> developed, or perhaps I could act generously but it would pain me to do so.
> So I cannot *now* be virtuous. But it is still up to me whether I become virtuous
> or not; for once I am convinced that it is important to become virtuous, I can
> take steps to enable myself to act virtuously—by thinking harder before the
> appropriate occasion and consciously resolving to do so, for example.[54]

The sort of virtue ethic Annas describes takes one out of one's comfort zone
and, necessarily, into the lives of other people. It seeks to recover, sustain, and
build onto a good that is always in danger of being lost to complacent entrench-
ment in what is familiar. It recognizes, as the privation thesis does, the dangers
of isolating oneself in what one knows, which is much narrower than the set of
things with which one is involved, whether one is aware of it or not. The great
democracy of sin on the Augustinian account, which exempts no one from sharing the burden of responsibility for everyone everywhere, is, at least on some

versions of the Aristotelian account, analogous to the unacceptability of simply allowing oneself to ignore the bigger picture. As Annas explains, when we choose to make a difference in the world or get involved in the plight of others in some way, this decision in turn commits us to make other pressing, and perhaps inconvenient, shifts in our priorities that will test all our developing other-regarding capacities. To ignore this pressure is to morally devolve. Conversely, the pursuit of the good is the existence of an individual in motion, ever attending to the problem that it is to be a human being.

Another objection about the synthesis I have drawn between Augustine and Aristotle hinges on my claim that the Augustinian emphasis on lack is what turns virtue ethics in the direction of other-regard. The critic might respond that this claim is underjustified. The characterization of evil as nothingness could lead one to empathize with others. However, it could also impel one to double down on one's pursuit of the City of God, resigned as one might be in one's belief that this life is limited. According to this critic, the thesis of privation might just as easily lead to a theology of personal salvation that does not place great emphasis on responsibility toward others. Moreover, the critic might further point out that the Aristotelian tradition has its own resources on other-regard and does not need Augustinian notions of caritas to improve it, particularly given that Aristotle talks about the friend in the *Nicomachean Ethics* as being like "another myself."[55] In light of these complementary reflections, with what confidence might one maintain that Augustine's privation thesis induces us to become more other-regarding, or that Aristotle's ethics requires a normative notion stronger than *philia* to propel the establishment of the virtuous community?[56]

The first thing to say in response is that nowhere have I claimed that Augustine and Aristotle unconditionally need each other as I have outlined, only that a synthesis of their ideas is justified by bringing to the fore a hitherto underemphasized feature of both of their ethical writings. This is the conviction that as human beings, regardless of circumstances, we are inadequate just as we are; we have work to do to bridge our current existence with our intended essence. I accept that it is possible to interpret the model of privation as a spur—in the case of some conversion-oriented Protestant traditions, for example—to relinquish investment in this world rather than to try to repair it. Likewise, I recognize that an Aristotelian ethics of virtue does not require the negative Augustinian motivation of the threat of being seized by nothingness to establish its communal emphasis on flourishing, particularly in light of the cohesive community of "friendships of character" toward which many of us, in Aristotle's view, already have the internal resources to be teleologically directed.

This said, emphasis in Augustinian anthropology on compassion and identification with the other, even if these impulses can be temporally misdirected, is enough to not give warrant to the follower of Augustine to forgo one's temporal existence altogether. As Eric Gregory points out, in the Augustinian picture human beings "are best understood as bundles of loves. Mortal creatures are lovers constituted by loving, and being loved by, others and God."[57] It is true that the self must learn to love rightly in this life, but this initial inadequacy increases the self's this-worldly burden rather than relinquishing it. Loving others rightly in the present is compatible with, and arguably even prerequisite for, one's quest for personal salvation. According to Augustine, we must love people for their own sake because they belong to God. Virtue is never considered by him to be a means to an end nor does it ever merely involve the needs of the self. So even if an Augustinian ethics depends on an Augustinian theology, it is a mistake to interpret Augustinian ethics as being encompassed strictly by personal ambition, including that to be saved. On the contrary, caritas is the principal reflection of undertaken discipleship. In light of this, "nothingness" becomes relevant to other-regard because, in the account of privation, nothingness signals a habitual series of missed opportunities to attend to the fundamental imperative to love all of God's creatures. The responsibility for others assumed by the self is ongoing, bearing down on the one who is ethically attuned and grace-seeking at all times. It is this condition that makes the Aristotelian aretaic meta-duty always to be improving oneself such an apt moral principle for the committed Augustinian.

An even stronger case is to be made that the telos of acquiring virtue in the Aristotelian account is served by an Augustinian stress on contrition, introspection, and humility to a greater degree than it would be merely by relying on its own resources. In Aristotle's ethics, only friendships of character exceed a threshold of virtuous interaction in which one is able to consider the friend as another myself. Also according to Aristotle, however, most associations between people are not friendships of character but the lesser friendships of pleasure or even more pedestrian friendships of utility, entailing significantly less enduring, worthwhile, and character-building relationships than the ideal sorts of friendships do. This implies that the pursuit of virtue in which the good life consists is restricted to those individuals who are able to cultivate these higher kinds of friendships. Virtue, and therefore the good life, is simply not as broadly accessible as it ought to be, according to the Aristotelian account. This is precisely where Augustine's insistence on the ubiquity of sin and polemic against complacency, equally applicable to everyone as finite creatures, has the potential to extend the activity of becoming virtuous to those who initially stand at a disadvantage. The attention given to self-knowledge in Aristotle as one requiring virtue to flourish is given an explicit boost in the Augustinian exhortation for one always to assess one's failings in a serious and forward-looking manner. In book 10 of *On the Trinity*, Augustine invokes the Delphic Oracle's instruction to know thyself so as to direct the self not to lose sight of the many paths to perversity on which the self, so easily, can come to forget itself.[58] To be sure, Augustine affords no leeway to the nonvirtuous individual to refer to his or her existing lack of virtue as a reason not to think more creatively about how to go about acquiring it than he or she so far has. Aristotle, by contrast, often speaks as though it is futile for the nonvirtuous person to try to become otherwise. As such, an Aristotelian ethic, which nonnegotiably attaches the acquisition of virtue to eudaemonia, is in this respect arguably better served by Augustine than by Aristotle.

In any case, I have in this book argued not for the strong claim that Augustine and Aristotle cannot do without one another, but rather for the more modest one that the respective objectives that emerge in their ethical writings turn out symbiotically to serve one another in a way perhaps not previously considered. The connection drawn between the two figures is intended to open a fruitful avenue for grounding our responsibility toward others in a way that probes the link between a certain characterization of evil and common way of thinking about how to go about pursuing the good. At the very least, it seems to me, a case can made that the similarities between Augustine and Aristotle should be examined at least to the same degree that the contrasts between them have historically been discussed in scholarship.

Undoing Wickedness

We have examined how one remains involved in the pursuit of the good to avoid becoming wicked, but something still needs to be said about the prospects for undoing wickedness once it has arrived. Is a stably developed wicked character incorrigible? If so, what does this say about the ability to exercise free will under circumstances, one would think, in which it becomes most important to do so, that is, in the case of the worst among us? If, through a combination of poor rearing and the exercise of bad habits over a long period, one develops an irreversibly wicked character, then how effective can a virtue ethic based on a thesis of privation be? How can it hold the person who has become evil accountable? Finally, what do we make of psychopaths, whose brains—as discussed in chapter 1—preclude them from forming the right kinds of habits, indeed, which preclude them from caring about caring? Are they, because of their incorrigibility, to be morally let off the hook because they are functionally unable to abide that aretaic meta-duty presumably borne by all of us?

Just yesterday I was waiting in a café when the woman at the front of the line badgered her server to make her specialty order just right. With admirable courtesy and patience, the server followed the customer's directions and handed her the iced coffee. I watched the woman (who was noticeably well-dressed and fashionably stylish) pay for the drink, walk away, furtively look around, and then steal a *New York Times*, which she stuffed in her bag. Thirty seconds later, as I ordered a black coffee, I was taken aback when the same woman appeared next to me and abruptly brushed me aside. Shaking the cup she had just received, she barked at the server, "I didn't pay for all of this ice! You're going to have to make my drink again." I felt an urge to remind her she had not paid for the newspaper she had taken either. Reading so much Augustine recently, however, and knowing that I surely live in my own proverbial glass house, I did not act on the impulse. Still, I wondered, how would this woman spend the rest of her day? The rest of her week? In how many more cafés would she make rude demands, and what are the chances, really, that her stealing this newspaper was for her the exception and not the rule? If she had been acting this way for some time, how realistic would it be to expect her to be able to change? If she were miraculously inclined to make an attempt to reform herself, where would she begin?

The anecdote I just relayed is a true story. Beyond asking myself the questions I mentioned, I was especially preoccupied with the chilling intuition that what I had witnessed was probably a common occurrence. By a certain age we have become who we are, and it is difficult to become someone else. This is what Aristotle means when he says that "vice resembles diseases such as dropsy or consumption" and is comparable to a "continuous bad condition." At some point in the lives of most people, one loses sight of the way one is.[59] What hope for reform is there for this sort of individual, the sort, let's be clear, who is not so uncommon?

For the privation thesis to serve as an inspiration for the acquisition of virtue, character must be malleable enough that it can evolve out of wicked states, otherwise the Augustinian judgment about our inevitable sinfulness risks lapsing into an unshakable despair to which we must, at best, resign ourselves. According to both the privation thesis and to the virtue ethic to which it leads, we are difficultly free. But we are not really free in any sense if, when we have disposed ourselves to adopting wicked traits (which is easier than adopting virtuous ones), we are then stuck with the character these traits have given us. In this case, we are less than difficultly free. Indeed, in this case we are miserable creatures consigned to wallow in our imperfection, like Dostoevsky's Underground Man. From such a pessimistic determination, it follows that there is ultimately no lasting sense of moral responsibility, for one might conclude those whose characters have become irredeemably spoiled might as well accept their fates and concentrate on surviving through an already hard life. Aristotle maintains that such individuals are incapable of true self-love. They lack the ability to engage in real reform or the incentive to want that ability. A question arises: What resources can those with a wicked character avail themselves of to address that character? Can the privation model, and the morally constructive virtue ethic to which it leads, be relevant to the wicked person who is all but lost to the world? Again, we are not talking about a psychopath, but instead the far more ordinary person who has passed from akratic to intemperate, and, as a result, has become accustomed to his or her own wickedness.

On the question of reforming a wicked character, Aristotle himself is rather pessimistic. As he suggests, individuals who have formed stably wicked characters lose the ability to recognize that they need to reacquire virtue, or acquire it in the first place. Yet, virtue is precisely what is required to gather the self-knowledge that will in turn inspire the search for virtue. The observation is disappointingly tautological, leading Aristotle to raise this concern:

> Someone might raise this puzzle: "What do you mean by saying that to become just we must first do just actions and to become temperate we must first do temperate actions? For if what we do is just or temperate, we must already be just or temperate. . . . [F]or actions expressing virtue to be done temperately or justly (and hence well) it does not suffice that they are themselves in the right state. Rather, the agent must also be in the right state when he does them. First he must know (that he is doing virtuous actions); second, he must decide on them, and decide on them for themselves; and third, he must also do them from a firm and unchanging state.[60]

In this response, it is as if Aristotle sets up disparate communities, the virtuous and nonvirtuous. These are two types of people who have little to do with one another.[61] This sentiment is not very Augustinian, for according to Augustine we are all fallen and guilty before one another. How can Aristotle's principal insight—that the telos of human existence is to become better, that the fight against evil is essentially one of occupying the good, which is Augustinian—be consistent with the essentially undemocratic, non-Augustinian assertion that intemperance is permanent because the intemperate one lacks the resources to know or care about his or her intemperance? To become better one must first know oneself as not good enough.

Although knowing oneself is a precondition of betterment for both Aristotle and Augustine, for Augustine it is inconceivable that the possession of some measure of virtue would qualitatively distinguish some kinds of human beings from others—in God's eyes, we are all profoundly wanting. Thus, on Aristotle's own terms, the question as to how to make virtue ethics more powerful—so it can apply to more than just those who are already virtuous—pressingly arises. No matter who one is, the ability to be self-aware of what is missing in one's makeup is of paramount importance for one to acquire virtue regardless of one's stage of moral development. What is needed is a mechanism for self-awareness, even in the case of the wicked individual Aristotle deems beyond redemption. It is at this point in the discussion that our religious traditions can become useful triggers in affecting what are admittedly improbable outcomes. I briefly delve into a couple examples of how this is possibly so.

In the Jewish tradition, wickedness is referred to as *yetzer ha-ra*, the evil inclination to which all human beings are believed to be subject. Built into the concept is the idea of a threshold beyond which real damage takes place. When someone yields to *yetzer ha-ra* it is not simply that they have harmed another; the term does not refer to a single act. Rather, sin has arrived to corrupt an individual's character and that individual is at this point threatened by the prospect of being eclipsed from rehabilitation. Thus, the concept of *yetzer ha-ra* does not merely entail but hones in on a wickedness seemingly beyond redemption. Indeed, the Jewish tradition acknowledges, with Aristotle, that there is a state more problematic than akrasia (when one succumbs to appetite) in which, because of the power of *yetzer ha-ra*, it no longer occurs to the one in sin that one is sinful. Yet, Judaism offers a resource for specifically addressing even the person Aristotle implies is lost—*teshuvah*.

In his recent work on repentance, Louis Newman discusses the process of atonement in the Jewish tradition, in which this sort of person—the wicked individual so habituated to his or her wicked habits that he or she no longer possesses a clear awareness of how far from decency he or she has strayed—still, improbably, is eligible for redemption.[62] Newman explains that Yom Kippur, the holiday in the Jewish tradition dedicated to atonement, is an opportunity that bears down equally on every Jew to cleanse himself or herself of the sinfulness inevitable in the previous year.[63] In other words, the tradition anticipates that one will have been seduced, at least to a certain extent, by *yetzer ha-ra*. It therefore seeks to insulate its members against precisely the sort of ignorance that for Aristotle makes the nonvirtuous individual unlikely ever to recover virtue. Quoting at length from the Torah, Newman effectively focuses on the prophetic writings of the Jewish tradition, particularly middle Isaiah, to admonish one against ever thinking that anyone is immune to straying from a once-healthy relationship, and yet not also able to return to that from which one has strayed. As Newman explains, the tradition assumes that we each turn away, albeit in varying degrees, and atonement thereby becomes the chance for us each to return and again catch the spark of goodness and purity with which we were endowed.[64] In this sense, two forms of self-knowledge become crucial to the type of redemption that in the Aristotelian account seems out of reach for the nonvirtuous. First is the communal self-knowledge that both sin and atonement are basic to human existence. We are hardwired to become unclean and therefore are meant to appreciate at the outset the importance of cleansing ourselves in the setting of a congregation. As the phenomenologist Paul Ricoeur puts it in *The Symbolism of Evil,* our fear of becoming unclean, of falling from grace, is always in the back of our minds and governs nearly everything we do.[65] This can be a good thing, however, if we assume at a basic level that no matter who we are we will tend to become enveloped by the *yetzer ha-ra,* but, having anticipated such a threat, are also prepared to address it. The second self-knowledge pertains to an awareness of the specific senses in which we have wronged others (and ourselves), dispositions and deeds of which we can be made cognizant only because of the prior humility encouraged by the tradition that asserts that all of us need atonement. As Newman puts it, the idea of *teshuvah* makes possible our ability to say to ourselves the "It is I" which is necessary to assume responsibility for atonement.[66] This is why, ironically, *teshuvah* is the opposite of avoiding wrongdoing, because to know oneself as one who has shunned the good, one must categorically embrace one's culpability and only then address one's transgressions.[67] Remorse, in this sense, goes hand in hand with moral responsibility.

What might seem irreversible is therefore reversible, despite the Augustinian adage that we are all sinners before God.[68] Furthermore, remorse, the idea that we are never fully worthy unto ourselves, seems key for it is what furnishes us with the ability to know ourselves as beings in need of forgiveness and in need of forgiving ourselves. Because sin is a natural condition, addressing sin by building into our psychological expectations that we are sinners must also become part of the moral life cycle. At the beginning of our moral consciousness in our adult lives, a religious tradition, such as Judaism, can help us do this.[69] We should relinquish all efforts to see ourselves as free of wrongdoing lest we become "slaves to an image of perfection that is unattainable."[70] We are all, in varying degrees, in the process of forming wicked characters, yet, paradoxically, it is precisely seeing ourselves this way that prevents a resistant characterological plaque transforming into an irremovable tarter. Aristotle fails to fully solve the puzzle of how the nonvirtuous can ever become virtuous, because his ethics do not conceive of the pedagogical value of human beings imagining themselves in the first place to be prone to straying from virtue. There is not enough emphasis on contrition and remorse in Aristotle's thought. Had there been more, Aristotle might have seen the character that becomes wicked as something we could better anticipate, and therefore something more likely to be understood as malleable.

A parallel may be drawn between the example of *teshuvah* from the Jewish tradition and that of redressing addiction to alcohol, especially if one understands Alcoholics Anonymous (AA) as a spiritual tradition that emphasizes the core value of humility in the face of the ubiquitous threat of sin. One of the key assumptions in both cases is the idea that a condition of being included in the spiritual community is that one is precluded from claiming ignorance about the wicked thing that threatens one's character. The Catholic theologian William McDonough, in his close study of the AA tradition, approvingly cites Ernest Kutz's claim that to its credit, AA has reintroduced into a therapy-obsessed culture of modernity the concept of sin.[71]

Through his analysis of *The Big Book* (AA's founding document), McDonough adduces textual evidence in support of the idea that again and again the alcoholic is encouraged to confront any tendency to feel self-pity or resentment over his or her predicament. As McDonough notes, the bias in the tradition against construing the alcoholic, despite his or her disease, as primarily a victim predetermined to suffer by some biological luck of the draw is deliberate. The assertion of powerlessness becomes escapism if one assumes that one is aware, always, of the possibility of becoming lost to the world within oneself. Alcoholism, which McDonough characterizes as a symptom of the sin of the one in deeper trouble, is, despite its paralyzing impact, never irreversible. What turns out to be the key in recovery is a familiar Augustinian motif:

> What does 'cure' alcoholics turns out to be exactly what cures all human beings, namely God's grace. . . . In the best classical theology, grace works to heal a broken human will in an instant. But, to use a wonderful phrase from German theologian Eberhard Schockenhoff, God's grace must 'reach all the way down into the deep strata of the person,' and this takes time. . . . AA shows the same deep understanding of how grace works when it invites the alcoholic into a lifelong membership in a fellowship dedicated to recovery, one's own and others'.[72]

McDonough's invocation of grace hinges on an emphasis of the Second Step to see oneself as a sinner and stand with other sinners before God, in a fellowship that enables afflicted addicts to see themselves in sin, which they cannot do on their own. But the Second Step is importantly also in advance of a crucial Fourth Step, which provides for a moral inventory of the self, an honest internal discussion after which one understands, where one previously had not, where one lost control. The Second and Fourth Steps can together be seen as the safeguards against the sort of self-ignorance that Aristotle thought precluded the stably nonvirtuous individual from becoming virtuous. In these two steps, one can acquire the motivational resources to undo vice even when one initially does not fully understand that one is in vice. To make a "searching and fearless moral inventory of ourselves" (Step Four)—to actually make good on this step—we must assume that there will be reasons or a temptation not to make such an inventory, particularly if we have gotten used to the way we are. This temptation must be resisted, and the AA tradition can help the afflicted alcoholic resist. As with *teshuvah*, the Twelve Steps of AA equip the soul that would otherwise seem lost to the world with a built-in mechanism for self-discovery. To be part of either tradition is to be forced to examine oneself introspectively. The traditions themselves, at the outset, serve as spurs to travel outside the self by looking within.

At this point, an objection may arise in defense of the skeptical attitude that Aristotle harbors about the possibility of character transformation of the nonvirtuous. The examples of atonement in the Jewish tradition and the Twelve Step Program as interpreted by Catholicism are intended to be available to all Jews and all alcoholics, respectively, in both cases large groups of people who, in the context of the infrastructure of their traditions, are either arguably not that badly off to begin with or have a reasonable chance of recovering in a fellowship of supportive congregants. However, what are the prospects for reform for the truly wicked individual who is alone, or only loosely associated with an institution, or fellowship, that could provide resources? How does one reverse the path one is on when one has done terrible things to isolate oneself from one's community? Is there not, furthermore, a distinction to be made between addiction to a substance and the foulest of character habits? James Keenan characterizes sin not as a wrong act but rather as a bad motivation, or a failure to strive to correct poorly formed motivations.[73] In this way of assessing moral culpability, which is essentially consistent with virtue theory, how does one whose good motivation has been supplanted by bad habit form good habits? Here we again rub up against a central tension between Augustine and Aristotle. Where Augustine puts us all in the same boat, as sinners before God, Aristotle recognizes that some individuals, sometimes because of influences and environment, and sometimes because of their organic moral abilities, are less capable than others, and so can only be lumped together insofar as they all share a duty to become better to the extent that they can. Traditions can go some distance toward bridging this gap between more and less morally capable persons, but only when a mechanism is available to make the sinner aware of his or her sin. What are the prospects for the evil character who is a loner and not substantively affiliated with any tradition in which others can catalyze self-reflection?

Here I think we must grant Aristotle his point that the likelihood of reform is dim. The prospect of changing from one sort of individual to another is paramount if an evil character is to be overcome. If one is shut off from positive influences, one's character will stagnate and bad habits will become more entrenched. Thus, religious traditions are effective in undoing even seemingly irreversible wickedness, on the condition that the wicked individual has formed a meaningful connection to his or her tradition.[74] Sin is exacerbated when one travels through life in isolation, Daniel Harrington and James Keenan explain. This is one of the most important respects in which, as human beings, we exist in interdependence. To the extent that this is true of all of us when we morally devolve, it is even more true with respect to the consistently wicked individual. Isolated, the one who is wicked has become so accustomed to not thinking about others that all attempts from the outside to make him or her see the value of other-regarding behavior in a different light will be in vain. In their study on the relationship between the Pauline tradition and virtue ethics, Harrington and Keenan affirm that even in religious settings, which couch an ethical value such as other-regard in the theological practice of surrendering to the divine, one must still be made to be open to this divine guidance. This, however, tends to happen in a communal setting, they point out, where crises of conscience are collectively addressed and the most wayward are kept in check through the "strong looking after the weak" (Corinthians 8–10).[75] The more one lives by oneself, the more plausible one's rationalizations to not seek the good become to oneself. In the end, we must conclude that religion is not a catch-all for the nonvirtuous individual set in his or ways and unable to get outside himself or herself, for such a person will never really be able to appreciate the resources of that religious tradition in the first place.

This consideration, finally, leads us to return to the case of the psychopath who makes a moral living perfecting the skill of appearing to care but not actually being affected. Technically, the difference between the stably wicked individual and the psychopath, is, as we discussed in chapter 1, that the psychopath is unable (likely due to a damaged amygdala) to care about people. What are the prospects for the application of a virtue ethic to the ones who, though not necessarily cognitively limited, are hardwired to never find themselves communally situated, regardless of how many people are or are not geographically or spiritually close to them? If the presuppositions of virtue ethics do not apply to the psychopath—because they cannot—then have I let the psychopath off the hook? Augustine's picture of evil hinges on the self-knowledge of seeing oneself as fallen and in need of grace and redemption. Aristotle's vision for moral recuperation and betterment fails to work without the attention to the habitual acquisition of virtue that flows from this self-knowledge. Both the diagnosis and prescription are of no use to the psychopath, who by definition lacks the internal resources to get the ball rolling. Worse even than the habitually wicked person, who at least is in principle eligible for reform, the psychopath does not have the free will to get outside of him or herself. Setting aide the question of how this affects the individual's moral accountability, it seems that the Augustinian-Aristotelian recommendation will fall on deaf ears with regard to the psychopath, who most needs to internalize that recommendation.[76]

Here again, we concede that Aristotle's skepticism about the limits of acquiring virtue when one has none to begin with is well founded. By conservative estimates, about 1 percent of the population of the United States is psychopathic.[77] This, though, translates to more than three million people.[78] Many of these, under the right circumstances, will torture or kill with impunity when they deem that doing so is a prudentially worthwhile opportunity. If indeed they are naturally disposed this way, and they consequently have no real sense of free will, then they should arguably be seen as ticking time bombs. This, however, leaves more than 300 million people in this country alone for whom the normal suppositions about the role of community, the effect of forming good or bad habits, and the possibility of free will, apply. For all of these individuals, we should conclude that the good is available, if hard to attain.

Evil: Our Problem

In *Evil in Modern Thought*, Susan Neiman defends the claim that evil is the most significant philosophical issue of the day, an unavoidable problem that the self-reflective individual has no choice but to consider every time he or she makes the judgment "this ought not to have happened."[79] This reflection simultaneously sheds light on clear missed opportunities and the bewildering unintelligibility of the world. Seeking to find the significance in occurrences gone wrong, William James identifies them in *The Varieties of Religious Experience* as "possibly the only openers of our eyes to the deepest levels of truth." These, he goes on to say, are revealed in nothing more overt than the "normal process of life" in which our wildest fears and fantastical horrors are "all drawn from the material of daily fact."[80] According to Neiman and James, the lesson of evil is not to notice the good for the sake of which bad things happen. It is rather, more modestly, that everything in this world is not as it should be. We can be certain of very little, but we can be certain that regardless of how much control wicked individuals have or do not have over their actions, they will act harmfully, and victims will suffer, in abundance. The good, by contrast, is, as Martha Nussbaum poignantly notes, "fragile": fleeting, elusive, and consonant with human frailty, vulnerability, and mortality.[81] Good is difficult to sustain when we do occupy it and is even harder to acquire. This asymmetry between evil and the good has interesting implications for the relationship between the descriptive enterprise of characterizing evil and the normative one of attending to it. That inertia is empirically on the side of evil according to the model of privation makes the distance between good and evil more vast than it is in other models, and, consequently, the overcoming of evil more pressing.

It is informed by this relationship between the descriptive and the normative that I have connected Augustine to Aristotle. Augustine's view of evil releases no one from its purview. Its application to a virtue ethic, according to which everyone is enjoined to take an inventory of him or herself in service of future betterment, naturally follows from this. To be sure, inherent truths in the first three models of evil discussed in this book make the connection between these two thinkers seem far from exhaustive of the possible ways of relating the descriptive and the normative spheres. There are, for example, instances of sadistic torturers to whom no one can get through with either reason or an affective appeal, which makes all-inclusive normative claims futile. In other instances we cannot distinguish evil from the good enough to have confidence in any normative agenda in the first place. After these instances, however, the sizable remainder of us can still reliably say that we are morally culpable and therefore have an opportunity to do good. Instances in which evil is the result of something we could have done but did not are plentiful enough, instances which on first glance may be superficially explained away as something else, that we should work on the assumption that we have something to do with the things in this world that go wrong.

What does this mean? It means that when any atrocity occurs, before its cause has been established, we ought to ask ourselves first what, if anything, we might have had to do with—to quote Neiman—the "this" that "ought not to have happened." Granting, as many of the thinkers I discuss in this book have pointed out, that there are sometimes reasons to be suspicious that anything labeled "evil" or "good" is what it is claimed to be, there are more instances in which we can be confident, through exposure to the evident suffering of one or some, that a terrible thing has in fact taken place. That the term evil is misused on occasion should not be taken to mean that evil does not exist. Adopting a proactive stance with regard to suffering and wrongdoing with which we potentially have something to do will ensure that we will have the best chance of becoming more self-reflective, virtuous, and finally caring about others and the world around us. We might end up occasionally blaming ourselves for something we had less to do with than we originally thought. However, we will protect ourselves against the much worse outcome of missing an opportunity to become involved in ourselves and others when we ought to have been involved.

What is the best way to train ourselves to begin our encounter with evil by looking for the ways in which we might be involved in the harms others suffer? The key is to think about what it means to be a bystander and to consider whether, indeed, any such a thing as a legitimate bystander in fact exists. In the context of an extended explanation of the degeneration of society in book 8 of Plato's *Republic*, Socrates says, "Societies are not made of sticks and stones, but of men whose individual characters, by turning the scale one way or another, determine the direction of the whole."[82] Plato is not referring here to the threatened European citizen, circa 1940, who needed to summon a heroic measure of courage to resist the Nazis. He is talking about all of us who have the opportunity every day to choose to focus on any situation that is developing ominously. Jonathan Glover's term for this individual is the "free bystander," the one whose failure to help when he or she otherwise could have is explained by no more than a lapse in moral imagination, bureaucratic ineptitude, or myopia.[83] The remedy for this unfortunate phenomenon, Glover explains, is to erect an other-regarding moral identity sufficient to shake us out of the institutional comfort zones and insular spheres of interaction to which we have become accustomed. Holocaust survivors observe that it was often the smallest gestures that made the difference between survival and despair. Glover relates that

> even a friendly face made a difference. Prisoners in Mauthausen working away from the camp noticed people who looked at them sympathetically. Austrian workmen used their position on top of scaffolding to warn prisoners when they needed to work hard and when it was safe to let up. Some villagers put out glasses of water for the passing prisoners and threw them apples. . . . Jean Améry remembered cigarettes. After he had been tortured in Breendonk, one soldier tossed him a lighted cigarette through the cell bars. Later, in Auschwitz-Monowitz, he shared the last cigarette of Herbert Karp, a disabled soldier from Danzig.[84]

Small gestures not only make a big difference. They are also a reminder that once we open our eyes we can almost always do something. That just a sympathetic gaze would positively affect a suffering individual indicates the enormous array of options available to anyone who is genuinely motivated to alleviate the sorrows of others. Although sometimes we are evil through our acts of commission, it is primarily through omission that we are responsible.

To become involved in the plight of others in a real way, one must first ask oneself how one might get involved. Intervention is typically perceived by the potential intervener as an unlikely course of action. It entails overcoming the common knee-jerk reflection: "what can I really do about this situation, a situation that seems so much bigger than me?" This is an easy and quite natural thing to say to oneself. We do not ask to become spectators to the miseries of others. It is also admittedly unpleasant to feel impotent about our ability to ameliorate the suffering of others when we have reasons to think we cannot. The, truth, however, is that we are almost never either fully uninvolved or impotent. Although the scaffolders in Glover's example who warned of approaching concentration camp guards and the compassionate soldier who gave a prisoner his cigarette were not the causes of the evils to which they bore witness, they understood that they became a part of these experiences by witnessing them.

There will be times when we can do nothing to help others because the opposing force is just too powerful. At still other times it will be best to do nothing. We cannot make a difference on every occasion. This said, at the outset of a situation developing for the worse, we can neither know what the real extent of our responsibility for its advent is nor when we stand to make a difference and when we do not. From this we might conclude that however much good we do, or realistically can hope to do, we should nevertheless go out of our way to choose the good.

Notes

1. See Jones, *Moral Responsibility in the Holocaust*, 90.

2. The historian Erich Goldhagen argued in 1971 that Speer had been present when Heinrich Himmler alerted Nazi leaders of the Final Solution, calling into question Speer's claim by which he stood throughout his prison sentence not to have known about the true nature of the Holocaust. See *Hitler's Willing Executioners*, 164. For a discussion of Goldhagen's and additional evidence attesting to Speer's possible additional knowledge of Hitler's genocide see Jones, *Moral Responsibility in the Holocaust*, 93.

3. Speer, *Inside the Third Reich*, 376.

4. Burrell and Hauerwas, "Self-Deception and Autobiography," 105. Burrell and Hauerwas cite several instances in which it appears that Speer *does* go so far to accept responsibility for his actions, if not his intentions.

5. Jones, *Moral Responsibility*, 92.

6. Speer, *Inside the Third Reich*, 342.

7. Ibid., 290.

8. Burrell and Hauerwas, "Self-Deception and Autobiography," 100.

9. Milgram, *Obedience to Authority*; Zimbardo, *The Lucifer Effect*.

10. Much has rightly been made of the human subjects ethical violations to which Milgram's and Zimbardo's experiments gave rise. For a classic critique of Milgram, see Baumrind, "Some Thoughts."

11. Milgram, "Behavioral Study of Obedience."

12. Milgram, *Obedience to Authority*, 123.

13. Ibid., 133.

14. Ibid., 155–56.

15. See, for example, Hallie, *Lest Innocent Blood*.

16. See Flescher, *Heroes, Saints*, 131.

17. Milgram, *Obedience to Authority*, 179–80.

18. Bonhoeffer's subversion of the fascist system to which he and his colleagues were seemingly helplessly subject was "diabolically" altruistic, diabolical not only because of the concealed manner in which Bonhoeffer's objectives of resistance to the Nazi regime were required to be carried out, but also because under the normal rules of civic engagement in this particular society and situation there was no possibility for goodness and flourishing. Under the pretext of *Abwehr*, Bonhoeffer was able to infiltrate and expose aspects of the German, fascist controlled, intelligence network and then position himself to attempt to establish possible terms of peace after the Allies had prevailed. I thank Stephen Post for helping me to think through the rich case of Bonhoeffer and for introducing me to the term of art *diabolical altruist*.

19. Milgram, *Obedience to Authority*, 182.

20. Flescher, *Heroes, Saints*, 246. Here I advocate a particular strand of neo-Aristotelianism that emphasizes striving over contentment in Aristotle's thought. In this view, I am joined by virtue ethicists such as Nancy Sherman and David Norton and opposed by, for example, Philippa Foot and Susan Wolf. See Sherman, "Common Sense"; Norton, "Moral Minimalism"; Foot, *Natural Goodness*; Wolf, "Moral Saints."

21. See Aristotle, *Nicomachean Ethics*, 1105a16–b20.

22. I and most ethicists would still accept that Aristotle is right about the possibility of the existence of stable character traits. However, a growing school of moral philosophers and psychologists—new situationalists—take no such thing for granted. See, for example, Gilbert Harman, who argues that "ordinary attributions of character traits to people are often deeply misguided and it may even be the case that there is no such thing as character, no ordinary character traits of the sort people think there are, none of the usual moral virtues and vices." See Harman, "Moral Philosophy," 316. See also Doris, *Lack of Character*.

23. For a discussion of the importance of rearing children in the right ways to the acquisition of virtue over a lifetime, see MacIntyre, *Dependent Rational Animals*, 70.

24. See, for example, Card, *Atrocity Paradigm*, 51.

25. Aristotle, *Nicomachean Ethics*, 1129a5–b10.

26. Ibid., 1166b1–b25.

27. See Post, *Altruism and Health*, for a collection of essays establishing these links. Some notable essays in this volume include Brown et al., "Close Relationships and Health"; Hirschfelder and Reilly, "Rx"; and Oman, "Does Volunteering Foster Physical Health and Longevity." Post and Neimark also published a companion book to this edited volume summarizing some of these and similar findings. See *Why Good Things Happen*.

28. Aristotle distinguishes three kinds of friendships: the lowest, "friendships of utility," which pertain to self-interested connections between individuals mutually using one another for some instrumental purpose; the second, "friendships of pleasure," which pertain to superficial hedonistic expression and fulfillment; and the highest, "friendships of character," according to which both parties make each other better by virtue of their connection, a connection justified in the first place by their independently demonstrating sufficiently virtuous traits in themselves such that they would be in a position to make a positive difference on one another. Aristotle enjoins us to strive for the latter while also acknowledging that the latter is not accessible to everyone. See Aristotle, *Nicomachean Ethics*, 1156a6.

29. Ibid., 1166b1, 1097b25, 1098a1–a3, 1170b13.

30. Augustine, *Confessions*, 251–53.

31. Augustine, *City of God*, 574.

32. Aristotle, *Nicomachean Ethics*, 1149b2–50b33, 1102b14–25; 1111b13–b16. See also Sarah Broadie, who discusses these passages in *Ethics with Aristotle*, 282.

33. Sherman, "Common Sense," 98.

34. Aristotle, *Nicomachean Ethics*, 1150b29, 1151a1–b5, 1150b35–36.

35. See Flescher, *Heroes, Saints*, 294n104.

36. Aristotle, *Rhetoric*, 1369b6, 1370a6.

37. Aristotle, *Nicomachean Ethics*, 1111b26, 1112b15–b26, 1139a21–b5, 1117a15–a22. Also see Terence Irwin's discussion of this distinction in his appendix where he talks about the meaning and different senses of *prohairesis*, 392–93.

38. The little-by-little theme comes through particularly in the writing of Dorothy Day, founder of the Catholic Worker's Movement. The phrase Day modifies from the nineteenth-century mystic and Carmelite nun, St. Thérèse of Liseux, whose "little way" pertained to the ordinary routine shared by twenty sisters in pursuit of a scrupulous and devout routine in the convent. The spirit behind the phrase, which conjures notions of effort and good-habit formation, appealed to Day. See Day, *By Little and by Little*.

39. See Sherman, *Making a Necessity of Virtue*, 136, and Korsgaard, "From Duty." As Sherman and Korsgaard both explain, Aristotle and Kant share a conception of wherein lies moral value, namely, in the capacity to choose deliberately for the sake of distinctive ends.

40. Sherman, *Making a Necessity*, 5.

41. The world bank estimated that this was the most expensive disaster ever, placing the cost at $235 billion. See www.accuweather.com/blogs/news/story/47459/top-5-most-expensive-natural-d.asp. The Japanese government upped this figure to $309 billion. See www.businessweek.com/news/2011–03–23/japan-forecasts-earthquake-damage-may-swell-to-309-billion.html.

42. Victor Kostev of the *Asia Times* quotes several examples. See, for instance, www.alternet.org/news/151440/fukushima%3A_world%27s_worst_industrial_disaster_reveals_how_nation_states_are_powerless_to_protect_us_from_advanced_technology.

43. Ibid.

44. As explained by Kirk Sorensen, a nuclear technologist, and one of the foremost experts on the dangers of nuclear power. See his Forbes article, "Explainer: What Caused the Incident at Fukushima-Daiichi," March 15, 2011, http://blogs.forbes.com/

christopherhelman/2011/03/15/explainer-what-caused-the-incident-at-fukushima-daiic
hi/. Sorensen also manages the site www.energyfromthorium.com.

45. Following the nuclear crisis at Fukushima, much has been made of the Japanese government's protecting TEPCO. An article on the World Socialist website says this, for example: "The Kyodo news agency this week reported that the government was examining the cost of TEPCO's obligations under the 1961 Act on Compensation for Nuclear Damage, which not only protects the interests of the private nuclear power companies but also of those, like the US giant General Electric, that have supplied and maintained its reactors." Mike Head, "Japanese Government Prepares to Protect TEPCO from Liability," March 25, 2011, www.wsws.org/articles/2011/mar2011/japa-m25.shtml.

46. Ibid. "The US Price-Anderson Act limits liability for nuclear power plant operators to $12.6 billion. The legislation, first passed in 1957, further authorises the Nuclear Regulatory Commission or the Department of Energy to indemnify nuclear companies for damages that exceed any required insured amount."

47. Two wonderful examples in film and television which deal comprehensively with the phenomenon of terrorism and inner city turbulence, respectively, are the movie *Syriana* and the HBO series *The Wire*. The latter won David Simon the coveted MacArthur Genius Award for the show's realistic and deep excavation of urban dysfunction.

48. This is not to say there are not innocents in the context, for example, of an ethics of war that distinguishes noncombatants from soldiers. Here specific roles figure into the rules of engagement, justifying noncombatant immunity. It is to say, however, that in lieu of specifically assigned roles it is not as easy to determine the guilty from the innocent as we tend to think it is.

49. Flescher, *Heroes, Saints*, 240–42, 256–60.

50. Wolf, "Moral Saints," 435.

51. See Hampton, "Selflessness and Loss of the Self."

52. Aristotle, *Nicomachean Ethics*, 1169a6–a8, 1177b35.

53. Norton, "Moral Minimalism," 187.

54. Annas, *Morality of Happiness*, 56.

55. Aristotle, *Nicomachean Ethics*, 1166b1, also 1171b33.

56. I thank the anonymous reviewers at Georgetown University Press for pressing me to defend my claim about the connection between Augustine and Aristotle along these lines.

57. Gregory, *Politics and the Order of Love*, 21.

58. For a detailed discussion of this passage, see Clark, "De Trinitate," 97–98.

59. Aristotle, *Nicomachean Ethics*, 1150a30–51a3, 1150b35.

60. Ibid., 1105a18–22, 1105a26–a34.

61. For an extended discussion of Aristotle's view that the virtuous have little to say to the nonvirtuous, see especially Annas, *Morality of Happiness*, 110.

62. Newman, *Repentance*.

63. Ibid., 58–61.

64. Ibid., 29.

65. Ricoeur, *Symbolism of Evil*, 25, discussed by Newman, *Repentance*, 29.

66. Newman, *Repentance*, 83.

67. Ibid., 86.

68. Ibid., 76. For a discussion of the notion of irredeemable sinners, see 165.

69. In *Fundamental Moral Theology*, Franz Böckle presents the confession of sinfulness as a comparably effective means of reversing the irreversible within the Catholic tradition. The articulation of one's fallenness to oneself is tantamount to clarifying how one is sinful in particular ways, due to its performative character. "If the psalmist," Böckle writes, "for example, tells us in a confession of guilt: *iniquitatem meam ego agnosco*, "I acknowledge my offence," he is combining the past and the future in the decisive moment of his present. He is also accepting responsibility for his action and its consequences" (89). Just as moral evil is malignant by virtue of the free act or inaction that precipitated it, evil's overcoming through confession, also a free act, has the capacity to return the sinner to his or her prior state before the commission of the sin in question. In this manner, Böckle sees confession, precipitated by guilt, as an existential line of defense against the equally existential default predicament according to which the human being in the first place lives as a sinner. This is how the one confessing can manage to turn his or her gaze from "past to future" (90). All the more effective if this happens in the context of community. "Faith is borne and made secure by the community of those who believe and in the same way sin prospers in the solidarity of sinners" (105).

70. Newman, *Repentance*, 84.

71. McDonough, "Sin and Addiction," 39–40.

72. Ibid., 43, 50.

73. Keenan, "The Problem," 410.

74. This perhaps accounts for why so many terrible people in this world undergo striking character reform when they find religion. It is not necessarily the case that the content of the faith doctrines to which they are attracted gives them the "born-again" experience that makes them appear to the outside world to be a brand new individual. Rather, it is their faith-community that collectively keeps honest the individual members of its flock by making that individual self-aware. Such self-awareness, in turn, can precipitate character reform along the lines that we have been discussing. This is not to suggest that the opposite cannot take place as well. Indeed, an individual of good character can become corrupted by a religious community which collectively espouses spurious values and transmits them, through coercion, to that individual. The point is that assuming we are *beginning* with a consideration of the wicked individual, that individual has a chance of recuperating, where he or she might not have, when thrust into a situation that structurally entails close connection to other individuals.

75. See Harrington and Keenan, *Paul and Virtue Ethics*, 156, 110, 133–37.

76. For an interesting discussion of the relation between free will and moral accountability (and defender of the view that the one who has compromised free will is still morally accountable), see several of the essays written by Frankfurt in *Importance of What We Care About*, particularly the first two: "Alternate Possibilities and Moral Responsibility," 1–10, and "Freedom of the Will and the Concept of a Person," 11–25. I thank Wai-Hung Wong for pointing Frankfurt out to me as a critic of the view that curtailed autonomous ability implies limited moral culpability.

77. Neumann and Hare, "Psychopathic Traits."

78. A 2009 study of British prisoners found a prevalence for "categorically diagnosed psychopathy" of 7.7 percent in men and 1.9 percent in women. See Coid et al., "Psychopathy among Prisoners," 32.

79. Neiman, *Evil in Modern Thought*, 5.

80. James, *Varieties of Religious Experience*, 163.

81. Nussbaum, *Fragility of Goodness.*

82. Plato, *The Republic*, 314.

83. Glover, *Humanity*, 391.

84. Ibid., 383.

BIBLIOGRAPHY

Adams, Robert. "Saints." *Journal of Philosophy* 81 (1984): 392–401.

Annas, Julia. *The Morality of Happiness*. Oxford: Oxford University Press, 1993.

Anscombe, G. E. M. "Modern Moral Philosophy." *Philosophy* 33 (1958): 1–19.

Arendt, Hannah. "Eichmann in Jerusalem: An Exchange of Letters between Gershom Scholem and Hannah Arendt." *Encounter* 22 (1964): 51–56.

———. *Eichmann in Jerusalem: A Report on the Banality of Evil*. New York: Viking Press, 1965.

———. *The Origins of Totalitarianism*. New York: Harcourt, Brace, Jovanovich, 1973.

———. *Life of the Mind: The Groundbreaking Investigation on How We Think*. Vols. 1 and 2. Edited by Mary McCarthy. New York: Mariner Books, 1981.

Aristotle. "Categories." Translated by E. M. Edghill. In *The Basic Works of Aristotle*. Edited by Richard McKeon. New York: Random House, 1941.

———. "Rhetoric." Translated by W. Rhys Roberts. In *The Basic Works of Aristotle*. Edited by Richard McKeon. New York: Random House, 1941.

———. *Nicomachean Ethics*. Translated by Terence Irwin. Indianapolis: Hackett Publishing, 1985.

Augustine. "On the Nature of the Good (Against the Manichees)." In *Augustine: Earlier Writings*. Translated by John H. S. Burleigh. Philadelphia, PA: Westminster Press, 1953.

———. *The Confessions of St. Augustine*. Translated by John K. Ryan. New York: Doubleday Books, 1960.

———. *On Free Choice of the Will*. Translated by Anna S. Benjamin and L. H. Hackstaff. Upper Saddle River, NJ: Prentice Hall, 1964.

———. *City of God*. Translated by Henry Bettenson. London: Penguin Books, 1972.

———. *On the Holy Trinity, Doctinal Treatises, Moral Treatises: Nicene and Post Nicene Fathers*. Vol. 3. Edited by P. Schaff. Peabody, MA: Hendrickson, 1994.

————. *St. Augustine's Anti-Pelagian Writings: Nicene and Post-Nicene Fathers of the Christian Church.* Vol. 5. Edited by Philip Schaff. Translated by Peter Holmes and Robert Ernest Wallis. Whitefish, MT: Kessinger Publishing, 2010.

————. *On Nature and Grace.* www.newadvent.org/fathers/1503.htm.

Barth, Karl. *Church Dogmatics.* 13 vols. Translated by G. W. Bromiley. Edinburgh: T&T Clark, 1956–1975.

————. *The Christian Life.* Edinburgh: T&T Clark, 1981.

————. *Ethics.* Translated by G. W. Bromiley. Edinburgh: T&T Clark, 1981.

Baumeister, Roy F. *Evil: Inside Human Cruelty and Violence.* New York: W. H. Freeman, 1997.

Baumrind, D. "Some Thoughts on Ethics of Research: After Reading Milgram's 'Behavorial Study of Obedience," *American Psychologist* 19 (1964): 421–23.

Bayle, Pierre. *Historical and Critical Dictionary.* Translated by Richard Popkin. Indianapolis: Bobbs Merrill, 1965.

Baynes, Kenneth, James Bohman, and Thomas McCarthy, eds. *After Philosophy: End or Transformation?* Cambridge, MA: MIT Press, 1987.

Bennet, Philip W. "Evil, God, and the Free Will Defense," *Australasian Journal of Philosophy* 51, no.1 (1973): 39–50.

Berger, Peter L. *The Sacred Canopy: Elements of a Sociology of Religion.* New York: Anchor Books, 1967.

Bernstein, Richard J. *The Abuse of Evil: The Corruption of Politics and Religion since 9/11.* Cambridge: Polity Press, 2005.

Böckle, Franz. *Fundamental Moral Theology.* Translated by N. D. Smith. New York: Pueblo Publishing, 1980.

Boyer, Paul. *When Time Shall Be No More: Prophecy Belief in Modern American Culture.* Cambridge, MA: Harvard University Press, 1992.

Broadie, Sarah. *Ethics with Aristotle.* Oxford: Oxford University Press, 1991.

Brown, Robert McAfee. "Introduction." In *The Essential Reinhold Niebuhr: Selected Essays and Addresse.* Edited by R. M. Brown. New Haven, CT: Yale University Press, 1987.

Brown, Stephanie L., Michael Brown, Ashley Schiavone, and Dylan M. Smith. "Close Relationships and Health through the Lens of Selective Investment Theory." In *Altruism and Health: Perspectives from Empirical Research*, edited by Stephen G. Post, 299–313. Oxford: Oxford University Press, 2007.

Browning, Christopher R. *Ordinary Men: Reserve Police Battalion 101 and the Final Solution in Poland.* New York: Harper Collins, 1992.

Burrell, David, and Stanley Hauerwas. "Self-Deception and Autobiography: Theological and Ethical Reflection on Speer's *Inside the Third Reich.*" *Journal of Religious Ethics* 2, no. 1 (1974): 99–117.

Byrne, Rhonda. *The Secret*. Hillsboro, OR: Artia/Beyond Words, 2006.

Calvin, John. *Institutes of the Christian Religion*. Translated by Ford Lewis Battles. Philadelphia, PA: Westminster Press, 1960.

Camus, Albert *The Fall*. Translated by Justin O'Brien. New York: Vintage Press, 1991.

———. *The Plague*. Translated by Stuart Gilbert. New York: Vintage Press, 1991.

———. *The Myth of Sisyphus and Other Essays*. Translated by Justin O'Brien. London: Vintage Books, 1991.

———. *The Rebel: An Essay on Man in Revolt*. Translated by Anthony Bower. New York: Vintage Press, 1991.

Caplan, Pat. *The Cultural Construction of Sexuality*. New York: Routledge, 1987.

Card, Claudia. *The Atrocity Paradigm: A Theory of Evil*. Oxford: Oxford University Press, 2002.

Chuang-Tzu, *Basic Writings*. Translated by Burton Watson. New York: Columbia University Press, 1964.

Clark, Mary T. "De Trinitate." In *The Cambridge Companion to Augustine*. Edited by Eleonore Stump and Norman Kretzmann. Cambridge: Cambridge University Press, 2001.

Coid, Jeremy, Min Yang, Simone Ullrich, Amanda Roberts, Paul Moran, Paul Bebbington, Traolach Brugha, Rachel Jenkins, Michael Farrell, Glyn Lewis, Nicola Singleton, and Robert Hare. "Psychopathy among Prisoners in England and Wales." *International Journal of Law and Psychiatry* 32, no. 3 (2009): 134–41.

Connolly, William E. "Beyond Good and Evil: The Ethical Sensibility of Michel Foucault," *Political Theory* 21, no. 3 (1993): 365–89.

Conrad, Joseph. *Heart of Darkness*. New York: W. W. Norton, 1988.

Conroy, John. *Unspeakable Acts, Ordinary People: The Dynamics of Torture*. New York: Alfred A. Knopf, 2000.

Cooper, Terry D. *Dimensions of Evil: Contemporary Perspectives*. Minneapolis, MN: Fortress Press, 2007.

Crumb, Robert. *The Book of Genesis Illustrated by R. Crumb*. New York: W. W. Norton, 2009.

Dawkins, Richard. *The God Delusion*. New York: Bantam Books, 2006.

Day, Dorothy. *By Little and by Little: Selected Writings of Dorothy Day*. Edited by Robert Ellsberg. New York: Orbis Books, 1992.

Dōgen Kigen. "Shobogenzo Genjokoan." Translated by Norman Waddell and Masao Abe. *The Eastern Buddhist* 5, no. 2 (1972): 129–40.

Doris, John. *Lack of Character: Personality and Moral Behavior*. Cambridge: Cambridge University Press, 2005.

Dostoevsky, Fydor. *The Grand Inquisitor.* Translated by Charles B. Guignon. Indianapolis, IN: Hackett Publishing, 1993.

Dyson, Michael Eric. *I Might Not Get There with You: The True Martin Luther King, Jr.* New York: The Free Press, 2000.

Eagleton, Terry. *On Evil.* New Haven, CT: Yale University Press, 2010.

Ehrenreich, Barbara, "Welcome to Cancerland." *Harpers Magazine* (November 2001). www.barbaraehrenreich.com/cancerland.htm.

Ehrman, Bart D. *God's Problem: How the Bible Fails to Answer Our Most Important Question—Why We Suffer.* New York: Harper One, 2008.

Eribon, Didier. *Michel Foucault.* Translated by Betsy Wind. Cambridge, MA: Harvard University Press, 1991.

Evans, G. R. *Augustine on Evil.* Cambridge: Cambridge University Press, 1982.

Flescher, Andrew Michael. *Heroes, Saints, and Ordinary Morality.* Washington, DC: Georgetown University Press, 2003.

Flescher, Andrew Michael, and Daniel L. Worthen. *The Altruistic Species: Scientific, Philosophical, and Religious Perspectives of Human Benevolence.* Philadelphia, PA: Templeton Foundation Press, 2007.

Flew, A. "Divine Omnipotence and Human Freedom." In *New Essays in Philosophical Theology.* Edited by A. Flew and A. MacIntyre. London: SCM Press, 1955.

Foot, Phillipa. *Natural Goodness.* Oxford: Clarendon Press, 2001.

Foucault, Michel. *Power/Knowledge [1972–77].* New York: Pantheon Books, 1980.

———. "Space, Knowledge and Power." In *The Foucault Reader.* Edited by Paul Rabinow. Harmondsworth, UK: Penguin Books, 1991.

———. *The Essential Works of Michel Foucault 1954–1988,* vol. 3, *Power.* Edited by James Faubion. Translated by Robert Hurley et al. New York: New York Press, 2000.

Frankfurt, Harry G. *The Importance of What We Care About.* Cambridge: Cambridge University Press, 1988.

Frankfurter, David. *Evil Incarnate: Rumors of Demonic Conspiracy and Satanic Abuse in History.* Princeton, NJ: Princeton University Press, 2006.

Freud, Sigmund. *The Standard Edition of the Complete Psychological Works of Sigmund Freud.* Translated by James Strachey. London: Hogarth Press, 1963.

Frykholm, Amy Johnson. *Rapture Culture: Left Behind in Evangelical America.* Oxford: Oxford University Press, 2004.

Galston, William A. "Cosmopolitan Altruism." In *Altruism,* edited by Ellen Frankel Paul, Fred D. Miller Jr., and Jeffrey Paul, 118–34. Cambridge: Cambridge University Press, 1993.

Gardner, Iain, and Samuel N. C. Lieu. *Manichean Texts from the Roman Empire*. Cambridge: Cambridge University Press, 2004.

Geertz, Clifford. *The Interpretation of Cultures*. New York: Basic Books, 1977.

Glassner, Barry. *The Culture of Fear: Why Americans Are Afraid of the Wrong Things*. New York: Basic Books, 2000.

Glenn, Andrea L., Adrian Raine, Peter H. Venables, and Sarnoff A. Mednick. "Early Temperamental and Psychophysiological Precursors of Adult Psychopathic Pesonality." *Journal of Abnormal Psychology* 11, no. 3 (2007): 508–15.

Glover, Jonathan. *Humanity: A Moral History of the Twentieth Century*. New Haven, CT: Yale University Press, 1999.

Goldhagen, Daniel Jonah. *Hitler's Willing Executioners: Ordinary Germans and the Holocaust*. New York: Alfred A. Knopf, 1996.

Gourevitch, Philip. *We Wish to Inform You That Tomorrow We Will Be Killed with Our Families: Stories from Rwanda*. New York: Picador USA, 1998.

Graham, Gordon. *Evil and Christian Ethics*. Cambridge: Cambridge University Press, 2001.

Green, R. M. "Theodicy." In *The Encyclopedia of Religion*. Vol. 14. Edited by M. Eliade. New York: MacMillan, 1987.

Gregory, Eric. *Politics and the Order of Love*. Chicago: University of Chicago Press, 2008.

Hallie, Philip. *Lest Innocent Blood Be Shed: The Story of the Village of Le Chambon and How Goodness Happened There*. New York: Harper and Row, 1979.

Hampton, Jean. "Selflessness and the Loss of Self." In *Altruism*, edited by Ellen Frankel Paul, Fred D. Miller Jr., and Jeffrey Paul, 135–65. Cambridge: Cambridge University Press, 1993.

Harcourt, Bernard. "Institutionalization vs. Imprisonment: Are There Massive Implications for Existing Research?" *The Volokh Conspiracy*, May 2, 2007. http://volokh.com/posts/1178086065.shtml.

Hare, John E. *The Moral Gap: Kantian Ethics, Human Limits, and God's Assistance*. Oxford: Clarendon Press, 1996.

Hari, Johann. "Gore Vidal's United States of Fury." *The Independent*. October 7, 2009. www.independent.co.uk/news/world/americas/gore-vidals-united-states-of-fury-1798601.html.

Harman, Gilbert. "Moral Philosophy Meets Social Psychology: Virtue Ethics and the Fundamental Attribution Error." *Proceedings of the Aristotelian Society* 99, no. 3 (1999): 315–31.

Harrington, Daniel J., and James F. Keenan. *Paul and Virtue Ethics: Building Bridges between New Testament Studies and Moral Theology*. Lanham, MD: Rowman & Littlefield, 2010.

Harris, Judith Rich. *The Nurture Assumption: Why Children Turn Out the Way They Do*. New York: The Free Press, 1999.

Harris, Sam. *The End of Faith: Religion, Terror, and the Future of Reason*. New York: W. W. Norton, 2004.

Harvey, Van. *Feuerbach and the Interpretation of Religion*. Cambridge: Cambridge University Press, 1995.

Hawes, Elizabeth. *Camus, A Romance*. New York: Grove Press, 2010.

Hawkins, Hunt. "Conrad's Critique of Imperialism in *Heart of Darkness*." *PLMA* 94, no. 2 (1979): 286–99.

Heidegger, Martin. *Being and Time: A Translation of Sein and Zeit*. Translated by Joan Stambaugh. New York: SUNY Press, 1996.

Hesse, Hermann. *Siddhartha*. Translated by Hilda Rosner. New York: New Directions Publishing, 1951.

———. *Demian*. Translated by Michael Roloff and Michael Lebeck. New York: Harper and Row, 1965.

———. "Thoughts on 'The Idiot'." In *My Belief: Essays on Life and Art*. Edited by Theodore Ziolkowski. Translated by Denver Lindley. New York: Farrar, Straus, and Giroux, 1974.

Hick, John. *Death and Eternal Life*. San Francisco: Harper and Row, 1976.

———. "Irenaean Theodicy." In *Encountering Evil: Live Options in Theodicy*. Edited by Stephen Davis. Atlanta, GA: John Knox Press, 1981.

———. *An Interpretation of Religion: Human Responses to the Transcendent*. New Haven, CT: Yale University Press, 1989.

———. *Evil and the God of Love*. Basingstoke, UK: Macmillan, 2007.

Hirschfelder, Adam S., and Sabrina L. Reilly. "Rx: Volunteer: A Prescription for Healthy Aging." In *Altruism and Health: Perspectives from Empirical Research*, edited by Stephen G. Post, 116–40. Oxford: Oxford University Press, 2007.

Hitchens, Christopher. *God Is Not Great: How Religion Poisons Everything*. New York: Twelve/Hachette Book Group, 2007.

Hobbes, Thomas. *Leviathan (or the Matter, Form and Power of a Commonwealth Ecclesiastical and Civil)*. New York: Collier Books, 1962.

Hume, David. *Enquiries concerning the Principles of Morals*. Edited by L. A. Selby-Bigge. Oxford: Oxford University Press, 1975.

———. *A Treatise of Human Nature*. Edited by L. A. Selby-Bigge and P. H. Nidditch. Oxford: Clarendon Press, 1978.

Huntington, Samuel. "The Clash of Civilizations?" *Foreign Affairs* (1993): 22–49.

———. *The Clash of Civilizations and the Remaking of World Order*. New York: Simon & Schuster, 1996.

Irenaeus. "Against Heresies." In *The Anti-Nicene Fathers: Translations of the Writings of the Fathers Down to A.D. 325*, vol. 1. Edited by Alexander Roberts and James Donaldson. Grand Rapids, MI: W. M. B. Eerdmans, 1956.

Isichei, Elizabeth. *Voices of the Poor in Africa*. Rochester, NY: University of Rochester Press, 2002.

Ivanhoe, Philip J. "Zhuangzi on Skepticism, Skill and the Ineffable *Dao*." *Journal of the American Academy of Religion* 59, no. 4 (1993): 639–53.

———. "Was Zhuangzi a Relativist?" In *Essays on Skepticism, Relativism, and Ethics in the Zhuangzi*. Edited by Philip J. Ivanhoe and Paul Kjellberg. Albany: SUNY Press, 1996.

James, William. *Pragmatism: A New Name for Some Old Ways of Thinking*. New York: Longman, Greens, 1907.

———. *The Will to Believe and Other Essays in Popular Philosophy*. New York: Dover Publications, 1956.

———. *The Varieties of Religious Experience: A Study in Human Nature*. New York: Penguin Books, 1982.

Jameson, Fredric. *Fables of Aggression: Wyndham Lewis, the Modernist as Fascist*. Berkeley: University of California, 1979.

Jones, David H. *Moral Responsibility in the Holocaust: A Study in the Ethics of Character*. New York: Rowman & Littlefield, 1999.

Kant, Immanuel, *Religion within the Limits of Reason Alone*. Translated by Theodore M. Greene and Hoyt H. Hudson. New York: Harper and Row, 1960.

———. *The Doctrine of Virtue: Part II of the Metaphysics of Morals*. Translated by Mary J. Gregor. Philadelphia: University of Pennsylvania Press, 1963.

———. *The Critique of Practical Reason*. 3rd ed. Translated by Lewis White Beck. New York: MacMillan, 1993.

———. *The Groundwork of the Metaphysic of Morals*. Translated by Alan Wood. New Haven, CT: Yale University Press, 2002.

Kaufmann, Walter. *Nietzsche: Philosopher, Psychologist, Antichrist*. 4th ed. Princeton, NJ: Princeton University Press, 1974.

Keenan, James. "The Problem with Thomas Aquinas's Concept of Sin." *The Heythrop Journal* 35, no. 4 (1994): 401–20.

Kellenberger, James. "God's Goodness and God's Evil." *Religious Studies* 41 (2005): 23–37.

Keller, Catherine. *Face of the Deep: A Theology of Becoming*. New York: Routledge, 2003.

Kelman, Herbert C., and V. Lee Hamilton. *Crimes of Obedience: Toward a Social Psychology of Authority and Responsibility*. New Haven, CT: Yale University Press, 1989.

Kent, Bonnie. "Augustine's Ethics." In *The Cambridge Companion to Augustine*, edited by Eleonore Stump and Norman Kretzman, 205–33. Cambridge: Cambridge University Press, 2001.

Kiehl, Kent A. "A Cognitive Neuroscience Perspective on Psychopathy: Evidence for Paralimbic System Dysfunction." *Psychiatry Research* 142, no. 2–3 (2006): 107–28.

Kiehl, Kent A., Andra M. Smith, Robert D. Hare, Adrianna Mendrek, Bruce B. Forster, Johann Brink, and Peter F. Liddle. "Limbic Abnormalities in Affective Processing by Criminal Psychopaths as Revealed by Functional Magnetic Resonance Imaging." *Biological Psychiatry* 50, no. 9 (2001): 677–84.

Kierkegaard, Soren. *Fear and Trembling.* Translated by Alistair Hannay. New York: Penguin Classics, 1986.

Kim, Hee-Jin. *Dōgen Kigen: Mystical Realist.* Tuscon: University of Arizona Press, 1987.

King, Martin Luther, Jr. *A Testament of Hope: The Essential Writings and Speeches of Martin Luther King, Jr.*, edited by James M. Washington. San Francisco: Harper Collins, 1986.

Kondoleon, Theodore J. "The Free Will Defense: New and Old." *Thomist* 47 (1983): 1–42.

Kopp, Sheldon. *Mirror, Mask, and Shadow: The Risks and Rewards of Self-Acceptance.* New York: Bantam Books, 1980.

Korsgaard, Christine M. "From Duty and for the Sake of the Noble: Kant and Aristotle on Morally Good Action." In *Aristotle, Kant and the Stoics: Rethinking Happiness and Duty.* Edited by Stephen Engstrom and Jennifer Whiting. Cambridge: Cambridge University Press, 1996.

Laato, Antii, and Johannes C. de Moor, eds. *Theodicy in the World of the Bible.* Leiden, The Netherlands: Brill Press, 2003.

Lactantius. *The Divine Institutes.* Translated by Mary Francis McDonald. Washington, DC: The Catholic University of America Press, 1964.

———. *Lactantius: The Minor Works.* Translated by Sister Mary Francis McDonald, OP. Washington, DC: The Catholic University of America Press, 1965.

Langer, Ellen J. *The Power of Mindful Learning.* Reading, MA: Addison-Wesley, 1997.

Lao-Tzu. *Te-Tao Ching.* Translated by Robert G. Henricks. New York: Ballantine Books, 1989.

Larrimore, Mark Joseph. *The Problem of Evil.* Oxford: Wiley-Blackwell, 2001.

Lee, Jung H. "Finely Aware and Richly Responsible: The Daoist Imperative." *Journal of the American Academy of Religion* 68, no. 3 (2000): 511–36.

Leibniz, G. W. *Theodicy: Essays on the Goodness of God the Freedom of Man and the Origin of Evil*. Translated by E. M. Huggard. New Haven, CT: Yale University Press, 1952.

Levenson, Jon D. *Creation and the Persistence of Evil: The Jewish Drama of Divine Omnipotence*. Princeton, NJ: Princeton University Press, 1988.

Levi, Primo. *The Drowned and the Saved*. Translated by Raymond Rosenthal. New York: Simon & Schuster, 1988.

Levinas, Emmanuel. *Totality and Infinity: An Essay on Exteriority*. Translated by Alphonso Lingus. Pittsburgh, PA: Duquesne University Press, 1969.

———. *Otherwise than Being or Beyond Essence*. Translated by Alphonso Lingus. The Hague: Martinus Nijhoff Publishers, 1974.

———. *Difficult Freedom: Essays on Judaism*. Translated by Sean Hand. Baltimore, MD: The Johns Hopkins University Press, 1990.

Lewis, Bernard. "The Roots of Muslim Rage." *The Atlantic*, September 1, 1990. www.theatlantic.com/magazine/archive/1990/09/the-roots-of-muslim-rage/304643.

Lewis, C. S. *A Grief Observed*. San Francisco: Harper Collins, 2001.

———. *The Screwtape Letters*. San Francisco: Harper San Francisco, 2001.

Lincoln, Bruce. *Holy Terrors: Thinking about Religion after September 11th*. 2nd ed. Chicago: University of Chicago Press, 2006.

London, Jack. *The Sea Wolf*. New York: Bantam Books, 1991.

Machiavelli, Nicolò. *The Prince*. Translated by David Wootton. Indianapolis, IN: Hackett Publishing, 1995.

MacIntyre, Alasdair. *Difficulties in Christian Belief*. London: SCM Press, 1959.

———. *Whose Justice? Which Rationality?* Notre Dame, IN: University of Notre Dame Press, 1989.

———. *Dependent, Rational Animals: Why Human Beings Need the Virtues*. Chicago: Open Court Press, 1999.

Mackie, J. L. "Evil and Omnipotence." *Mind* 64, no. 254 (April 1955): 200–212.

———. *The Miracle of Theism: Arguments for and against the Existence of God*. Oxford: Clarendon Press, 1982.

MacLeish, Archibald. *J. B.: A Play in Verse*. Boston: Houghton Mifflin, 1986.

Mann, William E. "Augustine on Evil and Original Sin." In *The Cambridge Companion to Augustine*, edited by Eleonore Stump and Norman Kretzman, 40–48. Cambridge: Cambridge University Press, 2001.

Mathewes, Charles T. *Evil and the Augustinian Tradition*. Cambridge: Cambridge University Press, 2001.

McDonough, Bill. "Sin and Addiction: Alcoholics Anonymous and the Soul of Christian Sin Talk." *Journal of the Society of Christian Ethics* 32, no. 1 (Spring/Summer 2012): 39–55.

McFague, Sallie. *Models of God: Theology for an Ecological, Nuclear Age*. Philadelphia, PA: Fortress Press, 1987.

Midgley, Mary. *Wickedness: A Philosophical Essay*. London: Ark Paperbacks, 1984.

Midlarsky, Elizabeth, and Eva Kahana. "Altruism, Well-Being, and Mental Health Late in Life." In *Altruism and Health: Perspectives from Empirical Research*, edited by Stephen G. Post, 56–69. Oxford: Oxford University Press, 2007.

Milbank, John. *Theology and Social Theory: Beyond Secular Liberalism*. Oxford: Blackwell Publishers, 1990.

Milgram, Stanley. "Behavorial Study of Obedience." *Journal of Abnormal and Social Psychology* 67, no. 4 (1963): 371–78.

———. *Obedience to Authority*. New York: Harper Collins, 1969.

Milhaven, J. Giles. *Good Anger*. Kansas City: Sheed and Ward, 1989.

Murdoch, Iris. *The Sovereignty of Good*. London: Routledge and Kegan Paul, 1970.

Neiman, Susan. *Evil in Modern Thought: An Alternative History of Philosophy*. Princeton, NJ: Princeton University Press, 2002.

Neumann, Craig S., and Robert D. Hare. "Psychopathic Traits in a Large Community Sample: Links to Violence, Alcohol Use, and Intelligence." *Journal of Consulting and Clinical Psychology* 76, no. 5 (2008): 893–99.

Newman, Louis. *Repentance: The Meaning and Practice of Teshuvah*. Woodstock, VT: Jewish Stock Publishing, 2010.

Niebuhr, H. Richard. *Christ and Culture*. New York: Harper and Row, 1951.

Niebuhr, Reinhold. *Moral Man and Immoral Society*. New York: Charles Scribner's Sons, 1932.

———. *An Interpretation of Christian Ethics*. San Francisco: Harper and Row, 1935.

———. *Faith and History*. New York: Charles Scribner's Sons, 1949.

———. *The Nature and Destiny of Man: A Christian Interpretation*. 2 vols. New York: Charles Scribner's Sons, 1949.

———. *Love and Justice*. edited by D. B. Robertson. Philadelphia, PA: The Westminster Press, 1957.

Nietzsche, Friedrich, *The Portable Nietzsche*. Translated by Walter Kaufmann. New York: Penguin Books, 1954.

———. *The Antichrist*. Reprinted in *The Portable Nietzsche*. Translated by Walter Kaufmann. New York: Penguin Books, 1954.

———. *Beyond Good & Evil: Prelude to a Philosophy of the Future*. Translated by Walter Kaufmann. New York: Vintage Books, 1966.

———. *Thus Spoke Zarathustra: A Book for None and All*. Translated by Walter Kaufmann. New York: Penguin Books, 1966.

————. *The Birth of Tragedy and the Case of Wagner*. Translated by Walter Kauffman. New York: Vintage Books, 1967.

————. *Will to Power*. Translated by Walter Kaufmann. New York: Random House, 1967.

————. *Twilight of the Angels and the Antichrist*. Translated by R. J. Hollingdale. New York: Penguin Books, 1990.

————. *Daybreak: Thoughts on the Prejudices of Morality*. Translated by R. J. Hollingdale. Cambridge: Cambridge University Press, 1997.

————. *Basic Writings of Nietzsche*. Translated by Walter Kaufmann. New York: The Modern Library, 2000.

————. *On the Genealogy of Morals*, in *Basic Writings of Nietzsche*. Translated by Walter Kaufmann. New York: The Modern Library, 2000.

Nishida, Kitarō. *An Inquiry into the Good*. Translated by Masao Abe and Christopher Ives. New Haven, CT: Yale University Press, 1990.

Norton, David. "Moral Minimalism and the Development of Moral Character." *Midwest Studies in Philosophy* 13, edited by P. French, T. Uehling, and H. Wettstein, 180–95. Notre Dame: Notre Dame University Press, 1988.

Nussbaum, Martha. *The Fragility of Goodness: Luck and Ethics in Greek Tragedy and Philosophy*. Cambridge: Cambridge University Press, 1986.

————. "Non-Relative Virtues: An Aristotelian Approach." *Midwest Studies in Philosophy* 13 (1988): 32–53.

————. *Love's Knowledge: Essays on Philosophy and Literature*. Oxford: Oxford University Press, 1990.

————. "Aristotle on Human Nature and the Foundations of Ethics," *World, Mind, and Ethics: Essays on the Ethical Philosophy of Bernard Williams*, edited by J. E. Altham and Ross Harrison. Cambridge: Cambridge University Press, 1995.

Oakley, Barbara. *Evil Genes: Why Rome Fell, Hitler Rose, Enron Failed, and My Sister Stole My Mother's Boyfriend*. New York: Prometheus Books, 2008.

O'Donovan, Oliver. *The Problem of Self-Love in Augustine*. New Haven, CT: Yale University Press, 1980.

O'Flaherty, W. D. *The Origins of Evil in Hindu Mythology*. Berkeley: University of California Press, 1976.

Oman, Doug. "Does Volunteering Foster Physical Health and Longevity?" In *Altruism and Health: Perspectives from Empirical Research*, edited by Stephen G. Post, 15–32. Oxford: Oxford University Press, 2007.

Osborn, Erc. *Irenaeus of Lyons*. Cambridge: Cambridge University Press, 2001.

Otto, Rudolf. *The Idea of the Holy*. 2nd ed. Translated by John W. Harvey. Oxford: Oxford University Press, 1958.

Pagels, Elaine. *Revelations: Visions, Prophecy, and Politics in the Book of Revelation.* New York: Viking, 2012.

Paul, Ellen Frankel, Fred D. Miller Jr., and Jeffrey Paul, eds. *Altruism.* Cambridge: Cambridge University Press, 1993.

Phillips, Adam. *Terrors and Experts.* Cambridge, MA: Harvard University Press, 1995.

Pike, Sarah. "Dark Teens and Born-Again Martyrs: Captivity Narratives after Columbine," *Journal of the American Academy of Religion*, 77, no. 3 (2009): 647–79.

Pinker, Steven. *The Blank Slate: The Modern Denial of Human Nature.* New York: Viking Press, 2002.

Plantinga, Alvin. "The Free Will Defense." In *Philosophy in America*, edited by Max Black, 204–30. Sydney: Allen and Unwin, 1965.

———. *God and Other Minds: A Study of the Rational Justification of Belief in God.* Ithaca, NY: Cornell University Press, 1990.

Plato. *The Republic.* Translated by H. P. D. Lee. Harmondsworth, UK: Penguin Books, 1955.

———. *Protagoras.* Translated by Benjamin Jowett. Cambridge: Cambridge University Press, 2008.

Post, Stephen G., ed. *Altruism and Health: Perspectives from Empirical Research.* Oxford: Oxford University Press, 2007.

Post, Stephen G., and Jill Neimark. *Why Good Things Happen to Good People: The Exciting New Research That Proves the Link between Doing Good and Living a Longer, Healthier, Happier Life.* Louisville, KY: Broadway Press, 2007.

Postel, Danny. "Gray's Anatomy." Book review for *The Nation.* December 22, 2002. www.thenation.com/doc/20031222/postel.

Raine, Adrian. "Psychopathy, Violence, and Brain Imaging." In *Violence and Psychopathy.* Edited by Adrian Raine and José Sanmartín. New York: Springer-Verlag, 2001.

Raine, Adrian, and Yaling Yang. "The Neuroanatomical Bases of Psychopathy: A Review of Brain Imagining Findings." In *Handbook of Psychopathy.* Edited by Christopher J. Patrick. New York: Guilford Press, 2006.

Ricoeur, Paul. *The Symbolism of Evil.* Translated by Emerson Buchanan. Boston, MA: Beacon Press, 1967.

Rist, John M. *Augustine: Ancient Thought Baptized.* Cambridge: Cambridge University Press, 1994.

Rorty, Amélie Oksenberg, ed. *The Many Faces of Evil: Historical Perpectives.* New York: Routledge, 2001.

Rorty, Richard. "The Historiography of Philosophy: Four Genres." In *Philosophy in History*, edited by R. Rorty, J. B. Schneewind, and W. Skinner, 49–75. Cambridge: Cambridge University Press, 1984.

————. "The Priority of Democracy to Philosophy." In *Objectivity, Relativism, and Truth*, 175–96. Cambridge: Cambridge University Press, 1991.

Rubenstein, Richard. *After Auschwitz: History, Theology, and Contemporary Judaism*. 2nd ed. Baltimore, MD: The Johns Hopkins University Press, 1992.

Rudolph, Susanne Hoeber, and Lloyd I. Rudolph. *Gandhi: The Traditional Roots of Charisma*. Chicago: University of Chicago Press, 1983.

Russell, Jeffrey Burton. *The Devil: Perceptions of Evil from Antiquity to Primitive Christianity*. Ithaca, NY: Cornell University Press, 1977.

Russell, John M. "Davis's Free Will Defense: An Exposition and Critique." *Encounter* 47 (1986): 245–56.

Russell, Mary Doria. *The Sparrow*. New York: Ballantine Books, 1997.

Sandler, Lauren. *Righteous: Dispatches from the Evangelical Youth Movement*. New York: Viking Press, 2006.

Sanford, John. *Evil: The Shadow Side of Reality*. New York: Crossroad Press, 1981.

————. *The Strange Trial of Mr. Hyde: A New Look at the Nature of Human Evil*. San Francisco: Harper and Row, 1987.

Sarot, Marcel. "Theodicy and Modernity: An Inquiry in the Historicity of Theodicy." *Theodicy in the World of the Bible: The Goodness of God and the Problem of Evil*. Edited by Antii Laato and Johannes C. de Moor. Leiden: Brill, 2003.

Sartre, Jean-Paul. "Literature in Our Time." *Partisan Review* 15, no. 6 (1948).

Seligman, Martin, and Mihaly Csikszentmihalyi. "Positive Psychology: An Introduction." *American Psychologist* 55, no. 1 (2000): 5–14.

Shakespeare, William. *Henry IV, part I* in *The Riverside Shakespeare*. Edited by G. Blakemore Evans. Boston, MA: Houghton Mifflin, 1974.

Sherman, Nancy. "Common Sense and Uncommon Virtue." *Midwest Studies in Philosophy XIII—Ethical Theory: Character and Virtue* 13, no. 1 (1988): 87–114.

————. *Making a Necessity of Virtue: Aristotle and Kant on Virtue*. Cambridge: Cambridge University Press, 1997.

Siegel, Bernie. *Love, Medicine and Miracles*. New York: Harper Paperbacks, 1990.

Speer, Albert. *Inside the Third Reich*. Translated by Richard and Clara Winston. New York: The MacMillan Company, 1970.

Stalnaker, Aaron. *Overcoming Our Evil: Human Nature and Spiritual Exercises in Xunzi and Augustine*. Washington, DC: Georgetown University Press, 2006.

Stocker, Michael. "The Schizophrenia of Modern Ethical Theories." *Journal of Philosophy* 73, no. 14 (1976): 453–66.

Straub, Ervin. *The Roots of Evil: The Origins of Genocide and Other Group Violence*. Cambridge: Cambridge University Press, 1989.

Stump, Eleanor. "The Mirror of Evil." In *God and the Philosophers: The Reconciliation of Faith and Reason*. Edited by Thomas V. Morris. Oxford: Oxford University Press, 1994.

Surin, Kenneth. *Theology and the Problem of Evil*. Oxford: Blackwell Press, 1986.

Swinburne, Richard. "Does Theism Need a Theodicy?" *Canadian Journal of Philosophy* 18, no. 2 (1988): 287–312.

———. *Is There a God?* Oxford: Oxford University Press, 1997.

Tankersley, Dharol, Jill C. Stowe, and Scott Huettel. "Altruism Is Associated with an Increased Neural Response to Agency." *Nature Neuroscience* 10, no. 2 (2007): 150–51.

Trout, J. D. *The Empathy Gap: Building Bridges to the Good Life and the Good Society*. New York: The Viking Press, 2009.

Urmson, J. O. "Saints and Heroes." In *Essays in Moral Philosophy*, edited by A. I. Melden, 198–216. Seattle: University of Washington Press, 1958.

Vidal, Gore. *Perpetual War for Perpetual Peace: How We Got to Be So Hated*. New York: Nation Books, 2002.

Viding, Essi, James R. Blair, Terrie E. Moffitt, and Robert Plomin. "Evidence for Substantial Genetic Risk for Psychopathy in 7-Year Olds." *Journal of Child Psychology and Psychiatry* 46, no. 6 (2005): 592–97.

Voltaire, Froncois-Marie Arouet. *Candide, Zadig and Selected Stories*. Translated by Donald M. Frame. New York: Penguin Books, 1981.

Waddell, Norman, and Masao Abe. "Introduction to the Shobogenzo Genjokoan." *The Eastern Buddhist* 5, no. 2 (1972).

Waller, James. *Becoming Evil: How Ordinary People Commit Genocide and Mass Killing*. Oxford: Oxford University Press, 2002.

Walzer, Michael. *Just and Unjust Wars: A Moral Argument with Historical Illustrations*. New York: Basic Books, 1977.

Wetzel, James. "Can Theodicy Be Avoided? The Claim of Unredeemed Evil." *Religious Studies* 25, no. 1 (1989): 1–13.

Whitney, Barry L. *Theodicy: An Annotated Bibliography on the Problem of Evil 1960–1990*. New York: Garland Publishing, 1993.

Wiesel, Elie. *First Person Singular*. Directed by Robert Gardner and David Grossbach. 2002.

———. *The Gates of the Forest*. Toronto: Holt, Rinehart, Winston, 1966.

———. *Night*. New York: Bantam Books. 1982.

Williams, Bernard. "Moral Luck." *Moral Luck: Philosophical Papers: 1973–1980*. Edited by Bernard Williams. Cambridge: Cambridge University Press, 1981.

Williams, Rowan. "Insubstantial Evil." In *Augustine and His Critics: Essays in Honour of Gerald Bonner*. Edited by Robert Dodaro and George Lawless, 105–23. New York: Routledge, 2000.

Wolf, Susan. "Moral Saints." *Journal of Philosophy* 79, no. 8 (1982): 419–39.

Wyschogrod, Edith. *Saints and Postmodernism: Revisioning Moral Philosophy*. Chicago: University of Chicago Press, 1990.

Zagzebski, Linda. *Virtues of the Mind: An Inquiry into the Nature of Virtue and the Ethical Foundations of Knowledge.* Cambridge: Cambridge University Press, 1994.

———. *The Lucifer Effect: Understanding How Good People Turn Evil.* New York: Random House, 2007.

Zimbardo, Philip. "The Power and Pathology of Imprisonment." *Congressional Record* (Serial No. 15, 1971-10-25). Hearings before Subcommittee No. 3, of the Committee on the Judiciary, House of Representatives, 92nd Congress, 1st Session on Corrections, Part II, Prisons, Prison Reform and Prisoner's Rights: California. Washington, DC: U.S. Government Printing Office.

———. "Pathology of Imprisonment." *Society* 9, no. 1 (1972): 4–8.

INDEX

absence, 16, 144, 171, 189, 197, 217; perspectivalist view of, 10, 118, 128, 139, 142; and presence, 14, 41, 93, 218; privation view of, 10, 14, 18, 48, 110, 165–66, 167, 197, 217, 218–19. *See also* privation model and thesis

absurdity, 210; Camus on, 7, 151, 183–84, 186

Abu Ghraib scandal, 6

accountability, 57, 70, 98, 166n100; moral, 245, 252n76

Adam and Eve, 166, 168, 173, 177–78, 201, 203n2

aesthetic, 132, 146, 154, 161n38; and ethics, 129, 154; and normative, 129, 130–34, 153, 161n38

After Auschwitz (Rubenstein), 73

agency, 36, 119, 121, 148; and evil, 24, 59, 77; and free will, 77, 169; and grace, 176; and personal responsibility, 70

agentic shift, 212–14, 215

akrasia, 222, 240

Alcoholics Anonymous (AA), 242–43

Al Qaeda and What It Means to Be Modern (Gray), 26

alterity, 26, 155; and other-regard, 153, 235–36

altruism, 15, 18, 49, 103, 154; cosmopolitan, 233; evil and, 17

American Beauty, 161n38

Amin, Idi, 50

Annas, Julia, 234–35

Antichrist, 43–44, 46, 47, 63n61

antisocial behavior, 48–49

antitradition, 121, 137–38

Apocalypse, 43–48

Arendt, Hannah, 36, 186–88; and Augustinianism, 14, 15, 187, 188–89; on

banality of evil, 14, 167, 187; works: *Eichmann in Jerusalem*, 5, 186–88, 190; *The Origins of Totalitarianism*, 188

Aristotle, 19, 217–26, 239; Augustine's common ground with, 11, 16, 18–19, 217, 221, 224, 225, 232–37, 246; on character, 52, 221, 243, 244; and eudaemonia, 217, 220, 233, 237; on evil and wrongdoing, 219–20, 222–23, 238; on friendship, 221, 236, 250n28; on reforming the wicked, 239; on self-awareness, 223, 224, 240; on self-deception, 221–22; on self-knowledge, 236–37, 239; on virtue, 147, 217–18, 220–21, 223–24, 233–34, 236, 239, 241–42; works: *The Nicomachean Ethics*, 19, 147, 219–20, 224, 235

atheism, 101, 183; and new atheists, 9, 20n18, 102, 115n83

atonement, 240–41, 243

atrocities, 25, 69, 100, 130, 148, 155, 246

Augustine, Saint, 14–15, 170–80, 219; Arendt and, 14, 15, 187, 188–89; Aristotle's common ground with, 11, 16, 18–19, 217, 221, 224, 225, 232–37, 246; on corruption and corruptibility, 15, 32, 56, 57, 180; on evil, 14, 19, 56, 166, 171–73, 178, 189; on finitude, 166, 176, 178, 233; on free will, 172–74, 176, 197; on goodness of God, 158, 200; on grace, 167, 173, 176–78, 179, 189, 197, 201, 222; on human nature, 165, 178, 203n1; on justice, 163n98, 174; on love, 177, 179, 189, 236; on lust and pride, 168, 170, 171, 174, 175, 177, 179, 221–22; and Manicheanism, 55–56, 158, 172–73, 176, 179, 180, 217; on man's wretchedness, 159, 163n98; on original

Augustine, Saint (*continued*)
sin, 166, 170, 180, 203n2, 216, 221; on
Pelagianism, 157–58, 217; on
redemption, 166, 167, 181, 183, 217; on
responsibility, 172–73, 175, 179, 222;
on salvation, 177, 178, 179, 183; on self-
awareness, 180, 192; on self-
knowledge, 237, 239, 244–45; on sin,
57, 177, 178, 222, 243; on suffering, 55,
158, 159, 166, 179; theocentrism of,
110, 150, 158, 159, 169, 176, 179; on
will, 166, 170–71, 176–77, 178; works:
The City of God, 14, 159, 163n98, 168,
171, 177, 181, 182, 188, 203n2; *The
Confessions,* 14, 170, 172; *On Continence,*
172–73; *Enchridion,* 200; *On Free Choice
of the Will,* 173–74, 175, 176, 178; *On
Rebuke and Grace,* 179; *On the Trinity,* 237

badness, 58, 222; and corruption, 57; and
evil, 5, 7, 14; evil as absence of, 10, 128,
139, 142; evil as presence of, 10, 27
banality, 36; of evil, 14, 167, 187, 212
Barth, Karl, 35, 194–96; on nothingness,
59–60, 66n103, 194–95
Baudelaire, Charles, 40–41
Bayle, Pierre, 29–30, 77–78, 79
beauty, 14, 41, 87, 146; perspectivalist
view of, 132, 153, 161n38
Beloved (Morrison), 152
Benigni, Roberto, 117, 120
Bennett, Philip, 100
Berger, Peter, 160n9
Beyond Good and Evil (Nietzsche), 13, 124
The Birth of Tragedy (Nietzsche), 154
blameworthiness, 23, 118, 153, 233
blindness, 209; evil as, 166
Böckle, Franz, 252n69
Bonhoeffer, Dietrich, 214, 249n18
born-again experience, 252n74
Boyer, Paul, 11, 45
brain, 49, 51, 57, 64nn81–82; abnormal-
ities, 53, 65nn94–95; of psychopath, 9,
21n20, 54nn94–95, 237
Brown, Robert MacAfee, 193
Browning, Christopher R., 36
Buddhism, 74; Zen, 141–45, 155
Burrell, David, 209, 210–11
Bush, George W., 43
Byrne, Rhonda, 119–20
bystanders, 4, 18, 229, 247; and complicity,
207–8; to evil situations, 186, 189–91,
231

Cain and Abel, 130–31, 153
Calvin, John, 37
Camus, Albert, 7–8, 76, 183–86; on
absurdity, 7, 151, 183–84, 186; August-
inianism of, 14, 15, 183–84, 204–5n50;
on Sisyphus, 105, 216; works: *The Fall,*
164–65, 184–85
Candide (Voltaire), 82, 111n8
Card, Claudia, 20n9, 151–52
character, 24, 249n22; Aristotle on, 52, 221,
243, 244; evil and, 164–69; Manichean
view of, 58–59; privation thesis on, 16,
165–69, 238; virtue ethics on, 218, 221,
225–26
Christianity, 11, 78, 125, 126, 170, 243
Chuang-Tzu, 138–41, 148, 157
Church Dogmatics (Barth), 194–95
Churchill, Winston, 51
Circle Limit IV (Escher), 5
The City of God (Augustine), 14, 159,
163n98, 168, 171, 177, 181, 182, 188,
203n2
clash of civilizations thesis, 42
Columbine massacre, 26, 32, 56, 62n30
commission-omission relation, 165, 167,
172, 247
compassion, 11, 32, 85, 88, 105, 165, 193,
226; Augustinianism on, 219, 236;
erosion and loss of, 33, 39, 187;
theodicy and, 91, 95
competition, 39–40, 183, 233
compliance, 213
complicity, 207–11, 213
The Confessions (Augustine), 14, 170, 172
Connolly, William, 134
Conrad, Joseph, 41–42
containment thesis, 24, 25, 69, 70–71
contrition. *See* remorse
Cooper, Terry, 27
Corinthians, 170, 244
corruption, 168–69, 187, 218; Augustine
on, 15, 32, 56, 57, 180; human nature
and, 15, 173, 180; and immutably bad,
57; sin and, 240; of the will, 32, 70, 200
creation, 33–34, 35–36, 88, 116n100
cross-cultural consensus, 124, 130
Crumb, R., 115n87
Csikszentmihalyi, Mihaly, 145–46

Dahmer, Jeffrey, 32
Daniel, Book of, 44
Dante Alighieri, 30

Darkness, King of, 28, 61n13
Davidman, Joy, 94
Dawkins, Richard, 20n18, 103, 115n83
Day, Dorothy, 250n38
death, 88, 132, 152, 158, 178; Bible on, 35, 37, 45; evil and, 7, 118; mortality and, 97, 157
Demian (Hesse), 130–32, 153
democracy, 123, 221, 234
despair, 157, 185; Augustinianism and, 158, 183, 184, 197, 201, 238; evil and, 19, 25, 60, 247; Great Conundrum and, 69, 75; Manicheanism and, 46, 59, 194; theodicy and, 85, 86, 89–90, 94, 101–2, 109–10
determinism, 8, 11, 44, 45, 49–50, 58; cosmic, 46–47; Manichean, 36, 59, 158, 167–68, 180; situational, 18, 212–14, 215
Deuteronomy, 103
devil. *See* Satan
dignity, human, 15, 24, 101, 224, 225; and efforts to heal world, 154, 163n91; and free will, 24, 97
disconfirmation crises, 7
disobedience, 30, 102, 103, 166, 177–78; moral, 213, 214
dissenters, 213, 214
The Divine Institutes (Lactantius), 113n52
Dōgen Kigen, 14, 141–42, 144, 148
domination, 136–37
doomsday chic, 45
Dostoevsky, Fyodor, 196, 238; Ivan Karamazov character of, 6–7, 71, 100, 101
dualism, 18, 37, 44, 87, 172; and human agency, 36; Manicheanism and, 11, 12, 28–29, 31, 33, 38, 53–54; Satan-God, 31–32

Eagleton, Terry, 149–50
Ecclesiastes, 104
Ehrenreich, Barbara, 156, 157
Ehrman, Bart D., 20n18, 102–3, 104, 105
Eichmann, Adolf, 5, 186–88, 199
Eichmann in Jerusalem (Arendt), 5, 186–88, 190
empathy, 1, 18, 58; human brain and, 49, 51, 53, 64n81
The Empathy Gap (Trout), 49–50
Epicurus, 77, 92, 111n16
Escher, M. C., 5
ethical naturalism, 153

ethics, 155, 195, 251n48; aesthetics and normativity in, 129, 135–36, 154; and morality, 154, 155; and theology, 176, 179, 197. *See also* virtue ethics
eudaemonia, 129, 137, 217, 220, 222, 233, 237
Evans, G. R., 176
evil: as absence of badness, 10, 128, 139, 142; as absence of goodness, 10, 14, 18, 48, 110, 165, 166, 167, 197, 218; and agency, 24, 59, 77; as all in one's head, 118, 147, 150–52, 155; and altruism, 17; Apocalypse and, 43–48; Arendt on, 14, 167, 187; Aristotle on, 219–20, 222–23, 238; Augustine on, 14, 19, 56, 166, 171–73, 178, 189; and bad, 5, 7, 10n27, 14; banality of, 14, 167, 187, 212; Barth on, 194–95; benign and malignant, 5; as blindness, 166; bystanders to, 186, 189–91, 231; Camus on, 184, 186; and character, 164–69; as commission and omission, 7, 165, 167, 172, 247; control over, 69–70; and death, 7, 118; definitions of, 4–8, 20n9, 118, 120–21; and despair, 19, 25, 60, 247; discourse of, 25, 26, 109; as evil, 73, 80, 92; Foucault on, 130, 134, 136; and free will, 7, 13, 18–19, 52–53, 97, 98–99, 166; and genetics, 50–53; God and, 3, 14, 96, 200–201; and human nature, 17, 58, 165, 196, 225; Hurricane Katrina and, 3–4; Kant on, 70, 96; and kindness, 5, 6; and knowledge, 175, 176; macro and micro aspects of, 216; Martin Luther King on, 11; natural, 7–8, 20n13, 99; naturalization of, 38–43; Niebuhr on, 192–94; Nietzsche on, 151; as nothingness, 59, 194–95, 235; as "othering," 149; participation in, 207–15; as part of human condition, 6, 7, 10, 38, 40–42, 165–67, 179, 196, 202; passivity in face of, 3, 5, 169, 187, 188, 189; as presence of badness, 10, 27; as presence of goodness, 10, 98; as problem for all, 245–48; as process, 58; and rebirth, 109; and religion, 25, 244, 252n74; Sartre on, 108; Satan and, 11, 13, 23, 199; seductive power of, 41–42; and selfishness, 4, 96, 144, 165, 167, 216; and self-knowledge, 110, 216; and sin, 196, 199; standard view of, 23–27; and suffering, 8, 151–52, 172; undoing,

evil (*continued*)
  237–45; use of word, 8, 149, 246;
  victims of, 82, 109, 151–52; virtue
  ethics and, 217, 219, 225–26; and will,
  166; Zen Buddhism on, 142, 143. *See
  also* good-evil relation
evildoers, 46, 115n80, 149, 150, 187, 197,
  200; defining and rating, 4–5, 199; and
  Satan, 11, 32, 199; Satan and existence
  of, 32
Evil Genes (Oakley), 50–52
Evil in Modern Thought (Neiman), 245
evil studies, 8–9
evil typology: comparison of models,
  17–18, 48, 118, 120, 180–81, 191–92,
  193–94; four models outlined, 10–11,
  116n100
Exodus, 79, 101, 115n80
Ezekiel, Book of, 44

Fackenheim, Emil, 73–74
faith, 7, 12–13, 25, 125, 252n69; blind, 82,
  102–3; and Great Conundrum, 72,
  75–76; and suffering, 68, 81, 82–83;
  theodicy and, 7, 81, 82–83, 107
The Fall (Camus), 164–65, 184–85
Falwell, Jerry, 19n2, 103
finitude, 81, 109; Augustine on, 166, 176,
  178, 233; and infinite, 79; Niebuhr on,
  193, 194; privation thesis and, 150, 153,
  157, 158, 181, 198, 220
Flew, Antony, 114n67
"The Flowers of Evil" (Baudelaire),
  40–41
forgiveness, 54, 69, 183, 192, 241
Foucault, Michel, 118; on evil, 130, 134,
  136; on power and judgment, 14,
  134–38, 149
Frankfurter, David, 25–26, 136
freedom, 99, 100, 164, 216; Augustine on,
  158, 170–71, 175, 176–77; Barth on,
  195–96; Camus on, 185–86; Levinas
  on, 15; Niebuhr on, 193; perspectivalism and, 121, 142, 157–58, 159;
  privation thesis and, 170, 175, 176–77,
  181, 184–86, 193, 195, 198, 238; virtue
  ethics and, 19, 238; will and, 170–71,
  175, 176–77; Zen Buddhism on, 142
free will, 24, 48, 57, 175, 216, 245;
  Augustine on, 172–74, 176, 197;
  containment thesis on, 71; as defense,
  73, 77, 97, 98–99, 114n67, 116n100,

191; and evil, 7, 13, 18–19, 52–53, 97,
  98–99, 166; God and, 97, 101, 114n67,
  115n80, 201; and human dignity, 24, 97;
  and suffering, 71, 100; theodicy and, 77,
  95–101, 114nn65–67, 116n100
friendship: Aristotle on, 221, 236, 250n28;
  Nietzsche on, 126, 160n20
Frykholm, Amy Johnson, 11, 43–44, 47
Fukushima, 226–31, 250n41, 251n45
future, 224; and past, 90, 91

Gandhi, Mahatma, 133, 202
The Gates of the Forest (Wiesel), 90
Genesis, 34–35, 103, 115n87, 166
genetics: and evil, 50–53; psychopaths
  and, 48–49, 50
genocide, 21n21, 90, 94, 97, 152;
  bystanders and, 189–90, 208–9; of
  Holocaust, 73, 94, 98, 151, 152, 189–90,
  213–14, 247; and Leibniz's theodicy,
  83, 112n26
The Genokoan (Dōgen), 141
Giuliani, Rudy, 228
Glover, Jonathan, 21n21, 109, 110n7, 155,
  191, 247
Gnostics, 28, 31, 60–61nn12–13, 87
God: anger and blame toward, 12–13, 68,
  90; and creation, 33–34, 35–36, 92,
  116n100; dualist view of, 31–32, 33; and
  evil, 3, 14, 96, 200–201; and free will,
  97, 101, 114n67, 115n80, 201; Gnostics
  on, 27–28; goodness of, 56, 84, 158, 159,
  200; grand design of, 81, 94, 111–12n24;
  and Great Conundrum, 72–77; and
  human suffering, 73, 78, 104, 113n57,
  179, 196; and *imago dei*, 88; Irenaeus on,
  87–89; and Job, 84–85, 87, 112n30;
  Kant on, 70, 100, 105–6; Lactantius on,
  12, 91–93; Leibniz on, 78–81; Manicheanism on, 28, 29, 53; new atheists on, 9,
  20n18; and omnipotence, 11, 28, 30, 35,
  53, 67, 68, 72, 114; as providential
  architect, 108–9; as solace, 69, 105;
  theodicy view of, 12, 91–93, 101–2;
  turning away from, 58, 166, 171–73,
  196, 201
Goebbels, Joseph, 199
good-evil relation, 2, 12, 92, 100; asymmetry in, 56–57, 246; Augustine on, 56,
  159, 172; complementarity in, 71;
  dualist view of, 11–12, 18, 31–32, 138,
  139, 172; evil as necessary for good, 12,

70, 99; Great Conundrum on, 72, 74–75; human capability for both, 15, 225; Kant on, 70, 96; Lactantius on, 92; Manicheanism and, 10, 11, 28–29, 32, 37, 57–58; perspectivalism and, 128, 139, 142, 153; privation model and, 10, 14, 18, 48, 110, 165, 166, 167, 197, 218; Taoism on, 138–39; theodicy and, 10, 71–72, 77, 82, 98, 106

goodness, 90, 202, 218–19; Foucault on, 136–37; fragile and elusive nature of, 246; free will and, 96; of God, 56, 84, 158, 159, 200; Irenaeus on, 91; in virtue ethics, 218–24, 225; Zen Buddhism on, 143–44

Good Samaritans, 2

Gothic, 26, 27, 29, 41, 44

grace, 37, 59; Augustine on, 167, 173, 176–78, 179, 189, 197, 201, 222; and ethical action, 196; fall from, 58, 88, 158, 166, 168, 173, 177–78, 179, 201, 203n2, 241; and redemption, 158, 167, 183, 197, 201; and suffering, 73, 78, 196; and will, 166, 178, 197, 242

Graham, Gordon, 32, 36–37, 56

Gray, John, 26

Great Conundrum, 111n16, 172; theodicy and, 72–77, 111n10

Green, Ron, 112n27

Gregory, Eric, 182, 188–89, 204n42, 236

grief, 90, 113n43, 144

A Grief Observed (Lewis), 89–90, 113n43

guilt, 58, 231, 252n69; and innocence, 185, 231, 251n48; and remorse, 153; and sin, 59, 196

Hampton, Jean, 233

Hanke, Karl, 209

happiness, 30, 105, 145–46, 202; suffering and, 90; virtue ethics and, 219, 232

Harcourt, Bernard, 52–53

Harman, Gilbert, 249n22

Harrington, Daniel, 244

Harris, Eric, 32, 62n30

Harris, Judith Rich, 65n84

Harris, Sam, 20n18, 115n83

Hauerwas, Stanley, 209, 210–11

Heart of Darkness (Conrad), 41–42

Heresies (Irenaeus), 87–88, 112n34

Hermes Trismegistus, 27–28

Hesse, Hermann, 17, 118, 130, 152, 154; on aesthetic and normative, 14, 130–34;

works: Demian, 130–32, 153; Siddhartha, 132

Hick, John, 88, 93

Himmler, Heinrich, 190, 191, 248n2

Hinduism, 74

Historical and Critical Dictionary (Bayle), 78, 79

historical reconstruction, 16, 17

Hitchens, Christopher, 20n18, 115n83

Hitler, Adolf, 50, 51, 94, 186, 189–90, 191

Hobbes, Thomas, 38–40

Holocaust, 73, 94, 98, 151, 152, 247; bystanders of, 189–90; obedience to authority during, 213–14

Homer, 97–98

Huettel, Scott, 64n81

human condition: Camus on, 15, 183; evil as part of, 6, 7, 10, 38, 40–42, 165–67, 179, 196, 202, 225; human nature and, 123, 165, 203n1; perspectivalists on, 109, 121, 122, 128, 198, 201; privation thesis and, 165, 196; theodicy and, 71

Humanity: A Moral History of the Twentieth Century (Glover), 155

human nature, 37–38, 123–24, 136, 173; Augustine on, 165, 178, 203n1; corruptibility of, 15, 173, 180; and evil, 17, 58, 165, 196; and human condition, 165, 203n1; Machiavelli and Hobbes on, 38–40; Manicheanism on, 56; perspectivalist view of, 198; and sin, 109, 157–58, 178; and will, 169

Hume, David, 111n16, 122, 123, 147

humility, 18, 54, 192, 193, 195, 241; Augustinian stress on, 56, 150, 158, 166, 179, 181, 198, 236; perspectivalist view of, 133, 142; theodicy and, 81, 85, 101, 104–5

Huntington, Samuel, 26, 42

Hurricane Katrina, 2–4, 19nn1–2, 98, 103

Hurricane Sandy, 207

imago dei, 88

Inner Chapters (Chuang), 14, 138, 140

innocence, 164; guilt and, 185, 231, 251n48

Innocent III, 37

Inside the Third Reich (Speer), 207, 209, 210

intemperance, 222–23, 239

Irenaeus, 35, 113n50; educative theodicy of, 87–91, 112n34

Isaiah, Book of, 35, 102

Islam, 42

Is There a God? (Swinburne), 97
I-Thou relationship, 85, 86, 90, 107–8
Ivanhoe, P. J., 139, 140

James, William, 31, 70, 86, 122–23, 191;
    The Varieties of Religious Experience,
    24–25, 146, 245; "The Will to
    Believe," 81
Jameson, Fredric, 136
J.B. (MacLeish), 107–8
Jekyll and Hyde, 27
Jesus Christ, 44, 60, 166; and Revelation,
    43–44, 63n61
Job, 12, 107–8; and educative theodicy,
    83–87; God and, 84–85, 87, 112n30
John 14, 43
Jones, David, 209–10
Judaism, 11, 240–41, 242
justice, 54, 182; Augustine on, 163n98,
    174; and love, 194; retributive, 192, 198;
    theodicy and, 79, 81
Justine (Sade), 40

Kant, Immanuel, 105–6, 150, 167, 225; on
    evil, 70, 96
Karamazov, Ivan, 6–7, 71, 100, 101
Keenan, James, 243, 244
Keller, Catherine, 35–36, 66n103
Kiehl, Kent A., 65n94
kindness, 88, 91; evil and, 5, 6
King, Martin Luther, Jr., 93, 94, 133, 202,
    217; on evil, 11; on fight for better
    society, 89, 163n91
Klebold, Dylan, 32, 62n30
knowledge, 82, 92, 105, 124, 140, 180, 202;
    and action, 170; and avoidance of evil,
    175, 176; and power, 129; of self, 195,
    217, 236–37, 239, 241; and virtue,
    20n10
Kotsev, Victor, 227–28
Kutz, Ernest, 242

Lactantius, 12, 111n16, 113n52; educative
    theodicy of, 91–95
language, 14, 149, 198; and power, 14, 120
Larkin, Philip, 21n21
Left Behind series, 43, 47, 63–64nn62–63
Leibniz, Gottfried: on God's grand design,
    81, 111–12n24; on theodicy, 12, 78–83,
    111n20
Levenson, Jon, 33–35, 55n103
Levi, Primo, 94, 109

Levinas, Emmanuel, 15, 140, 152, 162n62
Leviticus, 102, 103
Lewis, C. S., 93, 94, 168–69; *A Grief
    Observed*, 89–90, 113n43
Life Is Beautiful, 117, 151
Lisbon earthquake (1755), 83, 228
London, Jack, 63n52
love, 92–93, 182, 193, 202; Augustine on,
    177, 179, 189, 236; and justice, 194;
    self-, 18, 177, 179, 220, 222, 239
Love, Medicine, and Miracles (Siegel), 156
The Lucifer Effect (Zimbardo), 5–6
lust, 195; Augustine on, 170, 171, 174, 175,
    177, 179
Luther, Martin, 37

Machiavelli, Niccolò, 38–40, 50
MacIntyre, Alasdair, 114n67, 160n16
Mackie, J. L., 114n67
MacLeish, Archibald, 107–8
Mandean Ginza texts, 61n13
Mani, 28–29, 61n14
Manicheanism, 11–12, 23–60; Augustine
    on, 55–56, 172–73, 176, 179, 180, 217;
    Bayle on, 78; on character, 58–59; criti-
    cisms of, 53–60; determinism of, 36, 59,
    158, 167–68, 180; dualism of, 11, 12,
    28–29, 31, 33, 38, 53–54; evil as
    presence of badness in, 10, 27; on God,
    28, 29, 53; as heresy, 11, 53; on human
    nature, 56; Mani and, 28, 61n14; pers-
    pectivalism and, 14, 48, 118, 120, 137;
    pessimistic outlook of, 37, 38, 51,
    54–55, 179; privation model and, 48,
    158, 165, 167, 179, 197, 198–200; and
    redemption, 28, 33, 38, 44, 55, 59; on
    Satan, 27–33, 48; subjectivist view of,
    121; theodicy and, 17, 48; theological
    tradition of, 33–38
Mao Tse Tung, 50
Mark, Book of, 44
Mathewes, Charles, 121, 149, 193
The Matrix, 74–75
Matthew, Book of, 68
McDonough, William, 242
McFague, Sallie, 74, 76
McVeigh, Timothy, 133, 161n37
Midgley, Mary, 30–31, 63n56, 158n1
Milbank, John, 181–82
Milgram, Stanley, 17, 36, 191, 211–15
Milosevic, Slobodan, 50
Milton, John, 30, 31

Models of God (McFague), 74
modernity, 9, 47, 242
morality, 129, 130, 141, 195; Foucault on, 134, 135; Hesse on, 133–34; Nietzsche on, 118, 124–25, 126, 147, 154, 155; perspectivalist view of, 128, 155
Morrison, Toni, 152
mortality, 19, 81, 84, 98, 150; and free will, 97; Nussbaum on, 98, 110, 246
murder, 32, 40, 62n51, 122, 130–31, 153

natural disasters and calamities, 80, 81, 99, 156; Fukushima nuclear plant, 226–31, 250n41, 251n45; Hurricane Katrina, 2–4, 19nn1–2, 98, 103
natural evil, 20n13, 99; and moral evil, 7–8
naturalism, 53, 154; dualistic, 41; ethical, 153
nature-nurture relation, 18; Augustinianism and, 56–57; and vogue thesis, 65n84
Nazism, 195; bystanders of, 189–90; disobedience to, 213, 249n18; obedience to authority under, 208–11, 213–14
Neiman, Susan, 95, 105–6, 162n69, 187, 245
new atheists, 9, 20n18, 102, 115n83
Newman, Louis, 240–41
Newton, Isaac, 81
The Nicomachean Ethics (Aristotle), 19, 147, 219–20, 224, 235
Niebuhr, Reinhold, 14, 192–94, 202
Nietzsche, Friedrich, 17, 119, 124–29, 151–52, 233; on evil, 151; intellectual legacy of, 129–30; on morality, 118, 124–25, 126, 147, 154, 155; on nihilism, 126–27, 128; on pity, 13, 119, 125–26, 160nn20–22; on revaluation of values, 13, 17, 21n25, 137; on universal norms, 201–2; works: *The Antichrist*, 125; *Beyond Good and Evil*, 13, 124; *The Birth of Tragedy*, 154
Night (Wiesel), 90
nihilism, 123, 126–27, 128, 150
Nishida, Kitarō, 143–44
No Country for Old Men, 1–2, 19, 147
norms and normativity: aesthetics and, 129, 130–34, 153, 161n38; Aristotle's ethics and, 235, 246; Augustinianism and, 176, 183, 196–98, 231–32, 246; and descriptive, 246; Foucault on, 134, 135,

136; Hesse on, 14, 130–34; Nietzsche on, 129, 130, 161n29, 201–2; perspectivalist reevaluation of, 118, 128, 161n29, 201–2
Norton, David, 234
nothingness, 66n103; evil as, 59–60, 194–95, 235
nuclear power, 226–31, 250n41, 251nn45–46
Nussbaum, Martha, 97, 98, 110, 246

Oakley, Barbara, 23, 50–52, 65n84
Obedience to Authority (Milgram), 214
Ockham's razor, 32, 33, 56
The Odyssey (Homer), 97–98
On Free Choice of the Will (Augustine), 173–74, 175, 176, 178
original sin, 70, 221; Augustine on, 166, 170, 180, 203n2, 216, 221
The Origins of Totalitarianism (Arendt), 188
Otto, Rudolf, 86, 112n30

pain, 45, 90, 97–98, 101, 105, 110, 166; beneficial aspects of, 12, 94; Irenaeus on, 91; and pleasure, 25, 40, 79, 93; privation thesis on, 197, 202; and regard for others, 213, 232; and suffering, 82, 89
passions, 41, 108; Hume on, 122–23, 124, 147; Nietzsche on, 124, 127
passivity, 137, 186; in face of evil, 3, 5, 169, 187, 188, 189
past, 119; and future, 90, 91
Pelagianism, 157–58, 173–74, 176, 178–79, 204n40
Pelagius, 176
perfection, 120, 241; Irenaeus on, 87, 90–91, 113n50
perspectivalism, 13–14, 117–59; and beauty, 132, 153, 161n38; criticisms of, 14, 147–59; evil as absence of badness in, 10, 128, 139, 142; Foucault and, 134–38; and freedom, 121, 142, 157–58, 159; Hesse and, 130–34; and human nature, 198; Manicheanism and, 14, 48, 118, 120, 137; and morality, 128, 155; Nietzsche and, 124–29; positive psychology and, 145–47; privation model and, 48, 150, 167, 180, 193, 194, 198, 201–2; psychological basis for evil in, 118, 150–52, 155; on right and wrong, 150, 152–55; subjectivism and,

perspectivalism (*continued*)
120–24; and suffering, 150, 155–57;
Taoism and, 138–41; theodicy and, 48,
118, 120, 137; and will, 148, 150, 155,
157–59; Zen Buddhism and, 141–45
Phillips, Adam, 46
philosophy, 122–23, 124, 137, 145; and
theology, 102, 104
Pinker, Steven, 65n84
pity, 190, 242; Nietzsche on, 13, 119,
125–26, 160nn20–22
Plantinga, Alvin, 96–97, 99–100, 114n67
Plato, 247
pleonexia, 219, 220, 221
Pol Pot, 50
positive psychology, 145–47, 148, 155,
162n69; Character Strengths and
Virtues handbook of, 147, 162–63n78
"Positive Psychology: An Introduction"
(Seligman), 145–46
Postel, Danny, 26
power, 14, 118, 129, 202; Foucault on, 14,
135, 149; and language, 14, 120; and
punishment, 129, 130, 136
praiseworthiness, 23, 118, 153, 233
prayer, 177
predestination, 179
pride, 59, 194, 195; Augustine on, 168, 171,
177, 179, 221–22; and sin, 177, 193
The Prince (Machiavelli), 38–39
privation model and thesis, 14–15,
164–202, 231; Arendt and, 186–88;
Barth and, 194–96; Camus and,
183–86; and character, 16, 164–69, 238;
commission and omission in, 165, 167;
critical scrutiny of, 197–202; evil as
absence of goodness in, 10, 14, 18, 48,
110, 165–66, 167, 197, 218–19; on evil
and human condition, 165–67, 179,
196, 202; and finitude, 150, 153, 157,
158, 181, 198, 220; and freedom, 170,
175, 176–77, 181, 184–86, 193, 195,
198, 238; and good-evil relation, 15, 53,
246; Manicheanism and, 48, 158, 165,
167, 179, 197, 198–200; Niebuhr and,
192–94; as normative challenge,
196–97; and other-regard, 235–36; perspectivalism and, 48, 150, 167, 180, 193,
194, 198, 201–2; and redemption, 158,
181, 197; and responsibility, 166–67,
173, 175, 185, 189, 191, 231–32; and
salvation, 235, 236; and selfhood, 169,

170–71, 173, 181, 189, 196–97, 201;
theodicy and, 48, 116n100, 167, 179,
180, 194, 197–98, 200–201; virtue ethics
and, 11, 16, 18–19, 217, 221, 224, 225,
232–37, 246
prohairesis, 224, 225
prophecy, 11; of the rapture, 43–44, 46, 47,
63nn61–63
Psalms, 34, 37
psychopaths, 18, 197, 244–45; brains of, 9,
21n20, 54nn94–95, 237; existence of, 5,
149, 189; genetics and, 48–49, 50
punishment, 92, 166, 178; and power, 129,
130, 136; and sin, 79, 88, 101, 180; and
suffering, 80, 198

Raine, Adrian, 52
rapture, 43–44, 46, 47, 63nn61–63
Rapture Culture (Frykholm), 43–44
rational reconstruction, 16, 21–22n27
rebirth, 139, 142; and evil, 109
redemption, 69, 85, 188, 192, 240–41;
Augustine on, 166, 167, 181, 183, 217;
grace and, 158, 167, 183, 197, 201;
Manicheanism and, 28, 33, 38, 44, 55,
59; Pelagian doctrine and, 157;
privation model and, 158, 181, 197;
suffering and, 12, 83, 91, 94, 101;
theodicy and, 101, 105
reification, 118, 122, 136
Religion within the Limits of Reason (Kant),
96
remorse, 58, 141, 146, 196, 222; Augustinian stress on, 181, 236, 241
Reni, Guido, 24–25, 69–70, 86, 191
repentance, 58, 146; and atonement,
240–41, 243
responsibility, 70, 234–35, 238–39, 241,
248; Aristotle on, 223–24; Augustine
on, 172–73, 175, 179, 222; of
bystanders, 209, 229; privation thesis
and, 166–67, 173, 175, 185, 189, 191,
231–32
resurrection, 36–37, 78–79
Revelation, 43–44, 63n61; in *Left Behind*
series, 43–44, 63–64n63
Revelation, Book of, 11, 36, 44–45, 46, 103
Ricoeur, Paul, 107, 241
right and wrong, 38, 65n94, 128, 129; perspectivalism and, 150, 152–55
Robertson, Pat, 19n2, 103
Romans, Book of, 78, 204n31

Rorty, Richard, 16, 21–22n27, 123, 151
Rubenstein, Richard, 73, 76, 109
Russell, Jeffrey Burton, 31, 61n24
Russell, Mary Doria, 57, 67, 68–69, 160n15

Sade, Marquis de, 40, 41, 62n51
salvation, 37, 44, 45, 63–64n63, 89, 183;
    Augustine on, 177, 178, 179, 183;
    Gnostics on, 28, 60n12; privation thesis
    and, 235, 236; and sin, 60, 79; theodicy
    and, 108, 109
Sandler, Lauren, 46–47
Sartre, Jean-Paul, 108, 109
Satan, 3, 11, 37; evil as manifestation of,
    13; Jesus and, 11, 44; Job and, 84, 87; in
    literature, 30; Manicheanism and,
    27–33, 48; and Satanic possession,
    150–51; word for, 31, 61n24
satanic cults, 25–26
Schockenhoff, Eberhard, 242
The Secret (Byrne), 119–20
self-awareness, 53, 215, 241, 252n74; Aris-
    totle on, 223, 224, 240; Augustine on,
    180, 192; neo-Augustinians on, 193–94,
    196
self-centeredness, 93–94, 180
self-deception, 9, 54, 58; Aristotle on,
    221–22; Speer and, 208–11
self-determination, 57, 97, 120, 121
selfhood, 126; Eastern reconstruals of, 74,
    132, 150; Manicheanism and, 58, 120;
    privation model emphasis on, 169,
    170–71, 173, 181, 189, 196–97, 201; and
    suffering, 109
selfishness, 1, 38, 153, 211; Augustine on,
    199, 222; and evil, 4, 96, 144, 165, 167,
    216
self-knowledge, 80, 158, 189, 195, 217,
    241; Aristotle on, 221, 236–37, 239;
    Augustine on, 237, 239, 244–45; and
    evil, 110, 216
self-transformation, 13, 184, 189
Seligman, Martin, 145–46, 147
September 11 terrorist attack, 42–43, 95,
    103, 200, 228
Shakespeare, William, 86–87
shamanism, 74
Siddhartha (Hesse), 132
Siegel, Bernie, 156, 157
sin, 181, 182, 198, 234, 243, 244;
    atonement for, 240–41, 243; Augustine
    on, 57, 177, 178, 222, 243; Barth on, 69,

194; confession of, 252n69; and evil,
    196, 199; and guilt, 59, 196; and human
    nature, 109, 157–58, 178; inevitability
    of, 57, 158; as leading away from God,
    172–73, 196; Niebuhr on, 192, 193; and
    pride, 177, 193; and punishment, 79,
    88, 101, 180; and salvation, 60, 79, 178;
    and suffering, 78–79, 80, 101, 103. See
    also original sin
slavery, 128, 151–52, 186
Socrates, 20n10, 247
solidarity, human, 75, 183, 185, 231
The Sparrow (Russell), 57, 68–69, 160n15
Speer, Albert, 207, 209–11, 215, 224–25,
    248n2
Stalin, Joseph, 50
Stalnaker, Aaron, 173
Stowe, C. Jill, 84n81
Stump, Eleanor, 87
subjectivism, 120–24, 150, 179, 204n40
submission, 86, 198, 212
suffering, 3, 12, 86, 90, 103–4, 122, 190,
    246; amelioration of, 247–48; Augustine
    on, 55, 158, 159, 166, 179; and evil, 8,
    151–52, 172; and faith, 68, 81, 82–83;
    and free will, 71, 100; God and, 73, 78,
    104, 113n57, 179, 196; as mystery, 104,
    105; perspectivalism and, 150, 155–57;
    and punishment, 80, 198; and
    redemption, 12, 83, 91, 94, 101; and
    selfhood, 109; and sin, 78–79, 80, 101,
    103, 159; solace to victims of, 7, 102,
    104; theodicy and, 82, 86, 87, 93, 104,
    111n8, 144; threshold of, 81, 82, 83;
    world growth of, 9–10, 21n21; Zen
    Buddhism on, 144, 145
Surin, Kenneth, 100, 106, 107, 108, 109
Swinburne, Richard, 97
The Symbolism of Evil (Ricoeur), 241

Tankersley, Dharol, 64n81
Taoism, 138–41, 155, 156–57, 162n63
technology, 21n21, 191
terrorism, 4, 42, 200, 231; apologetics for,
    132, 133, 161n37; and September 11
    attack, 42–43, 95, 103, 200, 228; war on,
    54–55
Te-Tao Ching, 139
theocentrism, 114n67, 176; of Augustine,
    110, 150, 158, 159, 169, 176, 179
theodicy, 12–13, 24–25, 67–110;
    bystanders in, 190–91; and

0 1341 1487404 0

theodicy (*continued*)
  containment thesis, 69–71; criticisms
    of, 101–10; educative, 83–95; Epicurus
    and, 77; eschatological, 88, 89, 113n38;
    evil as presence of goodness in, 10, 98;
    and faith, 7, 81, 82–83, 107; and free
    will, 77, 95–101, 114nn65–67, 116n100;
    and Great Conundrum, 72–77, 111n10;
    Irenaeus and, 87–91, 112n34; Job and,
    83–87; and justice, 79, 81; Lactantius
    and, 91–95; Leibniz on, 12, 78–83, 79,
    111n20; Manicheanism and, 17, 48;
    Niebuhr repudiation of, 192; optimism
    of, 77–78, 89, 109, 179; perspectivalism
    and, 48, 118, 120, 137; privation model
    and, 48, 116n100, 167, 179, 180, 194,
    197–98, 200–201; quietism and
    passivity of, 110, 148, 159, 190; and
    redemption, 101, 105; and salvation,
    108, 109; subjectivist view of, 121; and
    suffering, 82, 86, 87, 93, 104, 111n8,
    144; theodicy *simpliciter*, 78–83, 93;
    typology of, 112n27; view of God in, 12,
    91–93, 101–2; Voltaire and, 82, 111n8;
    Weber and, 111n9
Theodicy (Leibniz), 12, 79, 111n20
theology, 33, 242; Christian, 12, 35–36,
  59–60, 63n61; and ethics, 176, 179; and
  philosophy, 102, 204; purposive, 104
Thessalonians, 43, 102
tradition, 121–22, 243; and antitradition,
  121, 137–38
transcendence, 74, 143, 159, 163n78, 192
Trout, J. D., 49–50
truth, 136, 137, 221, 246; as corrupted by
  power, 135; skepticism in search for,
  133, 140; as Truth, 123
two poles thesis, 11, 12. *See also* dualism

The Varieties of Religious Experience (James),
  24–25, 146, 245
victims, 82, 109, 151–52
Victorinus, 170

Vidal, Gore, 133, 161n37
virtue: Aristotle on, 147, 217–18, 220–21,
  223–24, 232–34, 236, 239, 241–42; and
  balance, 232; and knowledge, 20n10;
  Nietzsche on, 126; and vice, 31, 202,
  220, 223, 243
virtue ethics, 15, 147, 217–26, 234; character in, 218, 221, 225–26; culpability
  in, 241, 243; and evil, 217, 219, 225–26;
  and freedom, 19, 238; and happiness,
  219, 232; and other-regard, 235;
  privation model common ground with,
  11, 16, 18–19, 217, 221, 224, 225,
  232–37, 246
Voltaire, 82, 111n8
vulnerability, 82, 98, 218, 246; Augustinianism on, 150, 158, 166

Weber, Max, 111n9
When Time Shall Be No More (Boyer), 45
Whitman, Walt, 146
Whitney, Barry L., 114n65
Wiesel, Elie, 90
will, 156–57, 169, 199–200, 223, 224;
  Augustine on, 166, 170–71, 176–77,
  178; corruption of, 32, 70, 200; and
  freedom, 170–71, 175, 176–77; and
  grace, 166, 178, 197, 242; moral evil
  and, 166; perspectivalism and, 148, 150,
  155, 157–59. *See also* free will
Williams, Rowan, 58, 167, 199–200
"The Will to Believe" (James), 81
wisdom, 19, 78, 80, 83, 86, 120; Lactantius
  on, 91–92
Wolf, Susan, 233
The Wrath of God (Lactantius), 91–92

Xunzi, 173

Zen Buddhism, 141–45, 155
Zimbardo, Philip, 5–6, 17, 18, 36, 191,
  211–12
Zoroastrianism, 31

RECEIVED

OCT 1 4 2015

HUMBER LIBRARIES
LAKESHORE CAMPUS